The collected works of Ruqaiya Hasan

Volume 3 Language and Education: Learning and Teaching in Society

Edited by Jonathan J. Webster

Education is central to the knowledge base of society, groups and individuals. Yet education also, like health, is a public institution, central to the production and reproduction of distributive injustices. Biases in the form, content, access and opportunities of education have consequences not only for the economy; these biases can reach down to drain the very springs of affirmation, motivation and imagination. In this way they can become, and often are, an economic and cultural threat to democracy. Education can have a crucial role in creating tomorrow's optimism in the context of today's pessimism. But if it is to do this then we must have an analysis of social biases in education. These biases lie deep within the very structure of the educational system's processes of transmission and acquisition and their social assumptions.

Basil Bernstein, *Pedagogy, Symbolic Control and Identity: Theory, Research , Critique* (Lanham, MD: Rowman & Littlefield, 2000): xix.

The Collected Works of Ruqaiya Hasan

Volume 3

Language and Education

Learning and Teaching in Society

Edited by Jonathan J. Webster

LONDON OAKVILLE

Published by

UK: Equinox Publishing Ltd., 1 Chelsea Manor Studios, Flood Street, London SW3 5SR
USA: DBBC, 28 Main Street, Oakville, CT 06779

www.equinoxpub.com

First published 2011

British Library Cataloguing-in-Publication Data

A catalogue record for this book is available from the British Library.

ISBN 978 190476 837 1 (hardback)
978 190476 838 8 (paperback)

Library of Congress Cataloging-in-Publication Data

Hasan, Ruqaiya.
Language and education : learning and teaching in society / Ruqaiya Hasan ; edited by Jonathan J. Webster.
p. cm. -- (The collected works of Ruqaiya Hasan)
Includes bibliographical references and index.
ISBN 978-1-904768-37-1 -- ISBN 978-1-904768-38-8 (pbk.) 1. Language and languages--Study and teaching. I. Webster, Jonathan, 1955- II. Title. III. Series.

P53.H365 2010
418.0071--dc22

2010038544

Typeset by CA Typesetting Ltd, Sheffield, www.sheffieldtypesetting.com
Printed and bound in Great Britain by Lightning Source UK Ltd., Milton Keynes and Lightning Source Inc., La Vergne, TN

For my colleagues and students at Macquarie University, 1976–1994

Contents

Acknowledgments ix
Author's preface xi
Editor's introduction 1

I ON LEARNING AND TEACHING

1 On the process of teaching: a perspective from functional grammar 7
2 Modes of learning, modes of teaching: semiotic mediation and knowledge [2008] 48
3 The implications of semantic distance for language in education [1985] 73
4 Forms of discourse, forms of knowledge: reading Bernstein (with David Butt) 99

II LANGUAGE AND LITERACY

5 Literacy, everyday talk and society [1996] 169
6 Globalization, literacy and ideology [2003] 207
7 Literacy pedagogy and social change: directions from Bernstein's sociology [2007] 232

III MOTHER TONGUE AND OTHER TONGUE

8 Socialization and cross-cultural education [1976] 251
9 Some sociological considerations in second language teaching [1978] 270
10 Learning to function with the other tongue: A systemic-functional perspective on second language teaching (with G. Perrett) [1994] 288
11 English process, English tense: foreign learner, foreign teacher [1995] 336

References 380

Index 404

Acknowledgments

'Modes of learning, modes of teaching: semiotic mediation and knowledge'. In *SPELT Quarterly*, vol. 23, no. 3 (September 2008). Reprinted by permission of Society of Pakistan English Language Teachers (SPELT).

'The implications of semantic distance for language in education'. In *Indian Journal of Applied Linguistics*, vol. XI, no. 2 (June 1985), pp. 1-22. Reprinted by permission of Bahri Publications.

'Literacy, everyday talk, and society'. In *Literacy in Society*, edited by Ruqaiya Hasan and Geoff Williams, 1996, pp. 377-424. Published by Longman. Reprinted by permission of Pearson Education Limited. Copyright © Pearson Education Limited.

'Globalization, literacy and ideology'. In *World Englishes*, vol. 22, no. 4 (2003), pp. 433-448. Reprinted by permission of Blackwell Publishing Ltd.

'Literacy, pedagogy and social change: directions from Bernstein's sociology'. In *Knowledge, Power and Education Reform: Applying the sociology of Basil Bernstein*, edited by Rob Moore, Madeleine Arnot, John Beck and Harry Daniels, 2006, pp. 211-241. Published by Routledge Taylor & Francis Group. Reprinted by permission of Routledge Taylor & Francis Group.

'Socialization and cross-cultural education'. In *International Journal of the Sociology of Language*, vol. 8 (1976), pp. 7-26. Reprinted by permission of De Gruyter Mouton.

'Some sociological considerations in second langauge teaching'. In *Language Learning in Australian Society*, proceedings of the 1976 Congress of the Applied Lingusitics Association of Australia, 1976, pp. 50-62. Published by the Australia International Press, Melbourne.

'Learning to function with the other tongue: A systemic functional perspective on second language teaching' (with Gillian Perrett). In *Perspectives on*

Pedagogical Grammar, edited by Terence Odlin, 1994, pp. 179-226. Published by Cambridge University Press. Reprinted by permission of Cambridge University Press.

'English process, English tense: foreign learner, foreign teacher'. In *SPELT Newsletter*, vol. X, no. 4 (December 1995). Reprinted by permission of Society of Pakistan English Language Teachers (SPELT).

Author's Preface

The chapters that make up this volume consist of the written versions of talks[1] presented over half a century. In the nature of things, much should have changed during that long period – and, most probably, *has*. Not surprisingly, then, there is evidence of change both in the style of writing and in the choice of issues brought to attention. But, perhaps surprisingly, there is also evidence of *absence of change*: certain themes have remained constant over this long period. Thus, three major concerns occur repeatedly across the chapters: (i) educators' need to be aware of the identity of the learner; (ii) their need to understand why and in what ways language plays an active part in *all* the processes of learning and teaching irrespective of where and how those processes take place; and finally (iii) the connections between language, culture and the processes of education.

The focus on learner identity, foregrounded as the major issue in the earliest papers (chapters 3, 8 and 9) but raised in some form or other in each chapter, might surprise some readers – it might be seen as preaching to the converted. As evidence of this, one might point simply to a small though rich corner of the educational system, namely, the teaching of English to speakers of other languages (TESOL), where everything from curriculum to classroom practice today either claims to already possess or is on the verge of possessing the virtue of being 'learner centred'. One might further point to the fact that, in general, curricula have always paid attention to learners' identities by taking into account such factors as age, ability and even their social class. One might be tempted to cite here the staging of the educational process from kindergarten to primary to secondary and tertiary levels as proof of educators' awareness of the importance of the learners' maturational stages, just as ways of evaluating educational attainment might be seen as strategies for identifying learners' ability levels in order to establish the degree of commensurability with the challenges of the next stage of learning. As for the learners' identification by social class, note simply how anxious the British government is to help the 'socio-economically disadvantaged learners',[2] while fiercely determined to triple the cost of education across the board at the tertiary level!

Are these things really evidence of educators' awareness of learner identity? My answer would be: 'No'. There exists a world of difference between what I mean by *learner identity* and what is known as 'learner-centred approach' which aims to keep the learner entertained; similarly, such attention to factors of age, ability or social class does not mean that one understands the concept of learner identity. Whatever the potential relevance of these factors to learner identity, used as described above, they are just useful pegs to hang managerial decisions on. Education is about a deliberately designed programme for enabling learning; as such it necessarily involves mental labour on the part of the learner (cf. chapters 1, 2, 3 and 5 particularly). It is, therefore, reasonable to suggest that the central aspect of learner identity that should concern the educator has to do primarily with the learner's learning styles, and the formation of these to a very large extent rests upon those conditions of semiotic mediation (Hasan 2005) that the learner has experienced and is experiencing in his/her social life. It is such experiences that are central to fashioning individuals' ways of thinking and learning. It follows that the primary point of interest for educators has to be the learners' 'mental disposition' – the pathways of the brain used habitually for engaging with new information – because it is such 'habits of mind' that will deal with the information presented as educational knowledge.[3] Given this genesis of learner identity, variation is obviously inherent to the concept. It is in this sense that the complex concept of learner identity – or, more appropriately, *identities* – needs to inform every aspect of the educational process.

Through the experiences of teaching in Pakistan, ideas somewhat like a vague shadow of the above thoughts had suggested themselves to me in the late 1950s. They began to take a more definite shape in the mid-1960s as I first encountered the seminal work of Bernstein on the role of family, neighbourhood and education in the formation of human consciousness (Bernstein 1971c, 1973, 1975b). Even in those early days Bernstein's canvas was huge, his thinking multi-faceted and his orientation to his problems transdisciplinary – qualities that educators have needed and still need badly. My first attempt to use Bernstein's insights was to apply them in describing and critiquing the teaching and learning of English on the Indo-Pakistani sub-continent or as an overseas student in an English-speaking country; to my mind, the issues that these pedagogic contexts raised pertained basically to cross-cultural considerations in education. And that is how I approached them (see especially chapters 3, 8 and 9). These chapters argue that the culture created and maintained in educational sites must necessarily come face to face with the culture the learners live outside the educational sites – ignoring this fact is like sweeping dust under the carpet. Although the pretence of treating the outside culture as alien continues in educational institutions, I have not found any rational arguments for abandoning these views. However, in one respect my thinking about culture and language in relation to education changed considerably at the turn of the 1980s.

To talk of 'culture' is to talk of the universe of a people's social experience. This vast body of information is internalized and externalized semiotically, and as I have often argued, here 'semiotically' in fact means 'overwhelmingly linguistically' (Hasan 2005, 2009b; and nearly all chapters of this volume); the use of other semiotic systems, such as that of imaging[4], typically 'aids and abetts' linguistic meaning. Educators need an understanding of language not only to teach the learners how to process the valued registers of educational knowledge or how to teach specific patterns of language. Important as these considerations are, the need for the understanding of language is above all an essential aspect of understanding human ways of being, feeling, thinking and doing: these are as they are because humans talk. The entire fabric of education – every aspect of the production and dissemination of knowledge – depends on understanding the very close connection between language and culture. So, in a way, it is far from easy to address the issue of learner identity without understanding the language-culture connection – what part it plays in the production of individuals. In those early days, my work painted 'communal culture' in relation to the processes of education with a broad brush, and without support from any large-scale empirical research in the functioning of everyday meaning exchange in the community. In fact such research was conspicuous by its absence. As a result it was difficult to identify specific relevant elements of culture or of language to which one could assign some particular place in the learner's educational life; naturally, the chain of connection could not be made explicit.

I was naturally dissatisfied with this situation, but it is difficult to say what exactly caused me to move towards the study of linguistic meaning i.e., semantics. With hindsight I could name a number of factors, some or all of which might have pushed me in that direction: my interest in the study of literature, the publication of Halliday's *Learning How to Mean*, the refinement of Bernstein's work on the notion of codes putting meaning centre stage, teaching courses such as 'Discourse analysis', 'Language and the child', 'Sociolinguistics', and, of course, 'Semantics'. It would be futile to try and name all those great scholars from whose work I benefited, but with respect to culture, meaning and education, I feel obliged to mention the controversy between Labov and Bernstein, and its interpretation by Halliday, as decisive. In particular, Labov's mis/readings of Bernstein forced me in 1983–86 to conduct a fairly large research on *The Role of Every Day Talk between Mothers and Children in Establishing Ways of Learning*. That work – a semantic analysis of everyday talk – known now as Semantic Variation (Hasan 2009b and elsewhere), together with the research by Cloran (1994 and elsewhere) and by Williams (1995 and elsewhere) indicated beyond doubt the importance of ways of meaning in everyday life as a central factor in the formation of children's orientations to discourse production and reception. This focus on meaning, when seen in light of Vygotsky's theory on the role of semiosis in the sociogenetic development of higher mental functions and Bernstein's discourse on coding orientations in relation to social structure, together with Halliday's interpretation of children's language learning, has led me to suggest that the single most important factor in the formation of the identity of individuals in the context of education may be revealed by inspecting their 'fashions of speaking' in daily living. This is true notwithstanding the fact that educational knowledge is, as Bernstein (1975c and elsewhere) remarks, de-/re-contextualized: *whatever the context of saying and receiving, and whatever the history of the said, engaging with it is either engaging with its meanings or not at all.* Learners' ways of saying and of meaning are therefore of paramount concern in education, so long as education holds to its own definition as a complex process for facilitating the learning of deliberately selected elements of knowledge. This is not to underplay the principles of selection, instruction and evaluation in the educational context, but none of these are likely to make any difference unless the learner can make sense of what he/she is receiving as discourse.

The upshot of these conclusions for learner identity was that while the concept under any nomenclature continued to be a constant concern of chapters in this volume, the specific aspects of learner identity that are considered relevant in the context of education have become increasingly more specific and explicit. This has led to greater emphasis in the later work (say, since the mid-1980s) on what I have called 'reflection literacy' (chapters 1, 2, 5-7 and 11). Reflection literacy refers to the need to approach discourse with a conception of linguistic meaning that goes beyond the literal meanings of the 'words and vocables', insisting on a recognition of the assumptions that underlie what is said. Such probing necessarily involves taking into consideration the textual and social environment of the discourse under focus: instead of looking at formal construals of meaning unit by unit, it takes the paradigmatic and syntagmatic aspects of the whole discourse into account. Where reflection literacy is practised with such understanding of linguistic meaning by a teacher who 'knows' the learner, it helps the learner to 'read' (cf. Williams 2000) how through the spoken word the speaker positions the listener and indicates his/her own relation to the 'other' entities that are relevant to that discourse.

The need for reflection literacy is growing urgent by the day due to the global scope of significant socio-economic changes. While the benign face of globalization presents itself as the possibility of purchasing the fashions of Prada in Prague, Paris or Puerto Rico, and as the promise of easy access to multicultural music, entertainment and tourism, it does have a malign face as well. The toxic qualities of globalization are what provoke the riots and protests that are witnessed worldwide wherever global agencies for trade and commerce have met to determine how the principles of 'compassionate capitalism' should be translated into practice (Hasan 2003, 2004; included here as chapters 6 and 7). The Third World – where typically English is a foreign or second language – has noted with dismay that discussions on trade and commerce appear to be saying one thing while meaning another. The way this is achieved by a certain sub-section of the global community amounts to subverting linguistic meaning; the practice has given rise to a variety of language that effectively 'turns things upside down'.[5] I have referred to this variety as 'glib-speak'. Glib-speak is a variety spoken by the powerful managers of financial concerns; it allows them to present their exploitative and self-serving proposals packaged in language that hides the contentious nature of the contents. As an example, consider the Vice-Chancellor of Macquarie University, who describes the recent decision to treble fees in English Universities as 'New era dawns for UK higher education'.[6] It is a 'dawn' that many tertiary students and academics would unhesitatingly describe as ushering in not a bright day but a dark night. Some 'factual'[7] details of the 'new era' welcomed by Schwartz are described by journalist Derek Brown in the following words (see page 15, 'Present Week in Britain', *Guardian Weekly* 14.01.11): 'Universities are facing a financial squeeze, with funding for teaching cut by £300m, to £4.6bn. From next year, they will be expected to make up any funding shortfall by charging students up to £9,000 a year for their tuition. Students starting this year will pay £3,375 a year.' The features of the new era hailed by Schwartz become clearer still by putting the above information next to the headline 'Government abandons efforts to rein in bankers' bonuses' (see page 13 in the same issue of the *Guardian Weekly*): clearly an outstanding quality of the 'new era' seems to be that it thrives by dominating the helpless while cowering in the face of the powerful – a version of financial bullying. I hope this small example illustrates the need for emphasis on reflection literacy; future generations quite obviously must approach discourses with greater sensitivity to linguistic meaning – an aspect that is emphasized in most chapters written since the 1980s.

In one respect the chapters of this volume differ rather markedly from those in other books in the field of 'educational linguistics': they bear no direct relationship to classroom practices with reference to language. Certainly, many chapters contain some analysis of language, but these are presented more by way of 'straight language description' rather than a lesson on how to teach language. This is a deliberate decision on my part. In the SFL-inspired writings in the domain of educational linguistics, there is an abundance of such literature; it has seemed to me that rather than add to that literature it might be more useful to draw attention to theoretical considerations in language description, particularly with respect to the language-culture-education connection. This has seemed to me an urgent need. I believe it is important for the academic community to take serious interest in the management and maintenance of the educational system. As an institution, it is badly in need of change, and as Bernstein (2000) pointed out, a necessary condition of bringing a viable change in the institution of education is analysis and understanding of how the system actually functions today as opposed to its real functional potential. I believe this perspective is linked to a conviction that both short-term and long-term goals of education are equally important, but they will bear good results for a community only when the two kinds of goals are reviewed rationally in relation to each other, and calibrated logically. A short-term perspective views education as educating for life *here and now* in the community. It is, therefore, more susceptible to the fads and foibles of a specific time and place; note, for example, the so-called progressive countries of today where education is treated as the proverbial 'milking cow'. Today's management has a goal that suits today's corporate business ideology: cut cost, no matter what the cost; increase income to stay financially afloat even though large segments of the community might drown. While efficient and economic management of any institution is highly desirable, social institutions typically survive if they fulfil some social function. Whatever else the function of the institution of education may be, it is certainly not to exist in order to cut costs or to make profit. If the primary task of education is to produce and disseminate knowledge, then its long-term goal is to develop intellects capable of reasoning, thinking, and producing knowledge – that is to say, education is there to shape the nature of tomorrow's community. That being the case, educators need to know not simply about how to purvey knowledge, or what a certain level of knowledge is worth in terms of money, but also what makes knowledge a resource for a qualitative survival of the community. From this perspective, the community's material well-being matters but learning to be human matters more.

Much more needs to be said on these urgent issues, but let me close this preface now with sincere thanks to my editor, Professor Jonathan Webster, and to Ms Joey Wong at the Halliday Centre (City University of Hong Kong). My grateful thanks to Dr Annabelle Lukin for urgent help in persuading recalcitrant machines and for her cheerful moral support. Last but not least, many thanks to Ms Heidi Robbins, my Equinox editor, for careful reading and helpful suggestions.

Notes

1 The exceptions to this generalization are chapters 4, 8, and 10.
2 A descriptive label attributed to the British Prime Minister himself, who perhaps believes this to be the most efficient method of repairing the inequality in the distribution of resources.
3 In view of the rather inane cries of 'what can you do? This is how they have been brought up', it is important to emphasize that the pathways of the brain are shaped by habits, but habits are NOT unchangeable: all that is needed is understanding, effort and time to strengthen other pathways.
4 I use the word 'imaging' here to refer to a semiotic system instantiated by such signs as graphs, tables, and the like.
5 For some details of the lexicogrammar of glib-speak, see chapter 6 in this volume.
6 Issued by Macquarie University Vice-Chancellor's Office, written by Steven Schwartz on 15 December, 2010, http://www.vc.mq.edu.au/blog/2010/12/15/new-era-dawns-for-uk-higher-education/
7 I say 'factual' because, thanks to the glib-speak tradition introduced by the respected CEOs of powerful corporations, one no longer knows what to treat as a fact. Clinton is right in saying that loss of trust makes the world poorer, but loss of trust is not new; nor did it begin with Julian Assange – trust has been being eroded systematically ever since the fall of the Berlin Wall and the tragedy of Tiananmen Square, which was taken to announce the dawn of a new era, namely, that of globalized capitalism.

Editor's Introduction

When it comes to learning and teaching a living language, all parties to the process need to recognize that our ways of speaking cannot be separated easily from our way of life. Our understanding of the world around us is shaped through conversations in our community. Communities differ in their constructions of reality. There is no one single, correct interpretation. Hasan refers to such differences which serve as the basis of our alternative interpretations as 'semantic distance'. Awareness of semantic distance in the classroom and its implications for teaching and learning is one of the main topics covered in this third volume in the Collected Works of Ruqaiya Hasan on *Language and Education: Learning and Teaching in Society.*

This volume consists of eleven chapters spread over three sections, including one section on learning and teaching; another on language and literacy; and the third section on mother tongue and other tongue. Two chapters from the first section – the first chapter, *On the process of teaching: a perspective from functional grammar*; and chapter four, *Forms of discourse, forms of knowledge: reading Bernstein* (co-authored with David Butt) – are new and previously unpublished work.

Treating language as an autonomous structure defeats the purpose of educating learners into literacy in whatever language, whether it be their first, second or otherwise. 'Learning the so-called rules of grammar without relating them systematically to meaning is a waste of time,' writes Hasan, 'and talking about meaning without showing how you do it by putting words together is to deprive pupils from understanding; it is to deny them the power of reflection on how meanings are transacted in their community.' Instead, as Hasan persuasively shows, what teacher and learner need is an approach to language, such as one finds in Systemic Functional Theory, where the emphasis is on explaining 'how and why a saying comes to mean what it does'. The more aware we are about how our experience of the world around us comes to us mediated through meaning, the better we can critically reflect on the intangible bases of our interpretations.

Hasan refers to this as reflection literacy. She argues its importance in pedagogical practice, and its implications for bringing about social change. Becoming literate means being able to go beyond simply receiving information to learning how to interrogate and interpret not just the what, but also the how and why of what one is told.

In an endnote to the first chapter, Hasan remarks how it was her own experience as a teacher in Pakistan nearly a quarter of a century ago which prompted her to conclude the following as the goal of education: 'to produce such habits of mind in human beings which enable them to appreciate the nature of a problem, to examine the merits and demerits of proposed solutions, so as to act with discrimination not simply from the point of view of what's in it for me but from a consideration of the quality of life in the community.' The pursuit of knowledge in education should challenge our ways of meaning (whether in speech or thought) and expose habits of mind that limit our receptivity to other voices and new ways of understanding.

By reflecting on the role of language in human life, Hasan practices what she preaches. She acknowledges the limitations of specialization and the need for a meeting of minds between those working in the human sciences such as psychology, sociology, linguistics and education. She is, as she describes herself, 'a linguist interested in understanding society because society is the condition for the maintenance and evolution of language.'

Section One: On Learning and Teaching

Learning is more than just the replication of facts, as Hasan stresses in both *On the process of teaching: a perspective from functional grammar,* a new work appearing for the first time in this volume, and *Modes of learning, modes of teaching: semiotic mediation and knowledge* (2008). Instead, 'what the learner needs is to achieve interpretation, which will enable "logical thinking", which will bestow the ability "to go beyond the information" given.' Reflection literacy, as a mode of pedagogic practice, attaches importance to the learner's ability to examine, interpret and internalize concepts as one's own.

From infancy, one learns through experience and interaction, all of which is mediated through meaning in the context of community. When it comes to learning in the classroom, learners bring those same mental habits which have served them well in interpreting their experience outside the classroom. Because communities differ with respect to those 'habits of mind' which their members bring to the task of interpreting experience, interpretation does not necessarily lead to 'one single fixed and "correct" destination'. There will be different constructions of reality.

In *The implications of semantic distance for language in education* (1985), Hasan uses the term SEMANTIC DISTANCE to refer to those differences which form the basis of alternative interpretations across communities.

Beyond simply recognizing that semantic distance exists, Hasan addresses its implications for learning in the classroom. All parties to the learning process 'must be sensitized to the nature of the differences that exist in the criteria that lead to concepts of what is relevant to whom and why – what helps whom in making sense of how human behaviour is organised.' On the one hand, semantic distance may be made to play a positive role in the classroom if 'it can be directed towards the eliciting of alternative interpretations and examinations of their bases.' On the other hand, however, Hasan expresses concern over those speakers of disadvantaged varieties whose alternative interpretations may be ignored, or worse, belittled.

The fourth chapter in this section, *Forms of discourse, forms of knowledge: reading Bernstein*, co-authored with David Butt, focuses on Bernstein's (1999) paper, *Vertical and Horizontal Discourse: an essay*. With this essay, Bernstein closed out his writings with a thought-provoking look at the classification of discourse as horizontal and vertical. Noting the connection between Bernstein's work and Systemic Functional Linguistics, Hasan and Butt compare the two approaches with a view to achieving a better understanding of 'the role of language as a means of pedagogic action'.

Section Two: Language and Literacy

In *Literacy, everyday talk and society* (1996), Hasan discusses three facets of literacy: recognition, action and reflection. Each facet has a particular focus: recognition literacy focuses on language as expression; action literacy on language and content in relation to social processes; reflection literacy on making explicit the implications of the meanings said to be construed by language as active in a context relevant to some social processes.

The relation between each facet is not sequential but logical. Reflection subsumes action which in turn subsumes recognition. Literacy falls short if it fails to relate linguistic structures with their social functions, and likewise neglects reflection on the social significance of acts of meaning. 'What use is literacy,' asks Hasan in *Globalization, literacy and ideology* (2003), 'if it does not enable the literate person to decide how meanings are exchanged and how they fashion the world we live in.' Reflection literacy prompts one to examine how and why language's semiotic potential is actualized by socially positioned speakers.

Going one step further in *Literacy pedagogy and social change: directions from Bernstein's sociology* (2007), Hasan explores the possibilities for applying the outcome of reflection literacy to bring about social change. While acknowledging that reflection literacy 'will certainly not be an antidote to all social problems', nevertheless she notes the advantages of treating discourse as dialogic, and thereby cultivating in learners that most basic function of learning, 'namely to interrogate, rather than remain a docile recipient of information.' When the literate can 'see through the hypocrisy of the progressive and the civilized' therein lies hope for change.

Section Three: Mother Tongue and Other Tongue

The relationship between socialization and cross cultural education, with particular reference to the Indo-Pakistani sub-continent and England, is explored in *Socialization and cross-cultural education* (1976). As Hasan explains, by 'cross-cultural education' she is referring 'to the situation where an individual from one culture migrates temporarily to another culture in order to acquire some academic qualification.' Various intangible problems may arise in cross-cultural education as illustrated by the challenges faced by Indo-Pakistani students studying in the English educational system at the university level.

In the chapter, *Some sociological considerations in second language teaching* (1978), Hasan makes the point that we live 'a unified life in which action, interaction, understanding, learning and knowledge all work together: one's psychology is not set apart from one's culture; language is a part of human life, not an autonomous structure.' Likewise, when it comes to second language teaching/learning, it is important to consider the community within which the learners live and how the cultural patterns of the community will impact on successful language teaching/learning. As Hasan elaborates further in *Learning to function with the other tongue: A systemic functional perspective on second language teaching* (1994), success in language learning depends on the learner's ability to use wording for meaning for living. 'Learning the so-called rules of grammar without relating them systematically to meaning is a waste of time,' writes Hasan, 'and talking about meaning without showing how you do it by putting words together is to deprive pupils from understanding; it is to deny them the power of reflection on how meanings are transacted in their community.' Both teacher and student need a grammar which explains 'how and why a saying comes to mean what it does'. Such a grammar is illustrated in the last paper in this section, *English process, English tense: foreign learner, foreign teacher* (1995), in which Hasan focuses on how time is construed linguistically in English and Urdu, both through content words and the grammatical category of tense.

I

On Learning and Teaching

1 On the process of teaching: a perspective from functional grammar

1 Introduction

Let me begin by very warmly thanking the organizers of the Society of Pakistan English Language Teachers (SPELT) International Congress for inviting me to speak here today. This occasion is indeed special[1]. We are celebrating two decades of the Society's life during which it has distinguished itself by introducing innovations and improvements in language teaching and learning across the country. Indeed the theme of the present conference – *Teaching Learning, Learning Teaching* – sums up the Society's quest well. So, special congratulations are in order on this special occasion. But this situation is somewhat problematic for me: I have come here planning to speak *On the process of teaching*, which seems something like bringing coals to Newcastle. I assure you I gave the matter serious thought – but I have decided to hang on to my title for one good reason – a reason that makes sense in the context of this special occasion.

As I just said, SPELT has come of age today; with age must come a sense of maturity and independence, and for an organization as socially responsible as yours, this maturity and independence comes with a greater sense of responsibilities. It seems to me that if the Society's ideals are to be maintained, then the particular responsibility I have in mind today needs to be discussed. Indeed I would go so far as to say that this responsibility is so critical SPELT cannot afford to ignore it. Not taking it seriously will be almost like playing with the future of SPELT as well as with that of the wider society within which SPELT is embedded. This is not just a fanciful idea: teachers of any language – and particularly teachers of English, given the global status of that language today – have a central role to play in shaping the destiny of their countries. Now, I know many people are likely to think this is an exaggerated claim. After all, most of us believe that it is really those in the business of governing whose actions matter to shaping the country's future. What can language teachers do? They can hardly make any difference to such serious matters. Common as this view is, I disagree with it. Let me explain why.

2 Teaching in the age of information

We live today in the age of information – though there are people who say somewhat cynically that it might be truer to call it the age of disinformation. Whether it is the age of information, i.e., of giving listeners to understand what the case actually is, or of disinformation, i.e., deceiving them into thinking that something is the case when it is not – in either case, three things seem to be certain, and they are inter-related. First, the existence of both information/disinformation depends on the human ability to make sense of some experience; secondly, whether it is information or disinformation, its function in the life of human beings is typically to form the basis for reflection and/or action; and third, whether it is information or disinformation, its production and/or transmission involves the use of some kind of semiotic system(s) – i.e., systems of signs for making meaning. I will elaborate these points because understanding the meaning of this claim is fundamental to understanding why teachers may be said to possess the potential for contributing to their countries' future.

2.1 Making sense of experience

The simplest way to identify information quickly is to describe it as something one knows at some level of awareness. But equally important, it is a knowing that comes from experiencing, whether intentionally or unintentionally. Experience is perhaps the other name for living: so long as one lives, one cannot avoid experiencing. Take for example the new born infant: when the infant is born he[2] hardly knows anything that is not related to the working of his own body, but very soon a baby born with a normal brain begins to learn, i.e., to know about the world that exists beyond his body. He begins to accumulate new information making sense of his daily experience: the baby's information is completely mundane; he is sensing such things as *this is where food comes from* or *with this voice, comes comfort*, perhaps, a little later *crying brings help*, and much later *trying to reach something with the body brings that thing to me*; and so on. Attention has been drawn to such learning by well recognized scholars such as Vygotsky (1962), Halliday (1975a, 2003), Lock (1978), Trevarthen (1974a), and others who are all keenly aware of the part played by social environment in turning a human organism into an individual.

Now, I am not implying that the infant formulates these thoughts/words 'in' his head or is able to offer them as propositions in any way whatsoever. What is being claimed is simply that the baby is acquiring some sense of what happens; he is beginning to expect a patterning of sensuous experiences, because to live is to experience and most of the time for human beings, to experience is to learn. The condition for this to happen is two-fold: one, that the brain must have the affordance for 'recognizing' the experience in its full significance, and two, that the experience must be relevant to the experiencing self – it should be something that matters to the experiencer. If these conditions are met, the experiencer will come to 'know/learn' information based in experience whose 'value' has been mentally internalized in a useable form: this process of the transformation of experience into recognizably significant and useable value is what I am referring to as MAKING SENSE.

As we grow up in contact with the members of our speech fellowship (Firth 1957), we are surrounded by experiences that are SEMIOTIC: what we experience is some unit of a SIGN SYSTEM that signals something other than itself. We learn to attach some kind of meaning to such phenomena (Halliday 1975a; also chapter 2 here). For example, 'body language' such as a smile, a kind of eye contact, or a body posture all 'give some meaning'. There are other sign systems such as images, graphs and charts; we regularly make sense of these phenomena as well. And then, there is language – the most often used way of engaging people's attention; we effortlessly make sense of what someone is 'saying' whether by speaking or by writing: in fact we hardly ever give the matter a thought. Because we have grown up surrounded by these signs, working with them in the company of others day by day in the living of life, the meaningfulness of these signs seems natural. In learning language, we also learn what our immediate social world is like: experience is construed through meaning (Halliday and Matthiessen 1999). So putting it simply one might say: the words of a language or signs of other kinds 'have' some meaning which refers/relates to the world and it is these meanings that the human brain internalizes; this is how the world is 'translated' into the mind by signing systems.

Though as normal social beings, most often our experiences are of the kind just described above, yet there are other kinds of experiences which have nothing much to do with any established 'sign system', for example, the taste of food, stubbing your toes against a rock, or being scratched by a thorny bush, and so on. But these too are significant in our life, and they raise a rather interesting question: how is experience of this kind translated into some kind of sense? These bodily experiences to which we assign some meaning turning them into 'as-if-signs' do not seem to be part of any *recognized* semiotic system; and the question naturally arises: where does their 'value/meaning' come from? How are such experiences integrated into the processes of the brain? The question may sound simple but it is one that has been looking for an answer for centuries, because the answer has to be such as to satisfy the community of neurologists researching the working of the brain. It is not as if there are no answers at all, but those that have been presented so far (e.g., Edelman 1992; Deacon 1997; Edelman and Tononi 2000) still remain under debate.

Rushing in where angels fear to tread, I venture to suggest that there must be a considerable degree of resemblance in the processes of the brain as it makes sense of semiotic and non-semiotic experiences[3]: in both cases experience is mediated to the mind as making sense as defined above. This is only a conjecture on my part, or more charitably a thought metaphor: the idea is that in both cases a 'mental translation' or sense-making is needed, which suggests the need for postulating some mode of mediation. The brain, as the famous anthropologist, Gregory Bateson, remarked, has no monkeys or coconuts in it, nor is it a stage on which images of things and persons strut about: the significance of experience whether semiotic or non-semiotic must be transformed so as to become part of the working brain; such internalization is essential to survival. This would seem to agree with Greenfield's description of human mind as a 'personalized brain' – personalized by virtue of the unique experiences of each individual (Greenfield 2000). I conclude then that all information is relevant experience mediated to the continually developing mind in a useable form by a process that resembles SEMIOTIC MEDIATION[4] (Vygotsky 1978).

2.2 Synergy between information, reflection, action

To say that we live in the age of information is to say that information plays perhaps the most critical role in the management of human life today. Thanks to the ages of industrialization, invention and science, contemporary technology is now so advanced, particularly in the powerful nations of the West, that the possibility of mechanical error is considerably reduced; when things go wrong, this is overwhelmingly not because the machines are at fault, but it is rather due to some variety of information mismanagement,[5] which may or may not involve the human use of a machine, and which may be deliberate – a sabotage – or it may be a genuine error based in misinformation. In any case it is some variety of information that is at issue.

What this implies is that information forms the basis of the majority of our social practices – our actions, interactions, and such reflections as we care to engage in. The relationship between information and (inter-)action/reflection is, in fact, reciprocal: the greater the access to information, the greater the possibilities for engaging in effective (inter-)action and in viable reflection, and vice versa. The material success of individuals and communities depends to a great extent today on the production of useable information and the ability to exchange it to our satisfaction.

This makes information a SOCIAL GOOD, and because information is perceived as an element in bringing about social success, its quality comes to assume a critical importance: it matters whether we are dealing with information which corresponds to facts or not. Factually incorrect information whether given in good faith, i.e., some kind of misinformation, or given deliberately to deceive, i.e. disinformation, will at some stage make a difference to the effectiveness of the knower's actions and reflections. And precisely because information is so highly valued, the manufacture of counterfeit information, like counterfeit material goods, can bring about quick material gains to the manufacturer at the cost of those who are gullible enough to get caught in the web of disinformation, as for example the advertisements which offer us *freebies* – or allow us to buy now and pay later, or sell us 'melamine milk' as cheap and affordable nourishment for babies. The possibility of manufactured information – which will always contain some element of disinformation – is in fact the critical reason for differentiating between the three categories of information – MISINFORMATION, where the giver of information was unaware of 'faulty goods', DISINFORMATION, where the information was manufactured knowing it to be faulty, and INFORMATION. We do not live today simply in the age of information; we live also in a globalized world. This has meant that today the world offers vast opportunities to often 'respectable' manufacturers of disinformation (Klein 2007; McMurty 1999). This feature of our modern progressive world calls for special kind of attention to language (Hasan 2003, 2006, i.e., chapters 6 and 7 here), for often the disinformation is created skilfully by exploiting language.

2.3 Language and information

I suggested in section 2.1 that, to be internalized, all experience must be 'interpreted' as significant information. This mental process of turning experience into meaning is private to the experiencer in the sense that it is 'brain action'.[6] Section 2.2 drew attention to information as central to the management of social life. The social exchange of information naturally implies that some part of the internalized meanings must be made accessible to another, and this calls for some credible and cogent mode of externalizing the internalized information. This suggests, in turn, that as in the creation of information, so also in its transmission in society, the use of some kind of semiotic action is necessary.

Among the various semiotic systems, language is the most central to acts of transmission, simply because it is the most versatile: there are two important reasons for making this claim. First, it can construe meanings which are able to refer to what is being experienced here and now; to what has already been experienced and internalized as part of the mind's memory system; and even to those states of affairs which one hopes or imagines might come about under some circumstance some time in the future. Only a fraction of this vast range of meanings can be construed by the non-linguistic semiotic systems: instead of being 'time bound' like most other semiotic systems, language is 'time-binding' (Korzybski 1933), ranging over what is, what was, and what will be.

Secondly, there are significant differences in the quality of meaning construal: linguistically construed meanings tend to be more precise and can display a greater gradation of differentiation[7] amongst the members of the same class. It is due to these characteristics that language can be used for construing imaginary information as, for example, in verbal art (Hasan 1985a; Miller and Turci 2007; Lukin and Webster 2005; Butt and Lukin 2009), as well as for construing abstract structures containing elements whose referents might have no material existence, as for example 'network of relations' in linguistics: by this last comment I am referring to the role of language in the construction of theories. Behind each theory, there are hours of discourse: meanings are being exchanged among those who are interested in that field of study for some reason or another (cf. chapter 4 here). And, it needs to be added, that it is this quality of language which enables its speakers to exploit it for the construal of disinformation.

It follows that many of our experiences begin with language as saying or writing. But the fact that human social life cannot continue without people interacting linguistically, i.e., talking in friendship, in managerial capacity of some kind, in doing business and trade, in making theories to explain phenomena that impinge on human life and death, in commercially transacting information as in newspapers, TV and radio, and so on – all such interaction implies that meaning is being transmitted linguistically. In this way, *information goes around*: it begins as experience mediated to mind as sense/meaning and it returns in discourse as linguistic experience: in every discourse, information, i.e., (some part of) experience-based internalized meanings are transmitted to others as linguistically construed meanings. What this suggests is that to be transmitted as linguistic meanings, the experience based internalized meanings must be commensurate with linguistically construable meanings: it is *construing experience as meaning* that makes experience transmissible as meanings in discourse.

By these steps I have tried to argue that living in the age of information is largely equal to living in the age of 'languaging', which is not to say that other semiotic systems do not come into the picture – in non-pathological discourse most semiotic systems largely work together. The debate about the relationship of the various semiotic systems is complex and this is not the place to engage in it, but I hope I have managed to argue convincingly that today we live in the age of information, that in the construal and transmission of information linguistic meaning has a paramount position and that today language is the most powerful means of influencing the management of human affairs.[8] There is a need to understand the source of the power of language: this need has not arisen today simply because deceitful exploitation of manufactured information has become more prevalent, though this may be true enough. In fact the need has always been there because it is human acts of meaning that underlie social change and development across time. The need is recognized more clearly today perhaps partly because SFL, the functionally based model of language, has made it easier to perceive these connections so much more clearly.

If these meanings are beholden to language for their existence and transmission, then understanding the action power of language seems essential to a community's survival, and by implication, to the profession of language teaching. For who should be better equipped to teach the source of the power of language than the language teacher? It will be the quality of language teaching that will make the critical difference to the learners' ability to understand the nature of information.

3 Ideas about grammar

You might wonder what the GRAMMAR of teaching has to do with meaning, information, the power of language, or the part language plays in changing and developing societies; how could grammar, a set of rules, be relevant to such important social issues? Well, the word grammar, like most words in a language, means different things to different people. For example, simplifying the situation somewhat, the formalistic linguists think of grammar as a set of rules, universally applicable to all languages of the world; behind this lies a conception of language as a biologically inherited, so species-specific, *mental organ*; in this view, language is *autonomous*, i.e., has nothing or little to do with human social life (Chomsky 1965). Then, there are the teachers of language, particularly in countries forever described as *emerging/developing nations*: they, it seems, have inherited some of the canons of age-old educational systems. Their conception of grammar is typically as a set of rules which has very little to do with the working of the language that is being taught; often, therefore, the teaching of such grammar is viewed as profitless and irksome, simply a mistaken educational convention. Behind these views lie centuries of badly conceptualized grammar text books, a deep misunderstanding of the nature of language, and hardly any understanding whatsoever of the role of grammar in the internal organization of language or in the social exchanges of meanings. And yet, the exchange of meaning is the defining function of language in human life.

Naturally, then, a large number of both teachers and learners see grammar as extraneous to the business of language education: in their view grammar is something one is forced to learn, and it would be best ignored if only the evaluation criteria, i.e., passing the exam, did not require it! I would not be surprised if many members of my audience today actually sympathized with this view of grammar and grammar teaching. This was also *my* perception of the grammar that was taught to me in my student days – something to be ignored as useless rote learning. It is true that many of you have an advantage which I did not: there are now many occasions to listen to respected foreign experts, for example, on the SPELT conference platform. But unfortunately, they too are not necessarily well informed; so I have heard them pleading in favour of keeping grammar out of the classroom because they see it as a hindrance to successful teaching. Only yesterday, the keynote address entertained the general audience by reiterating this view about grammar and dictionary, both of which the speaker seemed to think were inflicted on the long suffering language teachers by some *little old people with pointy ears*. And I believe it was implied that neither learning about words nor about grammar is relevant to the success of language teaching; in the speaker's view, they interfere in entertaining classroom practices.

3.1 The role of grammar in language teaching

I am afraid I disagree with such views: they are most probably based in genuine misinformation, hopefully not in deliberate disinformation. A moment's reflection will make any normal human being realize that one cannot use language without using words and one cannot use more than one word without putting them in some kind of relation to each other, which is what grammar is for: to simplify the story, grammar informs us about how in a given community speakers put words together to make some desired meanings. If one fails to get such relations right, one would either not get understood at all or there would be genuine problems of interpretation. In other words, one would have failed to be meaningful to some extent. As Halliday (1975a) points out, *learning language is learning how to mean*: he said this in the context of a small child learning his mother tongue, but it is just as true for learning other tongues. We would have failed as teachers of language if after years of teaching the pupils fail to be understood. Our aim as teachers is to enable pupils 'to do things with words' (Austin 1980). But one cannot do things with words if they are produced as gibberish, i.e., used in such a way that they cannot be interpreted. To do things with words, the words have to be produced in some grammatical relation to each other – preferably relations that help in making the kind of meanings that are appropriate in that community for doing the desired thing.

3.2 Lexicogrammar as a resource for meaning

This is why I am proud to count myself as one amongst those 'little old people with pointy ears' who would deplore the shortsighted attitudes to understanding how words and grammar work together to produce meaning – which is a social good called 'information'. The work of my colleagues using systemic functional linguistics (SFL) to analyse texts has shown that, in the words of Michael Halliday, grammar is the 'powerhouse of language': nothing can ever be done with language without using words grammatically. This is why, in SFL, we think of these two aspects of language as closely related: together they count as the form of language, often referred to simply as WORDING or more technically as LEXICOGRAMMAR.

The lexicogrammar of a language is its resource for meaning; as such it is the heart of what teachers are trying to teach to enable the production and interpretation of meaning. If the success of language teaching is judged by how well students can do things with language, then such success depends on how effectively the language teacher manages to teach students to enable them to use their lexicogrammar to make meanings appropriate to the desired context of their discourse. And I am sure you will agree when I say that for teaching effectively how to make appropriate meanings with lexicogrammar, teachers themselves need to understand the nature of lexicogrammar: clearly, what one cannot understand reasonably well, one cannot teach effectively.

I am now going to embark on a discourse which will move towards its announced goal 'indirectly'. I will do a grammatical analysis of the process of teaching, hoping thereby to offer an insight into how grammar is done in SFL, and with the aim of showing how wording and meaning in language are inseparable. Through this exercise I hope to demonstrate that reflection on grammatically construed meanings leads us to an acute understanding of important social issues which make a difference to the quality of the survival of a society. By these related steps I hope to move from the grammar of the process of teaching to the significance of teaching as a social process.

4 Grammar construing 'states of affairs'

The aspect of grammar which construes the kind of relations that underlie a state of affairs is known in SFL as transitivity (for some discussion, see also chapters 10 and 11 in this volume; Halliday 1994a; Matthiessen 1995). A few words are needed here on this grammatical system,[9] since it is relevant to the analysis of the process of teaching. The term TRANSITIVITY refers to that aspect of the grammatical analysis of the clause[10] which resonates with the experiential metafunction[11] of language – that is to say, the function of language to construe speakers' experience of their world; whether this experience relates to the world outside the speaker or inside, it is realized in transitivity relations. To see how this is done, here is some 'real' language – real in the sense that it occurred in some natural context of discourse: a mother explaining to her daughter why she is being asked not to play with marbles when her little brother Andrew is awake and about:

> Chicky! I don't like you playing with marbles when Andrew is around, that's all … and you know what, yesterday I found a marble right there when Andrew was crawling around, now, it was one of those marbles that you were supposed to put back and you forgot.

When the mother says *yesterday I found a marble right there*, she is describing something that had happened – more technically, she is using language to construe a STATE OF AFFAIRS. On the basis of her saying, we know who did what, where, when and to what object: we had no other source of information but the mother's saying. But how is this kind of information construed? It is worth noting that we could produce the self-same words in a random string such as, say, *found right yesterday a there marble*. Whatever sense one makes of this collection of words, it is likely to be noticeably different from the original case – here, no part bears a recognizable relation to any others. The difference between this random string of words and the mother's original saying is precisely that in her wording there is a functional unity: the lexicogrammar creates a unified structure in which every constituent of the clause plays a significant role.

4.1 Process, participant and circumstance

So how is this functional order established in language? At the centre of every state of affairs, there is some kind of 'goings on'; in our example this is represented by the word *found* in the clause *yesterday I found a marble right there*. We refer to this transitivity element of the clause as PROCESS. The element process is the nucleus or the 'nub' of the transitivity structure of a clause, in the sense that the nature of the process is the most powerful indicator of what other elements may or may not form part of the transitivity structure of the clause under focus. The element itself is realized by the main verb of a verbal group. What we are calling 'main verb' here is traditionally described as a kind of 'content word'. These (content) verbs realize different process types, such as (i) MATERIAL, e.g., *find, lose, walk, run, give, bring, cook, kill* ..., (ii) MENTAL, e.g., *think, remember, understand, realize, see, hear, fear, hate, like* ..., (iii) VERBAL, e.g., *tell, narrate, ask, enquire, reply, respond, demand* ..., (iv) RELATIONAL, e.g., *appear, seem, be, become* ..., and so on. Teachers of language sometimes refer to such verbs as 'doing words'. In the course of discussing the process of teaching, I will present some details below about the material, verbal and mental process types in English. More detailed discussion of transitivity and of process types is to be found in Halliday (1994a); Halliday and Matthiessen (2004); Hasan, Cloran and Butt (1996); for a brief comparative Urdu-English account of material and mental process types, Hasan 1995b (and also chapter 11 in this volume).

It is a truism to say that where there is a process there must be some participants. Certain participant role(s) are entailed by a particular process type: they are either overtly present in the clause or implied/implicit. For example, with a material process, which refers to some kind of happening or action, the entailed participant role is ACTOR – putting it simply the actor is the doer of the deed; if there is a deed there must be a doer (though it is not true that the doer must be overtly mentioned in the same clause). Thus, in *yesterday I found a marble right there*, the actor function is realized by 'I'; in a clause such as *yesterday a marble was found right there*, it is still implied that there was some participant, who did the finding; reference to this finder can be built into the transitivity structure as in 'yesterday a marble was found right there by me' where 'by me' is indicative of the actor: but as the earlier example stands, the actor is not construed in the clause *yesterday a marble was found right there*.

By contrast, the participant GOAL is not entailed by every material process; thus when the material process is middle as in *Andrew is sleeping*, there can be no goal. Goal is permitted only with a specific sub-class of material process known in SFL as EFFECTIVE: in traditional grammars the term TRANSITIVE was used to refer to verbs which could 'take' an 'object'. In the example *yesterday I found a marble right there* the process is material: effective, and the function goal is realized by the nominal group *a marble*. Each participant in a clause plays a distinct role in construing the state of affairs; and each process type specifies some specific set of participants. These roles range from the more active, e.g., actor like *I* in our example to the less active, e.g. *a marble*, which functions here as goal.

Although the above is far from exhausting the topic of participants, we will close this section now with a word on CIRCUMSTANCE, which specifies such contingent facts as the place pertinent to the process, e.g., *here, there, in the playground*, …, or the time, e.g., *yesterday, now, tomorrow* …, or manner e.g., *quietly, quickly* …, or accompaniment e.g., *with granny, together* …, and so on. As the examples show circumstance is realized as an adverbial or prepositional phrase, capable of referring to the attendant circumstances in some state of affairs. Circumstance is seldom entailed, though the process type of a clause indicates which category of circumstance may be appropriately used with it (Hasan 1987a).

5 On the process of teaching: view 1

With his brief introduction to transitivity, let me now turn to the analysis of teaching. I will borrow an example from Halliday (1976d), particularly since I intend to traverse more or less the same path in my analysis[12] which was followed in that paper:

i: The teacher taught the student English.

It is obvious from the make up of this clause that it takes at least two to play the teaching game: no one just *teaches* as they *run* or *sleep* all by themselves; but teaching always suggests participation by someone else. And even a third entity is needed: one does not just teach someone; one teaches something to someone. In other words, if teaching is a material process, it has to be one of transaction (Hasan 1985b; 1987a): the process calls for an Actor who initiates the transaction – here, *the teacher*; it needs another participant who will receive the transacted entity, one which is realized here as *the student* (recipient) and 'English' (transacted entity), respectively. Let us now compare it with another clause whose process decisively involves transaction:

ii: Mary gave John the jacket.

We now need to ask if clause (i) and (ii) are identical in every respect other than the selection of lexical items in them. Figure 1 presents the analysis[13] of the two clauses: each cell in the first two rows presents the constituent groups of each clause; each clause has exactly the same number of constituents. The transitivity functions of these constituents are shown in the final row. Both clauses are assigned the same transitivity structure.

Figure 1: Is teaching like giving?

(i):	The teacher	taught	the student	English.
(ii):	Mary	gave	John	a jacket.
Analysis:	Actor: benefactor	Process: material: benefactive	Beneficiary: recipient	Goal: gift

According to Figure 1, the clauses are identical. The analysis in this figure assigns the function of actor: benefactor to *the teacher* and *Mary*: the process in both clauses is material: benefactive; *the student* and *John* are assigned the function of beneficiary: recipient; this leaves the final constituents, *English/ the jacket*, described here as goal. Semantically, certain general properties are associated with these functions. So, if the Process is material: benefactive, then an actor has the empowering role of benefactor, the giver of the gift; by contrast, the beneficiary: recipient has a comparatively reactive role of receiving that which is given. The goal, on the other hand, is entirely passive: being something that is moved from one participant to the other, it has the least active role.[14] According to this analysis, there is no difference between the two clauses in their grammatical meanings: *teaching* is a doing of the same kind as *giving, bringing, handing, lending*, and so on. Of course the meanings of the lexical items differ and one of these differences is that instead of transacting material goods, teaching is a process that transfers *semiotic goods* of some kind: giving moves an object from one person to another; teaching moves some kind of knowledge, expertise, or competence from the teacher to the taught.

5.1 Teaching a material process: socio-cultural arguments

This picture may strike some of us as strange. How can teaching be seen as the same kind of process as *giving*? But if we examine what goes on in schools, sometimes this image of teaching could not be said to be alien to the educational scene even in the progressive West. The idea of brains as empty vessels into which information is poured by way of education may have been put to rest, but the focus on information bytes remains; it would be unusual to find information being treated as something that has implications that go beyond the actual words, stretching the mind beyond the given to what can be imagined. And increasingly there is pressure on the schools and by the schools on its teachers to keep the lessons close to what is for assessment; if the pupils distinguish themselves at assessment time, schools get accolades in the form of merit points and higher funding. If success in education equals success in the recall of what one was told by the teacher, then passing the test is like producing a receipt for the safe arrival of the semiotic goods. So, yes! There is no exaggeration in saying that what we are witnessing is simply a transfer of semiotic goods – by the same token, it is what Bateson would have described as *zero learning* (1972: 283–308); something that is far from learning to learn. In keeping with the above stance, we talk about many aspects of the educational activity in a way that is quite reminiscent of handling material goods. What the pupils are to be given in the class are *materials*; the way the *materials* are arranged for *delivery* counts as *the packaging of materials* to which, rightly of course, much thought is devoted in terms of which segment is to follow which. We should, therefore, not be surprised to find that the dominant view of teaching in the forever-developing nations is overwhelmingly that of 'passing on' some kind of *packaged knowledge*. Here, additionally, the SOCIAL DISTANCE (Hasan 1973) between the pupil and the teacher might be greater: the teacher, given her expertise – but as likely, given her age – is not to be questioned. And it is not as if interrogation by the pupil and genuine discussions with the teacher in the classroom is a typical feature of the Western educational scenarios, either.

This account suggests that the common perception of teaching captured by the analysis in Figure 1 cannot be rejected on the ground that it does not correspond to truth. What is problematic in this factually correct situation is that it focuses simply on the most visible aspects of the process of teaching. But this too could be *explained away* on the ground that the business of teaching in most communities represents an INSTITUTIONALIZED activity; activities of this kind usually have 'multiple coding', i.e., they are indicated by material features as well as by semiotic patterns. Looking back into the history of humanity, we find arrangements were made, consciously and deliberately, in most cultures for imparting certain kinds of competencies to certain selected younger members of the community. These arrangements may not appear to be exactly alike everywhere at the visible level, but deep down certain features persist even today. For example, what will be taught to whom by whom for how long and where were issues that formed part of the story in most communities – ancient Indians, the Incas, the Egyptians, and the early Islamic Arabs. At some level, human beings recognized fairly early in their history the need for carefully organizing that group of activities which would educate the younger members, thus renewing 'the human resources' of the society – a condition of its continuity. So a great deal of cultural salience has always surrounded learning and teaching in societies, turning the ensemble into a recognized social institution which has always been regulated socially.

Nor is the situation very different today: we have inherited the preoccupation from the past, and in most countries there exists today a consciously designed, deliberately organized institution for administering the *transmission of specialized competences* (Bernstein 1990: 183). Following such sociologists as Bourdieu and Passeron (1977) and Bernstein (1990), I will refer to this socially regulated institution as OFFICIAL PEDAGOGY. Much more complex, especially perhaps in the advanced progressive societies, our educational institutions – said to be egalitarian – display some of the same concerns: they too design ways of determining what needs to be taught, to whom, of establishing criteria for who is competent to teach, and how the actual achievement of competence is to be assessed.[15] With the highly complex economic organization of modern societies, attainments in educational achievement appear to have visible material rewards: the perception is that higher educational attainments are in some way logically related to more independent and affluent existence, though it has also been argued that it is not what you know but who you are in terms of social status and power that determines your material well being (Luke 1996).

5.3 Education as a visible social institution

But what is a social institution? A social institution is known by the social practices that are associated with it; in the performance of INSTITUTIONALIZED practices, visible indicators of the staging of the process will often be found together with semiotic features. In other words, it is culturally multiply coded (Hasan 1981, 1999b; Cloran 1994): most aspects of the unfolding of such social practices, including the appearance and behaviour of its agents, are relatively routinized. Thus in the case of teaching, the location where the social practice will take place is socially identified; how the time will be organized is for the most part established prior to the act of learning and teaching and it has its own mode of announcement – the 'bell rings'; learners and sometimes teachers are distinctively dressed, the school bus has its own additional regulations, and so on. In these ways, visibly the process of education seems to be set apart from other mundane activities. And it is not uncommon for the visible to be taken to constitute what education is: governments pride themselves on the millions or billions they assign to building schools, to setting up committees of prominent citizens (irrespective of their qualifications for the job) to examine the way evaluation is carried out (without necessarily having engaged in any actual research about the significance of evaluation), and for setting up websites to name and shame *badly performing schools*, by which they mean schools where the pupils fail to return in tests what they were given in the classroom.[16]

Now, it would be silly to discount the value of visible educational resources such as transport facilities, providing good locations for teaching, making text books available at an affordable price, and so on, or to underplay the importance of invisible agencies that organize the mobilization of huge facilities such as the preparation of text books, the fair administration of evaluation, the orchestration of standards, and so on. But all of these activities are simply a means to an end: and that end is certainly not met in treating the process of education as analogous to the process of giving and taking some material object. In my view that end expressed in general terms is to *produce such habits of mind in human beings which enable them to appreciate the nature of a problem, to examine the merits and demerits of proposed solutions, so as to act with discrimination* not simply from the point of view of *what's in it for me* but *from a consideration of the quality of life in the community.*

6 Grammatical grounds for grammatical analysis

Even if my definition of what education is about were to be accepted,[17] this would not furnish a reason for revising the analysis presented in Figure 1. The grammatical analysis of some language unit is based on the language internal relations. So although in the last sections I have shown some 'logical' grounds for discrediting that interpretation of the process of teaching which is based on widespread socio-cultural views, neither the acceptance of these socio-cultural views nor the rejection of their significance bears much relevance to establishing the correct grammatical analysis of the clause under discussion: *the teacher taught the student English.* To find the grounds for rejecting that analysis we need to take a closer look at the two clauses.

6.1 Is teaching a material process? A lexicogrammatical view

One important difference between the grammar of *gave* and *taught* emerges from comparing their goal, i.e., *the jacket* and *English* respectively. Speaking non-technically, we may say that, in general, the goal of a process is that participant which is directly impacted by the process of a clause: the process always does something to the goal; if actor is DO-ER, then goal is DONE-TO. So, as Halliday (1994a) points out, the goal of a clause can be easily recognized by using a probe with *do to*, as for example in (ii): *what did Mary do to the jacket?* One appropriate answer could be she gave it (i.e., *the jacket*) to John. Consider, however, (i): *what did the teacher do to English?* If in response one said: 'the teacher taught it (i.e., English) to the student', then most speakers of English would most probably find the answer pretty odd! In fact, they might even be taken aback by the question itself! The process of teaching does not act on *English* in the way that *giving* does on its goal, *the jacket*. What exactly is the difference?

I will answer this question by considering both the lexicogrammar and the meanings it construes. To say that the process acts on the goal is to say that the coming about of the process would have a direct effect on the goal. This effect is not always identical: it varies systematically according to the more delicate sub-types of the material process. Although the description of the sub-types of material process has not yet reached this degree of detail in SFL, below are some examples of systemically distinct material processes which it seems very likely will need to be recognized in the study of 'lexis as most delicate grammar' (Halliday 1961; Hasan 1985b, 1987a; Tucker 1996, 1998, 2007):

	Example	Process material:	effect on goals
ii	Mary gave John the jacket.	dispositive: transactional	mediated to other
iii	He put the book on the shelf.	dispositive: non-transactional	changed location
iv	They make good furniture.	transformative: creative	comes to existence
v	John broke the vase.	transformative: disintegrative: partial	destroyed
vi	The bullet killed the man	transformative: disintegrative: final	becomes extinct

Table 1: Material process types and their effect on goal

At the primary degree of DELICACY, the process in all clauses in Table 1 would be described as material, but, more delicately, each is presented as having some systemic feature(s) which the others do not have.[18] For example, both *give* (ii) and *put* (iii) realize the systemic features material: DISPOSITIVE; any Goal, if it undergoes such a process, will have changed its location from that which it had held prior to the event. In this respect (ii) and (iii) are alike. The change in location of both *the jacket* in (ii) and *the book* in (iii) is specifically indicated. But at a more delicate level of analysis the processes differ: (ii) is TRANSACTIONAL, (iii) is not. So although both the goals have undergone a change of location, there is a significant difference between them. Being transactional (ii) implicates a participant other than the actor and the goal, viz., the beneficiary, whereas (iii) being NON-TRANSACTIONAL does not implicate any other party than the actor and the goal.

The material processes in clauses (iv), (v) and (vi) all have the systemic feature TRANSFORMATIVE. This process type is realized by verbs referring to a specific kind of physical change that implicates the entity referred to by the nominal realizing goal. Thus, if the material: transformative process is CREATIVE as in (iv) *they make good furniture*, the group functioning as goal refers to something that has/is about to come into existence as a result of the action[19]; if the material: transformative process has the features DIS-

INTEGRATIVE: PARTIAL, as in (v) *John broke the vase*, the group functioning as goal will refer to an entity whose physical structure has undergone or is about to undergo a change in appearance; if it is DISINTEGRATIVE: FINAL, the extinction of the entity referred to by the group functioning as goal is indicated as in (vi) *the bullet killed the man.* In light of these generalizations the question naturally arises: if *taught* is to be treated as material: dispositive: transactional: benefactive Process, with *English* as its goal, what would be implied about *English* as the entity that undergoes the process of teaching?

6.2 English as the goal in clause (i)

If someone says *Mary gave John the jacket*, then all else being equal, the semiotically *logical* assumption would be that thereafter John was in possession of that jacket and Mary was not. But the same cannot be said about English in the clause (i) *the teacher taught the student English.* There are at least three reasons for this: two of these pertain directly to the process of teaching, and the third concerns a requirement placed by a material... benefactive process on any nominal functioning as its goal.

Taking the first reason first, main verbs capable of functioning as process in English are either DURATIVE or PUNCTUATIVE. The latter category refers to a process that can be spatio-temporally delimited, while the durative ones have a cumulative nature, so their duration cannot be delimited. Thus *like, love, hate, care* – all main verbs which do not realize material process at all – like the verb *teach* are durative while verbs such as *give, hit, put, hear* are punctuative: it is possible to give someone a jacket at 3:27 p.m. but it would be laughable to say that someone hated someone at 3:27 p.m. When a teacher announces that she teaches geography at 10 a.m. on Wednesdays, speakers of English do not conclude that at two minutes past ten, this act of teaching will be concluded. The verb teaching is clearly durative, and technically speaking, there is a difficulty in determining whether/when it may be said to have unfolded.

Secondly, some actions with an assumption of exchange of goods/services in their history come in pairs: examples would be *buy/sell*; *borrow/lend*; and *give/take.* The relation between the members of such pairs I am going to call *symbiotic*: so, for example, if John buys a jacket, this implies some one sold John a jacket; if Jill borrows a book, then someone lent her a book and so on. The members of the pair are like two sides of the same coin: and just as in a coin, you do not have heads without tails, so in these pairs you do not have the possibility of one process but not the other. Each member refers to one 'face' only, but the other side has to be assumed as existing. So to say that

Mary gave John a jacket is to imply that *John took the jacket/John has the jacket*. Borrowing the botanical term *symbiosis* we may think of this relation as one of SEMIOTIC SYMBIOSIS. According to Lyons (1968: 25), pairs such as these are 'converse antonyms'; I am not clear whether semiotic symbiosis is a property of all converse antonyms, but it is quite clear that semantically *there is no such symbiotic relation between teaching and learning*. Although there is a pretty strong association between the verb to teach and to learn[20] (discussion 7.2 below), nonetheless, the processes are not coupled by semo-logic (Hasan 1999a). Without sounding absurd, you cannot say: *I did not sell my house but he has bought it;* but it is perfectly acceptable for a fond mother to say in praise of her son: *We did not teach him anything; he learnt everything by himself.* One might add: that the absence of a symbiotic relation between the two processes spells a continuing challenge to any education system truly setting out to educate its students. This, it would seem, constitutes a critical problem in the official pedagogic system, and we will return to some related issue below (section 8).

The above suggests that the analysis of *taught* as a material … benefactive process is subject to serious doubt; and there is yet more evidence to come in favour of rejecting that analysis. The material: dispositive: transactional: benefactive process requires its goal to be realized as a nominal group with some specific systemic features: whatever is able to function as goal of such a process must be CONCRETE: ALIENABLE. Consider verbs such as *give, lend, donate* which overwhelmingly often and quite indisputably realize this type of material processes: the goal in these cases is realized by a nominal which refers to an entity that is CONCRETE and ALIENABLE. If, however, such verbs occur in a clause with a nominal group which does not meet this condition, then notwithstanding other evidence such as the place of the nominal group in order of sequence, it will not function as goal; and, in fact, the verb realizing the process will be said to be a lexical metaphor (Hasan 1987a). A famous example is: *Friends! Romans! Countrymen! Lend me your ears*! Or *borrowing your expression, I would say* .... Or *well! I was considerably annoyed, so I gave him a decided what for*. Now, whatever the properties of the nominal group *English*, it is not concrete unlike *books, potatoes, shoes* or *houses*. Nor is it alienable; once English is learnt, it is like a part of the learner's being; it is an *in*alienable property of the speaker; it cannot be given away except when, in a manner of speaking, the speaker's *brain goes*: and yet there is no lexical metaphor involved in saying *I taught him English*.

The implication is that in relation to teaching or learning, *English* does not possess the properties that are necessary for a nominal group to function as the goal of a material process clause. The teacher may teach but the teacher is not endowing a gift, because English is incapable of being a gift. By saying that English is inalienable, and not 'given' by the teacher to the student', I do not mean to imply that in learning English, the experience of listening to other speakers of English is immaterial; or that English never changes; not even that teaching English could not contribute to some change in that language. But English is an instance of the semiotic system, 'language': as such it is subject to constant variation and change; the properties that define linguistic varieties as specific varieties or that lead eventually to the conclusion that the system of some language has changed sufficiently to be recognized as a distinct new language, tend to display themselves cumulatively; no single person, no single event can be identified as the one that could be credited with having actually changed English, or any other language.

As a semiotic system English is a resource for creating information – and sets of linguistic data called KNOWLEDGE (cf. the discussion in sections 2). Consisting of abstract structures, knowledge may deal with visible phenomena as physics does or with invisible ones, which are only intelligible such as most aspects of the semiotic – and perhaps, social – systems (cf. the discussion about 'experience' becoming mind in earlier sections). Elements of knowledge such as theories, concepts, ideas, beliefs, hypotheses, and so on are all created semiotically. We will return below (section 8) to the semiotic nature of English in relation to teaching. At this point, I simply emphasize: knowing that you have been teaching Johnny something is by no means the same as saying that Johnny has been learning that self-same thing. The grammatical patterns of the process of teaching show that teaching is not like giving.

6.3 The structure potential of two processes: *teaching* and *giving*

The arguments in 6.2 have thrown serious doubt on the status of *English* as goal and of *taught* as a material process that is also benefactive. In this section, I examine other differences between the processes of *teaching* and *giving*. These differences do not concern any one specific element of the clause; rather, they concern the possibilities of structure open to a clause type,[21] i.e., its STRUCTURE POTENTIAL.

In discussing the structure potential of clauses with the processes *taught* and *gave*, our focus will be limited to the transitivity structure only. As pointed out earlier (section 4), the element process is the nucleus of the transitivity structure. On the basis of the process, we can as a matter of principle predict what participant types – and sometimes what circumstance types – can be selected with it (Hasan 1987a). In the last section (6.2), we drew attention to those properties required in any nominal group capable of functioning as goal with a material...benefactive process; English had failed that test. In addition to this, on the basis of a process type, it is also possible to identify those elements which may or may not be left implicit.

Table 2 presents a partial picture of the structure potential of clauses (i) and (ii). The left column concerns the process of teaching; each of the clause types presented in the left column is 'replicated' element by element in the right column with reference to the process of giving. The aim is to see if the picture presented in the table will support the same description for both clauses:

	Clauses with Process *taught*		Clauses with Process *gave*
i	The teacher taught the student English	ii	Mary gave John the jacket
ia	The teacher taught the student	iia	? Mary gave John
ib	The teacher taught English	iib	Mary gave a jacket
ic	The teacher taught	iic	? Mary gave

Table 2: Structure potential of clauses with process gave/taught

The structure of (i) and (ii) in the first row of Table 2 have already been described in Figure 1. When (ia) and (iia) are compared, it appears that with the process of *giving* in clause (ii), the explicit realization of the goal *the jacket* is a requirement: in other words, it cannot be left implicit as in (iia). In fact, most speakers would find (iia) so unusual as to say that it makes no sense whereas (ia) by comparison is unremarkable. This implies that the range of things that can be taught is much wider than of those which can be *given, taken, sold, bought*, and so on. *Teachers teach students* all the time, and no one raises a question, but if *Mary gives John*, then listeners ask: what is it that the giver is giving the receiver; in other words there can be no beneficiary without the 'gift'/'benefit'. In clause (iib) *Mary gave a jacket* leaves something unsaid; on the basis of just this much information, the listener does not know who was given, but the assumption is that somewhere in the environment – most likely in the co-text – there is the information which makes clear the identity of the beneficiary, thus perhaps: *Everyone gave John a present. I gave a briefcase and Mary gave a jacket*. So it is not that the beneficiary is totally 'expendable' in this clause type: simply that it is possible for it to be left implicit, with the expectation/knowledge that the source of interpretation is very likely to be at hand. In the last row, clause (ic) and clause (iic), again, differ: the latter gives an impression of being incomplete, the former does not. In keeping with this, (ic) is much easier to contextualize – i.e., it construes its context as that of an expected action that was performed as, perhaps, in *the teacher taught and went back home*. This does not seem to apply to (iic) *Mary gave*: consider for example, *Mary gave and asked to take care of the book*. Even though this is an optimally helpful environment, it is to be doubted if many English speakers will interpret it as *Mary gave the book and asked for the book to be taken care of*. There are, however, conditions under which structure (iic) may be interpretable.[22]

The upshot of the above discussion is to establish that the structure potential of clauses with a clearly material … benefactive process such as with *give, donate* is remarkably different from that of the clause whose process is realized by the verb *teach*. This brings us back exactly where we began: what kind of process is the process of teaching? Section 7 is an attempt to offer another view.

7 On the process of teaching: view 2

Just as in section 6, I have attempted to offer grammatical grounds for saying that the analysis of the process of teaching in Figure 1 is not valid, so in this section I will attempt to offer grammatical grounds for suggesting an alternative analysis for it. My suggestion is that teaching is a VERBAL process. I will again follow Halliday (1994a) in my analysis, though at certain points the analysis presented here will need to go beyond the information given in Halliday (1994a). First, a few words on verbal process: as Halliday (1994a: 140) points out the verbal processes 'are the processes of saying, as in *what did you say? – I said it's noisy in here*. But "saying" has to be interpreted in a rather broad sense; it covers any kind of symbolic exchange of meaning, like *the notice tells you to keep quiet*, or *my watch tells me it's half past ten*.'

The three important functional elements associated with this process type are SAYER, RECEIVER and VERBIAGE. The function sayer is comparable to actor in the material process – i.e., it is the active –er function; in the above Halliday extract, sayer is *you, I, the notice, my watch*, respectively; these words refer to entities to whom/which the process of saying is ascribed. Secondly, the function of RECEIVER, the one 'to whom the saying is directed, e.g., *me, your parents, the court* in *tell me the whole truth, did you repeat that to your parents?, describe to the court the scene of the accident*, respectively' (Halliday 1994a: 141): this in some ways is reminiscent of the function beneficiary, being the receiver of a semiotic good. The third function is called VERBIAGE, and the closest function to this is the goal of a material: transformative: creative process. 'Verbiage may be **the content of what is said**; e.g. *the apartment* in *can you describe the apartment to me?…his plan of campaign* as in *the manager will outline his plan of campaign, the mystery* in *the mystery has never been explained*' (Halliday 1994a: 141; emphasis in original, *RH*).

As in the case of the material process so also with the verbal, it is possible to postulate sub-categories. For example, Halliday's identification of the function TARGET as 'the entity that is targeted by the process of saying; e.g. *him* in *she always praised him to her friends*, *my intelligence* in *please don't insult my intelligence*.' In this connection he points to a group of verbs capable of 'accepting' a TARGET, e.g., *praise, insult, abuse, slander, flatter, blame criticize*, and so on: these are instances of verbal: targeting process; and target is not the same as receiver. This sub-class of verbal process is known by implicating a target and typically being non-projecting[23] (for discussion Halliday 1994a; Halliday and Matthiessen 2004; also chapter 11 here). The verbs which realize the verbal process most generally are *say, ask* and *tell*; (compare them with *invite, announce, praise, accuse* and so on); on this ground we may consider the former as 'clearly' verbal as *give* is transactional: benefactive

7.1 Teaching as a verbal process

Employing the same strategy as used in Figure 1, I will present a verbal process clause where the process is realized by a verb which is clearly verbal, in this case *tell*; there can be no doubt that it refers to a verb of saying. In Figure 2, this verbal process clause (iii) will run parallel to clause (i) where the process is realized by the verb *teach*. The analysis of the pair will then be displayed in the final row as it was in Figure 1. I will examine the questions and implications arising from this analysis.

Figure 2: Teaching as a verbal process?

(i)	The teacher	taught	the student	English
(iii)	Mary	told	Julian	a story
Analysis	Sayer	Process: verbal	Receiver	Verbiage

According to this analysis, both clauses have a verbal process, which implies each is construing an interactive state of affairs in which two parties – the sayer and the receiver – exchange some meanings. They describe, in speech or writing, a semiotic event that took place in the past; the understanding of the nature of these states of affairs is revealed to the reader/listener by working out the meanings (i.e., semantics) of the wordings (i.e., lexicogrammar): it is the lexicogrammar of the language that has 're-created' the experiences of situations in the past. This is what we mean by saying that the semiotic system of language with lexicogrammar as its powerhouse is a highly potent resource for the exchange of information. In examining these verbal process clauses, we will also glean some information about how saying works in ordinary life.

The function of sayer, in both clauses, is realized by a nominal group which has the properties ANIMATE: HUMAN: SPECIFIC. But as Halliday's examples showed, the realization of the sayer function is not limited to only this type of nominal group: information can be relayed by other sources. Thus, first, instead of the feature 'specific', such a nominal group might refer to a COLLECTIVE, e.g., *crowd, class, committee* …; or to some entity that is IN-ANIMATE – perhaps an artefact of some kind which is used as a SYMBOL SOURCE e.g. *the notice board, the newspaper, the report, the book, the clock, the signal* … In fact, anything that is capable of representing sign/wording can be used to realize the function of sayer. In addition, going back to the discussion of the relationship between experience and information, I would suggest that events, reactions, semiotically interpretable actions e.g. smile, glance, look, expression etc are also able to function as sayer, as in *her look said more to me than his words did*; *the expression on his face told me what to expect*; *experience has taught me not to trust everyone*. Notably such sayer function typically co-occurs with projection as in all the examples here. As sayer both *the teacher* and *Mary* belong to the first category identified above: both are animate: human: specific.

The range of nominal groups capable of realizing the function of receiver is, in comparison, more limited. My watch may *tell* me that it is half past ten (cf. Halliday 1994a: 140), but I cannot tell my watch it's half past ten, and so on for many other examples. In fact overwhelmingly, the receiver role is realized by nominal groups with the features animate: human plus the feature specific or collective as for example *the applicant* and *the class*, respectively in *did you ask the applicant any questions at the interview?*, and *she asked the class to be careful with the maps*. Under certain specifiable circumstances, mammals (especially pets) might be co-opted in this function as *my dog* in *when I tell my dog to sit, he sits down*. This strong constraint regarding the nature of the receiver is highly significant and I shall return to it below (section 8—8.3). The receiver function is assigned in (i) to *the student* and in (iii) to *Julian*, both nominal groups have the features animate: human: specific.

The range of nominal groups capable of realizing the function of verbiage is the least constrained. In (i) and (iii) the verbiage is realized by *English* and *a story*, respectively: the selection of a semiotic entity as verbiage is quite unremarkable as in *Mary asked him a question* or *he teaches composition to the freshmen*. Both the processes used here permit not only the selection of verbiage in the clause but either could be projecting, as, for example in *the teacher taught the student how to write a report* (cf. clause i), and *Mary told Julian she was going to be out in the evening*. The constraint on what can be projected is still lower than that on verbiage. The latter is realizable by any nominal group referring to something made by/of signs, or a material referent with the implication that it in some way forms part of some state of affairs. For example, consider *he promised me a prize*. This can be expanded as *he promised "I will give you a prize"* or as *he promised to give me a prize*.

The analysis of teaching as a verbal process seems to be a good deal more satisfactory than its analysis as material ... benefactive process had been. Unlike the pair analysed in Figure 1, here the constituents of each clause have the properties called for by the elements of the structure of the clause. In Table 3, I present a comparative picture of the structure potential of the process of *teaching* and *telling*.

	Clauses with process *teach*		Clauses with process *tell*
i	the teacher taught the student English	iii	Mary told Julian a story
ia	the teacher taught the student	iiia	Mary told Julian
ib	the teacher taught English	iiib	Mary told a story
ic	the teacher taught	iiic	Mary told

Table 3: Partial structure potential of clauses with the process teach and tell

The structure potential of the two clauses runs parallel without any notable differences. Both (ic) and (iiic) sound somewhat strange. But (iiic) is in principle less problematic than (iic) had been in Table 2; in fact, a clause such as *Mary won't tell* or *Mary might be able to tell* is not likely to strike one as unusual, though of course for its interpretation it presumes the presence of some appropriate co-text, which is also true of (ic) as indicated in the earlier discussion (6.3): neither (ic) nor (iiic) could be the opening utterance of a dialogue but the point of the comparison was to simply find out whether the two clauses appear to be alike in the possibilities open to them by way of a verbal process clause, and it seems that unlike the earlier case discussed in section 6.2 the answer here is 'yes'. The obvious implication is that the analysis of teaching as a verbal process is better ratified by the lexicogrammatical relations.

In the following sections I will discuss the significance of the relations between some elements of the structure of verbal process clauses. The examination will reveal that the verbal process clause 'reaches out' semantically to other clause types in a way that is highly significant for understanding the nature of teaching. It is a discussion that will take us beyond the examination of the clause internal structure into a consideration of another process type and other structural elements.

8 Sayings, sayers, receivers and verbiage

Well described as the grammar of English is, it is necessary to begin with the simple statement that the lexicogrammatical description of most process types, including verbal process, still stands in need of more delicate analysis. In the following account, my focus will be on the semantics of the various elements of a verbal process clause,[24] in the hope that such an examination will allow us to understand the complexities of the processes of teaching and learning – an understanding that is a central issue in any functional theory of pedagogy.

8.1 Understanding the nature of verbal process

To begin with the element process, its wider interpretation as covering 'any kind of symbolic exchange of meaning' (Halliday 1994a: 140) brings into its orbit all experiences of semiotic interaction. The difference such processes make to the social world is axiomatic in the social sciences, but the possibility of making such difference depends on the possibility of making sense of the messages exchanged: as pointed out earlier (cf. section 2 above): to be usable, semiotic experiences have to be internalized, which is to say, the experiencer has to make sense of them.

Now the activities of making sense/understanding/interpreting – call them what you will – are activities of the brain, and they are central to the formation of human consciousness, i.e., to the making of mind. In the face of any new experience, semiotic or otherwise, some such activities are undertaken *naturally* by all human beings,[25] and naturally the languages of the world have words to refer to them. SF linguists typically categorize such words as MENTAL PROCESS (Halliday 1994a: 112–119; Halliday and Matthiessen 2004; also chapter 11, this volume). It follows that if semantically a relation between the actions of saying and sense making is claimed, then it is highly likely that verbal and mental processes are linked by some kind of semiotic logic. What is the nature of this logic?

Put very simply the basic relation between the two processes is that they work together. For a verbal process to take effect mental process must also occur in a specific kind of calibration with the saying process: I will refer to this relationship between the verbal and the mental process types as that of SEMIOTIC SYNERGY: as a semiotic relationship, it differs remarkably from the relation of semiotic symbiosis (Section 6.2). The symbiotic relation exists between members that belong to the same primary category of process; this is not the case with the relation of synergy which brings two distinct primary categories of process together. Although, in order to have its effect, saying *has to be* understood, it is far from true that every act of saying is necessarily followed by understanding the saying. Highlighting the *first* difference then: in a synergic relation one process, e.g., *tell,* does not necessarily imply the other, e.g., *understand* – in this respect the relation is quite unlike that between *buy/sell, lend/borrow*... With *tell/understand* there is no necessity, only an expectation based on probabilistic tendencies, which allows the claim that saying will *typically* lead into the activity of making sense on the part of the listener/reader. The last sentence points to a *second* difference: unlike *buy/sell* in the case of semiotic synergy we have *unidirectional dependence*: understanding of the saying logically depends on the saying but not in the way that an effect necessarily follows a given cause. *Saying does not ensure understanding*; it simply provides a semiotic object as a focus towards which the process of understanding may be oriented. Note also, in passing, that if saying is done by the sayer without prior understanding then the quality of the saying is likely to be affected. In some way mental process is pivotal to verbal process though without the logical relation of necessity. *Thirdly*, the process of *understanding* is an essential part of the process of *knowing*, especially where the object of knowing is only *intelligible*, i.e., the object is not accessible to the five senses. Meanings, ideas, concepts, beliefs, theories, and other such semiotically construed 'objects' are of this kind; they are not sensed, i.e., not apprehended sensuously; they have to be understood to become known. The implication is that the synergy can be seen as extending beyond the first pair of actions, i.e., from 'saying—understanding', to a triplet of processes 'saying—understanding—knowing'. Note, it would be absurd for someone to say *I understand what you are saying but I don't know what you are saying,*[26] while it makes perfect sense to hear someone say: *I don't know (the meaning of) what you are saying because I can't understand a word (of what you are saying)*.

Coming to the *final* point of difference, *buying/selling* type of verbs refer to actions which manifest a clear point of completion; by contrast, the actions of understanding as well as of knowing do not display this certainty – that is to say, these actions lack a definitive completion point, so that this stage is not as easy to identify here as it is in the case of *selling/buying, giving/taking, lending/borrowing* ...We might say with Sapir (1944) that both understanding and knowing are INHERENTLY GRADABLE[27]: one may understand something *not at all, a little, quite a lot, very well, perfectly* and so on; the same applies to the process of *knowing* as well. I would suggest tentatively that it might be better, in fact, to think of the main verbs *to understand* and *to know* as stages in internalization: the mental action of knowing is a viable possibility at a certain degree of understanding. Knowing happens when the internalized meaning has been integrated in the cognitive framework, allowing it to be recalled voluntarily and to be used in ways other than those already encountered by the user.

One further point needs to be made before leaving this section: the situations that are construed by clauses used in exemplifying points of grammar are pale copies of what happens in real life: one important aspect of the operation of saying in the living of life is the reversibility of roles between speaker and addressee (the human sayers and receivers); in real life, most addressees adopt the role of speaker – often within the same interaction if it is dialogic – and most speakers 'become' addressees in their turn. The relation of synergy is as central to the verbal act of saying as it is to the mental act of receiving: recall the first, informal mention of synergy (section 2.2) in the description of the spiralling relationship between experience, information, interaction (i.e. semiotic experience), and making sense (i.e. a form of mental action). The role reversibility is an important condition of continued interaction.

8.2 Sayer, receiver and verbiage

The discussion of semiotic synergy has revealed a good deal about verbal processes. The verbal process is an important part of a complex cycle, in which understanding/interpretation, i.e., the mental act of making sense of the message is necessarily linked to remembering and knowing, which, keeping in mind the principle of role reversibility, is a necessary condition for social agents to act as acculturated members of the society with an awareness of their socio-cultural history. *The verbal process will act on its receiver only if the receiver's mind can act on the message conveyed* – whether that message is overt or implied, presented as verbiage or as its projected counterpart. This perspective highlights the close, and yet different relationships, between sayer, verbiage and receiver. Let us begin the discussion with receiver.

It was said earlier (Section 7) that typically the receiver role has to be assigned to an entity with the features animate: human. Special circumstances are called for in assigning the function to other entities, including even non-human mammals. Your watch may tell you that it is half past ten (cf. Halliday 1994a: 140) but you can hardly ask your watch what time it is. Interacting with even advanced electronic machinery is still more demanding than talking to very young children; for this reason all acts of speaking semantically implicate someone with human consciousness as the receiver, which opens up a range of mental responses typical of human beings. Thus maintaining the relation of semiotic synergy implies that to successfully continue an interaction, the receiver must adopt a specific relation to verbiage. Figure 3 is one attempt to display these relations across the two process types.

Figure 3: Covert relations between Receiver and Senser

	Sayer	**Pro:verbal**	**Receiver**		**Verbiage**
(iv)	Mary	has told	Julian		The story of the Red Hen
(v)			Julian	Knows	The story of the Red Hen
			Senser	**Pro: mental**	**Phenomenon**

The first row in Figure 3 displays the structure of clause (iv) *Mary has told Julian the story of the Red Hen*, which is a variant of clause (iii) *Mary told Julian a story*. As an instance of a verbal process type, there is no difference between them despite some differences in the make up of some of their constituents. Thus the elements of structure are the same for both (compare entries in last row of Figure 2 with those in first row in Figure 3). In both, *Mary* is sayer, the process is verbal event realized by forms of the verb *tell*, the receiver is *Julian* and the verbiage in both refers to *story* though in (iii) the story has no definite identity while in (iv) it is well identified. Row three of figure 3, presents clause (v) *Julian knows the story of the Red Hen*. This clause differs from all the clauses analysed so far: it is a mental process clause whose structure is shown in the last row of the figure; here the function of SENSER is realized by *Julian*; the Process is MENTAL: COGNITION realized by a form of the verb *know* while *the story of the Red Hen* realizes the function PHENOMENON, that which forms the focus of the mental process.

The two clauses displayed in Figure 3 form something of a 'mini recount' – an interactive event and its sequel. Note in particular column 4: here we witness the synergy relation whereby the receiver is transformed into the senser, whose job it is to make sense of the verbiage; engagement in this process turns what was verbiage into a phenomenon, i.e., that which is subjected to mental process: the implication is that *if all goes as it should then the sayer's saying must become the receiver's knowledge*. Notable in this mini recount is the absence of the act of making sense, or understanding. Its inclusion might have created a recount perhaps as follows: (iv) *Mary has told Julian the story of the Red Hen* (iva) [and] *Julian has understood the story of the Red Hen* (v) *[so] Julian knows the story of the Red Hen.*[28]

However, if [*and*] in (iv) and [*so*] in (v) were switched around, the sequence of clauses would appear questionable. This is significant; it shows up how unconscious we are of the act of understanding as an essential step in knowing what was said. In real life, we take it for granted that the transformation of someone's saying into another's knowledge is a 'natural' happening. The success of the majority of human communication which hardly calls for a conscious hiatus for understanding supports the impression that sayings are transformed effortlessly into knowing, which makes the intermediate mental process of understanding quite invisible. Taking the context of teaching as my point of reference, I briefly discuss below the significance of the receiver 'turning into' senser – and what it says about the nature of classroom activities.

8.3 Receiver as senser in the context of teaching

There is no question that the teacher has an active role in the classroom: she is the major performer. Looking semantically at the kind of activities initiated by her, it is easy to see that in the majority of cases the aim is the transmission of some information. The immediate output is utterance, the destined goal is instruction leading to competence in the learning student. In this perspective teaching is primarily a form of semiotic action.

However, the relation of synergy between saying and sensing points us to the fact that there is a systematic division of labour in the classroom. The teacher is certainly the source of instructional messages, but if the uttered instructional messages are 'going to get anywhere' then the student too has to be active in a particular way – as the senser of those messages. He may be the intended receiver but he cannot 'receive' without exerting his intelligence; and a condition of learning the specific competence being taught by the teacher is for the student to exert his intelligence on precisely what is said. In fact, as Figure 3 shows, the student's real relation to the teacher is via the verbiage: as the one who is supposed to understand the verbiage, it is the verbiage that relates them to each other. We can go beyond the central classroom activity of 'the transmission of knowledge/competence' and add that in the context of the wider educational situation, it is the ways in which the student mentally 'deals with' the different varieties of verbiage/message that make the difference to his life as a learner. From this perspective, the textbook's presentation, the teacher's classroom discourse, the elaborations and clarifications during revision, the exercises that evaluate understanding, all of these interactive engagements represent forms of what is said to and by the student: a large proportion of life as a learner is simply submersion in discourse, which calls for mental labour by the student. In this view, the teacher is not a benefactor bestowing a free gift on the student – as in the earlier analysis (cf. discussion, section 6); if there is to be a gift the student must work to receive it. As for all of us, such mental labour is a condition for the acquisition of information/learning/knowledge as argued in section 2 above.

Now, mental processes are typically ego-based: what this means is that unlike verbal process where someone tells/asks someone something, in mental process a human participant other than the senser cannot be implicated except as a phenomenon; one cannot understand/learn someone something. One interpretation of this situation is to place the responsibility for understanding with the student alone. This aspect of the image of the student is quite familiar to most educational systems. With privileges attached to certain grades, the grading of students by reference to their intelligence, competence, and ability indicates that the onus for success is on them. Some extremely relevant questions in the context of this discussion are: (a) what is the genesis of human mind (consider here the views put forward by Vygotsky 1962, 1978); (b) what part does semiotic experience play in this genesis (consider here Bernstein 1971c; Cloran 1994; Williams 1995; Hasan 2009b); (c) is change in the quality of mental processes possible; and (d) if so, how (consider here reports on genre based pedagogy, e.g., Martin 1986, 1989; Martin and Rose 2003; Christie 1991, 1999; Christie and Martin 2007; Williams 1998, 2000, and numerous others)?

It is not that the questions raised above are new, or that answers to them have never been considered. Quite the contrary, they have been raised and by eminent scholars as the pages of this volume indicate again and again; and they have been considered to the extent that the research controlling scholars representing funding bodies have permitted. That serious, comprehensive, longitudinal research on these issues is relevant to improved instruction cannot be doubted. In light of these facts, one most important question is: why has there been no funding to resolve these issues? With specific reference to Australia in recent years, why has the use of billions of dollars for the construction of school buildings been deemed more important than increased funding for understanding the place of linguistic processes in education? Of all the resources valued in societies today, the development of the quality of human mental processes appears to be the most expendable. Every time we lay the responsibility on the student, we are in fact also holding the society responsible, for the student as a growing member of the society represents the working of that society by way of developing human potential. What the neonate brings in the world is malleable; it is shaped in a large measure by society as pointed out by many scholars (naming a few: Lewontin *et al.* 1984; Greenfield 1997, 2000; Vygotsky 1962, 1978; Luria 1976; Bernstein 1971c, 1975b, 1990, 2000; Halliday 2003, 2007a, 2007b; Halliday and Matthiessen 1999; Matthiessen 1993; Hasan 2005, 2009b; Bateson 1972; Mead 1934).

8.4 Sayer in relation to verbiage and receivers in the context of teaching

The above discourse returns us once again to the teacher by focusing on the relation of the message, i.e., instructional discourses of one kind or another, and the addressee, i.e., the learner, an apprentice who needs to learn how to learn as much as he needs to learn skills and expertise. A massive part of the active role the teacher has in the classroom consists in acting as the sayer, and as sayer and source of message, she is the one responsible for the verbiage, which, given the context, is what is said by way of instruction. Not surprisingly, she too has been singled out as the source of the problem in the educational system. And yet she does not have as free a hand as accounts of the teacher's power might suggest. Take the content of the instructional message: as Bernstein's concept of 'recontextualizations' (1975a, 1990, 2000) suggests, the first pass at the selection of 'materials' is made somewhere else. That is also the site where decision is taken about other elements of the curricula: the agency responsible for this primary recontextualization is responsible not only for determining what is to be said by way of instruction but also for when it is to be said and to whom. The process is arcane and teachers who will be actually doing the teaching are in the majority of cases out of the 'consultation loop' – this is especially so in the 'emerging countries'.

All the same, it is significant that the parole in the classroom is mainly in the hands of the teacher; so in a very real sense what is said becomes her responsibility. It is true that the receiver of the message has to engage in mental labour, but the focus of this labour is the produced message, and the quality of the message is critical in determining what sense can be made of it. How would one judge the 'quality of the message'? Well, the same parameters of the context of discourse are relevant as anywhere else: these will involve a judgment of the teacher's language by reference to (i) what one is attempting to do, which largely determines the content, (ii) who else is involved in the doing, and (iii) how the message is being made accessible to the receiver. A few words on the first two of these issues, below.

8.4.1 *The content of the instructional message*

In the first perspective, what is at issue primarily is engagement in some field of knowledge, a facilitation of learning, an effort to provide semiotic experience which can be made sense of and appropriated by the student. Once again, no one can teach something they do not understand; and the degree of their understanding is directly relevant to what they might say by way of 'instructional' discourse. Here again, to a large extent, the decisions are, in a manner of speaking, taken away from the teacher. This is done, not by 'on the job' instructions regarding appropriate behaviour as teacher, though that too is a factor. Mostly, however, what matters here is the fact that the teacher too has to be taught the very competencies which she will be attempting to teach: it is that educational experience that 'produces' her identity as teacher. In other words how she herself has been educated will bear a good deal of relevance to what she will say, and how she will organize the content of her messages in the classroom.

Ignoring for lack of space the huge debate which this opens up, I will comment briefly on the most important issues: there is a highly significant difference in the learning and understanding required of teachers who are learning to teach one group of subjects as opposed to some other. For example, no one is going to let a person loose in a mathematics classroom, or in physics, or geography, or human anatomy without proof that they possess sufficient knowledge in the requisite area. This contrasts starkly with the near absence of a well articulated knowledge requirement when it comes to teaching some of the subjects in humanities and social sciences, especially for teachers preparing to engage with the early stages of schooling. And if some requirement is put in place, then often what is required of teachers appears counter-productive. The complexity of the task is regularly underestimated. Let me show how this is done with reference to language, since language teaching is the primary concern of the present discussion.

Playing a variation on Halliday (1980), there are at least three perspectives for examining the involvement of language in the classroom: (i) teaching language, (ii) teaching about language and (iii) teaching through language. The concern in the first case is strictly speaking with enabling the learner to speak the language. This aim has different meanings in different contexts: learning English at school, when you are a native speaker of that language, cannot be about being able to speak that language in everyday mundane contexts; for this, fortunately no help is needed from official pedagogy. So it has to be about something else: this may be about speaking 'proper English', about being able to read and write, about being able to pursue higher education, and/or it may be about being a useful member of the society. In the context of learning a language, say, English as a foreign or second language, the aims are different yet again. One might wish to learn it for 'cosmetic' purposes – to enjoy life better as a tourist in English-speaking countries, which, with the global status of English, covers a great deal of ground! But today, learning another tongue – usually English – is tied very much to the student's aspirations: for higher education/training abroad (which would involve living in some community other than one's own), for competitive higher education at home. In these cases, the learner has to learn what the native speaker learns naturally as a child – i.e., MUNDANE language – but also the additional elements needed for higher education – i.e., the SPECIALIZED forms of language. So today more than ever before we need to stress that the teaching of any language calls for an understanding *about* language in general and *about the particular language* being taught. A concerted effort is needed to explode the myth, alive even today especially in the 'emerging countries', that the native speaker is a person who naturally knows *about* the language: this is typically quite untrue; knowing a language – i.e., how to speak a desirable variety of a language – does not bestow this expertise about language any more than the ability to breathe proves knowledge about the physiology and the functions of the lung.

The competence for teaching language whether as mother tongue or as another tongue requires certain specific kinds of understanding: it requires an understanding of the inner structure of language, how linguistic meanings are construed, what part is played in this by the lexicogrammar, what is the relation of phonology – the speech patterns – and graphology – the patterns of writing – to construing meaning with lexicogrammar. Understanding the nature of linguistic meaning – that, for example, it is not enclosed within single words, that it changes according to where a word is used in the discourse, and that every linguistically construed meaning brings in its train a number of inferred meanings – these issues are highly important to the teaching of language, and to showing how language plays such a crucial role in human life. And, further, it requires also an understanding of the relationship of language and society within which is embedded linguistic variation and valuation of such variation; the varieties of language, whether according to use, i.e., REGISTER/GENRES or according to users, i.e., ACCENT, DIALECT and SEMANTIC VARIATION need to be understood, because much of social valuation of varieties is not about the wording in use, it is about social uses and users' social adjustment to their positioning. By enumerating these things, I do not mean to say that the teacher needs to teach each of these things in the classroom; what I mean is that expertise such as this is what would enable the teacher to decide with confidence which part of such information is relevant where, for whom, at what stage and how it can be appropriately built into the instructional discourse. Today even in the advanced nations of the world such understanding, regretfully, does not constitute a necessary requirement for teaching language, not even a pale copy!

The third perspective – teaching through language – in a sense applies to the whole pedagogic effort: the expert imparts the secret of her expertise largely by using language. Take the case of mathematics, the most advanced 'language' has developed to encode mathematical meanings (O'Halloran 2007). Even so, 'natural' language has to be still called upon in teaching and discussing mathematics. What this suggests is that ideally, the teacher of any discipline should have experience of the different varieties of that discipline: what does a discussion in physics look like in terms of how language is used in it, how much is it like the language of the text book, how much is the spoken presentation like the discussion or like the experts' theoretical written up accounts of the same phenomenon? What do reports look like when experts build them into their books, how do they differ from the reports the student produces when called upon to do so, and how does that report differ from the essay the student might write, and so on. To introduce such understanding of language across the curriculum is perhaps the most important step in improving the quality of education by improving the quality of the teacher's message with reference to what she is trying to achieve; it might even bring the myth of education as an egalitarian system somewhat closer to reality.

8.4.2 *The instructional message in relation to the addressee*

When it comes to judging the message with reference to who the instructional message is addressed to, pedagogic discourse is in a class by itself. Let us begin with the obvious observation that the exchange of messages between the interactants does *something* significant in their life: discussions around terms such as 'aim', 'goal', 'purpose' of activity/discourse/genre (Hasan 1981, 1985c, 1999b, 2005, 2009b; Martin 1985, 1986, 1992; Martin, Christie and Rothery 1987) bear witness to the complexity of what is achieved in the exchange of meanings. Thus as a general principle, speakers are normally highly sensitive to their addressee, and, in their turn, addressees have, more often than not, a stake in attending to the message. There is something like an element of self-interest in the speakers' regard for their addressee. On the assumption that they do not want to have their parole 'blowing on the wind', it seems reasonable that speakers would invest effort in making the message accessible both materially by making sure that it gets across physically – one reason for the teacher's great concern with maintaining order in the classroom – and equally important, speakers would also ensure that the wording of the message does not become a semiotic hurdle: it meets the addressee at least halfway in his struggle to make sense of it. To achieve these aims, wherever possible, the speaker would pay attention to the addressee as a person with some specific abilities, understandings, inclinations and needs; in short the speaker must have some sense of the addressee's social identity. This aspect of speaker-addressee relations opens up another huge discussion which cannot be pursued here; but one important point worth bringing to attention is that repeated interaction in the same field or in many different ones by the same speaker-addressee typically tends to create fairly minimal SOCIAL DISTANCE[29] (Hasan 1973, 1980, 1999b), allowing the speaker to craft the kind of message which is likely to meet their communicative needs.

The teacher-pupil relation in many ways presents an anomaly. I do not know of any 'opinion polls' from the classroom, but it is very obviously open to doubt that the majority of students representing the addressee role – especially at the post-primary and pre-university stages – behave as if they have 'a stake' in making sense of the communication. A significant reason may lie in the distance between the long-term aims of education as conceptualized by the system of education and the short-term interests of the adolescent/young adult population, now often known in the trade as 'clients'. There is therefore a need to 'put the student at the centre': instruction, we are told, has to be made 'learner centered', an expression common among those who try to tell us how to succeed in teaching. But the learners are in the classroom mostly because in a just and healthy society learning is a human need, not a luxury – despite the fact that at that early age the learners might not sympathize with that aim. So to alter the instructional message in such a way that learning takes second place or is lost in the 'fun' is to defeat the purpose. The slogan one needs is *make learning maximally interesting to the majority of the class*. What makes the message interesting does not inhere in the message as such: it resides in the relation of the message to the message receiver. So the most important question is how to make interesting to a classful of learners such things as the principles of heat conduction, of food chain, of rain cycle, of blood circulation, the value of coins, or what the English verb does in a sentence or the function of the pronoun. Clearly, for this the teacher has to 'know' her addressee!

And it is here that the issue of the development of social distance between the teacher and the learner becomes highly important: in general, as the social distance between the speaker and the addressee decreases their understanding of each other in respect of some activity increases. Teachers do interact with the same individuals; why does social distance not decrease, or put it less technically, why do they not get to know each other better? The answer may depend a good deal on keeping track of so many different listeners. One message catering for a class of even twenty individuals seems a considerable challenge for one speaker, but that figure is generally exceeded even in the progressive countries, leave aside countries such as Pakistan. No one would suggest a system that has a one-to-one teacher-student ratio, but it is certainly desirable to create resources where more time can be devoted to real discussion, where discussion is more important than 'handing out information'. Although the real aim is to inform this is more likely to happen when the experience is one that the students can engage in. What lies behind this problem is how official pedagogy is administered, who decides where the investment of the community's material capital is critical and why. Governments that deny education the funding it needs to enable teachers to excite the love of learning in the younger generations of the community will end up with a nation that is incapable of understanding, discrimination and invention. To understand the way students in the class are receiving an instructional message, the teacher needs to be able to not just 'present' well-crafted information relating to some discipline under focus – this is a necessary condition but not a sufficient one for students' engagement – she also needs to be able to talk them through, to understand what problem they might have in making sense of the information, in short, to build a picture of their specific abilities, understandings, inclinations and needs. As things stand, in the classroom communication, teachers and students alike are, in effect, asked to meet a challenge that absolutely no other communicative situation places on speakers and addressees. The setting up of commissions, of naming and shaming websites to improve the performance of the school, in fact misses the point by a very wide margin: very often, it is not schools but governments that fail the pupils; the ultimate responsibility rests with them.

9 Concluding comments

I am aware that what has been said here about the process of teaching is far from foregrounding many of the central issues in the system of education – how it is viewed by whom, how close to reality the various views are, what are its shortcomings, and much more. But the aim was not so much to present a full account of the system of education. It was rather to show first and foremost that lexicogrammatical analysis is not about 'rules' which are designed to control what speakers should or should not say. In the last resort, speaking is one game where the proof of the pudding is definitely in the eating: the need to communicate means that communication should be such as to be understood. An understanding of language, the way its forms function, is necessary if what one wants to do is to teach the language. I hope I have also demonstrated what decides whether some grammatical analysis 'fits the facts'. In discussing the alternative views of the grammatical analysis of *teaching*, the arguments for grammar in my presentation came from a consideration of the lexicogrammatical organization of the language. This is not just following rules for the sake of controlling the behaviour of ordinary persons. When it comes to language, there is no other court of appeal but how things are done in a language. I demonstrated socio-cultural 'facts' do not determine the correctness of a grammatical analysis. Much of our understanding of what the world is like depends on how our language presents 'the' world to us. Arguing from 'realities' is thus only a way of showing what belief systems are operative in a society; it is not necessarily a good recipe for doing the grammar of the clause! And though semantic enquiries into the significance of some aspect of language can be an impetus toward further enquiry into grammar, the semantic claims have to be validated by the grammatical patterns, precisely because linguistic meanings do not have a being independent of the workings of linguistic form. I have shown that the implications of teaching as a process of saying are not respected fully in the educational practices of most societies: this is a social claim about the educational systems. The claim that teaching is a process of saying is a grammatical claim: it is upheld or not by looking into the patterns which the verb *to teach* can perform.

I began this presentation by saying that we live in the age of information. I have attempted to show that language furnishes the most important means of creating exchangeable information. If one wishes to teach one's students to succeed in the required exchanges of information, this cannot be done adequately without an understanding of how the form of language enables you to perform many actions by using your language. Literacy is a buzz word, but literacy is also the most important quest for the language teacher – not least because literacy interpreted as making sense is relevant not only to language learning but for learning everything. Educating for literacy is educating to make sense of the linguistic meaning in its fullness; it is to go beyond the information given by reflecting on the implications of what is being said. This reflection has to do not only with the meanings of words as entered in the dictionaries, or simply in the initial lexicogrammatical analysis of some sentence, paragraph or text. In my opinion literacy achieves its full effect when it enables enquiry into the inferences of what the analysis is 'saying'. Meanings inferred from actually worded meanings are as much part of the language system and as pertinent to language education as other forms of literacy such as recognition and action literacy. I moved on from such inferred information to discuss the implications of such meanings. I have interrogated the implications of what teaching as a verbal process would mean if its significance was understood and acted on – this is an aspect of literacy education that to my mind represents the conception of literacy I have referred to as reflection literacy (Hasan 1996b, chapter 5 here), not *instead of* recognition or action literacy, but as the *culmination of responsible educated behaviour* of social agents in society. *Learning is not the replication of facts even though facts are important. Therefore, if teaching is to be of any relevance to learning in the true sense of the word, we must resist all efforts from any direction whatsoever that threaten to reduce teaching to that mechanical status.*

Notes

1 The contents of this chapter are based on notes made for three versions of the same plenary talk delivered to the SPELT Annual International Congress, September 21 – 25, 2005 in Karachi, Lahore and Multan (Pakistan) on the 21st anniversary of the Society of Pakistan English Language Teachers (SPELT). The grammatical analysis of teaching was first presented at a Faculty of Education Seminar, Hong Kong University, June 2004.

2 To avoid possible ambiguities, I will use the masculine pronominals to refer to the baby, leaving the feminine ones to refer to the caregiver.

3 Most human experiences integrate the semiotic and the non-semiotic phenomena; we separate them here because the potential for experiencing purely the one or the other is open at least in some cases, such as the ones I have mentioned here, which is what gives rise to the important question about how they get internalized.

4 In using the words 'resembles semiotic mediation', on the one hand I acknowledge my debt to Vygotsky's concept, and on the other attempt an extension of its scope: as I understand (Hasan 2005; also chapter 3 here) Vygotsky (1962, 1978) used this expression to refer to the making of mind through the internalization of semiotic – mostly linguistic – interaction. The point I am making is that the internalization of any social experience depends on some kind of mediating activity, and that this activity must resemble the activity of mediating meaning with wording.

5 It should be granted, though, that often it is not easy to apportion blame between machine and man as instruments of error, as in Chernobyl or the friendly fire in Afghanistan that kills harmless civilians rather than the hated enemies.

6 In saying this, it is important to remember with Vygotsky's that human brains turn into minds – higher mental functions develop – through sociogenesis (Vygotsky 1978; Hasan 2005).

7 Certainly experience of material phenomena present to the senses, as well as first person experience of pain, pleasure, sorrow, wonder etc., possesses a vividness which cannot be matched by any semiotic construal. By the same token, out of the situational setting in which they occur, these vivid experiences are able to be transmitted to another person only to the extent that language can do justice to any of those feelings.

8 From this perspective, the macho gestures of war indicate actions and reflections still arrested in a by-gone age where brawn rose above brain and technology was more important than intellect.

9 The information to be presented here is highly selective: I focus only on those aspects which are relevant to the analysis of the process 'teach'.

10 In SFL, *clause* refers to a grammatical unit which is made up of groups/phrases, and which acts as the point of origin for choices from a set of system networks such as MOOD, MODALITY, TRANSITIVITY, THEME, INFORMATION FOCUS, and others. For further detail, Halliday 1994b, Halliday and Matthiessen 2004. For short definition and exemplification, see Matthiessen *et al.* 2010.

11 There is a good deal of literature on metafunctions. For detailed discussions,

see Halliday 1970a, 1979b; Matthiessen 2007 etc. For brief accounts of these, see chapters 11 and 12 here.

12 Halliday (1976b) had also used the TRANSITIVITY analysis of this verb in order to consider the meaning of the grammatical functions assigned to the constituents in terms of their implications in relation to the social process of teaching. However, there are at least three important differences between my presentation and Halliday's: (a) my analysis uses a more recent version of Transitivity analysis which is based on further research (Halliday 1994a); (b) Halliday presents three possible analyses of *taught* as material process, deliberately avoiding any discussion of their grammatical merits; this paper offers only one analysis of the verb as a material process, and attempts to show why this would be grammatically undesirable; (c) in addition to the three analyses of *taught* as material process, Halliday also considers *taught* as verbal and mental process; by contrast, this presentation suggest, that the only viable analysis of *taught* is to treat it as verbal process, and it goes on to develop a theoretically based connection between the verbal and the mental process in English which it is hoped will 'fit' all cases of verbal process.

13 For the specific terms for transitivity functions see Halliday 1994a.

14 A discussion of the cline of dynamism based on experiential considerations will be found in Hasan 1985b: 45-47.

15 The most generalized descriptive model of official pedagogy is presented by Basil Bernstein 2000, with detailed observations on what is taught, how it is made available for teaching, how the success of transmission is assessed and what the process of teaching actually involves.

16 The assumption seems to be that schools fail in educating out of their free will; they would not fail if they did not want to – this is in keeping with the belief that the disadvantaged remain disadvantaged because they do not have the motivation for improving their lot.

17 I have pushed this concept of education for at least a quarter of a century. I first came to this conclusion while I was myself a teacher in Pakistan long ago. My message about education has not exactly been warmly welcomed amongst my colleagues, who fear there is not enough linguistics or description of language in it. My response is that this view of the role of language in education is the most potent and the most widely applicable to education anywhere, simply because it shows the true value of the importance of the concept of semiotic mediation in the educational processes, particularly because they are not being foregrounded anywhere else in the SFL literature to the best of my knowledge.

18 Even so, the description is not complete since that would require time and space not available to this contribution. For discussion on some of the terms used here, see Hasan 1987a; Halliday and Matthiessen 2004.

19 The implication is that something pre-existed which has been transformed into something else. As a recognition of this kind of relation, I paraphrase an Urdu proverb I heard my mother using, namely 'ghi hota gewlgewla pəkaty, gwʀ laty wdhar, kja karũ bəhən, ghər aTa nahĩ' (translation: if I had some 'ghi' I would cook sweet dumplings, I would have borrowed some brown sugar, but sister! the problem is I don't have any flour!). so if someone says məỹ ne gwlgwla

pəkaja (I cooked sweet dumplings) the implication is that an action was undertaken which transformed certain ingredients into the sweet dumplings

20 In some dialects of English *learn* is used interchangeably with *teach* as in *learn me how to ice the cake, please*.

21 It is important to clarify that in SFL every clause is analysed from the four distinct metafunctional perspectives: EXPERIENTIAL, LOGICAL, INTERPERSONAL and TEXTUAL, (for some discussion, chapters 10 and 11 this volume; Halliday 1970a; Matthiessen 2007); the set of possibilities of structure open to a clause may therefore be discussed by reference to some one specific metafunction or by reference to all four. Here we consider only transitivity which is related by realization to the experiential metafunction.

22 One condition I have in mind here is the addition of a circumstance of manner as in *Mary gave generously.* The presence of such a circumstance seems to alter the situation perhaps because recurrence is implied, hence the specification of gift seems unreasonable. This explanation need to be tested.

23 What is said may be a portmanteau utterance, e.g., *the chaos at the scene of the accident* in *he described the chaos at scene of the accident*, *a book* in *he promised me a book*. Here *the chaos at the scene of the accident* and *a book* have the function of verbiage and the verbal process is non-projecting. By contrast, in *he said 'there is complete chaos here at the scene of the accident'*, or *he promised he would buy me a book*, the sayings are the projection of the meanings construed by the sayer's discourse; less is left to inference by the listener and a *qua si* utterance is present either in a QUOTED form as in '*there is complete chaos here at the scene of the accident'* or REPORTED as in *he would buy me a book*.

24 Wherever possible I will attempt to relate the semantic generalizations to some formal – i.e., lexicogrammatical patterns, but clearly the latter are presented only as a tentative description awaiting further studies in the lexicogrammar of the verbal process.

25 The only condition for engaging in this *natural* activity is a brain free of pathology.

26 There is always the issue of 'slippage' in the use of words such as *understand*, *know*; *know* is also used to refer to acquaintance e.g., *oh I know this chair from your house in Killara*. This use is significantly different from *I know the meaning of this sentence*. All verbiage is accessed as meaning.

27 I extend the notion of gradability to verbs here with apologies to Sapir (1944: 93- 116) who, to the best of my memory, used the term for nominal words only (e.g., see Lyons 1977).

28 Of course, in 'real life' no one speaks like this. What I am hoping to achieve by this degree of artificial repetition of the actual words is to show the alignment of the constituents of one clause with those of the other.

29 The term SOCIAL DISTANCE is used here as defined by Hasan 1973, 1981, 1985c; it is based on the significance of the interactive biography of the specific speaker and addressee and differs considerably both from *social contact* (Poynton 1984) and from *social distance* as used in sociology and social psychology at the turn of last century.

2 Modes of learning, modes of teaching: semiotic mediation and knowledge[1] [2008]

1 Introduction: meaning in education

Education has been a primary focus of interest for responsible, democratic governments, and it goes without saying that teaching and learning form the heart of educational practices. However, thoughtful educators have always recognized that teaching does not necessarily result in the learning desired, nor is all learning the outcome of deliberate teaching: in fact, the basic problem in ensuring the successful outcome of educational activities lies precisely in this possibility of learning without teaching and of teaching without leading to desired learning. It is necessary to understand the sources of this asymmetry if we wish to take constructive steps towards solving this perennial problem which confronts the educational systems almost everywhere, but especially so in the so-called 'developing' countries of the world. This paper attempts an analysis of the asymmetry between teaching and learning, in order to suggest some elements of a possible solution.

The foundation of this analysis will lie in clarifying the place of talk in the educational system; I hope to establish that speaking is the most important activity in the educational process (cf. chapter 1 here). Basil Bernstein, an internationally renowned British expert on the sociology of education (1975a, 1990, 2000), used to say that universities are institutions built around talk, while Michael Halliday has defined talk as the exchange of meaning in social contexts (Halliday 1974a, 1974b, 1976a). My line of argument will be that there is an inherent relationship between society, talk, teaching, learning and education. Any discussion of the pedagogic activities associated with the educational institutions anywhere in the world must, therefore, strive for a clear understanding of the ways in which saying and meaning – which is really what talking amounts to – play a critical part in the kind of contribution made to a society by the educational institution. It is important to point out at the start that, like all social institutions, the educational institution too has two salient lines of organization: the functional and the administrative. The functional academic aspect concerns what we do by way of education – e.g., the selection and organization of the contents which make up the curriculum, the sequencing of its presentation, the determination of the instructional practices suitable to the production of competencies at these stages, and the systems of evaluation which legitimize moves from one stage to another – these constitute the defining characteristics of the educational institution. It would be a mistake, though, to underestimate the importance of the administrative aspect. The administrative arm of the institution is devised not only to provide material support for the day to day working of the various educational institutions, but it also turns out to be a powerful reminder of the ways in which the politico-economic concerns of a society penetrate the basic and critical elements of the academic aspects of the educational process. I will return briefly to this theme in concluding my presentation.

2 Semiotic mediation: social interaction, meaning and mental development

One might well ask: if this presentation is about the importance of talk in education, then what are all these words doing in the title of my talk? I have already drawn attention to LEARNING and TEACHING – and everyone would agree on the close relationship between teaching, learning and KNOWLEDGE – these things reportedly constitute the business which occupies schools, colleges and universities anywhere; and it would be also widely accepted that both the processes of teaching and of learning take place overwhelmingly by engaging in talk, just as knowledge of all kinds involves the use of language for its creation, transmission and its preservation through the ages. But how about SEMIOTIC MEDIATION?

I am assuming that my psychologist colleagues will be familiar with this expression as well, which was first coined by another famous European scholar, Lev Semyonovich Vygotsky (1962, 1978), a Russian psychologist, who worked in Moscow in the early years of the Communist revolution. He used this expression to refer to that central quality of human social interaction which is essential to the formation of our human-ness. Simplifying somewhat, Vygotsky pointed out that all human interaction is made up of meanings – every social activity in which we participate with others depends on the EXCHANGE OF MEANINGS. Vygotsky did not stop at this point – which, by the way, had been made by some European linguists too. He went on to argue that meaning is an 'abstract tool' for mediating all forms of experience to the human mind, and this naturally implies that *the mental life of human beings depends greatly on the process of semiotic mediation*: according to Vygotsky, even the ability to form concepts, and logical connections between thoughts, as well as other such 'higher mental functions' have their foundation in the experience of social interaction.

> Every function in the child's cultural[2] development appears twice: first, on the social level, and later, on the individual level; first *between* people (*inter-psychologically*), and then *inside* the child (*intra-psychologically*). This applies equally to voluntary attention, to logical memory, and to the formation of concepts. All the higher functions originate as actual relations between human individuals. (Vygotsky 1978: 57)

Perhaps now it may be obvious why I included the terms 'semiotic mediation' and 'knowledge' in my title, and why I am beginning my talk with the place of talk in education. Simplifying a little, here is what the theory of semiotic mediation implies: from early infancy, human beings participate in a large number of social experiences; experience of any kind is mediated to the mind as meaning; this constitutes the essence of learning, which in turn is the key to the internalization of knowledge – the nature of human MENTAL DEVELOPMENT consists in the continued iteration of the sequence of these inherently related processes. According to Vygotsky, acts of learning in social life and the knowledge that this learning produces form the foundation of the individual's mental development.

2.1 The brain-mind relation: human mind as a product of social interaction

In making these claims Vygotsky was going against some of the widely held 'scientific' beliefs of his time. The majority of scientists had believed at that time – and some still do – that mental maturation depended automatically on biological maturation, and that learning could only occur when the mind had matured. Today's theories of 'learning readiness' seem to echo this same position. Also, Vygotsky's contemporaries believed that each human being was born with some specific mental capacities, the true nature of which became progressively more visible as the growing persons moved from infancy to childhood, to adolescence and to adulthood. In other words, for them, the essential quality of mental development depended on inherited capacities and pre-determined programs of nature[3]; it was thus seen simply 'as the elaboration and substitution of innate responses' (Vygotsky 1978: 80). As if this much confusion was not enough, there also existed a long-standing debate about the relationship between brain and mind: they were thought of as two distinct things – brain was the physical location where mind, the mysterious object, 'lived'. However, these beliefs did not agree with the observable facts.

Vygotsky took a major step in clarifying the relationship of the physical organ we know as the 'brain' to that human faculty which we call 'mind'. A powerful thinker, he sidestepped the troubled debate in which brain and mind were pitted against each other. Instead, he put forward a theory which united brain and mind as locked together in a life-long dialectic whereby what is inherited by individuals because of belonging to the human species, i.e., the brain, develops into a faculty, i.e., the mind that is socially fashioned by the individual's own cultural experiences. Here is an extract that indicates his position:

> Within a general process of development, two qualitatively different lines of development, differing in origin, can be distinguished: on the one hand the elementary [mental] processes, which are of biological origin and, on the other, the higher psychological functions of socio-cultural origin. *The history of child behaviour is born through the interweaving of these two lines*. (Vygotsky 1978:46; my emphasis)

The phenomenon that Vygotsky is talking about can be easily observed across the world. All babies are born with a brain, but at birth it would not be too far from truth to refer to this physical organ as 'a mind-less brain'. Note that cultures around the world agree with this observation: they recognize that the neonate has 'no sense'. Thus, no one holds the infant responsible for what s/he might do. But as day by day, month by month and year by year, the newborn grows, the fact widely observed in all human societies is that the infant's mind-less brain is turning into a 'mind-ful brain': increasingly, the growing child develops a sense of the universe that he/she is living in; this manifests itself in the child's visible recognition of what others are doing, an anticipation of what they might go on to do, and above all in the child's increasing ability to participate in different kinds of social interaction. Not surprisingly, as this change continues cultures also begin to hold the growing person responsible for their actions and their locutions – which is to say, a mind is attributed to the growing human being. This little sketch presents a highly simplified picture of what Vygotsky meant by saying that the development of human mind is SOCIOGENETIC; that in fashioning the mind for each individual, it is the exchange of meaning with other social beings in the community that has played the most important part.[4] Modern research on the development of the human brain by renowned neurologists (such as Damasio 2000; Edelman and Mountcastle 1978; Edelman and Tononi 2000; Greenfield 1997, and others) supports Vygotsky's position that brain and mind are not two distinct things: they are simply two different states of the same thing. In fact, the famous neurologist, Susan Greenfield, has described the human mind as a PERSONALIZED BRAIN – 'personalized' in the sense that each mind is unique due to the unique interactive experiences of the owner of the brain.

To sum up: the brain we come with in this world is, in a manner of speaking, a gift of God to humanity; by contrast, the mind that this brain develops into is produced by us: we ourselves and those around us with whom we habitually interact are the joint architects of the mind which guides us in all aspects of the living of life. The brain is our biologically inherited potential: at birth, a largely malleable physical part of the body, with the same biological potential in all normal human beings; it is this universally shaped brain that is re-shaped into our very own unique minds through the working of our own unique social experiences in life. The fashions of thinking this mind develops, the modes of reasoning that become habitual to it, these things are not natural: they are created by the specific kinds of meanings exchanged by each person in the course of their life. What links the developing mind to the meanings of social experience is the process of semiotic mediation.[5]

2.2 Semiotics: the scientific study of signs making meaning

Before going further, let me try to define what I mean by the term 'SEMIOTICS', from which the adjective 'semiotic' derives. I will approach this definition by linking the term to expressions I have been using, such as 'exchange of meaning', or 'mediation of experience by meaning', and so on. Very simply put, what I am referring to is an ability to INTERPRET THINGS which all normal human beings seem to possess. I want to highlight two features of this normal ability to interpret what we might be experiencing: one, that it *appears* to involve no attention to the individual elements of the experienced phenomena; and second, that it *appears* to demand a holistic focus on whatever experience is engaging the attention. For example, when we hear someone speak, or note a gesture, or take in a facial expression, or look at a room with some furniture arranged in it in some manner, we appear to become aware of the meaning of these things almost instantaneously without having the same awareness of its individual parts. Speaking metaphorically, *these sensed phenomena convey some message as a whole: experience is being mediated to the mind as meaning*. For example, perceiving a facial expression, one does not typically recall it to oneself or describe it to others as: 'I see a face; it has two eyes, a nose, a mouth …'; rather, one is much more likely to describe the experience as 'this person is happy', or 'sad' or 'puzzled', and so on. The point of the perception is in interpreting some configuration as a whole; it is this understanding that we typically make connection with and which amounts to getting some message. Similarly when we hear a sentence we typically do not describe our experience as 'this bit of language has five 't' sounds, two 'p' sounds, or three verbs and six nouns', or whatever. What we get almost immediately from the sentence is a whole message – for example, we perceive that a statement is being made or a command is being issued; perhaps that the utterance is praising or denigrating someone or something; and that it is telling us of a state of affairs which involves one entity or more, and so on. So when I talk about exchange of meaning, I am thinking of the holistic meanings of a series of such experiences to which we human beings attend and which we interpret as one unified event. 'Getting the meaning' is the key, because the mind has no way of storing any experience except as meaning. So instead of saying that we learn from what our five senses experience, it is probably far more precise to say that we learn from what an experience has meant to us – i.e., how we have interpreted it.

Note that I highlighted the word 'appears' above in talking about the individual elements of experiences: this is because I wanted to emphasize that the ignoring of the individual elements is *simply an appearance, not a fact*. It does *seem* to be true that what we attend *to* and what we attend *for* in normal everyday contexts of living is the meaning of a pattern as a whole, which is what most of us are able to recall when we tell others of some experience. By contrast, not many would be able to recall the details of its structural configuration. Nonetheless, the fact remains that the meanings we perceive in this way are actually made by a configuration of individual patterns; and it is important to emphasize that without those individual elements and their modes of coming together *there would be no exchangeable meanings*. To put it simply, what cannot be 'coded' cannot be meant, and what cannot be meant cannot be made known to anyone except the experiencer: our 'raw sensations' are never the heard discourse; what we hear is sensation/reflection refracted through meaning-making signs. From this it follows that in order to get the meaning of an experience, we must at some level have decoded, therefore we must have attended no matter how subconsciously to the elements; we must have known at some level what these elements were and how they came together to form a structure. Without this we couldn't have got the meaning. On the face of it, this presents us with a conundrum; we are forced to ask: what exactly is going on?

I am inclined to say that because the meaning of experienced phenomena is central to the human mental development and so to the quality of the survival of the human species, very possibly there is a quasi-natural adaptation to coded meanings, so that the getting of meaning from the constantly emerging configurations of sign patterns appears to be natural and effortless. To the person 'getting' the meaning, it seems as if there is nothing between the experience and what the experience means. But the fact is that between the experience and the meaning of the experience lies the entire formal potential of the sign system(s): the principles of coding – i.e., the network of relations which bring elements together into a configuration – are essential to the making of meaning but in the majority of cases, the facts of coding remains largely invisible. While every normal human being is conscious of having derived some meaning or other from an experience, not all of us are at the same time conscious of the individual elements that have configured to produce that meaning: so far as lay persons are concerned, this kind of information as a rule does not enter the conscious level of the mind; therefore the ability to voluntarily recall those elements in the same relations in which they occurred is pretty rare.[6]

More than any other species, human beings are inclined to treat a large number of different sorts of material phenomena as signs, as patterns, which according to the members of a community can be interpreted as having this meaning or that. Nearly a century ago, Ferdinand de Saussure (1966), a great European scholar, recognized the need for a science whose job it is to study the nature of such meaning-making sign systems – this science of meaning-making signs, Saussure called SEMIOLOGY; later this same field of endeavour became known as semiotics. Saussure had suggested that the aim of this science would be to develop ways of establishing precisely those principles whereby patterns are constructed – what elements underlie a sign, how the signs are expressed (so that they can be physically apprehended), under what conditions they come to make meanings, what relations the meanings bear to the social subject's life in community, how, over time, the sign's expression form and/or the meanings construed by that form tend to change, and so on. Saussure proceeded to define linguistics as one branch of the science of semiology. It is not surprising that today most linguists think of Saussure as the father of modern linguistics.

Perhaps it is clear from the above discussion that language is not the only system for making meanings: semiotics is by definition multi-modal because there are many other kinds of sign systems such as gestures and expressions, pictures, tables and graphs, even the clothes we wear, the kind of houses we live in, the ways in which we organize our material environment and so on – all of these are interpreted by social beings as having some meaning or other. But amongst the different systems for making meaning, human language has turned out to be the most versatile: it is the most capable of conveying different sorts of meanings. Not only is it able to refer to concrete phenomena that are around us here and now, but it can also recall the past, and describe the future; it is capable of creating abstract concepts and structures which refer to phenomena that exist either in memory and/or in the world of imagination – the five human senses may not be able to make any contact with some phenomena but so far as language is concerned, it has no problem referring to them. It would seem that language is not bound by any physical constraints of time and space; logic or truth: the domain of the operation of language knows no other limit than human imagination. What is more, we can use language to describe any and all systems for making meaning, including language itself; it is, however, impossible to use any other semiotic system for discussing even the major attributes of language. All this appears to furnish a cogent argument for maintaining that, amongst the semiotic systems, language offers much the widest scope, and clearly the possibilities of the mediation of meaning depends on the power of the meaning-making system.

3 Language and learning

Vygotsky's concept of semiotic mediation is tied to the power of language, and since the power of language for making meaning exceeds that of any other semiotic system, it follows that the reach of this concept is highly pervasive. To make an estimate of its scope, all we have to do is to ask: when and where do human beings encounter linguistic meaning? The obvious answer is: almost everywhere! And wherever language is in use, there has to be the presumption of semiotic mediation. Although Vygotsky paid attention to other sign systems, not surprisingly language has had a critical place in his theory of the sociogenesis of higher mental functions. Of course cultures vary in how soon strangers will speak to each other, but complete silence between co-present acquaintances is everywhere regarded as unusual, if not a sign of tension. So there is no exaggeration in saying that to be with someone is to exchange some linguistic meaning.

We conduct most of our daily activities with someone or other, and as we engage in these activities, we also exchange meanings. Sometimes this is made necessary because of the nature of the activity we are engaged in, for example, you might be measuring something and I might be recording the measurements. But often we talk without such necessity; consider, for example, much of the talk that goes on around a dinner table – which is by no means about eating. Often our talk might concern just ordinary everyday things such as the habitual experience of greeting others, of buying a bunch of bananas or a kilo of potatoes, or getting a child to do something, such as 'put your toys away where they belong', or 'let granny sit there because she finds that chair comfortable'. On other occasions, our exchanges of meaning might involve specialized activities that we think of as serious business such as writing a paper on a topic in physics or linguistics, discussing the latest change on the political scene, debating the comparative merits of several applications for a vacant post, and so on. Irrespective of whether language is being used in doing some everyday ordinary activity or a special one, semiotic mediation must occur; that is to say the meanings of the social experience(s) will be mediated to the mind, which will lead to learning and knowledge of some kind. But the kind of learning in the two different environments is not likely to be identical, and the differences between them are significant. In the following sub-sections, I will foreground some of the differences between the kinds of learning that is done in these two environments, which are common to most contemporary societies: the special focus is on language learning.

3.1 Learning in everyday environments: learning the mother tongue

The most spectacular act of learning performed in everyday environments by every normal child born anywhere in the world is the learning of the language of his community, i.e., the mother tongue. Indeed so impressive is this phenomenon that it persuaded the world famous linguist, Noam Chomsky (e.g., 1965), to suggest that the neonate is actually born with a blueprint of the human language. Simplifying somewhat, his theory maintained that all the deeper syntactic patterns of human language are innate; what remains for the child to learn is how the patterns need to be manifested in accordance with the child's mother tongue. The argument for the claim of innateness went something as follows: human language is a highly complex system; children begin the acquisition of their mother tongue when they are about two years old; and by the time they are four years old, they have mastered that language (Brown 1973). If the principles of the syntax of human language were not an innate part of the children's mental make up, it would be impossible for them to learn the complex system of their mother tongue in such a short time; it follows that they must possess a 'language acquisition device' (=LAD) to manage this difficult task.

As it turned out, these views have come to be questioned. First, research in neurology points out (Edelman 1992; Deacon 1997; Greenfield 2000) that neither the innateness hypothesis nor the existence of LAD is supported by the structure of the neonate's brain: the brain does have a biogenetic line of function (see extract from Vygotsky above); but the structure and functioning of the brain from infancy to early childhood appears not to be in keeping with the hypothesis of a 'mental organ' dedicated to 'storing' the universal syntax of human language. Secondly, research on pre-speech communication in neonates (Bullowa 1979), initially stimulated by the

Chomskyan hypotheses, caused scholars to ask questions about the significance of the continuities they observed between 'action, gestures and symbols' (Lock 1978).

In the early 1970s when Michael Halliday began his case study of a child learning his mother tongue (Halliday 1973a, 1975a), he departed radically from the dominant Chomskyan approach. Like others he pointed out that babies engage in exchanges of meaning long before they are able to speak a single simple sentence of their mother tongue. He went further when he suggested that between the early simple action of crying and the performance of a linguistic act of meaning, the child passes through a highly creative communicative stage which is at once both like a human language and yet markedly different from it. This mode of meaning, he referred to as PROTOLANGUAGE, or as CHILD TONGUE because according to him, the noise patterns a child produces at this stage in attempting to mean, though displaying a systematic patterning, are not recognizable as pertaining to the sound system of any human language; in fact, at the protolinguistic stage, each child creates his/her own child tongue which s/he uses to exchange meanings with his/her adult care-giver(s).

Halliday identified four main categories of action that Nigel, the child whose language development he studied, was able to perform with the use of his protolanguage around the age of ten and a half months. Simplifying his detailed descriptions (2003: Appendix 2 pp 391), at that early stage, Nigel could make a demand by producing a sound sequence *na* on a mid tone, and was 'pacified' when whatever he was looking at or straining towards was given to him, from which it is justifiable to suppose that what he 'meant to say' by *na* was something close to the adult utterance 'give me that'. Halliday called this the INSTRUMENTAL function, where the child is using his protolanguage as an instrument for getting something. The remaining three such functions were identified as the REGULATORY, INTERPERSONAL and PERSONAL. In the regulatory function, the child's noise *aa* said on a mid tone needed to be interpreted as 'do that (again)', thus regulating the behaviour of some specific person; the interactional function was indicative of social contact and consisted in indicating the recognition of some close other by producing the noise *o* or *do*, the analogue to which in the adult language would be something like 'hello there' and/or 'nice to see you', thus establishing an interpersonal relationship between him and some caregiver. The personal function was expressed by uttering the noise *o* on a low tone and its interpretation that satisfied the child was for the other to attend together with Nigel to something that was at that moment engaging his interest, as if what he meant to say was 'lets look at this together'. Halliday (1975a) produced detailed descriptions of what Nigel was able to do with his 'language', presenting an account of its functional development at six weekly intervals from 9 to 18 months of age – a period that began with proto-language and made a transition into the early stages of the mother tongue.[7] Using his functional perspective, he reviewed his own observations of Nigel's pre-protolinguistic behaviour together with those of the contemporary researchers, and offered a cogent interpretation as shown in Figure 1:

Figure 1: Moving and meaning (Halliday 2003: 9)

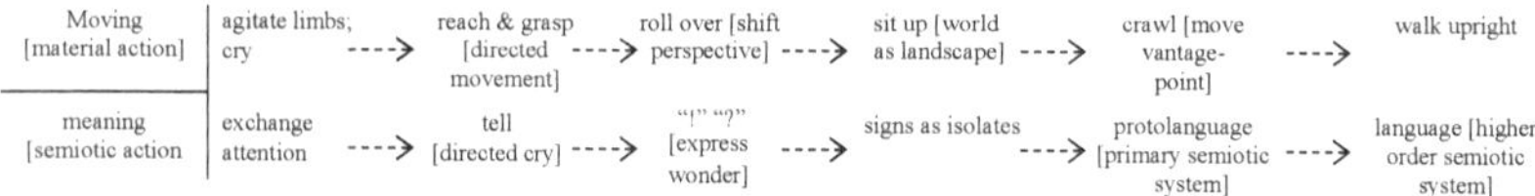

Halliday finds 'notable parallels between phases of moving and phases of meaning' from birth to 18 months. While, the first row of Figure 1 offers an account of continuities in material processes which begin with the agitation of limbs and culminate in the process of walking upright, the second depicts an interweaving of material and semiotic action. Thus the material action of crying coincides with the exchange of attention with a caregiver; this humble process is followed by the use of gestures as symbols; crawling coincides with the use of protolanguage which culminates in entry into the mother tongue bringing in linguistic signs, a stage which coincides with walking upright as shown in the rightmost columns in Figure 1. Throughout this period, the child has been engaging in 'acts of meaning', has actually been treated as doing so by his caregivers, and has overwhelmingly been successful in getting his meanings across. From this perspective, learning the mother tongue is not so much about 'the acquisition of syntax' as it is about LEARNING HOW TO MEAN (Halliday 1975a).

Halliday rejects the metaphor of 'acquisition' because in learning how to mean, neither do children just collect something that is already there, readymade to be 'acquired', nor do they act alone: from infancy onwards, they actively co-participate in exchanges of meaning with someone in their immediate community. This co-participation is important, because for the newborn, the world is a new place: to survive in it s/he needs to 'know' it – not as an object of analysis out there, but as an internalization of her/his immediate environment. Language is important to children because it is the richest resource. Three facets necessarily inhere in language development: LEARNING LANGUAGE, LEARNING THROUGH LANGUAGE, AND LEARNING ABOUT LANGUAGE (Halliday 1980); this is so because language is for the living of life, not for the production of structures. This makes learning the mother tongue an even more complex business than scholars marvelling on the complexity of syntax had ever imagined.

3.2 Learning through language in ordinary everyday environments

By the end of their pre-speech stage (see Figure 1), babies have already learned a good deal about their environment. For example, they can recognize the faces of their caregivers and the voices of those close to them, they differentiate persons from objects, night from day, and have some idea of what is 'usual' or 'unusual' in their world. Halliday (1975a: 82–119) presents an impressive description of Nigel's grasp on 'reality'. As the above brief account of Nigel's language development has indicated, quite early in life he knew how to get certain things done by his protolanguage, which means he had expectations about how persons and objects in his immediate meaning group behaved. Naturally, much of this 'knowledge of the world' Nigel did not present to the adult in declarative syntax; for example, he did not say 'I recognize those steps: they belong to my mother'. Instead, on hearing his mother's steps, what he did say was: 'mummy come' on a falling tone, which in adult language would be glossed by his caregivers as 'I am telling you my mother is back; I know this because I recognize her steps'. By contrast, if he said 'mummy come' on a rising tone, this would be interpreted as 'I want my mother to come here to me now!'

Children as young as three to four years have such an acute understanding of the meanings exchanged in their everyday life it belies the adult's concept of 'child language' as evidenced in text book sentences such as 'your hen has my blue pen'! Extract 1 is taken from a longer conversation. The child, Julian, is just three and a half years old. His language has drawn reasonably closer to the language of his immediate meaning group, thus rendering unnecessary the additional level of interpretation called for in the discussion of Nigel's language during transition from protolanguage.

Extract 1:

1	Mother:	d'you love daddy? … d'you love daddy?
2	Julian:	mmm (= yes)
3	Mother:	d'you love Rosemary? (ROSEMARY IS JULIAN'S SISTER)
4	Julian:	no!
5	Mother:	why don't you love Rosemary?
6	Julian:	(LAUGHS)
7	Mother:	why don't you love Rosemary?
8	Julian:	(CONTINUES TO LAUGH)
9	Mother:	you're a [?rat-bag] (REALIZES CHILD WAS TEASING)
10	Julian:	I do
11	Mother:	(UNINTELLIGIBLE)
12	Julian:	who else do you want me to love?
13	Mother:	you can love whoever you want to love
14	Julian:	can I love Peter? … Can I?
15	Mother:	no, I think that's more like friendship

16	Julian:	pardon?
17	Mother:	I thought you'd say that. It's like friendship, isn't it? You're friends with Peter, aren't you?
18	Julian:	yep ... (DRINKS NOISILY FROM HIS GLASS; PAUSE SEVERAL SECONDS)
19	Julian:	when I get old as you and [? Maree likes me] could we marry each other?
20	Mother:	no because Maree is your cousin
21	Julian:	oh!
22	Mother:	'cause cousins aren't allowed to marry
23	Julian:	why?
24	Mother:	'cause the law says they're not
25	Julian:	who is that?
26	Mother:	the law? (= do you mean who is the law?)
27	Julian:	yeah
28	Mother:	the policeman ... (CONVERSATION CONTINUES BEYOND THIS POINT).

Extract 1 forms part of a set of naturally occurring dialogues, audio-recorded and transcribed[8] for a sociolinguistics research that I directed at Macquarie University[9] in the 1980s. All recordings were made by the subject mothers themselves (for details, Hasan 2009b). The present segment was recorded while Julian was having his snack and the mother was attending to him; at the same time they were also engaged in a conversation. In a light-hearted game of who loves whom how much, Julian had just told his mother that he loved her lots. Extract 1 commences just at this point.

Let us first note the little teasing game played by this three and half year old: he clearly knows that his response 'no!' (turn 4) will tease the mother into some kind of protest. As it happens, the mother's concern features as repeated demands for an explanation 'why don't you love Rosemary?' The child simply laughs, until finally, the mother realizes (turn 9) that she was being teased. And Julian confirms her interpretation of the situation with 'I do' (turn 10). To appreciate why the child asks 'who else do you want me to love?' (turn 11), we need to examine more closely the wording of the QUESTION[10] the mother has asked: grammatically, her questions in turns 1 and 3 would be described as a YES-NO INTERROGATIVE, and those in turns 5 and 7 as WH-INTERROGATIVE. Typically, but not always, the yes-no interrogative is used to seek confirmation: i.e., to find out whether some state of affairs is or is not the case, while the WH-interrogative is typically used to seek information, i.e, to find out the identity of who/what did what to whom/what, why, when etc. Both types of interrogatives can be either POSITIVE or NEGATIVE, which is indicated respectively by the absence or presence of the negative word 'not/n't'. Thus the interrogatives in turns 1 and 3 are positive – 'not' is absent – while those in 5 and 7 are negative – both have 'n't' in them. The little word 'not/n't' changes its meaning somewhat according to whether it occurs in a clause with the function of statement or of command: dictionaries in general recognize this in their description of 'not' as 'a word expressing negation, denial, refusal or prohibition'. But the fact is that the semantic potential of 'not/n't' is much wider: it has many other meanings depending on its semantic environment (Hasan 2010), most of which remain generally unrecorded in grammars and dictionaries.[11] I will draw attention to one such semantic environment, namely that of negation in a subset of questions. Consider first Table 1:

	Function	*Affirming*	*Negating*
1	STATEMENT	He sold it.	He didn't sell it.
2	COMMAND	Do that again!	Don't do that again!
3a	QUESTION	Did you speak to him?	Didn't you speak to him?
3b	QUESTION	Why did you speak to him?	Why didn't you speak to him?

Table 1: Negation in statement, question and command

Example 1 presents an AFFIRMING STATEMENT: the 'not/n't' is absent; by contrast, the interpretation of its NEGATING counterpart 'is a' DENIAL/CONTRADICTION from the point of view of its meaning. Example 2 shows that while an affirming COMMAND 'is an' INJUNCTION, i.e., it demands a particular action be undertaken, its negating counterpart would be interpreted as a PROHIBITION, i.e., it forbids the undertaking of the mentioned action. This is true even if the command is grammatically realized not as an imperative but as a DECLARATIVE clause. Compare the following: (a) 'you must leave this afternoon' (injunction), and (b) 'you must not leave this afternoon' (prohibition). But neither of these interpretations can be applied to clauses which function as question. In 3a the affirming question would be interpreted as an attempt to find out if the process of 'speaking to him' occurred; in 3b, it would be interpreted as seeking an explanation for 'speaking to him'. When the word 'not' is inserted in these questions, then in both cases the typical interpretation is what I have called ASSUMPTIVE (Hasan 1983, 2010). The negating question 'didn't you speak to him?' would be interpreted as the speaker saying 'I had expected you would have spoken to him', while 'why didn't you speak to him?' is like saying 'you should have spoken to him'. This is true even when the question is realized as a declarative, as with 'you didn't speak to him?' said on a rising tone, which assigns it the function of question.

When his mother says 'why don't you love Rosemary?' (turns 5 and 7), Julian is not slow to get her meaning, as is clear from the question he himself asks: 'who else do you want me to love?' (turn 12). As a part of the dialogue, Julian's question needs to be interpreted as saying: 'from the way you ask this question I assume that you think I should love Rosemary which implies that you know whom I should or should not love. So who else do you want/expect me to love?' Receiving in response the mother's blank cheque on loving 'whoever' he wants (turn 13), Julian sets out to test the limits of 'whoever': in the questions-answers that follow, he receives an early lesson on the difference between friendship and love, and the implied unacceptability of loving a friend of the same sex; he further learns about the limits his society imposes on love with a female kin, including the rules forbidding marriage between cousins. He learns of the power of law and the role of the policeman as its enforcer. Clearly all of these things – many would call it 'knowledge of the world' – have been presented to the child's mind THROUGH language, more precisely through language in everyday talk.

But did he learn anything ABOUT language during this segment of an ongoing dialogue? Going back to Julian's questions about love, we might ask: when Julian is learning whom he could legitimately love and what meaning is attributed to that love, depending on his relation to the loved ones, is he learning about the world he lives in or about the meaning of the word 'love'? This, in terms of Rorty (1981), is a 'bad question'. A moment's reflection will reveal that the use of 'or' is inappropriate: what Julian is learning about love is both practical – i.e., relevant to life in his community – and linguistic, i.e., he is learning the meaning of the word, the senses in which his community uses it. I am not claiming that participation in one such dialogue provides a perfectly learned 'lesson'; the knowledge acquired through language use in everyday environments is cumulative: it changes, grows and takes root – or not – as the child continues participating in daily life, which is to say it grows with all the variation and indefiniteness typical of daily discourse. Nonetheless, it is in daily discourses of these kinds that children's mental habits take shape; they receive their early lessons in forms of reasoning (Hasan 1992a, 2004), and in what is relevant to their ways of living (Hasan 1986, 2000). There is much more to this fascinating story (Cloran 1989, 1999a; Painter 1989, 1996; Williams 1995), but enough has been said to allow us to now examine the nature of learning in everyday environments from the point of view of teaching and learning.

3.3 Learning and teaching in ordinary everyday environments

Learning language, learning through language and learning about language points unmistakably to the powerful impetus underlying the *first* major act of learning a child ever performs in his life. Looking at the complexity of this task, it has to be admitted that every single child with a normal brain is an awesome learning machine – he is designed to absorb the relevant aspects of the social environment that impinge on him, until the social world he has been experiencing becomes a reality that is truly *real* for him – in fact, it becomes *the* reality on the basis of which he is able to act with others in his immediate community. Awesome as the talent for such learning is, every normal child – and that is a very high percentage of babies born – displays an equal capacity for such learning: it is learning that comes naturally to all children. This important fact, we shall need to recall when we encounter learning in environments created by the educational systems of the world.

When placed side by side with learning in the specialized environments of education, this first kind of learning seems to be lacking in many ways. Take first the fact that it does not have a 'proper' teacher; add to this the absence of an orderly programme of instruction; consider also the difficulty of knowing what has or has not been learned. So there is neither a curriculum, nor a program of conscious instructional strategies, nor is there any easy means of evaluating the success in learning – and as for the outcomes of learning, the picture is at best hazy, at worst no one seems to be giving it a thought! All the processes are invisible: if it is by interaction with the caregivers that children learn these things, then the teaching is unconscious and unplanned; no one bothers about the learner's IQ or about his learning readiness, and the learner himself is not aware of making special efforts towards attaining knowledge. The knowledge itself is fragmentary and no one has a clear idea of the details of what is known, what remains to be learned. It is, nonetheless, obvious to any observer that learning is being attained successfully.

So what is special about learning in ordinary everyday environments? Why does it succeed? The temptation is very strong to attribute this success to knowledge that is innate, already built into the neonate's brain. But that solution has a serious problem: the kind of knowledge that the baby born in a Bilawal House[12] displays is considerably different from that displayed by the baby clutched in the arms of a mother who begs from drivers of cars speeding along the wide streets of such 'cosmopolitan' cites of Pakistan as Karachi, Islamabad or Lahore. What is more, both these babies would have a considerably different form of knowledge from that a baby might learn in the black ghettoes of America or in the White House. It is difficult to see how these deeply disparate forms of knowledge could be innate. What seems to be universally true is that the ability to learn is something that comes naturally to all children; they will learn so long as nothing gets in the way of their learning. In this respect, all children are born equal; what will swiftly make them unequal is their social environment. And more specifically, what makes the greatest difference to children's life and learning is the nature of their social interactions – first with their meaning group (Halliday 1975a), then their speech fellowship (Firth 1957) and finally the wider social community whose structuring impacts from a distance but effectively. Depending on these social aspects of their environment, the internalized picture of the world will vary from one grouping of children to another: their view of what is relevant will differ, as will their ways of thinking and reasoning. So when we talk of some children as 'good' learners, others as 'bad', some having high IQ, others as lacking in intelligence, we are unknowingly often making judgments about different socially generated patterns of learning (Gladwell 2007) rather than any inherent innate quality of the child in question. We must note also those things which will remain the same across different social environments: this is, first, the quality of the mediation of meaning to the child's mind – irrespective of what that meaning may be; second – and just as important – the internalized meanings will relate to the ways of living familiar to the learner's meaning group; what is being learned is what is being lived. There can hardly be a better condition for learning!

4 Learning in a specialized environment: the educational system

The knowledge the child gains in the ways described above is what educational sociologists have described as COMMONSENSE KNOWLEDGE, or everyday knowledge. The boundaries of this knowledge are unknown both to those who learn and those whose behaviours teach them; the unconscious teaching that is thus taking place is called LOCAL PEDAGOGY. Very often experts in education ignore both common sense knowledge and local pedagogy as irrelevant to what goes on in educational institutions. Their concern is with knowledge described in educational sociology as EXOTIC or SPECIALIZED KNOWLEDGE; the pedagogy they favour, called OFFICIAL PEDAGOGY, is anything but unconscious. There is reason to doubt the wisdom of this attitude. But first let me describe briefly some elements of official pedagogy.

4.1 Official pedagogy: planned teaching and learning

If learning and teaching in local pedagogy are unplanned social activities, official pedagogy presents an extreme contrast; it is carefully 'designed'. Three critically important concepts pertaining to it are particularly relevant here: one logically pre-dates teaching, i.e., the CURRICULUM, the next concerns actual teaching of competency, i.e., PEDAGOGY, and the third concerns assessment of the success of such teaching, i.e., EVALUATION. In Bernstein's words (1975b: 85):

> Curriculum defines what counts as valid knowledge, pedagogy defines what counts as a valid transmission of knowledge, and evaluation defines what counts as a valid realisation of this knowledge on the part of the learner.

The knowledge resources of any given society present a wide spectrum at any given historical moment. To be used effectively in the educational context, some selection from this vast spectrum is needed. And wherever there is selection, criteria for selection are needed. Criteria discriminate what is 'good': in the nature of things, persons with authority get to choose what domains of knowledge will be 'good' in the curricula, and their choices are guided as much by convention as by the dominant ruling ideas regarding what would be 'good' for the society. So curricula across societies are seldom identical, though as a rule the less advanced societies strive to duplicate those of the more advanced ones.

Selection of knowledge presupposes its CLASSIFICATION, i.e., what element of knowledge 'goes with what other'. It thus concerns the relationship between various categories; so in the context of curriculum, history may be classified as bearing no relation to sociology, and neither of these as having any bearing on linguistics, which may be seen as separate from applied linguistics, and so on. Curricula differ from each other according to how jealously the boundaries between categories are guarded and kept apart. With STRONG classification, categories will be clear cut, creating a CLOSED CURRICULUM. Where classification is WEAK, i.e., the boundaries are not sharply defined, points of contact between categories are recognized, yielding a relatively OPEN CURRICULUM. Closed curricula are created in societies which, as a rule, favour strong boundaries: they tend to be more HIERARCHIC, given to maintaining established traditions, therefore discouraging negotiation and tolerance of variation. And importantly, all knowledge categories are not accorded the same status in the curriculum: some form its compulsory elements, others remain optional; some are allocated five periods a week, others just one. The main point to note is that neither the curriculum nor the timetable are 'natural' phenomena. They are subtle indicators of a society's predispositions and the social beings who design them need to understand the nature and consequences of honouring existing predispositions.

Moving to the next aspect, pedagogy – it concerns the discourse of competency as well as teacher-pupil relationship. Bernstein (e.g., 2000: 32) described classroom talk as 'instructional discourse embedded in regulative discourse', implying thereby that the regulative element of the discourse is primary. The teaching of some content – i.e., instructional discourse – is popularly viewed as a teacher's primary concern, but at least equally important is the regulation of the students' internal and external conduct, teaching what it means to learn and to assume the role of student. Like curriculum, the organization of classroom discourse too varies across and within societies. Bernstein's concept of FRAMING is a good tool for analysing how teacher-student communications are negotiated – how it is decided and by whom what is to be discussed, what comes first, what next, how is the discourse paced and who prevails in deciding such issues.

However, the teacher–pupil relationship is not entirely manufactured within the classroom – societies vary in the extent to which the age and authority relation between interactants affect who says what to whom, when. In the traditional classroom, the teacher was in full control; the framing was strong giving her the right to decide all issues. Such framing is typical of authoritarian societies, where the hierarchic status of speakers is a decisive factor. Strong framing can distort pedagogic discourse to such an extent that pupils might hesitate to raise a question about anything said by the teacher. This would naturally encourage the spread of doxic knowledge, leading to what Bateson called zero-level learning – learning the item rather than the principle. By contrast, in most Western countries over the last half century, progressive schools have given relatively greater discretion to pupils who participate in negotiating the selection, sequencing and pacing of the discourse. On the other hand, with the erosion of respect for age or expertise, many contemporary Western schools are experiencing difficulties in maintaining the kind of environment in the classroom which would be conducive to teaching and learning.

The discourse of competency is overwhelmingly performed simply by language in use in a specialized domain. Knowledge is coded as language whether as content of classroom transmissions or for putting it on display for evaluation. Teacher's awareness of the patterns of language specific to the various categories of knowledge would be a tremendous advantage in instructional practices; in the forever developing countries, such as Pakistan, this aspect of the teacher education leaves a good deal to be desired. If the teacher herself does not know what features of language use make a definition a definition, if she herself has no explicit understanding of the structuring of an essay or a report, she would be unable to give effective help to pupils. There is perhaps no exaggeration in the claim that in teacher education, the understanding of language – the relations between wording and meaning – are least emphasized, least well taught because the teachers of the future educators are themselves lacking in understanding; the value of such understanding is seldom recognized. Archaic ideas about grammar are as harmful as the lack of understanding concerning the role of grammar in the construal of meaning and the role of meaning in the successful accomplishment of activities pertaining to the living of life.

The third aspect, evaluation, has sometimes been described as a 'necessary evil': it is essential to the structure of official pedagogy, and yet its effects are not always benign. Its primary function is 'gate keeping', establishing which learners have reached some designated state of knowledge. Educational systems strive to set up assessment schemes which test the required standards of performance, are objective, and fair. The pressures on the education system are many, and these demands are not always mutually reconcilable, so that the evaluative schemes become a balancing act. Consider, for example, the assessment of the comprehension of some piece of writing. A multiple choice test will save time, and so reduce the cost of examining, and it will certainly be objective, so far as it goes but – and this is important – it seldom goes far enough; so it can hardly be credited with the ability to examine the 'standard of performance'. Evaluation can exercise undue control over the educational enterprise – passing the exam may become the point of the exercise, more so in the current climate where the worth of an institution is judged on the basis of the rate of student success. Rather than focusing on the production of knowledge, instruction may be 'tweaked' to meet the demands of success: competency may be translated as attainment of skills rather than the internalization of principles. In this way, an evaluation system may defeat its own purpose: it may become a test of the state of knowledge rather than of ways of knowing, though the latter is arguably more beneficial to the society.

4.2 Official pedagogy: omissions and problems

All over the world specific branches of the educational institution have been set up, where experts discuss and determine the principles for the formation of curricula and for the standards of assessment; both pre- and in-service teacher training seems to be thriving – at least in the western world, though I see it flourishes in parts of Pakistan as well. Elementary as the above discussion is, it shows how much thinking, planning, decision making – all of which come at a material cost to the community – has to be devoted to the 'good' functioning of official pedagogy, which is now a universal concern. But one central figure is absent – the one for whom all the planning, all the thinking has been done – *and that is the learner*. Of course there is recognition of the learner in the mention of pupil/student, but it is a faceless abstraction whose antecedent experiences are overlooked.

But the child's meaning group, his history and his experiences, do not just disappear simply because official pedagogy ignores them: they enter the classroom with the child because they have played an important part in shaping the habits of his mind. As Vygotsky (1978: 84) said: 'Any learning a child encounters in school has a previous history': ways of dealing with that category of learning are already in place. In our sociolinguistic research at Macquarie University (see section 3.2 above), we found that mothers from two different sub-communities from the same general culture talked remarkably differently to their children. For example, the 24 children we studied asked their mothers a little over three thousand questions in all. Significantly more often, one group of mothers gave more information than the child had actually sought, while the other group preferred to give a minimal response rather than elaborated ones; one group answered why questions in full, the other was as likely to say 'because' as to just ignore the question. In follow up research we found that the children's experience of engaging in different sorts of question-answer routines bore a close correlation to the children's own behaviour during the question-answer routines in the classroom. We found also that mothers in one group have a good sense of the kind of instructional discourse that is typically found in schools: their interaction with their children had presented, as it were, a preview of what they would encounter in the official educational system. Not surprisingly, these children appeared to the teacher and other listeners as more 'intelligent' because of how they talked in the classroom interaction. The learners' past cannot be ignored, because its consequences are reflected in the present. To understand behaviour we need to examine the history of behaviour.

It would be a gross error to imagine that 'habits of the mind' (Lave 1997) are graven images incapable of being modified; but an informed nudge is needed as impetus to desired change; this would naturally be missing from the classroom scene if official pedagogy continues to ignore the variation in the children's past, instead of enabling teachers to understand the nature and effect of social structure during their education, for it is this feature that underlies these variations. Superficially, ignoring the difference between learners seems non-discriminatory, an indicator of equality, but in actual fact its effects are recidivist. Because the formation of curricula is heavily tilted in the favour of those with material power, the materially disadvantaged are also robbed of semiotic power. Effort does not go into eradicating the difference through careful teaching because they are branded 'sub-standard', 'unmotivated' and 'dull'. It is an axiom that nothing attracts success like success, so it probably follows that success is repelled by frequent failure. We cannot blame pupils for turning away from discourses that do not appear relevant to them. Both the failure and drop out rates are known to be considerably higher for pupils from disadvantaged background. This suggests that those who plan and design the shape of classroom discourse need to develop sensitivity and understanding for other, different modes of interaction. Instead of pointing to the child as a failure, it might be more useful to ask: how come the system of education universally fails more often to teach precisely those who are more in need of help?

5 Concluding remarks

Many third world countries, including Pakistan, mired in doxic beliefs and behaviours, look up to the system of education as the talisman – something access to which will bring about social change. Perhaps the brief description of the three fundamental elements of the educational system has pointed out that the education system may itself be viewed as iconic of the nature of the society in which it is located: for example, authoritarian societies create authoritarian social structures, which in the end maintain its pathologies thus maintaining the status quo, especially in respect of the hierarchies be they based in socio-economic distinction, in gender distinction, in ethnicity or in religion. So it is important to build into the educational system some element(s) which will counteract its tendency to march in step with what *is* rather than what *could be*. This is where once again we might usefully return to the message implicit in the concept of semiotic mediation.

The emphasis of semiotic mediation is on 'achieved interpretation', which is the essential condition for the internalization of concepts and the relationships between them: it is this process that we call understanding. The internalized concept enables the internalizing subject to appropriate that concept as his own and to act freely with it where and when, in his judgment, its use is called for. I am suggesting that in order to counteract the reproductive tendencies of official pedagogy, pedagogic practice must focus on the interpretation being achieved by the pupil. And this can be managed effectively by encouraging enquiry. Interpretation is not a simple activity with one single fixed and 'correct' destination. Pupils bring those habits of the mind which have earlier in life assisted them in interpreting the encountered experiences. And I emphasized above that these mental habits vary across distinct social groups. The presence of distinct groups in the classroom is therefore a rich resource: it can be directed towards the eliciting of alternative interpretations and examination of their bases. This pedagogic practice I referred to some time back as REFLECTION LITERACY (Hasan 1996b). It is a mode of teaching that will undoubtedly make many demands: it will demand time; more time for educational practice will demand higher funding; having more time for educational practice will be useful only if the pedagogy is worthy of this expense; to ensure the latter our focus must be on the educators. We need to create an effective method of *educating the educators*:

- So that they understand their learner which implies understanding the nature of the society to which both the teacher and the taught belong;
- So that they understand the content areas deeply enough to enable them to bring its concepts in relation to the learners' understand-

ings, which implies understanding how language works across the curriculum;
- These demands imply an understanding of how language functions in the life of the community.

It is not difficult to meet these demands. There exists a good deal of work in Systemic Functional Linguistics to illuminate both the functional nature of language and its working across the curriculum. Acquaintance with a social semiotic model of language would also open the door to an understanding of society in relation to language – how language plays a critical role in maintaining and changing social structure. It is not impossible to teach the language of official pedagogy to the learner in such a way that the understanding can be used for the production of knowledge: what the learner needs is to achieve interpretation, which will enable 'logical thinking', which will bestow the ability 'to go beyond the information' given. What may prove more problematic is the education of the educators. For this what is needed is cooperation from the boundary maintainers in the community. They have to ask: what are those social material conditions that will change the communal conditions of living so as to give freedom to think, open up spaces for the mind to stretch to explore beyond here and now to what it truly means to be human. This would provide a good model for the learner-centred teaching and learning.

Notes

1 This is a slightly revised written version of an invited talk presented to the Department of English Language, Linguistics and Literature at the Fatima Jinnah Women's University, Rawalpindi on 26 May, 2008. My thanks are due to the Vice-Chancellor Professor Dr Saeeda Asadullah and to the Pakistan Higher Educational Commission for sponsoring the talk.

2 In Vygotsky's writing 'cultural development' and 'higher mental development' refer approximately to the same/similar phenomena: both are equally central to the development of human mind (Hasan 2005).

3 Current debates on whether human intelligence as measured by IQ should be attributed to nature *or* to nurture show that this debate is not yet over; even today there are scholars such as Hernstein and Murray (1994) who claim that IQ is genetically inherited, while scholars such as Flynn (2007) and Lewontin, Rose and Kamin (1984) give credit to social environment for a person's mental abilities.

4 Powerful as Vygotsky's theory of the role of semiotic mediation in the making of human mind is, it is not amenable to definitive empirical proof. What can, however, be empirically proved is that where communities habitually differ in their semantic orientation, there the nature of human consciousness differs systematically (Luria 1976; Cloran 1994; Williams 1995; Hasan 2005, 2009b).

5 The reason that despite our unique minds we are able to continue interacting with others in our community is to be attributed to the fact that (i) in the first place, the 'biogenetic' capital, i.e., the brain with which we begin life, is largely the same for every normal member of the human species; and (ii) secondly, the general design for living in a particular segment of the community has enough in common to allow the members of that community to continue interacting with each other: our socially developed mind furnishes us with a blueprint for successful navigation within the boundaries of our own community. By contrast, when a common design for social living is not shared, interaction across such communities and even sub-cultures often becomes a different ball-game altogether (Tollefson 1991; Hasan 1976, 1978 etc.).

6 Some confirmation for these claims is provided by Day (1971) who has investigated modes of 'information processing'. Day claims that there are systematic differences between individuals in this respect: for example, a small percentage are able to attend not only to the meaning of an utterance but also to its 'form'; they are therefore able to recall the individual elements and their ways of coming together in a structure; by contrast, the majority attend to the meaning with the form being pushed in the background, so they are not able to recall details of structural configuration with the same degree of facility.

7 Two major studies replicating Halliday's highly demanding methodology are provided by Painter 1984; Oldenburg-Torr 1997.

8 The conventions for transcription are as shown below:

- Each number in the left column indicates a new turn in consecutive order;
- Entries in capital letters within parentheses, e.g., (LAUGHS) provide contextual comments based on audio evidence;
- Entries within square brackets, e.g. [? rat-bag] represent a segment not clearly intelligible; the entered item is the best guess based on co-text and imperfect phonological cues;
- Entries within parentheses preceded by equal sign, e.g. , (= yes) provide the analyst's interpretation based on textual and/or phonological clues;
- Three dots between items, e.g., in turn 1 of the extract indicate a pause greater than would be normal at that point.

9 The title of the research was 'The Role of Everyday Talk between Mothers and Children in Establishing Ways of Learning'. Funded by the Australian Research Council and Macquarie University Research Grant Scheme, the research was directed by Ruqaiya Hasan, with Carmel Cloran as her main research officer. I hereby gratefully acknowledge both the financial and the intellectual help. The full description and reports of this research have been published in a number of articles which are reprinted in Hasan (2009b).

10 I am making a theoretical distinction between the semantic term 'question' and the grammatical term 'interrogative'; the latter names the pattern of wording, which realizes the former, i.e., the meaning pattern. The distinction is important because not all questions are realized as interrogative and not all interrogatives function as question (Hasan 1988, 1989, 1991, 2010).

11 It would take us too far afield to discuss the semantic potential of 'not' here in detail, though I have presented my findings on this issue on a few occasions; (see also Hasan 1989, 2010).

12 Bilawal House is the residence of the late Benazeer Bhutto, daughter of a wealthy landlord who was the ruler of Pakistan in Pre-Zia-ul-Haq era. Benazeer Bhutto (called BB by her followers) was herself twice the prime minister of Pakistan in the 1990s, and the owner of rich properties not only in Pakistan but also abroad.

3 The implications of semantic distance for language in education[1] [1985]

1 Introduction

It does not take a linguist to recognize the fact that languages differ from each other, but the exact nature and extent of this difference – and the implications of such difference – are much more difficult to pinpoint. There does appear to be general agreement that two distinct languages do not have the same sound system and they do not have the same words: beyond this there is confusion and often violent disagreements, even among linguists. With some oversimplification, two current positions on the question of difference between languages can be isolated. According to one, such differences are confined to details at the level of lexicogrammar, phonology and phonetics; they thus pertain only to 'surface' matters: the SEMANTIC SPACE, that is to say, the DEEP STRUCTURE[2] of all languages is identical. According to the other view, entertained by functional linguists in particular, saying and meaning are inalienably related; the distinction between surface and deep structure is spurious; therefore any difference between two languages at the lexicogrammatical level is indicative of difference at the semantic level. Let me refer to these two positions as the UNIVERSALIST and the PARTICULARIST, respectively.

The difficulties in *conclusively* confirming or disproving either the first or the second hypothesis should be quite obvious. And the situation is not improved by the fact that the universalist statement is often apt to slide from the actual to the possible. Clearly there is a qualitative distinction between what is hypothetically possible and what is observed to be the actual case. To claim that semantic space *can* be made identical for all languages is a different assertion from saying that it actually *is* identical: the acceptance of the former claim does not entail the acceptance of the latter, which, it so happens, has some critical characteristics of an ideal hypothesis; it cannot be confirmed though it can be falsified without difficulty, which should please the devotees of Popper (1972) – all one needs to falsify it is to find just one pair of languages that show any significant point of semantic difference.

But crucial to this whole enterprise of accepting/rejecting one of the two views would be the notion of semantic difference: what exactly would count as semantic difference between languages? Is such a difference between Urdu and English established as a matter of fact because where English has *aunt*, Urdu has non-synonymously *phuphi, chachi, khaala, mumaani*; where English has *toe* and *finger*, Urdu has just *ungli*; and where Urdu has *suraj* and *dhoop*, English has only *sun*. If 'yes', then one might ask: how many such differences are needed to assert conclusively that the two languages differ semantically. Obviously if the slightest appearance of such distinction is taken as proof positive for recognizing difference at the semantic level, then the notion of semantic difference becomes tautologous. Complete equivalence of meaning across the unitary symbols of two languages has never been found so far, and may well be impossible to find, as many scholars have argued while reflecting on problems of translation (Sapir 1921; Malinowski 1923, 1935; Prochazka 1942; Saussure 1966; Halliday 1962). Besides, a quantitative definition of semantic difference is likely to pose some obvious problems – too obvious to spell them out here. In any event, far more fundamental is the question whether such a view of semantic difference truly disproves the hypothesis it set out to disprove. After all, the universalist could argue that the hypothesis of 'the same semantic space' is not concerned with distinctions in the inventory of elements of meaning: such distinctions can be seen as simply a difference in coding. One could go on to argue that in English it is possible to say *paternal aunt*, instead of the Urdu word *phuphi*, or to use *the wife of paternal uncle* instead of the word *chachi*. This must surely imply that the same set of minimal semantic distinctions are actually present in both languages, to be drawn upon as and when the occasion demands. And surely this suggests strongly, though it perhaps does not prove it beyond doubt, that if such paraphrases were always possible then the totality of the elements/components of meaning would have to be seen as identical across all languages: the difference would lie only in how the various elements/components are concatenated and synthetically coded as lexical items in distinct languages. On this argument the universality of semantic space will be always a demonstrable fact: there seems to be no condition under which such an interpretation of the phrase could possibly be falsified. The possibility of approximate translation equivalence cannot be denied even by the most ardent particularist.

This brief discussion indicates the dilemma in an atomistic approach to the question of semantic difference. The acceptance of the position that semantic difference can be claimed on the basis of differences in the meaning of unitary symbols leads to a tautology: to say that two languages exist would then be tantamount to saying that there is semantic difference between them. And the rejection of the position is equally unprofitable: it resolves nothing and it moves the focus from the habitual and the actual to the possible, so that one is arguing not from what meanings people *actually* transact but from what meanings they *could* transact if they wished to. It is tempting to suggest that Whorf (1956) who repeatedly warned linguists against attaching too much importance to lexical comparisons must have been aware of the inconclusive nature of such data. It is therefore all the more ironic that Whorf's own hypotheses should have been tested mostly (e.g., Lenneberg 1971) at the level of language Whorf referred to as 'merely lexation'.

2 Beyond the meaning of unitary symbols

One may be willing to grant with the particularist that in the last resort, the difference between *sun* and *suraj* or that between *sun* and *dhoop* is essentially semantic, in that it indicates how the elements of meaning are concatenated in one language as opposed to another. But this would still not be the entire story: I would suggest that languages can differ from each other at the semantic level in such a way that the differences transcend the semantics of the unitary symbols, relating instead, to the total semantic potential of the language, or at least to sizeable portions of it which can be explicitly specified. The kind of differences I have in mind can best be described as consistencies in the style of meaning (Hasan 1984a). It must be noted that even if we were to conceive of the semantic level as consisting of a vast array of minimal elements of meaning, upon which certain rules operate to permit acceptable concatenations, this view would itself raise further questions, such as wherein lies the rationale for these rules? Which came first the semantic elements or the rules which allow them to be concatenated into that semantic configuration which is perceived as a semantic unity in some language?

My aim in asking these questions is not to examine the various tortuous and non-tortuous ways of combining and re-combining the minimal semantic features of a language; instead, the interest is primarily in exploring the notion of 'consistency of meaning'. And in this exploration, the primary concern will be only with that body of meanings which is habitually and characteristically transacted within a community – in other words, with *aunt* rather than *the wife of paternal uncle*. The question under consideration is: if there is such a pattern as 'consistency of meanings', what are the principles along which such meanings are organized; what motivates such habitual selections? The hypothesis I put forward here is that communities differ in respect to those meanings which appear relevant; it is only relevant meanings that the speakers actually attend to – and they are the ones that are transacted habitually in most settings. The principles underlying the semantic consistency in the language of one community would differ from those underlying the semantic consistency of another. I shall use the term SEMANTIC DISTANCE to refer to the difference between the organizing principles that create consistencies within the various styles of meaning. In elaborating the concept of semantic distance, I shall adopt an indirect approach: so the starting point will not be the formal mechanisms of a language – the devices which are critical to linguistic meaning (Halliday 1973a) – but rather on how language functions within human communities.

2.1 Communities, cultures and linguistic meaning

Let me begin then with the widely accepted axiom that language plays a crucial role in the transmission of culture. This is not to say that language does not have other functions in social life or that other socializing institutions do not exist; it is simply to reassert the unparalleled position of language in this process. No matter what other socializing agency is cited, the acts of socialization themselves are largely mediated through language; and, equally, no matter what other functions of language are cited, each of them can be related to the business of socialization. Scholars have suggested that communities differ in the distribution of the symbolic modalities for socializing into distinct areas of communal life (for example, Philips 1972); nonetheless, a community that does not use language in any act of socialization is unknown.

It follows from the role of language in socialization that there is a two-way relationship between language and culture. The totality of a community's knowledge and beliefs – its culture – can become transmissible only when they are 'externalized' in some sign system (Berger and Luckman 1966). To play a critical role in socialization, language must encapsulate those elements which are vital to the identity of that particular culture. Therefore language must reflect in its semantic and lexico-grammatical structure, no matter how indirectly, that community's preoccupations and its perceptions of relevance – of how the universe makes sense. In the words of Berger and Luckman (1966) these preoccupations and perceptions must be 'objectivated' in that symbolic system which is the language of the community. What is encapsulated is not this or that particular individual's experience at some particular moment in time: language can truly arrive at the status of a communicative system for a community only by being freed of particularities relating to specific persons, events, experiences. Instead, it must typify experiences, allowing them to be subsumed under such broad categories as can have meaning for the many users of the language in general. Thus the reality that language projects is not an exact mirroring, reflections or re-creation of reality by any one member of the community; rather, from the very beginning, this projected reality is communal.

2.2 'Facticity': the objective reality of language

Once the communal preoccupations and perceptions – the speakers' relevancies – have been built into language, they acquire the quality of objective reality, what Berger and Luckman (1966) refer to as the quality of FACTICITY. Let me hasten to add, this is not a particular trait of language alone; rather, it is a characteristic common to all social institutions: what starts as a human-made product ends as the shaper of reality, the mover of social practices for the community. In the cultural history of any community there is sufficient data to support this generalization. Thus it comes to pass that the world which is actualized through the mediation of the humanly constructed, communally organized linguistic sign system acquires an inevitability for its speakers in so far as their views of work-a-day reality are concerned. And this is particularly so for the infant just embarking on the course of life in society, being initiated into it by already acculturated adults. For most of us the shape of reality remains as it is actualized by our language; it alters only when some part of it becomes an object for reflection, perhaps by being exposed to an alternative reality in one of the many possible ways. However, for the child during his/her formative years, this socially constructed reality, mediated through the patterns of his/her caregivers' language, attains a palpable character. Seen in this light, the literal-mindedness of the five-year-old (Chukovsky 1971) is just another expression of the faith the child puts in the absolute, undeniable facticity of the classification of reality mediated through the categories of his/her language. To the child, language is not a metaphor for reality; it is its representation – what names the phenomena that are really real. Thus the encapsulated reality projected by language becomes actual reality; what was externalized by the community is internalized by the growing infant. Language thus pays back with interest what it borrows from the community for projection and reflection.

I find no difficulty in believing that there must be some property specific to the human brain which permits these operations of externalization and internalization through the signs of a symbolic system; but equally undeniable appears the fact that the bases for behaviour, beliefs and therefore for concept formation are essentially social. Reality as known to human beings is not *sui generis* (Hjelmslev 1961). We may say with Mead (1934) that the human mind is a social artefact; or, less flatteringly, that all primary socialization is a form of brain washing, to which no one objects because – or rather as long as – the result is an approximation towards an inter-subjectively recognized communally accepted reality. It is in this sense that language may be said to have the potential of determining the limits of 'habitual thought and behaviour'. Whorf's picture of the effect of language upon cognition appears far more easily tenable where that kind of common-sense knowledge is concerned which is largely a product of primary socialization. There is a large amount in everyday life that we take for granted without reflection, without question, and largely upon faith simply because everyone else does, just because seemingly this-is-how-it-actually-is. It can be argued – and many well known anthropologists have done so – that the 'thus-ness' of the universe is a construct (Douglas 1972); it is construed by the various symbolic systems available to the members of a community. This construct will retain an aura of truth so long as it is not confronted by an alternative reality. It is important to emphasize that in this game of identities, there is no impostor; and if there is a conjuror, then its name is language. So in the last analysis, one may be allowed to make the largely speculative statement that the child does not set out to learn the language of his/her community simply because the linguistic system is aesthetically pleasing in its formal logic, in its near-perfect self-consistency, though this may perhaps be what makes the child's task easier. The child learns language because language turns out to be the most potent means of defining his/her everyday universe, and therefore, his/her own identity. It provides him with a stable basis for the ways in which he/she can be, behave and believe.

2.3 Language, socialization and cognitive frameworks

On the basis of the above arguments, we may derive the limited postulate that the end-product of primary socialization is the creation of a COGNITIVE FRAMEWORK which controls the appropriate forms of existence, of beliefs and knowledge pertinent to everyday common-sense reality. What is the nature of such a cognitive framework? What statements, if any, can be made about it such that they are generally applicable hypotheses about the crucial properties of a mental structure which can operate as a culture-specific blueprint for action, reaction and interaction?

One suggestion that appears highly plausible is that such a structure could not consist entirely of myriads of dissociated facts, since dissociated facts/concepts could never function successfully by themselves as a blueprint. Instead, to function as a blueprint, a cognitive structure would have to contain something more abstract, more easily detachable from the particular, capable of acting as a guide to type rather than attending to the specificities of tokens. The validity and usefulness of a mental map would depend on such habitual replications of social practices within personal histories as will be found even in the most internally differentiated societies. But instead of myriads of specific events, behaviours and beliefs, the cognitive framework has to rise to a set of principles along which are organized cultural institutions and, therefore, members' forms of behaviours and belief systems. Only such a conceptualization of the cognitive framework would permit the possibility of accounting for the appropriate forms of behaviour by social beings in situational settings which in their material content may appear quite non-identical but which in their symbolic status will have to be treated as the same by the normally socialized members. Take one example: as a Muslim woman in Pakistan, you would cover your head when saying your prayers; you would also cover it when you enter the presence of your grandfather or father.[3] These are not the only situations calling for respectful behaviour nor is respectful behaviour always manifested by covering the head. If in this maze of diverse situations and actions, resemblances are perceived, then I suggest it is due to some guiding principle(s) which the socialized beings use so as not to walk too far out of step.

2.4 Cognitive framework and semantic distance

Once the above position is accepted, we can approach the notion of semantic distance by relating it to cognitive framework. If for an individual, the cognitive framework is the blueprint for whatever s/he can mean in whatever modality, then a similar blueprint applicable to the community as a whole may be referred to as a SEMIOTIC POTENTIAL (Halliday 1973a). The semiotic potential represents a community's meaning resources as a whole: all orders of relevance have been constructed and mediated by this resource. In this sense the history of the use of these resources is the history of the community's orders of relevance through time. What has been referred to as cognitive framework is a subset of this communal semiotic potential: the cognitive framework has an immediate reality for *some* individual in the community, thus it represents only a part of what is introduced here as the semiotic potential. The same relation holds *mutatis mutandis* between semantic potential and semantic framework: the latter is a subset of the former, having an immediate reality for some individual. What is the difference between semiotic and semantic potential? I would suggest that if the semiotic potential is the communal blueprint, all that can be meant in using any semiotic modality, then semantic potential refers to that subset of communal meanings which can be expressed only by means of language. In other words, semantic potential consists of verbalizable meanings only. The relationship between the four terms discussed above may be graphically displayed as in Figure 1.

Figure 1: Semiology and language in relation to community and individual

sign systems / sign users	semiology		language
community	semiotic potential	↔	semantic potential
	↕		↕
individual	cognitive framework	↔	semantic framework

In Figure 1 both the horizontal and vertical arrows indicate a part-whole relation. The semantic potential is a subset of the semiotic potential: as pointed out above, it is that subset of communal meanings which can be realized only by languaging. A similar relation holds between cognitive framework and semantic framework: the latter is a subset of all those meanings which have the immediacy of apprehended reality to some individual. Both the frameworks are INTERNALIZED structures and pertain to the individual, whereas the potential are communally externalized structures, which underlie the community's ways of being, believing, saying and acting. The horizontal arrows indicate that the organizing principles which order and integrate the diverse domains of meanings comprising the semiotic potential must also be relevant to the semantic potential.

Making the above claims is tantamount to asserting that both at the communal and the individual level, serious dissonance in the organization of meanings is not very likely: there is likely to be a consistency between the semiotic and the semantic styles of meaning (Hasan 1984a). To offer an example again from the Indo-Pakistani sub-continent,[4] if the newly-wed bride is expected to let herself be displayed like an object for inspection by select members of her newly acquired husband's community, if she is to remain mutely passive during any overt criticism of herself while being so inspected, if her worth is to be assessed in terms of the dowry she brings, if her selection as a daughter-in-law is the prerogative of her husband's parents, if she should refrain from initiating conversations with older members of her husband's family, if greetings should take a ritualized form whether expressed verbally or non-verbally; if she should not express strong personal preferences, and if she should not address her husband or his elders by their name – these many conditions are not individual verbal and/or non-verbal acts: instead, they are so many expression of the same relevancy criteria. The consonance of semiotic and semantic styles follows logically from the acceptance of the definitions and relations discussed above. Further it appears valid to assume that when the criteria for relevance and integration of meanings vary from one culture to another – or indeed within the same culture – we would encounter two (or more) distinct forms of semiotic potential. By these steps the notion of semantic distance can be shown to be related to that of cultural variation: significant semantic distance between two languages obtains only if, and to the extent that, each (sub-)culture represents a distinct externalization of social 'realities'.

2.5 Atomistic semantics and the concept of semantic consistency

With this definition of semantic distance, the comparison of languages symbol by symbol, semantic element by element in isolation from each other no longer appears to be the desired goal. One is freed from concentrating on randomly segregated facts of a somewhat quixotic nature, e.g., how many terms for camel in this language or that, how many for colour in that one, which often leads to such naïve 'cultural' explanations as for example: camels are economically important to the Arab community hence the elaboration of the terminology referring to the animal. This completely disregards the fact that the same general principle cannot be applied to the terminology for rice in Chinese, though rice is probably as important to the economy of that community as camel to that of the Arabs. Even more absurd appear the attempts to relate such randomly picked out differences to variation in 'the physical perception of reality'. So speakers are asked: can you perceive the difference between blue and green colours, between your toes and your fingers, if your language 'has' but one lexical item to refer to the two members of each pair?

Contrast this with the concept of semantic distance between languages – or language varieties. Here, the comparison of language or language varieties at the level of lexation would be treated as beside the point. And this is as it should be: a moments' consideration will show that in demonstrating differences between the meanings of unitary symbols, one is doing no more than affirming Saussure's principle of the arbitrariness in the relation of the

SIGNIFIER to the SIGNIFIED (Saussure 1966; Culler 1976). For the examination of semantic difference, the focus should be on patterns of consistency in the selection of meanings. One such study was undertaken by Whorf (1956), who suggested that one of the prominent principles for the organization of meanings in Standard Average European (SAE) languages was that of 'OBJECTIFICATION', i.e., the use of the concrete as a metaphor for the abstract. I read Whorf as attempting to demonstrate that the form of human language is not amenable to a once-and-for-all clear categorization with water-tight boundaries. What from a purely formal point of view may be distinct categories – e.g., those of plurality and tense in English – can be thus seen to be inter-related, their inter-relation resulting from the principle of objectification. Other analyses attempting to bring apparently disparate formal facts under the umbrella of semantic consistency can be found in the work of the Prague School linguists, particularly that of Mathesius (1928).

It is significant that Whorf was able to refer to SAE languages as if they constituted one single entity. I would grant that in the context of his discussion, they certainly appear to do so: each of these languages appears to have objectivated a form of reality which is closer to that of the other languages within the SAE group, than it is to the reality projected by any Native American languages. What is being implied is that the difference between the two culture types – the European and the Native American – was considerably greater than that which could be found within each of the two general types. The semiotic style of the two groups would therefore differ in correlation with this difference and so the semantic distance between the European and the Native American languages would be more noticeable than that which could be found between, say, English and French on the one hand and that between the Hopi and the Navajo, on the other.

3 Variation in culture and in language

The sequence of arguments underlying the differences discussed above suggests that the starting point of linguistic difference is cultural variation, which is logically related to what we are calling semantic distance. Certain questions can be pertinently raised at this point. For example, if cultural variation always implies semantic distance, is there any advantage in introducing this new term? Is it not a tautology, even as the atomistic approach to semantic difference is a tautology from another point of view? Also, how does the concept of semantic distance fare in view of the fact that the culture of any speech community as a whole is often not just one totally integrated structure? What happens to semantic distance in complex communities where multiple integrated structures can be traced as making up one macroculture? This in turn raises the question whether one and the same language can project more than one model of reality? Let me attend to these questions briefly in the order in which they are listed above.

3.1 Cultural variation and semantic distance

If semantic distance is paraphrased as the linguistic expression of cultural variation, then it would follow that the relationship between the two is not accidental, that it is likely to be logical.[5] However, cultures can vary from each other in many different ways, and not all cultural variation is relevant to semantic distance. Semantic distance between languages would be said to occur only if the cultures vary in the principles of relevance which integrate the various institutions. Throughout this paper my concern has been not with item by item comparison, whether in the linguistic or the cultural systems: when I talk of the principles that integrate a large number of apparently varied instantial details, this necessarily implies rising above the consideration of isolated singularities. What one is after are general characteristics, some informing principles which can be used to give sense, to bring into inter-relation vast minutiae of disparate appearances. Systematization of this kind appears to be an essential condition for human communal existence: and systematization presupposes the recognition of some general basis. It is not, then, culture in all its concrete manifestations that is primarily relevant to the discussion of semantic distance – only that aspect of culture that is concerned with the organization and integration of cultural institutions. Thus, for example, if we accept that Whorf's grouping of SAE languages was valid, then we accept implicitly that the criteria for the integration of institutions in the cultures of the SAE speech communities were much closer to each other than they were to any criteria that might have been considered relevant to the integration of Native American social institutions.

In the last resort the usefulness of the notion of semantic distance can be judged from the light it is capable of throwing upon the important characteristics of the linguistic and the cultural systems. And I would maintain that the notion is important in that respect. For example, I know of no heading referring to the analysis of language under which we can simultaneously account for such disparate facts as the following:

i. a marked preference for elliptical forms;
ii. the extension of ellipsis to all elements of information that can be possibly gathered from the situational configuration;[6]
iii. certain patterns of modification within the nominal segment, especially those involving reference to definite identities;

iv. the use of honorific forms;
v. a clear cut distinction between the formal and informal sub-levels of the lexicogrammar.

I have argued (Hasan 1984a) that the bundling of these disparate facts – which are to be found in Urdu – can be accounted for by relating them to one of the widely recognized main preoccupation of the Indo-Pakistani sub-continental culture, namely that of its insistence on rigid role differentiation by reference to ascribed attributes such as those of sex, age, kinship relation, social status and the principles controlling the participation of certain individuals in certain social practices. Once we accept that this principle is an important one in the sub-continental semiotic style, a large number of individual facts – linguistic and non-linguistic – fall into place. Seen in this light, the kind of elaboration of kinship terminology one finds in Urdu – and in other Indo-Pakistani languages – assumes a deeper significance. Such significance cannot be assigned to members of the above bundle had they been arrived at atomistically, one by one as unitary coding of some element(s) of meaning or by an ad hoc relating of linguistic facts to cultural ones (as, for example, in the case of camels and colours!).

3.2 The poly-systemic nature of culture and language

This discussion leads one quite naturally into a consideration of the next problem. The postulate of a perfectly integrated cultural system is, perhaps, nowhere as open to doubt as in the context of the Indo-Pakistani sub-continental culture. In what sense can one maintain the notion of harmony between the various institutions and that of culture-wide principles of relevance? At the risk of repeating much debate that has already taken place in this field, let me add here that in talking of the integration of cultural institutions I do not imply that cultures are monolithic systems. The typical situation would seem to resemble more that of language as a system: if a culture is to be regarded as a unified system, this would be because the value and identity of each of its institutions is determined by that of the others. Such a unified system can be poly-systemic, as is amply exemplified by human languages (Firth 1957). The sociologist Durkheim (1964) points out that the multiplicity of organizational principles leading to the integration of the cultural institutions within a community correlate with the degree of the division of labour. The wider the range of specialized institutions, the wider the range of differentiated roles and the more likely it is that the criteria for relevancy would vary from one section of the community to another. As Berger and Luckman point out (1966) what happens is as follows: 'a segmentation of the institutional order, with only certain types of individuals performing certain actions, and, following that, a social distribution of knowledge, with role-specific knowledge coming to be reserved to certain types'. According to these authors, there arises, as a result, a problem regarding the integration of the total body of meanings within the community[7]: 'the problem of establishing a stable symbolic canopy for the entire society' may vary greatly: in some cases it is increased, in others not. Thus within the SAE culture, there may simultaneously exist distinct sets of integrative principles, each set having a 'reality' for a distinct section of the community. It logically follows from the definition of the concept that under such circumstances, semantic distance will obtain between the varieties of language specific to each such section of the community.

3.3 Inter-lingual and intra-lingual semantic distance

Up to this point, I have deliberately talked of semantic distance as obtaining between two (or more) distinct languages. However, now in the context of the immediately preceding discussion and its logical conclusion, it is obvious that the term is applicable to the varieties of the same language so long as the basis of variation is semantic, i.e., so long as there exists semantic variation as the ground for recognizing linguistic variety. In other words, semantic distance can obtain both inter-lingually and intra-lingually. As an example of intra-lingual semantic distance – i.e., semantic distance between the varieties of the same language – consider Bernstein's restricted and elaborated CODES. The codes are distinguished from each other by virtue of being associated with distinct semiotic styles. The criteria for relevance for members oriented to the two codes differ; the ground rules for being, behaving and saying show consistent distinctions across the two sub-communities (Bernstein 1971c). It perhaps needs to be emphasized that the overlap in the distribution of codes and social dialects is largely irrelevant – especially in view of current definitions of the term 'social dialect' (e.g., see Labov 1970; Gumperz 1971; Fishman 1971; Trudgill 1974; Halliday *et al.* 1964; Halliday 1974a; Hasan 1973). From the knowledge of the orientation of a section of the community to one particular code, one could never predict features of the so called social dialects (cf. the Labovian sociolinguistics) that may be in use in the speech of the members of that community. The reason for this is clear: these varieties are typically what Abercrombie (1965) would have referred to as ACCENT VARIETIES rather than dialects: accents are a-semantic, whereas the linguistic basis for code distinction lies in the principles that regulate meanings. On this basis, today's social dialects differ remarkably from codes. However, the recognition of the possibility of intra-lingual semantic distance such as obtains between the two codes raises an important question: what exactly is the nature of language difference from the point of view of the total system of language? Do members oriented to distinct codes have a somewhat distinct access to the system of their native language?

3.4 Competence, performance and codes

Recall Whorf's discourse on 'fashions of speaking'. His concern was not with varieties of the same language, but mainly with distinct languages, and in the context of his discussions the phrase can be validly reworded as 'characteristic ways of realizing meanings' in some given language. The famous Whorfian phrase was thus used to focus upon the actual and mundane linguistic behaviour across languages as opposed to the potential or the specialized behaviour, since it was only the former that was relevant to Whorf's arguments regarding language and cognition. With the rise to fame of the famous twins COMPETENCE and PERFORMANCE, Whorf's phrase has come to be seen as an informal, non-technical way of referring to 'performance'. If in this changed interpretation Bernstein's coding orientation is paraphrased as fashions of speaking, this would naturally imply that the distinction between orientations to two codes is really based on a distinction in performance, not in competence. Is this really the case?

To my mind the entire debate is somewhat pointless due to the confusion that surrounds the two terms 'competence' and 'performance'. It has been assumed perhaps even without an explicit assertion that competence is identical for all speakers of a language. If, therefore, there are variations, they belong to the domain of performance. Since competence in one of its guises is also identical to the system of language itself, the view encourages the belief that there is no significant distinction between competence as the system of language and competence as an individual speaker's competence. For sociolinguistically informed studies, various serious problems arise from such a conception of competence, performance and linguistic varieties. Hymes' idea of communicative competence may be seen as a step towards solving some of these problems, but even with that modification, it does not appear possible to use the concepts of competence and performance to throw light on the questions under discussion here.

3.5 Code, competence and 'language deficit'

In one respect serious harm has been done by the use of 'competence' to refer both to the language system as a whole and to a specific individual's competence in drawing on the language system. The confusion has lead to attaching a greater weight to the notion of LANGUAGE DEFICIT – a notion that has sometimes been used – though not by scholars who understand Bernstein's work – to describe the language abilities of members oriented to the restricted code. However, language deficit as a notion is not capable of differentiating any variety as a genuine variety of language so long as language system and the individual's habitual use of language are referred to as 'competence'; moreover, if used, it could have no stigma attached to it but for the confusion of an individual's 'competence' with the language system as a whole.

The view I have presented here maintains that the language system transcends all individuals qua individuals; in this respect language is no different from other human institutions. The individual's competence over the total language system can never be complete; his/her internalized knowledge of language is never a replication of the entire communally externalized system. Thus compared with the total language system each individual suffers from some kind of language deficit; and the degree of this deficit would vary with reference to distinct sections of the community, as well as to distinct spheres of language use. In this view, then, one possible definition of the term 'language deficit' would be to say that it is the name given to the difference between the externalized system – the total language system – and the individual's language. Thus we could express it as a formula: total language system minus individual's (communicative) competence equals language deficit for that individual. On this view *language deficit is a universal condition for all speakers of any language* – the stigma attached to individual's 'language deficit' does not even begin to arise. Language deficit and language variation are indicative of norms – a view that I believe is supported by reflection on Labov's work (e.g., 1966, 1970). Being the norm they neither call for explanation nor merit stigmatization; if anything stands in need of explanation or justification it is rather the notion of total homogeneity of language or its complete knowledge in any individual anywhere. This position lacks observational adequacy as Labov (1970) has so brilliantly demonstrated.

It seems then that reference to competence/performance and/or language deficit, however defined, fails to provide a convincing description of the crucial linguistic differences that exist in the condition described here as intra-lingual semantic distance; fashions of speaking comes nearest, but, as pointed out before, in its original application in Whorf's work the expression is used to refer to inter-lingual semantic distance.

4 Semantic distance and coding orientations

The arguments on the basis of which semantic distance is recognized presuppose that the main difference lies at the level of meaning. The speakers of the varieties separated by semantic distance must have immediate access to distinct subsets of the same total semantic potential. This in turn implies that the total system of language is capable of objectivating distinct social alternative realities simultaneously (Halliday 1976c). What can be described as one integrated system in which all the lexicogrammatical categories hang together must yet be so fashioned that it can be utilized by distinct sections of the community for the structuring of distinct universes of meaning. There must be the possibility of picking non-identical paths within this vast system, each of the paths being associated with one specific variety of the type in question.

Vexation seems to set in at this point in the debate. It is all very well to say that when varieties of the same language display semantic distance, the speakers of the distinct varieties have immediate and 'automatized' access to some distinct set of the semantic potential of their language, and that they also have immediate and 'automatized' control over certain well-defined paths of the total language system. But how are all these facts manifested? Where is the objective correlative to these assertions? It is argued, and with much empirical fervour, that if such objective correlative cannot be found, then the entire idea of codes needs to be abandoned. I am not concerned here with the vindication of codes except in as much as I have presented them as examples of varieties distinguished by semantic distance. It therefore seems appropriate to say a few words on the question of the realization of intra-lingual semantic distance.

If it is true that the atomistic approach has proved fruitless in the examination of semantic distance across languages, it should be more than obvious that the approach could not even be entertained as suitable in the study of intra-lingual semantic distance. In neither case can one elevate just one formal pattern – or even one pattern type – to the status of crucial marker of some variety. Thus the semantic style of Urdu and French do not become identical because the *tum/aap* distinction is mirrored in French by *tu* and *vous*. In Urdu the distinction between *tum* and *aap* forms part of a configuration of patterns – a syndrome – each element of which points in the same direction. To mention but a few: we find a parallel distinction both for the first and the third person pronouns, the activation of distinct levels of lexicon in formal as opposed to informal environments, an elaboration of kinship terminology, a tendency for inferential assertions by way of demand for goods and services addressed to certain category of persons, in other words an avoidance of imperative structures as realizing a command, and so on.

4.1 A configurative approach and the realization of codes

The discussion shows that Whorf's differentiation of inter-lingual variation depends not on some single formal feature but rather on a configuration of features: it is the latter that proves relevant in establishing inter-lingual semantic distance. This suggests that in trying to establish the identity of codes differentiated by intra-lingual semantic distance, it might be more sensible to use a similar configurative approach. According to this approach what matters is not the simple presence or absence of, say, causal conjunctives, but the entire relevant environment – what is treated as cause for what, what kind of backing is provided for what kind of cause-effect relation. In this perspective, what we are looking for are bundles of semantic patterns co-occurring and relatable to the same (set of) principle(s). It follows that there is no easy list of lexical items, or even structural patterns by which either of the codes may be characterized: the situation is fundamentally different from that of identifying accents found in certain geographical areas or in distinct social groups. Consider for example the following examples:

(i) well you are not to play with those guys cos your dad told you not to and you mustn't go against what your dad's told you cos that would be very wrong you know.

(ii) Well, I'd like you not to play with those guys cos I don't like the kind of games they play; you could even hurt someone, and that would be wrong you know.

I take (i) to be an example of Bernstein's restricted code and (ii) as that of the elaborated code; and this fact would not change if (i) were said with the most royal version of educated English accent. Note, however, that neither the grammar nor the lexicon can be easily distinguished by simple formal means. So what is it that tells us that (i) and (ii) are instances of distinct code varieties? It is only the appeal to the way meanings are organized. In (i) the case is presented as external to the prohibited deed, and the rationale for the acceptance of the prohibition – its legitimation – depends on regard for ascribed authority. In (ii), by contrast, the cause for banning the deed is presented as arising from the nature of the deed; the restriction for the prohibition on the deed – i.e., the rationale for the command – lies in the nature of the deed itself. In other words, its moral basis does not lie in ascribed authority; it lies instead in appeal to personal affect. The child in whose experience most control is of the first type cannot truly be said to construct the same picture of social reality, which is likely to be constructed by the child whose typical experience of control is of the type exemplified by (ii). It is true that the linguistic difference to which I am drawing attention is not as concrete, as simple or as easily visible as the presence or absence of some specific formal 'bit' such as the vocalic or consonantal features of items, the presence/absence of the copula or the singular/plural difference in English. However, I see no reasonable basis whatever for denying that differences such as identified between (i) and (ii) do actually exist, and that it is a 'true' linguistic difference requiring attention and study.

The modes for the realization of semantic distance – whether inter-lingual or intra-lingual – present a challenge to linguistics. The examples I have provided here are preliminary, but I hope the discussion has succeeded in establishing the validity of the category of semantic distance. What now needs to be shown is that the category is not simply of theoretical interest: its relevance becomes obvious when we shift attention from language as a formal system to language as resource for living. This is true not only in such specialized areas as those of language teaching, translation, stylistics and developmental linguistics: it is true of any occasion where language is used for non-casual communication. But perhaps nowhere else has the notion as much relevance in its application as in the sphere of education. I will devote the remainder of this paper to an examination of this aspect from two distinct but related points of view: one may examine the role of this concept in the interaction of language and education, and secondly, the relevance of the notion could be examined from the point of view of the use of language for the transmission of such specialized knowledge as the educational institutions normally consider their duty and their privilege to impart.

5 Language and the transmission of knowledge

It is well recognized that for most members of society, language plays an important role in the transmission of culture (discussion, section 2). To live in a society is to learn its culture, and cultures tend to have multiple agencies for socialization: one institution that has been traditionally recognized as central in the process is that of education (Durkheim 1938; Parsons 1964; Bernstein 1975b; Barnes 1974; Berger and Luckman 1966). However, despite the functional similarity between these two culture-transmitting institutions, i.e., language in everyday life and formal education, it is important to draw attention to a qualitative difference between the two agencies.

I noted above that the system of language is capable of being used for the objectivation of distinct alternative realities – this much is obvious from an examination of complex societies. This attribute of language makes it possible for the language of primary socialization to be always in harmony with the total semiotic style of the section of the child's immediate meaning group which is precisely where the very small child is socialized. There can be no conflict between the socialized person's cognitive framework and his semantic framework, the part which is relevant specifically to his linguistic behaviour. By contrast, education as a socializing agency, i.e., formal institutionalized education,[8] appears to have a more restricted status. This is true in two respects: first, the system of education is concerned with the transmission of specialized, uncommonsense knowledge, and secondly, both the definition and the selection of what counts as specialized knowledge as well as what count as the legitimate modes of its transmission have traditionally been recognized to have been monopolized by a small but powerful subsection of the larger community. The relevance of the system of education to the community as a whole is conditioned by these two facts taken together.

5.1 Education and society

The education system of a community comes to represent social reality as apprehended by the specific sub-section that controls it. Although there are reasons for suggesting that the cleavage between commonsense and uncommonsense knowledge might not be as sharp as commonly believed – the latter is in complex ways a continuation of the former – the fact still remains that the definition of knowledge is the monopoly of only a sub-section. If it is generally agreed that knowledge is power, this may be largely because it is the powerful who define what counts as knowledge.[9] Both in itself and in the relation it bears to everyday commonsense reality, the knowledge imparted by the schools appears less problematic to those for whom the system of education is a continuation of reality as they have always apprehended it. For those who do not share this reality, the knowledge imparted in school appears not to impinge on 'real' life problems as they know them. This is an important difference which could by itself render the socializing agency of education much less effective in the fulfilment of its proclaimed function than the socializing agency of language in everyday life. But this is not all. While it is true that the major thrust of the educational system is towards imparting specialized knowledge to all, the fact is that nothing can be imparted where there is lack of readiness to receive.[10] It is the school's responsibility to enable learners by creating such readiness: the pupils will succeed in learning to the extent that the educational system succeeds in fulfilling this duty. In the end, the fulfilling of this duty entails changing the learner's perception of reality, their orders of relevance, their preferences and plans. By these steps the school comes to have the role of the shaper of the pupils' character. Not only the knowledge, but also the mode of imparting it, as well as the ways of evaluating the achievements of the pupils – all these aspects of the educational process come to have an equal importance as an expression of a particular view of self in relation to one's social universe.

5.2 Semantic distance and the educational system

Given that the educational system represents the reality apprehended as really real by one segment of the community, the workings of the system – what it tries to socialize the pupils into – do not have the character of inevitability about it for those who are on the fringes of this reality. The possibility is always open that those who do not share the semiotic style of the purveyors of education might end up as aliens in the system. The alienation from the system impinges upon the participants of the process of education in many significant ways, depending upon the degree of semiotic dissonance that may be experienced. I have argued elsewhere that there is a serious semiotic dissonance between the Western educational system and the sub-continental view of the world (Hasan 1976, chapter 9 in this volume). As one manifestation of this, consider the distinct conceptions of the roles involved in the process of education – the contrast in the perception of the rights and obligations of the roles differ sufficiently to cause problems in learning. However, in order to find semiotic discord affecting the efficient conduct of education, it is not necessary to examine cultures so obviously different as the Western and the sub-continental. Dissonance of a similar intensity can be found easily within what would be generally perceived as one single larger community – and that is precisely what is at issue since the education systems do not really vary according to distinct sub-communities within the same wider culture. There is convincing discussion of problems ranging from inter-ethnic situations (John 1972; Philips 1972) to those involving sociologically differentiated sub-communities of the same ethnic community, i.e., differentiated by social class (Bernstein 1971c).

Wherever semiotic discord is found, there semantic distance must exist. One result of semantic distance between the purveyors of education and the learners can be put quite simply as frequent break down in communication (Butt 1989; Hasan 2004). In situations where distinct cultures are involved, where inter-lingual semantic distance appears to be implicated, the break down is often explained away as arising from 'language difficulty'. And in fact it *is* language difficulty – but not in the sense in which the phrase is usually intended. What the learner really needs is an understanding of the language of those who control the selection and organization of educational knowledge, but this understanding goes beyond such matters as errors in concord, correct ordering of constituents, and correct pronunciation. The learner certainly needs this kind of knowledge but it is likely that the difficulty concerns other issues: it might often concern bewilderment about where the discourse began, where it is headed and how it is getting there – in other words, the shape that social practice takes.

When semantic distance is experienced by those involved in the educational process within the same general culture, the resulting problems are once again described as 'difficulty with language'. And once again the phrase in itself is true enough but not in the sense in which it is intended, for once again the problem is not at the level of literal decoding; it is more importantly at the level of making sense of the whole interaction. For the system of education to operate successfully – and there are those who doubt that maximum success is the true goal of education – the teacher and the taught need to function on the same wave-length; this is precisely what cannot happen if there is semantic distance between the two. We can examine almost any area of education – the methodology, the evaluation, the selection and organization of instructional materials – the over-powering impression is that of a search for *the* correct way of doing things. I am suggesting that if semantic distance is a reality and if its effects are as described here, then what is needed is far more than attending to language alone. It may be important to ask if there might be different ways of presenting information to pupils with decidedly different kinds of semantic orientation, and whether the right way to encourage learning in the context of one community might not necessarily be the best way in the context of another.[11]

The optimal learning environment is one where the pupil feels at home, where s/he experiences no semantic distance between himself and the teacher. To quote Halliday (1975b):

> … in our own culture, in our own environment, we know most of what the other person is going to say – or rather, what he is going to mean, whether or not and in what way he says it. The significance of an incoming message lies not in the fact that we do not know what it [the message, RH] contains, as in the mathematical model of communication, but in the fact that we do know. … If a pupil cannot predict about 90% of what a teacher is going to say, he is unlikely to learn very much.

The ability to predict with success what the other person is going to say presupposes sharing to some extent the same picture of reality, having largely the same criteria for relevance. One knows that in theory drawing a hard and fast line between two sub-cultures is not easy, but for the child in the classroom the theoretical aspect of the problem has little or no reality: what has immediacy is the realization that s/he cannot get the hang of things.

5.3 Semantic distance and the concept of register variation

Where the use of language in the transmission of specialized knowledge is concerned, one area to which inter-lingual semantic distance is primarily relevant is that created by dissimilarities in register repertoires (Gumperz 1971) of the two languages. It is often assumed that the creation of a new register in a language is just a matter of finding the right terminology for the technical concepts. I doubt if the matter is as simple as this. If registers are the expression of social processes (Halliday 1977; Hasan 1973, 1976; Gregory and Carroll 1978), it seems fairly obvious that the presence or absence of a register goes much deeper than the finding of new vocabulary. The presence of a register is proof that some particular social process has some standing for some members of the community, that there is some recognized CONTEXTUAL CONFIGURATION which is inherently associated with some specific meanings that are habitually exchanged in the course of that process. Conversely its absence proves that the particular social process has no standing in the community; then, naturally enough the meanings associated with it are not the familiar habitual ones. The specialized knowledge of that register is not the continuation of the commonsense knowledge of any section of that community. In the context of the third world educational scene, familiarity with new registers common to the educational system is gained usually not through mother tongue, but through another tongue – and given the politico-economic history of the subcontinent, most often through English. But such familiarity is often fairly restricted; it has no roots in the indigenous culture as such.

While discrepancy in register repertoires across languages is fairly well recognized as a substantial barrier to educational success, it is not very often that such discrepancy between the repertories of the varieties of the same language is taken seriously. And yet, the assumption is unwarranted that if one speaks, say, English, then to that speaker all the registers of English – its entire repertoire – is equally accessible. Nothing could be further from the truth in actual practice. For each sub-section of the community – especially where the social system as a whole displays complex patterns of division of labour – there are certain social processes which remain outside the common run of things. Given the speaker's place in the social structure certain activities and certain accompanying roles fall outside the habitual range of behaviours. For this reason, if we know the register repertoire of an individual, say, in the Western cultural context, then on the basis of such knowledge we would have little difficulty in predicting fairly successfully the relative placement of that individual in the community.

When the registers most frequently used in the educational context are examined, it becomes immediately obvious that their semantic style is in consonance with the semiotic style of that sub-section of the community which has control over other agencies of cultural transmission, e.g., the media, the institutions for the production and distribution of national wealth and resources. This is only natural, since the educational system represents that view of reality. Those who fall outside this section, then, are faced with this well-integrated structure, which is largely inaccessible and yet which tantalizingly appears to reject any ideas of its inaccessibility due to any easily visible process of language. Education, we announce righteously, is for everyone and everyone has an equal chance of success in it. But the real power, the true resource through which the 'equal chance' can come to have a tangible reality is language. What the system professes to make available to everyone is in fact available to everyone only if they have access to the language which is characteristically and habitually used in constructing that information. The solution seems easy: create awareness of the features of the academic registers.

5.4 What is the solution?

On the surface this injunction seems sensible, but reflection suggests that the solution has been based on fairly shallow reasoning. In actual fact the solution is not as easy as it is made to appear: problems arise because of the relationship between registers, social processes and social structure. In mastering an academic register – no matter what field of specialized knowledge that register pertains to – the pupil is not just mastering so many words and syntactic structures; s/he is also learning at the same time a new mode of thinking, a new approach to ways of meaning. This enterprise is likely to meet with success in direct proportion to how close the new approach to ways of meaning is to any that the student is already fluent in. Thus the implications of semantic distance, whether intra- or inter-lingual, go far beyond the question of form in language: they require an examination of what lies beyond the selection of specific formal patterns, whether they pertain to the structure of the text or to that of a clause. I agree completely that a greater clarity is introduced in understanding problems in learning and teaching when they are presented in terms of formal features of the text or of the clauses/sentences in the text. I would also accept that the kind of issues and problems in education I am raising are not very easy to investigate – and so far as their solution is concerned, I do not believe the question has engaged much serious attention. But none of this implies that the problems I am drawing attention to do not exist; nor does it mean that by concentrating on the form of language alone – because it is easy to grapple with, objectively accessible – we are going to solve the specific problems created by semantic distance. What the teacher's report describes as 'fails to engage with the problem!' or 'irrelevant!' or 'poor organization!' has very little to do with errors in operations on the form of language. If anything, it is drawing attention to the fact that the student is not able to see the rationale for the organization, is not able to grasp the principles along which facts are ranged in a hierarchy of relevance, or maybe the central issues constituting 'the problem' elude the student altogether. The phenomenon of lack of relevance, poor organization, failure to get 'the point' occur more typically in the case of those for whom the semantic style of the educational system is foreign. Whether the language itself is foreign or not appears of secondary importance so long as the teacher himself/herself has a coherent understanding of the formal resources of the language the student is using. To have this understanding implies that the teacher is capable of linking the form to meaning in context; linking form to meaning in context implies the teacher knows how the student is 'visualizing' the context of his/her discourse.

6 Closing remarks

It follows from steps in the arguments concerning the importance of semantic distance that I do not believe such distance to be eternal, impervious to change. The human mind may be in the grip of language (Bolinger 1975), but language itself is neither static nor unalterable. The presence of semantic distance across and within societies is a function of the construction of social realities, differing pictures of what the social and physical universe is like. The construct may have a facticity but its legitimacy – its fact-faithfulness – is open to question by the very fact that it is a social semiotic construct, not something that is given in nature. There are conditions in which such questioning occurs quite naturally, as for example when two substantially distinct cultures come into contact. The history of colonization is the history of culture change, though culture change does not take place only in the context of such cross-cultural contact.

The reminder is of relevance to us here for one simple reason: in colonization of whatever kind, the ascendant community has always behaved – and still goes on behaving – as if the construct of reality to which it subscribes is not just a construct, as if this reality is really real. By the same token – given the nature of the power relation – the purveyors of education have so far always behaved as if the alternative realities which some pupils bring into the school are so many counterfeit systems, which in the interest of progress and civilization, need to be destroyed. There has been no dialogue, although we claim there has been a beneficial spread of egalitarian democracy – that the claim is spurious is evident to an impartial observer.

The only means of counteracting the consequences of semantic distance is to create conditions in which the two realities in question can be viewed side by side. To span semantic distance the parties must be sensitized to the nature of the differences that exist in the criteria that lead to concepts of what is relevant to whom and why – what helps whom in making sense of how human behaviour is organized. If a teacher is willing to accept that the legitimacy of 'inherent cause-effect' relation is no greater than that of 'non-inherent, extrinsic cause-effect' – and why this is so – progress has already been made towards explanation rather than denigration of the one as against the other. It may be that the structuring of arguments in the academic registers gives priority to the former, but such priority has its domain in this particular context, and it is possible that it is not a mode of argument that should be given priority everywhere.

To talk about semantic distance is no more divisive than to talk about social accent/dialects. To understand the causes of semantic distance might possibly orient us in the right direction towards doing something more sensible about the problems faced by speakers of disadvantaged varieties than has hitherto been possible, despite, or perhaps because of, the well-meant but short-sighted and sentimental views from critics who would suppress this discourse due to a professed respect for equality and a desire to abolish 'judgmental' discourse – when in all essential matters, social equality is actually denied; and the judgments regarding dominated varieties of behaviour are so well known, that hardly any one who practices them would admit to doing so! This does not help the disadvantaged; it merely maintains the *status quo*.

Notes

1 This paper was accepted for presentation at a Post-Plenary Session of the Xth International Congress of Anthropological and Ethnological Sciences held at Mysore in December 1978. Riots in India and the erratic behaviour of my chosen airlines prevented my attendance. Much later in 1985 the paper was published in the *Indian Journal of Applied Linguistics* (xi. 2, 1-22); reprinted a year later in Anvita Abbi (ed), *Studies in Bilingualism*, New Delhi: Bahri Publications, 1986. I am grateful to Gunther Kress for his comments on that last version. However, the responsibility for the views expressed here is mine. References were up-dated for the 1986 publication; some were further corrected for the present version along with other errors and omissions; some highly condensed parts of the original version have been elaborated (author's note, 2008).

2 Up to the mid-1970s these terms were much in vogue in the dominant formalistic models of language which originated in early Chomsky (1957, 1965).

3 During the last three decades this particular custom has changed especially in the Westernized segments of the Indo-Pakistani community: one no longer respects age to the same extent as one did before. On the other hand with fundamental Islamism gaining strength other much more virulent forms of behaviour to show respect and to safeguard the honour of the family have become more prevalent (note added by author, 2008).

4 Again as for the earlier example, the situation is now different. As a distant observer of the scene, it seems to me, it would be true to say that the difference in behaviour between segments of the Pakistani community in most of these ways has been further exaggerated: there is the segment of the community that rejects many of these older conventions, while there are other segments where the objectification of the female has grown much stronger.

5 This claim is indicative of my early recognition of the fact that the REALIZATION relationships obtaining at the levels arising from the analysis of Saussure's signified and Hjelmslev's PURPORT, CONTENT-SUBSTANCE and CONTENT FORM (now in SFL referred to as CONTEXT, SEMANTICS and LEXICOGRAMMAR) is qualitatively different. Later I introduced the notion of REALIZATIONAL DIALECTIC which has informed my work at these levels consistently (e.g. Hasan 2005, 2009b) (author's note, 2008).

6 Situational configuration is not identical with material situational setting; for some details Hasan 1973, 2005, 1976 (chapter 6 in this volume), and 1978.

7 With Bernstein's discussion of the 'circulation' of different kinds of knowledges in the culture, it is clear now that it plays an important part in cultural 'integration' as it does in creating specializations and group identities (note added 2008).

8 The current term used for formal education system is 'official pedagogy' (note added 2008)

9 Certainly such knowledge as is produced in the educational system contributes to the greater power of that class which happens to be in control of the pedagogic system.

10 The unfortunate fact is that this principle has been treated as a licence to teach different things rather than to devise ways of enhancing the receiver's ability to receive the many type of knowledges available to everyone.

11 With hindsight I note these injunctions might be read as recommending 'streaming' in education. A better question to ask may be: why should the system of education ignore the learner, attaching greater importance to the understanding of every other aspect of education?

4 Forms of discourse, forms of knowledge: reading Bernstein

> A man demonstrates his rationality, not by a commitment to fixed ideas, stereo-typed procedures, or immutable concepts, but by the manner in which, and the occasion on which, he changes those ideas, procedures and concepts.
>
> [Stephen Toulmin, *Human Understanding*, 1972: vi]

1 Introduction

Discourse on knowledge – its ontogenesis, maintenance and change – is fraught with challenge not only because so many diverse issues surround the concept pressing urgently for attention, but also because the issues themselves are so complex due to being closely woven into the politico-economic fabric of human existence. The danger is that one might be swept away by the recurrent waves of these complexities, never to come up with a coherent breath. We hope to avoid this fate here,[1] first, by *minimizing* attention to any detailed discussion of how the politico-economic considerations pervade the processes of knowledge, since this has been a recurrent theme in many of the social sciences.[2] Secondly, we are setting ourselves a severely limited goal: our aim is to externalize our understanding of one slender piece presented by Basil Bernstein (1924–2000) in the last years of his life (Bernstein 1999) before commenting on some aspects of its content. Attention to his other writings – both his early CODE THEORY (1971c, 1975b) and his discourses on aspects of official pedagogy (1990, 2000), so skilfully linked to central aspects of the earlier work on codes[3] – will be subsidiary to this enterprise. This self-imposed limitation does disadvantage us, since in ignoring the recent work of his colleagues,[4] we will lose the most recent perspectives, but we hope this may enable us perhaps to attend more thoroughly to Bernstein's own *parole.*

The Bernstein (1999) paper, called *Vertical and Horizontal Discourse: an essay*, which forms the focus of our interest, is no more than 20 pages long. Concerned with his thoughts on a mode of classifying discourse and knowledge, it in effect closes his writings, and is without doubt as thought-provoking and perhaps as controversial as the concept of CODES with which he opened his scholarly career (Bernstein 1959). The sad difference is that Bernstein's code theory received four decades of keen attention and revision by its author – and the word 'revision' is not being used here pejoratively, as evident from the introductory extract above (Toulmin 1972); rather it indicates our admiration for his integrity and commitment which drove him repeatedly to deepen and widen the scope of that theory. By contrast, the relatively new concepts of HORIZONTAL/VERTICAL DISCOURSE (henceforth HD and VD, respectively) and HORIZONTAL/HIERARCHICAL KNOWLEDGE STRUCTURES (henceforth HOKS and HIKS, respectively) will remain bereft of that careful attention.[5] In turning to these concepts we are, therefore, acutely aware of a duty to read him with deep care, but with an honest scholarly detachment which Bernstein himself would have appreciated. One of us, Hasan, has engaged with Bernstein's work almost throughout her professional life (2005, 2009b; the present volume), but always as a linguist, using Bernstein's theory for exploring the reach of language in social life – and this is precisely the perspective we propose to maintain here as well. As Hasan has argued elsewhere (2005: 51-52) in fruitful dialogues between EXOTROPIC theories of the social and the semiotic, each theory contributes to further elaboration of the same sphere of human experience; but each does so with a distinct perspective arising from its serious understanding of its own specific object of enquiry and the nature of its relation to the other's 'subject matter'. We believe a multi-perspective focus is likely to be richer, providing a more viable comment or support than the homogenization of the distinct languages of description pertaining to the distinct objects of enquiry.

It would be a fairer description of our efforts here to say that the following pages are simply an account of how, as linguists, we interpret[6] what we read in the pages of Bernstein's *Vertical and Horizontal Discourse: an essay*. We intend to first explore the significance of the classification of discourse as horizontal and vertical (1999: 158-163). On the basis of our interpretation we would like to ask a series of questions: how the term 'discourse' is used – is it explicitly placed in relation to some specific social context? How is the relationship between discourse and knowledge conceptualized? If discourse is language operative in some social context, then it should be possible for us as linguists to examine the RECOGNITION and DEFINITION CRITERIA (Halliday 1984) for any distinct postulated category of discourse, such as HD/VD. Turning to horizontal and hierarchical knowledge structures, we have three major concerns: one, how does the classification of forms of discourse calibrate – if it does – with the classification of forms of knowledge (Bernstein 1999: 164-166); secondly, how does this classification fare when confronted with the history of the evolution of knowledge, and third, does this way of classifying knowledge shed a clearer light on the processes of knowledge in the community, and if so in what way? Last but not least, we would like to ask if/how Bernstein's conception of discourse and knowledge as presented here (and in Bernstein 2000)[7] prove relevant to the elaborate architecture of his code theory carefully developed over four decades[8]: how does the classification of knowledge structures as either horizontal or hierarchical fit into Bernstein's 'theory of educational transmission' (Bernstein 1975b), or with his views about the 'structuring of pedagogic discourse' (Bernstein 1990) or his concern with forms of social control as capable of leading to 'distributive injustices' (Bernstein 2000: xix). There are, it seems, three possible scenarios: one might believe (i) that this 'latest' work on categories of knowledge forms an element of the elaborate theoretical framework encompassing both his early discourse of primary socialization (sometimes known as the Code Theory) and his later theoretical approach to educational transmissions, the nature of pedagogic discourse, symbolic control and identity, best exemplified in the last two volumes of his work (1990, 2000); or (ii) that this new work is neither an integral element of any earlier work by Bernstein nor does it run contrary to it: it represents a completely different direction; or (iii) that this new work contradicts certain specific part(s) of Bernstein's earlier work. No matter which of these three positions is adopted, the questions we raise here have significant bearing on reading Bernstein, researching Bernstein and exploring the sociological landscape painted by Bernstein.

We realize that in the end it will most probably not be possible to address all the questions here that we have raised above; but perhaps our efforts may prove useful in another way. First, in the act of mentioning them, the paper does draw attention to issues open for discussion. Secondly, we are motivated in this undertaking by another important consideration: Bernstein's work makes important connections with SFL which has always seen language as a *social* semiotic, treating human interaction as one of the most important factors underlying the nature of language both as system and as process. It follows that Bernstein's work needs to be familiar to the SFL readers *but not as unprocessed labels*: understanding Bernstein's discussion presupposes a degree of familiarity with sociology; we fear we are not well-qualified interpreters in that respect. However, we might succeed in unpacking some of Bernstein's important concepts putting them side by side with ideas from SFL, which in our view would be highly relevant to understanding the role of language as a means of pedagogic action. These, in the end, are our justifications for embarking on this highly ambitious project.

2 Horizontal and vertical discourses

A few words before we embark on what we understand from Bernstein's discourse. We, like all systemic functional linguists, use the word 'discourse' to refer to (groupings of) instances of SEMIOSIS – i.e., acts of meaning, which is by definition situationally located. As communicative activity, such interaction is typically realized by multiple semiotic systems operating in concert, i.e., with each instantiated semiotic system playing some part in the production of the total communication[9]; this is especially true of the *in situ* spoken variety as opposed to the written ones, also known sometimes as dis-embedded/displaced/de-contextualized discourse (for discussion, section 5 below). To describe satisfactorily what is going on, the analyst will need to pay attention to more than language.[10] Thus, by way of doing 'discourse' analysis, many linguists will today engage with the analysis of at least some semiotic system(s) *other than that of language*. We accept also that Bernstein would not have limited the words 'text' or 'discourse' to their linguistic realizations only. Nonetheless, in our discussions here, we plan to focus only on the *linguistic* aspect of HD/VD.

There are good reasons for this decision. First, language has always had a more significant place in Bernstein's theoretical framework (Hasan 2005, 2009b) than any other semiotic system – he could just as easily have foregrounded the role of, say, some kind of 'body language' which does play a quite important part in most interactions – but he chose not to do so. We take this to be indicative of Bernstein's view that language is central to human social existence. Secondly, many scholars, including Bernstein, have assigned language a critical role in the formation of consciousness[11] whether through local or official pedagogic actions, e.g., Vygotsky (1978), Luria (1976), Mead (1934), Whorf (1956), Wittgenstein (1953), Halliday (1975a, 2007a) and Bernstein (1971c, 1975b, 1990, 2000). While, in general, in any serious examination of human social life, attention to the part played by language is unavoidable, this is truer still when it comes to the examination of how acts of learning by normal human beings relate to the process of knowledge internalization: Hasan (2008, 2010, Chapter 1, this volume) has argued that the meaning of the term 'semiotic mediation' goes beyond the 'mediation of just semiotically construed experiences to the mind'; she suggests, instead, that this Vygotskian term has to be reinterpreted, since irrespective of the kind of experience being mediated to the mind, *mediation must itself be a variety of semantic action* (Halliday and Matthiessen 1999; Hasan 2005, 2009b, Chapter 1, this volume). Third, consideration of limited space forces choice, and as linguists our choice naturally is to focus on language. Finally, the 'language of description' for describing language is arguably far more developed than that for describing instances of other primary or secondary[12] semiotic systems such as gesture or images.

2.1 Horizontal discourse in relation to 'commonsense' knowledge

With these justifications for focussing on language, we turn now to Bernstein's discourse on discourse and knowledge. In this section and the following, we present our understanding of his ideas on horizontal and vertical discourse, respectively.

Bernstein 'take[s] "forms of knowledge" as criteria' (158)[13] for classifying a discourse as horizontal (HD) or vertical (VD). We understand from this formulation that the *division between HD/VD is based on the forms of knowledge these varieties are able to produce and/or disseminate*. Thus the discourse type HD is known by the fact that it produces and disseminates 'everyday or "commonsense" knowledge'. If discourse types are defined by reference to forms of knowledge, the obvious implication is that in this theoretical discourse, forms of knowledge themselves will be unmistakably recognizable. Using discourse and 'forms of knowledge' *almost interchangeably*, Bernstein examines the discourse of everyday knowledge in its different aspects, amongst which the most crucial is its SEGMENTAL organization.

> This form has a group of well-known features: it is likely to be oral, local, context dependent and specific, tacit, multi-layered, and contradictory across but not within contexts. ... *the crucial feature is that it is segmentally organized.* (159) [emphasis added, *H&B*]

The aetiology of HD's segmental nature resides in the relationship between discourse and social practice. It is the social practice that not only furnishes the occasion for the occurrence of the discourse, but also 'varies with the way the culture segments and specialises activities and practices. *The knowledge is segmentally differentiated*' (159) [emphasis added, *H&B*]: to say that HD realizes, at least partially, the various everyday activities and social practices is to say also that each (kind of) social practice is the site for the re/production or transmission of some knowledge. Bernstein reiterates that there are many such differing knowledge segments unrelated to each other, and embedded within differing social practices. The collection of such segments is what constitutes 'commonsense' or 'segmental knowledge'[14]: the two descriptors 'commonsense' and 'segmental' are describing two distinct aspects of the same phenomenon. Thus each instance of HD is also an instance of some segmental commonsense knowledge; what is responsible for the segmental differentiation and organization of this knowledge is its being embedded within distinct set of social practices.

The critical feature of segmental organization which identifies HD also determines most of its functions and attributes. 'The segmental organization of the "knowledges" of horizontal discourse leads to segmentally structured acquisitions' (160). If social practice is where commonsense knowledge is acquired, and if each context of social practice varies from others, then by the same token the varied social contexts are the site for varying pedagogic action as well. It follows that, on the one hand, HD, 'in its acquisition, becomes the major cultural relay' (160) for everyday knowledge, with each social practice calling for the acquisition of a different knowledge, a different competence; and, on the other hand, given that 'the pedagogic intervention is the function of the different "knowledges" required to be acquired' (160) by the learner, the pedagogy *naturally* has to be segmental:

> These 'knowledges' are related not by integration of their meaning by some co-ordinating principle, but through the functional relations of segments or contexts to the everyday life. It then follows that what is acquired in one segment or context, and how it is acquired, may bear no relation to what is acquired or how it is acquired in another segment. Learning how to tie up one's shoes bears no relation to how to use the lavatory correctly. (160)

These and other such comments emphasize the segmental nature of everyday knowledge, creating by association the impression that HD – i.e. everyday talk – which is constitutive of these many un-connected knowledges is just a collection of segments. One might conclude that according to Bernstein no HD segment bears any 'logical' relation to another – and the word 'logical' would be interpreted here as 'having a relation on the physical, material or practical basis'. And yet, there are occasions when fleetingly, and by implication, it may be being suggested to those who know/value his early contributions that the management of life might not be so massively disjointed due to the over-arching principle of coding orientation:

> Furthermore, as acquisition arises from discrete segments, pedagogic practice may well vary with the segment. Thus, similar segments across social groups/classes may differ in the code modality regulating acquisition. Or, to put it another way, *vertical discourse may regulate more segments of acquisition in one social group/class than another, and this entails a different mode of learning and context management*. (160) [emphasis added, *H&B*]

Beyond the safe closed orbit of the small baby's 'meaning group' (Halliday 1975a) where the very early learning occurs, the question of communication within the community is an important issue: how do these segmental knowledges circulate across distinct wider group such as the ones Firth (1950) referred to as 'SPEECH FELLOWSHIP', and even wider still, the sociolinguists' 'speech community'? The circulation of knowledge across a community depends on how open the lines of communication are – who is able to talk to whom and what constraints there are on what may be communicated. There are no known communities without a number of speech fellowships, sometimes also referred to as sub-communities, established by reference to such varied contextual features as those of sex, age, kinship, profession, status, and class. Irrespective of the basis for their formation, the existence of many speech fellowships in the wider community may or may not act as a barrier to open communication: the degree to which lines of communication may be open depends on aspects of the organization of the society. In this context, significantly, there is no established, institutional mode of circulation for segmental knowledges associated with horizontal discourse: the circulation depends on the degree of facility in inter-group communication – failing this, such knowledges may circulate largely within the bounds of the immediate local MEANING GROUPS (Halliday 1975a), with each group maintaining its own set of strategies for coping with everyday situations, without any possibility of learning in this segmental way from experiencing how others in the wider community cope with the same/similar kind of problems.

2.2 Vertical discourse and knowledge structures

As with HD, so also with VD, Bernstein takes forms of knowledge as the defining feature of the variety. However, there is a difference: VD is not unequivocally related to just one form of knowledge [emphasis added, *H&B*]:

> a vertical discourse takes the form of a coherent, explicit and systematically principled structure, hierarchically organized, as in the sciences, *or* it takes the form of a series of specialized languages with specialized modes of interrogation and specialized criteria for the production and circulation of texts, as in the social sciences and humanities. (159)

We thus have one single discourse variety, namely vertical discourse, and two distinct forms/varieties of knowledge: (i) hierarchical knowledge structures (HIKS), and (ii) horizontal knowledge structures (HOKS). Whatever the difference in these two classes of knowledge,[15] one thing that brings them under the same umbrella for Bernstein is the fact that neither of these forms of knowledge is segmental. Their integration is not based on an accidental collection devoid of any 'logical' principles as is that of segmental knowledge; rather, the integration of this discourse variety/and its defining knowledge types is an 'integration at the level of meanings' (161), whereas what brings together the various segments of everyday segmental knowledge is the fact that they all pertain to 'a common history in the sense of arising out of common problems of living and dying' (159). The pedagogy of vertical discourse is OFFICIAL, supported institutionally; it has a well articulated structuring and unlike commonsense knowledge, it is 'an on-going process in extended time'. 'The social units of the pedagogy of vertical discourse are constructed, evaluated and distributed to different groups of individuals, structured in time and space by 'principles' of recontextualising' (161).

Although in the identification of the discourse types, the system of language appears to play little or no part in Bernstein's treatment, nonetheless he provides a good number of linguistic criteria that are said to identify each of the two classes of knowledge (for discussion section 5). Table 1 presents our systematic summary of what is considered important in understanding the nature of HD/VD. Of course, a summary is never equal to what it summarizes; note, however, that much of the wording in columns 2 and 3 of the table is taken directly from Bernstein (1999: 159-163). This table shows the recognition of (i) two discursive varieties, HD/VD; (ii) each with certain associated linguistic features; but (iii) the defining criterion for each is some form of knowledge. It remains to be clarified what is achieved by the strategy of talking about HD/VD as one pair of contrasting concepts and HOKS and HIKS as another.

3 Vertical discourse as hierarchical/horizontal knowledge structures

Having identified two major classes of discourse – the horizontal and the vertical – Bernstein turns in earnest to the classes of knowledge which, as it were, *define* the latter discourse type and are relevant to official pedagogy: we understand it is this kind of discourse that would be 'subject to pedagogic transformation' (157). After a brief comparison of the two types of knowledge structures in general terms, Bernstein moves to his main focus i.e., a comparison of the hierarchical and horizontal knowledge structures, within which he is particularly concerned with the varieties of LANGUAGES[16] (discourse types?) which represent sociology as an array of knowledge structures. This particular focus on sociology will not be pursued here to the same extent since neither of us is competent to comment on the entire range of even the many contemporary Languages generated for its description, let alone going back to those distant times when modern sociology

Table 1: Summary of Bernstein's discussion of forms of discourse and knowledge

DISCOURSE FEATURES	HORIZONTAL DISCOURSE (HD)	VERTICAL DISCOURSE (VD)
ATTRIBUTES:		
critical	segmental knowledge; segments embedded in social practices; culturally governed; implicit; unstructured; no principle of coherence across context/practice/segment	(i): coherent, systematically principled structure; hierarchically organized as in the physical sciences; (ii): serially specialized languages; specialized modes of interrogation; with specialized text production criteria
associated	oral; local; context dependent; specific; tacit; contradictory across contexts but not within; multi-layered	integrated at the level of meaning; specialized symbolic structure of explicit knowledge; procedures linked to procedure hierarchically
FUNCTIONS:		
acquisition	determined by context; strategies context specific; acquired knowledge not transferable across segments	units of acquisition constructed, evaluated and distributed to different groups of individuals over time
pedagogy	segmental pedagogy meeting needs of each context governed segment; exhausted with the context; no recontextualising; no evaluation; pedagogy not transferable across segments	institutional organization i.e. official pedagogy; structured in time and space by principles of recontextualising; not consumed at the point of its delivery
circulation	depending on lines of communication; across social grouping possibility of barrier in communication; segmental knowledge lacking institutional pedagogy; acquired strategies/k might have limited circulation	circulation regulated by arbitrary distributive rules
evolution	change may be problematic for reasons above	what counts as evolution is for (i) development of hiks hierarchic integration of new knowledge into already existing hiks; and for (ii) by invention and circulation of new languages

began to take shape in the writings of Saint-Simon (1760–1825) and Comte (1798–1857): the examples in our discussion (sections 4-6) may focus on linguistics, though we will from time to time refer to the 'subject matter' of sociology.

3.1 A general comparison of hierarchical and horizontal knowledge structures

The outstanding attribute of a hierarchical knowledge structure (HIKS) is that (162):

> it attempts to create very general propositions and theories, which integrate knowledge at lower levels, and in this way shows underlying uniformities across an expanding range of apparently different phenomena. Hierarchical knowledge structures appear, by their users, to be motivated towards greater and greater integrating propositions, operating at more and more abstract levels. Thus, ... [they, *H&B*] could be said ... [to be, *H&B*] produced by an 'integrating' code.

The paradigm case of such a knowledge structure is the domain of knowledge known as physics. The figure of a triangle with its apex, suggestive of verticality, is used in 'the essay' as a symbolic representation of HIKS (see page 162); it shows that here scholarly efforts move to an integrated point of unity in the development of knowledge. By contrast, the horizontal knowledge structures 'consist of a series of specialised languages' (162), which 'are based upon collection[17] or serial codes'. One may think of them as a series of Ls existing side by side, without any upper limit in theory to the actual number of such structures. In this perspective, most linguists would recognize the following list of labels as naming one variety or another of the discipline called, 'linguistics' today: *structural linguistics*, *glossematics*, *generative linguistics*,[18] *systemic functional linguistics*, *West Coast functional linguistics*, *cognitive linguistics*, and so on. These various Ls are said to be 'not translatable': one cannot assume that a word-shape necessarily refers to the same concept across two distinct Languages which might be said to be describing the same phenomenon, say, human language. This has remarkable consequences for acquisition: the acquirer of HIKS is introduced to, and acquires, elements of an integrated theory, whereas the acquirer of HOKS is logically incapable of mastering such a wide array of differing Ls, each of which represents the knowledge about some domain only partially. Being restricted to attend to just one of the knowledge structures from the entire array, one's knowledge of 'linguistics' would be bound to be 'partial' because (presumably) no L would present an exhaustive account of the object of enquiry for linguistics (for discussion, section 5).

It follows that development in HIKS is synonymous with development of *the* theory: it suggests that here 'oppositions in theory' are 'played out in the attempt to refute positions ... or to incorporate them in more general propositions ..., because of special investments, a choice is possible provided the issue can be settled by empirical procedures' (163). By contrast in HOKS development often equals the development of yet other Ls. This inheres in the conceptualization of horizontal knowledge structures: they are viewed as necessarily consisting of the many Ls – each protecting 'its discreteness, its strategies of apparent uniqueness, and its non-translatability' (163). Apparently what is being valued is difference rather than a unified view about the centre of attention. Difference in views is valued more highly than unity of perspective; efforts at the latter are often viewed as hegemonic moves and denial of originality.

3.2 On the acquisition of hierarchical/horizontal knowledge structures

Bernstein argues that the above basic difference between hierarchical and horizontal knowledge structures pervades all aspects of their process in society: in HIKS 'in the end, it's the theory that counts' (165); the power of the theory is demonstrated both in its empirically validated achievements and in its imaginative, predictive power. One outstanding advantage of this 'clear-cut' approach among the practitioners of hierarchical knowledge structures is that 'the acquirer does not have the problem of knowing whether she/he is speaking physics or writing physics, only the problem of correct usage. The strong grammar [of HIKS][19] visibly announces what it is' (164).

The situation has to be obviously different with respect to horizontal knowledge structures: notably, the grammar of the various 'Ls' differs, so that the HOKS pertaining to any one domain in the social and human sciences may be further sub-classified by reference to the 'strength' of its 'syntax'. Taking contemporary linguistics as an example, Bernstein identifies the Chomskian L as possessing the strongest syntax. The strength of the syntax may sometimes be achieved by a rigorous 'ruling out' of concerns which may produce a 'tidy' though limited account of the discipline under focus (for discussion, section 6). In the social sciences both the existence of multiple Ls comprising the HOKS of some discipline and the variability in the strength of their grammar constitute a source of problem for the acquirer. For example, the weaker the syntax of the language of description, the greater the acquirer's uncertainty in identifying whether some specific discipline, say, sociology or linguistics is being pursued: for example, is hermeneutics a variety of linguistics? Is pragmatics? Is CDA? By the same token, the existence of so many competing Ls forces the issue of choice in the context of official pedagogic transmission (164); the selection of the chosen L for that purpose may be based on the 'dominant perspective': 'thus, a perspective becomes the principle of the recontextualisation which constructs the horizontal knowledge structure to be acquired' (164). In order to relate to some L as legitimate, 'A "gaze" has to be acquired, i.e., a particular mode of recognising and realising what counts as an "authentic" sociological reality' (165).

For the reader bemused by the use of the term 'horizontal' as classifier of both 'horizontal discourse' and 'horizontal knowledge structures', Bernstein draws attention to 'a resemblance' between the two, especially where the latter 'display a WEAK GRAMMAR' (165). Their common features are that HD and HOKS (165):

> both are horizontally organised, both are serial, both are segmented. In both the contents are volatile. In the case of horizontal discourse volatility refers to the referents of this discourse, and in the case of horizontal knowledge structures, especially of the weak grammar modality, volatility refers to additions and omissions of the specialised languages of a particular horizontal knowledge structure. *Perhaps there is a deeper resemblance* [emphasis added, *H&B*]. Acquisition of horizontal discourse is a tacit acquisition of a particular view of cultural realities, or rather of a way of realising these realities. *The way itself is embedded in the unity latent in the contextual segmentation of this discourse* [emphasis added, *H&B*]. The way may be likened to the 'gaze' as it becomes active in the experience and on-going practices of the speaker. This is similar to the 'gaze' embedded in the acquisition of the specialised languages of a horizontal knowledge structure with a weak grammar.

The above represents our account of Bernstein (1999: 163-166). We are aware that certain quite significant issues have not been included here. In fact, as we suggested in the introductory section of this chapter, Bernstein (1999) has opened a highly significant discourse which demands serious attention by scholars interested in the nature and origin of the varied forms of pedagogic disciplines seen in relation to each other as well as to 'commonsense knowledge'.

3.3 Hierarchical and horizontal knowledge structures: changes and orientations

With characteristic acuteness, Bernstein points to the interesting fact that although the concerns of the disciplines within humanities and social sciences are certainly far from identical, all these 'knowledges' still use generally the same kind of procedures; they may all be said to 'have' horizontal knowledge structures: the only knowledges that fall outside this form are the hierarchical ones. This leads Bernstein to suggest that if we assume there is no need to 'explain' a practice that is pursued in general, then 'what has to be accounted for is the shape of the hierarchical knowledge structures' (166). Instead of asking why there exist horizontal knowledge structures for the description of the objects of enquiry in the domain of the humanities and the social sciences – as many philosophers have done – we should really be asking: why is there this integrated structure of the hierarchical knowledges?

In these last pages Bernstein's discourse is indicative of a central concern that logically arises from the acceptance of the remarkable difference between the hierarchical organisation of the structuring of the physical sciences on the one hand and the horizontal array of structures found in the humanities and the social sciences, on the other: why is there this significant difference and how does it affect the pedagogy of these areas, with what consequences for the acquirer? Within the confines of this paper, we might regretfully not be able to revisit this segment of 'the essay' (pp. 166-169).

4 Language, social context, text and discourse

With the above (partial) account of our understanding of Bernstein's 'essay', from this point onwards we will be concerned with the discussion of issues arising from its presentation of discourse and knowledge. There are problems in this pursuit pointed out in George Bernard Shaw's humorous remark about England and USA as two countries divided by a common language – a saying applicable *mutatis mutandis* to any two of Bernstein's horizontal knowledge structures within any one discipline; *and* not surprisingly, no matter how close they might be in their general perspective the same situation would typically obtain between any two disciplines in the social sciences and humanities. So our first concern is to interpret the word 'discourse' as used by Bernstein (1999) in relation to forms of knowledge.

Discourse, as in 'discourse analysis' is the bread and butter of the theory and practice of SFL: Bernstein's sociological insights on social practice, social relations and the ontogenesis of consciousness have contributed much to SFL's thinking on the context of culture and the context of situation (for discussion, Halliday 1973c, 1974c, 1975a, 1978; Hasan 2005, especially 4-156, 2009b; Cloran 1994, 1999b; Williams 1995, 2001). Similarly, Bernstein has commented on the contributions of this Language of linguistics to his sociology (Bernstein 1971c, 1973, 1990, 2000). Both disciplines use the term *discourse*. This, however, does not mean we can feel confident about the status of that word in the discipline of Basil Bernstein's Codes, Control and Consciousness Sociology.[20] Some clarification will be needed.

4.1 Context, text and discourse in relation to knowledge

Recognizing the handicap of working in horizontal knowledge structures, we begin here by identifying the specific L of SFL we use in this discussion: our L within SFL – with specific reference to the concept of CONTEXT – is the one that has been worked out in the writings of Malinowski (1923, 1935: 3- 74), Firth (1957: 177-89, 1964: 93-118), Halliday (1959, 1977, 1991), Halliday (in Halliday, McIntosh and Strevens (1964: 75-110), Halliday and Hasan (1985), Hasan (1973, 1980, 2005: 68-105, 2009b: 8-40); Cloran (1994). This is not the place to justify this choice (for discussion Hasan 1995; Lukin 2010; Bowcher 2010); suffice it to say in our view this approach is better integrated in the theoretical modelling of the object of enquiry for SFL –language – and, logically, *that* is the basic move in the foundation of that theory.

In SFL both the terms TEXT and discourse will be found in use. However, text is treated as a theorized category: it refers to language operative in some *specific* CONTEXT OF SITUATION. The notion of context of situation (abbreviated to 'context') is seen as a tripartite construct of situational parameters, each of which is always relevant to every text. The stipulation that *context is always relevant to a text* has theoretical consequences for the conceptualization of situation as an extra-linguistic phenomenon and textual context, which are briefly discussed in 4.2. Here a brief word on the three contextual parameters, known as FIELD OF DISCOURSE, TENOR OF DISCOURSE, and MODE OF DISCOURSE. The first, i.e., field[21] of discourse, concerns the social activity – what is going on, in which language is playing some part. This parameter comes nearest the concept of *social practice* in sociology such as that of Bernstein's, Bourdieu's and their colleagues'; it also appears to echo the concept of *activity* in the sense of 'activity theory' (Engeström *et al.* 1999).

The second parameter, i.e., tenor[22] of discourse, concerns the interactants – who is acting with whom *a propos* the goings-on, in what relation to each other and to the relevant action(s): it thus concerns human relations. Now, although human relationship is central to the sociology of Bernstein, we believe we are right in saying that its relevance to discourse, context, or social practice is not always brought to notice overtly,[23] particularly in the discourses of the sociology of education. And it is a related fact, we believe, that in this sociology the undertaking of actions, such as eating, putting on clothes, or tidying one's garden, would all be treated as instances of social practice: the ways of accomplishing them are certainly socially significant in positioning the one who undertakes these actions. In fact, with the exception of reflex physical actions, it would be difficult to identify any human action which would not qualify as an instance of social practice. The lack of differentiation among three categories of social practices – those which *necessarily* involve linguistic interaction, those which *may*, and those which *just cannot do so* – is particularly surprising in a sociology to which the concepts of codes and control are central. This is not to say that codes are only linguistic or that control is only exercised by speech. And yet, it remains true that no sociologist has written more eloquently than Bernstein about the role of *linguistic interaction* in fashioning forms of human consciousness, or who has made such a remarkable contribution to our understanding of interpersonal relations.

The situation is different with respect to the context of discourse in SFL, where the qualifier 'of discourse' necessarily implies the presence of language and therefore interaction. In this view, then, no action is of any consequence *to linguistics* unless there is some linguistic exchange of meanings relevant to that action. In our understanding, linguistics does not presume to explain the nature of non-language. Thus, the act of kissing may be a datum for the analyst of the semiotic system of kinesics; the linguist, *qua* linguist, has no means of describing that event, though the most delicate semantics of the item 'kiss' as verb or noun would be best described by the resources of linguistics, not kinesics. We are not claiming that one is more 'real' or 'important' than the other, simply that the 'kiss' as bodily action is a different order of phenomenon from the linguistic item 'kiss'. So unlike social practice in sociology, the question of the context of discourse arises only where there is linguistic interaction, which naturally presupposes some relation between the interactants. From this point of view, the dyad – speaker and addressee – is functionally *always* there as part of the context, though in some cases, the speaker may be 'anon.', or the addressee may be physically absent as when a telephone message is being left on someone's message bank or when someone is being written a letter. And sometimes the addressee may have no physical 'being' in the material universe: s/he may be simply VIRTUAL (Hasan 1999b), a stereotype of some category of addressee defined by certain feature(s). To say that the speaker and addressee are functionally always there is to say that the formation of the text *announces* some aspects of the nature of their relation: the addressee, whether present, physically absent or having only a virtual 'presence', exercises 'semantic pressure' (Butt 1985) on the text's wording; this is one significant condition for successful communication. The last parameter, i.e., the mode of discourse, refers to the mode of material and semiotic contact between the speaker and the addressee; the physical 'channel', 'aural' or visual', has important implications for how language will be used as 'medium' of interaction.

Each of these parameters can be conceptualized as representing a POTENTIAL[24] in the sense that it is a reservoir[25] of possible features, and the manifestation of any of these draws recognition in some way from the members of (some identifiable group belonging to) the community whose context of culture is under description. Logically no single text is able to realize all of these features, any more than, for example, any one English clause is able to realize *all* features represented in the transitivity system network of English at the level of lexicogrammar. However, every text must be a realization of some features from each of the three parameters: together these contextual (sociocultural) features may be referred to as the CONTEXTUAL CONFIGURATION of that text. The contextual configuration construed by a text is the relevant context of that text on the assumption that every text (whether complete or incomplete) is a record of some process of language (whether completed or abandoned) in some context of discourse. In other words, the texture and structure of each text (Halliday and Hasan 1976, 1985) linguistically represent those features of socio-cultural context that appeared relevant to the interactants.

4.1.1 *Situation, context and text*

'Situation' is a large word: the above discussion shows that speaking theoretically 'situation' and 'context of situation' are not synonymous. On any given occasion of talk, the referents of the word 'situation' can potentially cover a large number of phenomena within the reach of (at least some of) the interactants' capacity to see and/or hear – and it is always worth remembering that the interactants are acculturated beings. Not only do a large number of phenomena surround the interactants, but social practices of different types could also be going on concurrently, particularly in public places (for examples and discussion, see Cloran 1982, 1994, 1999b; Hasan 1981, 1999b). The impossibility of describing the entire material surroundings of a linguistic event – the 'situation in the raw' – was aptly described by Guy Cook (1990) as 'transcribing infinity'. Cook is, in principle, right: it is not feasible to exhaustively describe raw, untheorized situations. However, the main problem does not lie in the feasibility of an exhaustive description of a raw situation in which the verbal interaction is occurring; the real problem is to locate criteria/principles for deciding which elements of the situation are to be treated as relevant, for clearly there is no sense in describing phenomena that happen to be of no interest whatsoever for the focus of one's analysis, namely, the text. What is needed is to ask questions, for example, what exactly did Firth (1957: 182) mean by talking about 'the *relevant* features of participants' and 'the *relevant* objects'? Elements of raw situation *in themselves* clearly do not announce their own relevance. So there is a need to establish how we identify what aspects of the surrounding situation will be said to form the relevant context of the text being formed or the one already formed.

The answer to this problem is already implied in the last sentence: *all those sociocultural features of the situation form (elements of) the* RELEVANT CONTEXT *of a text which can be identified by reference to the process of language on any social occasion of talk.* From the linguist's point of view, the primary interest is in those events, persons and objects *a propos* which languaging can occur/is occurring/has occurred[26]: it is these that make up the relevant context of a text. For example, it does not matter to the structure and texture of this chapter where it is being composed – at the workplace or at a private residence – or what the working table is made of, or which printer the authors use, and so on for myriad phenomena. We say this because these phenomena of the material situation are not relatable to any aspect of the present text as a semiotic construct. In other words we can make a generalization: *only those parts of the situation can be seen as transformed into elements of the relevant context to which the language of that text assigns some place within the three parameters of field, tenor and mode.* This clearly separates out the relevant context of the text from the remaining elements of its material situational surrounding – irrespective of whether the text is actual, hypothetical, crafted as an example or addressed to virtual beings. Hasan (1973, 1985c) coined the term MATERIAL SITUATIONAL SETTING (MSS) to refer to this negatively identified part of the situation. The assumption is that the MSS of an ongoing text will typically consist of phenomena at least some of which cannot be viewed as pertaining to the values of the three contextual parameters, nor can their identity be known for already produced displaced texts. This hedged way of identifying material situational setting has been adopted here due to the fact that MSS of an *ongoing* text cannot be described as outright 'irrelevant': the MSS happens to be 'a dormant force', and there exists the possibility of some of its elements becoming 'active'[27] which might have appeared as no part of the relevant context at the start of an interaction. If and when that happens the analyst would be faced with an interrupting text or a 'sub-text' (Cross 1991), or even what Hasan (1999b) has called a 'parallel text'. One difference between interruption/parallel text and sub-texts is that while the former bear no relation to the already established relevant context, sub-texts usually do so by 'importing' some new element from the MSS, though this is not the only source for the genesis of sub-texts (for examples of both, Hasan 1999b).[28]

To conclude, the process of language is embedded within some immediate material situation,[29] which can be seen as being differentiated into two different categories by the process of language: MSS and relevant context (or 'contextual configuration' of a completed text). With every text seen as an ongoing process of language both relevant context and MSS are 'co-present'; however, seen as a *displaced text*, only some elements of the situation will be illuminated as part of its relevant context; the process of no text can be dissociated from the speaker,[30] the one element of the situation that must necessarily be imported into the relevant context, e.g., others will remain unknown unless they have been activated during the same spatio-temporal occasion of talk and are capable of being integrated into the on-going text (for discussion, Cloran 1994; Hasan 1999b). In this perspective, the term 'discourse' will be taken to refer to a body of texts whose relevant context *as a whole* is as unknown as their MSS is; by contrast there is no well-made text that will fail to construe (substantial parts of) its own relevant context – so long as the text consists of at least one MAIN MESSAGE,[31] some elements of the immediate situation will be encapsulated within the text. In light of these comments, it will be necessary to pay closer attention to Bernstein's ideas of CONTEXT DEPENDENT and CONTEXT INDEPENDENT DISCOURSE (discussion, section 5).

4.1.2 *Discourse, text and context of situation*

'Discourse', to the best of our knowledge, has never been theorized.[32] It is used so often in so many different COTEXTS that its use in any theoretical discourse, unless rigorously defined at least for that specific occasion of use, simply creates a category of convenience; we may think of it as 'languaging' as for example in expressions such as 'the discourse of earth sciences/of feminism/of everyday knowledge', all this means is that some element of the earth sciences/feminism/everyday knowledge will be referred to explicitly or implicitly in an instance of that 'discourse' whose identity is given by its qualifier. Thus, a particular earth science text may be concerned with volcanic eruptions or with the hydrological cycle or with global warming. From the perspective of a particular kind of knowledge structure, the identity of each such different topic is obviously highly significant to that domain of knowledge; however, the significance of such variation is of no consequence to the status of the instance each of which would be referred to as 'the discourse of the earth sciences'. In this sense, the category of 'discourse' is general; it has a low degree of specificity; in terms of SFL, at best the description is at the primary level of DELICACY and at worst it is 'under-described'; in either case, there will be consequences for its predictive potential. The possibility of prediction is, as it were, the theoretical returns from the difference in ways of talking about the terms 'text' and 'discourse'.

We may – and many often do – use the two terms as if they are simply interchangeable, but in the context of specialized discussions the difference between them may be relevant depending on the field of discourse. Commenting on this situation Halliday (2008: 78) suggested 'we can use either ['text' or 'discourse', *H&B*] to define the other: "discourse" is text that is being viewed in its sociocultural context, while "text" is discourse being viewed as a process of language.' We accept that with text the primary focus in SFL is on language. However, as a theoretical category, text in SFL represents 'the process of language', by virtue of its construal of some recognizable 'sociocultural context' in terms of the three parameters, field, tenor and mode, as introduced above. The socio-cultural context is not expendable if one is doing comprehensive 'discourse analysis'; the logic of the reciprocal realization relation between text and context must carry this implication: the difference is only in the strength of orientation which depends on the analyst's aims. What can be said in the light of this discussion on the use of the word *discourse* in Bernstein 1999?

4.2 The context and the content of discourse: forms of knowledge

In talking about discourse, Bernstein cannot be said to ignore its linguistic attributes; but at the same time the fact remains that his primary focus is on certain 'sociocultural' features of context. The critical distinctive feature of HD is its expression of commonsense knowledge, and that of VD its expression of structured knowledge (see critical and associated attributes in Table 1, Section 2.1). Seen in the light of the above discussion, to us it seems that Bernstein's use of the word 'discourse' is oriented to the content, or to certain features of its context, and finally to some properties of language. We see the strength of orientation in that order, the first being the strongest, the second less so and so on. We shall return once again to the linguistic features of 'discourse' in section 5 to ask if any features specified in the essay relate to the content – whether they play a part in the construal of that content – and if so, which they are and how they do it. In this section, following the statements in the essay, we specify first the contextual features of horizontal and vertical discourses and then proceed to comment on Bernstein's view of the content of horizontal discourse, i.e., commonsense knowledge.

4.2.1 *Contextual features of discourse*

The sociocultural features relevant to 'discourse' in the essay may be described by reference to the choices in the field of discourse (Hasan 1999b: 311). For HD, they are VERBAL ACTION: ANCILLARY – i.e., some languaging is occurring to assist in performance of some material action which forms part of some social process – which belongs to the QUOTIDIAN SPHERE i.e., the said social process pertains to everyday life. For VD, the sociocultural values may be described as VERBAL ACTION: CONSTITUTIVE – i.e., *the category of social process is defined wholly on the basis of the properties of language*; further the process is CONCEPTUAL – paraphrased briefly here as: it is not concerned with some practical action but requires focus on the semiotic construal; the verbal action is REFLECTION BASED, which may be paraphrased here as attention is devoted to some states of affairs, their logical relations and implications; the action would pertain to the SPECIALIZED SPHERE – i.e., where the social process involves some action requiring expertise of some kind. By way of tenor of discourse, with specific reference to horizontal discourse, there is fleeting mention of mothers and children but clearly everyday discourse cannot be limited to just this interactant dyad. No other features of the tenor of discourse are referred to, which validates our comments (in section 4.1 above) regarding the dissociation – at least in practice – between social relation and social action. The mode of discourse is referred to briefly, as in the linguistic feature 'oral'. We will return to some of these issues in section 5.

The description of these two kinds of discourse mainly in terms of the field of discourse, together with Bernstein's focus on 'referents' suggests that knowledge in this view is entirely ideational. This is a conception of knowledge that sits well with the already produced knowledge structures – and of course, it is the already produced knowledge structures that act as the resource for pedagogic recontextualizations. They are thus significant from the point of view of official pedagogy. Nonetheless, as Bernstein (1990, 2000) shows, some attention to the sociocultural features pertaining to tenor and to mode might become unavoidable, *when thinking of the processes of knowledge* – how it is produced, how maintained and how it might change, either developing further or being discarded, as happens often in the case of horizontal knowledge structures but is not entirely unknown, by any means, in the domain of hierarchical knowledge structures either: consider for example the fate of astrology, now reduced to 'mumbo jumbo'. Someone might argue that, all the same, knowledge itself remains purely ideational; human relation and the channels for transmission and preservation of knowledge may have a facilitating role, but they are not the stuff which knowledge is made of: they make no difference to the *nature* of knowledge. We would be inclined to disagree with this position. It is a disagreement based on a chain of reasoning – the assumption that human minds are essential to the processes of knowledge production as well as transmission, and that these human minds are never produced except in interaction, and, above all, that no interaction is without human relation.

Since Popper has been such an influential force in the discussions of knowledge as an entirely ideational phenomenon, we note also that Popper's 'World 3' (Popper 1972) would not survive but for the technologies which transform the 'mode of discourse' as that expression is used in SFL – reinventing the wheel gets one nowhere as the fate of horizontal knowledge structures sometimes so poignantly exemplifies. For all we know, the Incas knew better ways of guarding themselves against the havoc caused by earthquakes; however, the technology that has transformed the mode of discourse today came too late for them – there is no World 3 that contains the seeds of that knowledge. Even more important, Popper's World 3 could not bear fruit without readers with a particular kind of semantic orientation. Whorf (1956: 248) tells us that 'speech is the best show man puts on' – one must add, it is so largely if/because there are human beings capable of listening and reflecting on what they hear, before doing or saying something in their turn. Much of the magic effects of speech would be lost but for the mental labour (discussion Chapter 1 here) the listeners put into it.

We believe that no sociology of pedagogy – official or local – is likely to survive unless it is capable of explicating not only the *systems* pertaining to it but also of attending to the *processes* that sustain it – i.e., acts of showing that which is known, viz., 'transmission of knowledge', and also acts of getting to know, viz., its internalization by the other, which has to be a central condition in the 'acquisition of knowledge'. As Bernstein (1971c, 1975b) pointed out, at least in official education, transmission – teaching – and internalization – learning – do not form an automatic sequence of the kind desired; there are complications in the plot of this story, especially when we turn to the question of what kind of minds get to produce knowledge and why. Description of the kind that leads to the understanding of the nature of the various kinds of knowledges existing in a society is certainly valuable; nonetheless, after all is said and done, a highly significant question hangs in the air for any theory of pedagogy: *whether the sayings occur in everyday discourse or in pedagogic discourse, what is it that is involved in the acquirer's transformation of these sayings into knowledges of different kind*? For some indicative answers to that question, we suggest revisiting Bernstein (especially part III of 1971c and 1975b); when the indications from such work are pursued, it will be found that they lead us to such scholars as Vygotsky (1962, 1978), Mead (1934), Bateson (1972), Donaldson (1992), Greenfield (1997, 2000), Halliday (1975a), Hasan (2009b) and this is by no means an exhaustive list of those concerned with the original question. For lack of time and space, any detailed pursuit of these lines of discussion will not be possible here. Let us add, however, that in holding these views, we feel we are more closely in tune with Bernstein: he would accept our interpretations, as a careful reading of his 'work'. There is nothing 'natural' about knowledge structure of any kind and from this perspective Bernstein is certainly right to make a clear distinction between what is known as commonsense knowledge and structured knowledges – categorized here as horizontal and hierarchical knowledge structures.

4.3 The content of horizontal discourse: commonsense knowledge

The highly condensed remarks in the last three paragraphs indicate that reading Bernstein's 'essay' with a keen interrogative attention is likely to pay high dividends. In this section, we will selectively approach Bernstein's discussion of commonsense knowledge with the same spirit of enquiry. Bernstein's emphasis on segmentation tempts us to examine the concept closely as the first step in this enterprise. There exists an assumption in the essay that each specific segment in commonsense knowledge occurs in the course of a specific social practice. But how should the term 'segment' be interpreted?

4.3.1 *An enquiry into the meaning of segment/ation*

One thing is certain: 'segments' in this context could not refer to INSTANCE alone. Our yesterdays and tomorrows – without being replications – are more like our todays than we care to admit in a world so devoted to novelty and change; in a close-knit speech fellowship, the same types of social processes recur in practically everyone's life, sometimes on a daily basis and sometimes over longer or shorter periods of time. Sometimes the typicality of a social practice might extend even across the wider speech community: the latter are very likely the social practices that get viewed as 'institutional', for example, 'walking out' with a member of the other sex some hundred years ago. One reason small children internalize their immediate practical world with such apparent ease is the regularity of the social practices that impinge on them. In listening to about a hundred hours of naturally occurring interactions between a number of mothers and their pre-school children in their everyday life, no researcher on Hasan's research team[33] was ever at a loss to figure out what was going on, even though visual evidence was absent. This implies a complex principle of regularity: variation is not across segment instances but segment *types*. Differences across the instances of a type would in that case be immaterial to their membership of that category: it might not matter whether you learn to tie shoelaces or to put on socks. Categories, as Basil Bernstein so effectively reasoned, are defined not by what is contained *within* but by the critical differences *between* (1975a, 1990). The differences *between* are the 'markers' of a type; instances, as individuals, will always vary in other respects which make no difference to their type membership. This principle applies to variant categories across the board.

Once we begin to examine segment types, it becomes evident that some types of social practices are more alike than others: what you do with your school shoes when you get back home is in principle very much like what you do with your school cardigan or tie, though neither of these bear any direct relation on how one might treat the pet pussy cat. Strange as it may seem to suggest, the treatment one metes out to the pussy cat may be quite similar to how one treats one's siblings, especially if they happen to be nearer in age. It would seem then that the category of referents is less central than how the principle governing the category of objects and processes is established. 'My school things' is a category containing referents as different from each other as the school shoes and the crayons. We accept there certainly is segmentation, each segment type being relevant to some particular type of social practice, but type is sensitive to DELICACY and open to 're-drawn boundaries'. We suggest that there exist grounds for putting together segment types since logically principled lines of inclusion/exclusion are far from improbable for certain types of social practices, such as, for example, arranging flowers in the sitting room and shopping at the delicatessen: though superficially very different social practices, they both relate to the superordinate social practice of entertaining guests. The cohesion between them has not so much to do with the 'referents' on the scene as it has to do with some superordinate concern, such as the principle for managing one's belongings be they shoes or clothes, books or toys.

With such complex lines of *natural connections* between certain segment types of knowledge, born out of participation in social practices, it should not surprise that the naturally occurring daily discourse of groups of mothers and children examined in Hasan's research on SEMANTIC VARIATION revealed distinct consistencies in semantic choices across clearly different social practices. The consistently strong statistical results (Hasan 2009b) that revealed systematic semantic variation in ways of meaning correlating with the two distinct speech fellowships of mother–child populations indicate that each such group acted by reference to a different 'semantic code'. What is more, each group revealed semantic congruence in their behaviour *across* significantly different types of social practice such as in giving information or controlling the children's action or in chatting to their male or female child. The high correlation between semantic choices in such distinct types of social practices are impressive (see for example, Hasan 2009b: e.g., pp 115-116, and elsewhere).[34] These results indicate that, in the last analysis, their practices were guided by some 'logical principle'; following Bernstein's insights regarding interaction in speech fellowships (1971c, 1975b), we call it 'coding orientation'. We are thus led to claim that in order to convince us that there are no principles of consistency in what is being called commonsense knowledge or horizontal discourse, what we require is some equally strong evidence which clearly contradicts the results of our studies, thus throwing them in doubt.

4.3.2 *Differentiating unstructured and structured knowledge*

We have argued above that commonsense knowledge is not an undifferentiated mass; nor is learning based on a collection of millions of unrelated memories: it has its own complex principle of internal order outlined by Basil Bernstein (1971c, 1975b). That said, there is no doubt in our mind that Bernstein is drawing attention to a significant qualitative distinction between the unstructured commonsense knowledge on the one hand, and on the other, the distinct types of knowledge structures. Further, we would add other distinct points of difference: first, some form of everyday knowledge, which is what defines HD, is *acquired without deliberation by each individual in the course of everyday communal life*; whereas knowledge structures, which define VD, are *created mainly by the efforts of some specific individuals doing deliberate and persistent theorizing,*[35] *the taste for which is most probably carefully cultivated and developed in specific cultural institutions*. These cultural institutions today turn out to be those dedicated to the administration of official pedagogy, whereas in ancient times they pertained to the maintenance of some religion and used to be dedicated to the gods – and if Lloyd (1983) is to be believed, for the 'ancients' the initial point of departure for almost any kind of knowledge lay in 'folklore and ideology' (discussion, section 6).

The outstanding difference between commonsense and structured knowledge is not that the former has segments and the latter, an integrated mass as Bernstein suggests. Perhaps a more relevant distinction is that the former is not considered to have been created by *any single individual;* it has emerged from the community's 'management' of life, and so to echo Douglas' (1971) excellent title of her inaugural lecture, it appears to exist 'in the nature of things' – and being NATURAL, it naturally appears to require no explanation. By contrast, knowledge structures, whether hierarchical or horizontal, are DEVISED by some specific individual(s): it is irrelevant whether their names are known to posterity or not[36]; they are not the product of everyday living by every member of a whole community. More important, this devising consists in setting up a chain of theorization around an object of enquiry, prioritizing the evidence of senses – the clinching factor being the proof in application/simulation (discussion, section 6). Thinking of the distinction between hierarchical and horizontal knowledge structures, what matters most are characteristics of theorization and methods by which the theory might be shown to be proven. Significantly, the presence or absence of segmentation plays no part in this differentiation.

There seem to be good reasons for underplaying segmentation as a significant distinguishing criterion of distinct forms of knowledge. We say this because every single object of enquiry in 'devised knowledge structures', when viewed analytically, will display segments/components/parts – call them what you like: there seem to be no domains of knowledge without divisibility. Take, for example, MEANING, WORDING and SOUND: no matter what one calls them in the different Ls of linguistics, they are, in some sense of the word, simply parts or 'segments' of that phenomenon which forms the object of enquiry for linguistics, known in common parlance as '(natural) language'. The hierarchical science of chemistry could hardly exist without recognition of segments/components which create compounds from simples; the horizontal knowledge structure of earth sciences has many segments, but consider simply the example of evaporation, condensation and precipitation as segments/components in the water cycle.

4.3.3 *Sites of segmentation and of integration*

One might object to this suggestion by pointing out that segments/components in knowledge structures have logical relations. They cannot be treated as items in an inventory because there exists some *principle of integration* to unite them; it is only when it comes to natural – i.e., commonsense – knowledge that no such inherent relation is found to exist. The observation appears so true, that it needs to be examined more closely. Take for example, components in SFL: they are 'brought together' by the principle of REALIZATION, so one might claim that in linguistics there exists a principle for integrating the component of language known as meaning, wording and sound. Before one treats this as 'proof' that structured knowledge has no components, two connected points need to be noted. First, not every L of linguistics follows such an overt recognition of some principle linking the components – in fact most Ls of linguistics have simply referred to them as components as if no principled relation existed between them: the issue of recognizing the components without identifying an integrating relation has not been seen as of any importance: the components are just components. Secondly, and related very closely to the foregoing: the recognition of a principled relation between the segments/components appears to be a function of the structuring of knowledge. In other words, the principle underlying the relation is not sensuous – not an attribute 'visible' to the senses ordinarily. If and when the relation is 'perceived', this will happen originally in the pursuit of theorization as it happened with Hjelmslev, Firth, Halliday and Lamb concerning the relation of realization. In other words, the existence of the components is pre-theoretical; the *principle* for integrating segments/components is an 'intelligible' phenomenon. It arises out of interrogating some aspect of the object of enquiry; further, its being 'intelligible' and non-sensuous does not negate the possibility of testing.

In the context of present discussion, the fact that the integration principle arises in the course of some problem solution appears to have considerable significance: it may be viewed as suggesting that the logic of integration is an operation in the deliberate reflection which contributes to the structuring of knowledge. The principle of integration is *not found*; it is *discovered* in the process of theorization, which, however, does not mean that all theories necessarily work out all such principles[37] – and this may well be one means of judging the strength/weakness of a language of description. The principle of divisibility inheres in the object of enquiry, but the principle of the co-operation, i.e., integration of the segments/components, is essentially part of the process of understanding and explicating the nature of a chosen object of enquiry: it forms a step in the production of devised knowledge structures, such as the ones Bernstein considers critical to the definition of vertical discourse. As Bernstein very clearly shows, and we agree with his claim, natural knowledge does not belong in that league because it is not structured. What we are emphasizing is simply that this is not because commonsense knowledge is segmental – no matter how the term 'segment' is defined. We hope we have already shown that other devised knowledges too have divisibility; without it, specialization in some part of the same discipline would be a contradiction in terms.

Commonsense knowledge is not structured knowledge simply because from the social subject's point of view engagement in social practices is a way of being, doing, and saying; it does not call for reflection nor is it seen as a problem in need of explanation: it is simply something that just happens. The subject-mothers in Hasan's research (2009b) did not listen to all or even part of their recording though expressly invited to do so if they wished. When asked to comment on what they had recorded, most admitted they had not listened because 'it was really not anything special; just ordinary stuff!'[38] The process of daily living where social subjects move from one social practice to the next often without a conscious design does not present itself to everyone as a site for deliberate theorization in order to explain 'why things are in life as they are' (Hasan 1992a): it takes thinkers such as, say, Marx, Whorf, Vygotsky, Firth, Halliday, Douglas, Bernstein, and others of similar calibre to identify that there is 'in the nature of things' something to be explained, that what happens in every day life is open to interrogation, and can form an object of enquiry.

This takes us to what we consider the most important point about 'common sense knowledge': it is *definitely not structured knowledge* and may not be welcome in the sites set aside for the propagation of 'esoteric'/'reasoned' knowledges, but it is certainly where *the subject matter of the many structured knowledges is located*, especially those in the areas of humanities and social sciences in the production of which human beings have employed deliberate and persistent reasoning. In every age and in all known cultures, human beings have been known to devote time and energy to understanding and explaining the nature of only those phenomena that appear significant to them, be that in search of the divine or the mundane: which is to say, it is everyday life some aspect of which forms the object of enquiry for the humanities and the social sciences. Seen thus, there are a large number of knowledge structures whose object of enquiry is rooted in the daily living of life – such as sociology, anthropology, linguistics, economics, politics and many others; there are others that enquire into the working of the human body and brain – such as biological sciences, neuroscience, psychology, logic in as much as it is concerned with reasoning, and inference; there are still other knowledge structures that enquire into natural phenomena such as physics, astronomy, mathematics, the earth sciences and so on – whatever the motivation for entry into the latter, their prestige in communities is based on their reputation for making reliable predictions which affect aspects of human living and dying (section 6.4, cf., astronomy in China and in Babylon). In one way or another, these knowledges are essentially 'about' human life. Together they increasingly impact on so much of the living of everyday life as to persuade us to take Marx's suggestion seriously when he says that:

> Natural sciences [i.e., Bernstein's hierarchical knowledge structures, *H&B*] will eventually subsume the sciences of man [i.e., Bernstein's horizontal knowledge structures, *H&B*] just as the sciences of man will subsume the natural sciences: *there will be one single science.* [source Habermas 1987: 46; emphasis *H&B*]

Human learning and scholarship in nearly all forms – theorizing, research, critique – is essentially linked to life in society. This is not to say that the production of knowledge has always been so overtly 'goal directed' as today's much touted accountability of research in the universities has made it – simply that it is human knowledge, created by human beings, for human beings, and in the end, much of it impinges everyday on nearly every life, though not necessarily in ways intended by those who actually helped develop some of these specific knowledge structures. To appreciate the truth of these comments we need examine only the dilemmas arising out of access to nuclear armaments, or the threat to the survival of the world arising from the discovery of fossil fuels, or the 'fundamentalism of capitalism' which has rendered thousands homeless in the recent 'money melt down'.

4.3.4 *The demarcation of the ordinary/mundane and the extraordinary/esoteric*

This in turn raises a difficult question: what exactly can be meant by the term 'everyday life', especially in today's world? The heart of the issue is this: if the experience of everyday life is somehow transformed into knowledge, what does the act of such 'knowledging' do for the knowledging individual? Thinking of only *the early stages of the learning of the natural unstructured everyday commonsense knowledge*, we are inclined to say it enables the internalization of one's social universe (Hasan 2002, 2009a): ways of being, doing and saying begin to get established. It is reasonable to ask then: is the learning of this knowledge specific to a particular stage of human life? Does this function alter as time passes by? If so, in what way? Does it, for example, change direction? Does this knowledge ever cease to come into existence?

Up to the early/mid 1970s, a significant distinction was implied in sociology by the terms PRIMARY SOCIALIZATION, which was clearly different from SECONDARY SOCIALIZATION: the learning in these two stages was thought to be different in important ways (Bernstein 1975b; Vygotsky 1978). It appeared to be implied that 'everyday life' concerned life within Halliday's 'meaning group' or at best no more than Firth's 'speech fellowship'; that as the social subject moved into the wider community, the orders of learning changed. Now, with the term socialization out of favour, we are no longer sure how far into the life of social subjects the so-called 'everyday life' extends. Is having to put in an appearance in the courts because you were found vandalizing public property a part of everyday life? Is it part of ordinary life to know that the taking of easy loans might threaten your security? If such things do not pervade everyday life, then how does the 'money melt down', the 'credit crunch', affect thousands of ordinary beings in their ordinary pursuit of life? Is it part of everyday life to watch the national and international news? Is it part of everyday life to listen to a programme on topical issues which allows voluntary participation in discussion to the listening audience? In what ways are these experiences similar to and different from those one grew up with while interacting within one's meaning group, as that term is used by Halliday (1975a) in the discussion of learning how to mean in the first few years of one's life – i.e., during primary socialization?

The questions above draw attention to the fact that apparently there are many ways in which vertical discourse and glimpses of hierarchical knowledge structures can make an appearance in everyday life through a variety of everyday life experiences. In this context, it is a matter of interest that the influence of the disciplines belonging to the humanities and the social sciences is far less obvious than that of the physical sciences. This unplanned introduction of vertical knowledge structures might lack the order, the clarity of the goals, and the meticulous management specific to official pedagogic introduction of the recontextualizations of vertical knowledge structures, but that it happens and happens in systematically variable ways (Hasan 2009b; Cloran 1994; Williams 1995) in Western societies is beyond doubt. The simple question is whether such learning through these experiences too is the learning of commonsense knowledge, whether it is viable to act as if commonsense knowledge is completely sealed off from all intimations of verticality? These issues seem so important to any sociology which takes seriously the modelling of everyday life in society to which the notion of commonsense knowledge is hitched. We believe that research on these important issues needs to be made more widely available: the expression *everyday life* has been used widely in social science research – we ourselves have used it liberally (Hasan 2005, 2009b) – nonetheless it appears on reflection that as a theoretically important term, it is perhaps less transparent than it has been assumed to be.

4.3.5 *Teaching, learning and knowledge*

Some serious issues are linked to the above thoughts on everyday life; this concerns the nature of what is learned as well as the relation between learning and teaching. Just as the term 'knowledge' is perhaps somewhat problematic as a description of what one 'acquires' by the living of life, so also is the term (local/segmental) pedagogy as an explanation of the occurrence of *all* learning that occurs in it (see chapters 1 and 2 for further discussion).

In the first place, learning does not necessarily presuppose deliberate teaching: in ordinary everyday social practices, a good deal of the so-called knowledge is not the result of any kind of direct teaching by a human; rather, there is substantial evidence that a good deal of such learning arises from being able to make inferences which are based not on some deliberately taught bit of knowledge but simply from a direct experience of a semiotic or non-semiotic event. The value of direct experience as a 'teacher of lessons' cannot be ignored; the range and variety of these experiences – sometimes material and impersonal, at others emotional and intimate – act as formidable teachers as they encounter the innate human abilities to remember, to compare and contrast, and to infer. In our understanding, Vygotsky (1978) ascribed the initial manifestations of such mental functions to the learner's *bio-genetic* foundation; their *continued development*, he viewed as *socio-genetic* in nature – i.e., arising in living with other acculturated persons. So at least some part of the process of learning has been seen as initially independent of what is known as LOCAL PEDAGOGY, especially if that expression is interpreted as intentional teaching by some human teacher. The suggestion is not that there is no connection between teaching and learning, but simply that whatever the nature of what we learn in the living of life, not all of it can be attributed to local/segmental pedagogy because, first, the process of learning is not inevitably the result of teaching; this is evident from the failure of pupils to learn that which is being deliberately taught with a good deal of careful preparation. Secondly, even when there is deliberate, carefully organized teaching as in official pedagogy such as described in Bernstein (1990), the 'mental labour' on the part of the learner has to be harnessed for the actual learning of competence to occur. That some learning is always taking place is not in question; what is in question is its relation to teaching.

Having closely examined hours of maternal discourse with very young children, we are not about to deny that what is called 'local pedagogy' is active in everyday life, and that it is considerably different from official pedagogy (Bernstein 1999: 161). We add some further points of difference between the two. Unlike official pedagogy, local pedagogy seldom fails to teach – not because the human pedagogue in everyday life is always a skilled teacher, but mostly because there is a great deal of redundancy and recurrence of same/similar 'strategy' which helps the learner in recognizing that which has to be learned. It may be important also that in local pedagogy the human teacher knows a good deal better than the teacher in official pedagogy what the acquirer is actually like; moreover, the 'teaching agenda' in local pedagogy is subordinate to the child's concerns in the sense that it arises from something that involves the child in the first place.[39] These traits are absent from official pedagogy. Whether this absence inheres in the nature of that social practice, we are not sure. What is known as a fact is that only selected learners can feel at one with this highly orchestrated system – a characteristic common to most institutionally set agendas.

Local pedagogy is certainly segmental, but in light of earlier discussion (sections 4.3 – 4.3.4), the segmentation of pedagogy is perhaps not as serious a point of difference: according to the reasoning presented above, all pedagogy – whether local or official – is of necessity segmented. The important difference is in its aetiology and its manner of integration: in one case – i.e., local pedagogy – the time boundary and the 'domain' of teaching is determined by what is going on, in the other – i.e., official pedagogy – the boundaries and the sequencing within the domain is subordinated to material and disciplinary considerations. What time of the day it is; who the learner is in terms of age, sex, class, pedagogic attainment; how is the 'material' related to the domain of knowledge as a whole, are some of the considerations that apply in official pedagogy. As Bernstein has shown (1975b, 1990) recontextualization is an essential element of instructional discourse in official pedagogy, which implies dependence on already produced vertical knowledge structures, whether horizontal or hierarchical. The sequential integration of segments in official pedagogy arises from the deliberate structuring of knowledge. By contrast, the happenstance occurrence of local pedagogy appears to lack any principle for integration. We have suggested above (section 4.3.1) that this lack is imaginary rather than real – there are integrating principles in the shape of coding orientation which determine the orders of relevance for local pedagogy. This pedagogy seems to have only one mission – to enable the learners to participate in social practices which are central to the ways of living specific to the child's speech fellowships – it is a device for the 'naturalization' of one's SOCIAL POSITIONING.

This is one reason for suggesting that perhaps 'knowledge' – especially as used in 'knowledge structure' – is not the point of what is called local pedagogy: the process of the living of life with the members of one's community makes one not knowledgeable, but perhaps, 'cognizant' of how living is done. Such cognizance is at a considerable distance from knowledge, especially if what is meant by the latter word is persistent, deliberate and principle-based probing in search of irrefutable evidence in favour of certain principles. Terms such as 'know-how', 'folklore', 'ideology', 'mother wit', and 'common sense' (*without* the qualifier 'knowledge') have sometimes been used precisely because 'knowledge' in some sense appears a rather 'inflated' description for what is generally learned: for the majority of human beings, living and dying are things that *happen* in life, not things one enquires into systematically. Above all, this is the site where in primary socialization the earliest form of consciousness takes shape (Bernstein 1971c, 1975b); this is well supported by Hasan's research on semantic variation (1999b). This is not to say that the earliest form of consciousness is unchangeable or unchanging – informal narratives provide 'evidence' galore of change happening. What we need is simply a clear account of such changes, based on empirical sociological research regarding how this transformation occurs; how we characterize those who are transformed; how we describe the ways in which the transformation reveals itself.

5 The linguistic features of horizontal/vertical discourse

In this section we turn once again to horizontal and vertical discourse – this time with the aim of discussing some of their linguistic features. Recall, the 'brief definition' of 'the two discourses' is said to 'take "forms of knowledge" as criteria. *Different forms of knowledge will be realized in the two discourses*' (158). We interpret this as a claim that the two forms of discourse construe the two forms of knowledge: the linguistic features of horizontal discourse construe 'commonsense knowledge', and those of the vertical discourse construe either hierarchical or horizontal knowledge structures. The use of the term 'realization' as the relation between forms of knowledge and forms of discourse[40] supports the interpretation that the relation between them is non-arbitrary. So it is valid to ask if the linguistic features relate to the 'forms of knowledge', and if so how? Most of these features were presented in section 2.1 and summarized in Table 1, for ease of reference we reproduce below first the two major segments of the essay containing the linguistic description of HD, followed by two major segments concerning VD, which are said to realize commonsense and vertical knowledge, respectively.

Extract (i): HD features (Bernstein 1999: 159); [emphasis added, *H&B*]
This *form* has a group of well-known features: it is likely to be oral, local, context dependent and specific, tacit, multi-layered, and contradictory across but not within contexts. *However,... the crucial feature is that it is segmentally organized.* By segmental, I am referring to the sites of the realization of this discourse. The realization of this discourse varies with the way the culture segments and specialises activities and practices. The knowledge is segmentally differentiated.

Extract (ii): HD features (Bernstein 1999: 161)
Thus in the case of horizontal discourse, its 'knowledge', competences and literacies are segmental. They are contextually specific and 'context dependent', embedded in on-going practices, usually with strong affective loading, and directed towards specific immediate goals, highly relevant to the acquirer in the context of his/her life.

Extract (iii): VD features (Bernstein 1999: 159)
Briefly, a vertical discourse takes the form of a coherent, explicit, and systematically principled structure, hierarchically organized, as in the sciences, *or* it takes the form of a series of specialised languages with specialised modes of interrogation and specialised criteria for their production and circulation of texts, as in the social sciences and humanities. [emphasis added, *H&B*]

Extract (iv) : VD features (Bernstein 1999: 161)
vertical discourse ... has two forms: one is coherent, explicit and systematically principled structure, hierarchically organised and the second takes the form of a series of specialised languages with specialised modes of interrogation, specialised criteria for their production. ... The integration of a vertical discourse is not integration at the level of the relation between segments/contexts as in horizontal discourse, but integration at the level of meanings. Vertical discourse consists not of culturally specialised segments, but of specialised symbolic structures of explicit knowledge.

5.1 On linguistic features

Before turning to the 'well-known features' of the form of the horizontal or vertical discourse, we offer a word in general about the term 'linguistic features'. The term can potentially refer to a wide range of linguistic patterns which may belong to different linguistic strata. In terms of SFL, human language is a potential for MEANING – i.e., a device for the construal of a set of abstract categories instantiating 'meanings'. Linguistic meanings are not 'objects, processes or qualities' out there in the world; they simply REPRESENT categories of phenomena whether belonging to the 'real' or imaginary world. The representation relation itself is not bound to any time or place. In this way meaning is that stratum of the language system which functions as an interface between the semiotic system and the speech community's conditions of living; in this perspective, linguistic meanings (semantic categories) are realized as wordings (lexicogrammatical categories), which are realized as some sound patterns[41] (phonological categories). These strata and the internal systemic relations of language signs have been discussed fairly often in SFL.[42] Here we want to clarify two things, that, first, *linguistic* features may occur at the level of meaning (semantics), or wording (lexicogrammar) or sound (phonology; phonetics); and secondly, that if the discussion is focussed on meanings as for example it has to be in the case of knowledge as the 'realized' category, then by default, the linguistic features considered most relevant to the debate are those which pertain to the level of lexicogrammar: this is because the latter are non-arbitrarily related to linguistic meanings (for discussion Halliday and Matthiessen 1999; Hasan 1996c, 2009b, 2010). Meanings, to use an expression favoured by Firth, are neither immanent nor transcendent, they are simply semiotically created categories familiar by use to the members of that particular community; they are artefacts of the lexicogrammatical relations, expressed by the phonological ones, which ensures the two faces of the sign – the *intelligi-ble* and the *sensi-ble*. This is the reason for insisting that a linguistic meaning be seen as the construal of some lexicogrammatical features.

5.2 Context dependent/independent discourse

We open this discussion with the pair of terms mentioned earlier (4.1.1), namely, 'context dependent'/'context independent'. There is an excellent reason for turning to this pair first: as descriptive features of language, they are over-arching concepts, from which may be derived a set of lower order linguistic features such as 'oral', 'local', 'explicit', '(context) specific', 'tacit', and other such features. As antonyms, the two over-arching concepts have much in common semantically, and the description of one invokes the qualities of the other, though obviously they or the features derived from them cannot be attributed to the same discourse type. The two terms were introduced in Bernstein's research as early as the 1960s. During this early stage of his 'work', they were used primarily to characterize aspects of the realization of RESTRICTED and ELABORATED CODES. And though the focus of research moved from primary socialization to the structuring of pedagogic discourse, the concept of code has appeared in the literature consistently (cf. coding orientation), building upon their respective original meanings (Bernstein 1971c, 1975b, 1990, 2000). Like many other Bernsteinian concepts, in terms of Langer, these too proved 'productive'. This was perhaps particularly true of the term 'context independent' which has been used widely due to its relevance to processes of the construal and internalization of knowledge – issues that cannot be ignored in planned knowledge transmission, i.e. official pedagogy (for a brief review of literature on this topic see Cloran 1994). However, true to the cherished conventions of horizontal knowledge producers, scholars have chosen different labels to refer to approximately the same concept including terms such as DECONTEXTUALIZED or DIS-EMBEDDED language (e.g., Donaldson 1978). If we are not mistaken, the latest arrival on the scene is Maton's SEMANTIC GRAVITY (2008, 2009). We are not aware of any effort to elaborate on this concept since an early effort was made briefly – though with the wisdom of hindsight not very clearly – by Hasan (1973: 284) to explain the special sense in which the terms were being used by Bernstein and his colleagues at the Sociological Research Unit (SRU). At that stage the role of language in construing relevant context, and the relations of the relevant context to material situational setting (MSS) (4.1 – 4.1.1) were far from clear: context was being seen then as a 'determiner' of linguistic choices, which made the terms 'context dependent' and 'context independent' difficult to explain. Today when, thanks to the work of SFL colleagues,[43] the situation appears somewhat clearer the two terms may perhaps be described linguistically with greater clarity. This is what we hope to achieve below.

5.2.1 *One linguistic interpretation of context independent*

Given the principle in SFL today that every natural use of language has some specific context, the term 'context independent', paraphrased literally as 'being independent of context', would have to be treated as a contradiction in terms (Halliday *et al.* 1964; Hasan 1973: 284; Cloran 1994:17-83). So, what exactly did Bernstein mean in using this term? Any reading of Bernstein that claims he thought of 'context independent texts' as having *no* context is simply a misreading: what he claimed was that the language of texts with this characteristic would not need to depend on their situation in order to be understood. If this paraphrase strikes the reader as confusing or self-contradictory, then we suggest the genesis of the confusion lies in a common slippage: the discourse of most social scientists, including sociologists and linguists, which regretfully includes us as well, is likely to display a slippage between the words 'situation' and 'context'. The terms are used interchangeably as if they were synonymous, though they are not, and that forms the source of a good deal of misunderstanding.

To elaborate on this statement, we return to two earlier sections (4 – 4.1.1) where it was suggested that the language of a text illuminates its own context of situation; this is a metaphorical way of saying that *context is a linguistic construal*, or that *the context of a text is typically encapsulated in the text*, or that *a text typically reveals the nature of its field, tenor and mode*. This does *NOT* mean that a text carries with itself information about all of its raw situational setting. In other words, distinction has to be made between the context of a text and the spatio-temporal situational setting in which it may have taken place, which is what we argued in 4.1.1. If we examine the construed contexts of DISPLACED texts, one as simple as say 'my parents have just left for London', it is obvious that most of the entities, processes and their attributes (call them 'referents', if you prefer) construed by the language such as 'parents', 'left', 'London' *logically could not have formed part of the material situational setting* (MSS) where the utterance was produced. When we produce a recount, reference is made in the talk to many entities which logically could not be part of the situational setting of the interaction – in history, biography, recount and other such registers, the 'referents' are furnished from resources other than what is present in the here and now – memory whether communal or individual plays an enormous part. And this is true not just of recounts. In other words, we are suggesting that relevant context does not consist simply of phenomena which form part of the situational setting of some verbal interaction: material situational setting may or may not be a resource in the formation of a textual context. In fact the extent to which a text receiver may be able to recover information about the nature of a text's material situational setting correlates systematically with different categories of textual context. Such variation is, thus, significant as a factor contributing to the definition of certain register types (for discussion of some examples see Cloran 1994, 1999a, 1999b). However, given the slippage between the words 'context' and 'situation', if the word *context* is used as a synonym for *situational setting* then naturally texts which make no reference to any part of their MSS are independent of their "context", i.e., of their material situational setting. What this means is that Bernstein's context independent texts are texts *which logically could not depend for their interpretation on (the knowledge of) any part of the situation in which the texts might have occurred.*

5.2.2 *Context in context independent discourse*

This raises an interesting question: (i) what allows this degree of independence from situational setting, and (ii) on what ground can such texts be said to have any context? We believe both these questions – which are, in fact, intimately related – are of considerable interest to a sociology of pedagogy so long as it does not set itself up as simply a formal device without a functional basis in the life of the community. To answer the first question briefly, we will invoke the term MSS again. This degree of independence is possible because invoking any part of the MSS is unnecessary for construing the appropriate structure and texture of such texts; *all meanings that are necessary for the interpretation of that text are text-internally available*. This includes its TEXTUAL STRUCTURE, instantiating a GSP (Hasan 1979) – approximately the same as SCHEMATIC STRUCTURE in Martin's terminology (1985) – as well as its TEXTURE, i.e., lines of cohesion and coherence which are realized as COHESIVE HARMONY (Hasan 1984b) – in some respects close to but not the same as Martin's RETICULUM ANALYSIS (Martin 1992). *The complete construal of the structure and texture of texts of this kind can, in principle, be arrived at by interpreting the lexicogrammatical patterns which realize the text's semantics*.

But if this response to the first question is accepted, then the answer to the second question is implicit in it: texts of this kind must construe some context of their discourse. This claim is made on the assumption that it is impossible to arrive at a text's global/schematic structure and to interpret all relations of relevancies in it, without understanding what is being done (what the field of discourse is), with/for/to whom (what the tenor of discourse is) and by what semiotic means (what the mode of discourse is): they are simply two sides of the same coin. This naturally depends on the deployment of linguistic patterns in some particular way. True that Bernstein's 'essay' (1999) does not foreground the feature 'context independent', but as extracts (iii) and (iv) show, what he does is to name at least some of those semantic properties of language which are essential in a text capable of construing its context simply on the basis of the text's lexicogrammatical choices: the language has to be 'coherent', 'explicit', capable of interrogating, refuting, in short building a well structured account of the speaker's argumentations. The implications of the interpretative self-sufficiency of a context independent text is discussed below, where we also turn to context dependence as a linguistic feature.

5.3 Context dependent language, situation and context

One might assume that being the other member of the antonymous pair, *'context dependent discourse' would refer only to those entities, processes and their attributes all of which have formed components of that situational setting in which the language use occurred*: the ongoing situation is supposed to be the primary source for understanding what is being said. If that were the case, then such language could be said to be CONTEXT/SITUATION BOUND and indeed this descriptive phrase was used interchangeably with 'context dependent' in the writings of the members of SRU. Interpreting context dependent language in this way would logically imply that once the original text is taken out of its situational setting, no one who was not party to its production would be able to make much sense of it: the text should be largely/totally implicit, its referents unknowable. Now the expression 'context dependent' or 'context bound' is used typically to characterize everyday discourse. But even a cursory examination of discourse which takes place in everyday life will in no time at all show this description to be invalid. It is in fact quite difficult to find texts which lose intelligibility the moment they are displaced; one only has to consider such discourses as, say, that between adults and children, or between adult friends having a chat while sitting round a dinner table. So what did Bernstein mean by this term?

Everyday language covers a huge spectrum of human life – strong generalizations about language such as 'context dependent' to an under-described category are not likely to stand up to scrutiny. To be valid, they have to be applied to a more delicate category, identified by some other equally strong properties. Indeed the early use of the term did precisely that: it is worth noting that it was applied to language governed by the principles of restricted code in significant contexts – not to the daily language of everyday life in the *whole community* engaged in *any social practice whatever*, but to the language of a specific subset of the community,[44] in certain social contexts, the range of whose social processes is 'naturally' constrained by their positioning in society (Bernstein 1971c, 1975b; Hasan 1999a, 2009b). Describing everyday language as a whole either as 'context bound/dependent' or 'implicit', as it is in the 'essay', is likely to expose the claim to sure refutation.

But even if context dependence is said to be a characteristic of only the discourse governed by restricted code, the claim would not be valid if the term is interpreted as *language referring* ONLY *to those entities, processes and their attributes which functioned as components of its situational setting*. Further modifications must be made to the meaning of the term. We are fairly confident that Bernstein would have agreed with our characterization of context independent language (section 5.2.1) in terms of its relation to its MSS, but he would have strenuously objected to the account of context dependent language offered in the opening lines of this section. He would have countered that context dependent language is IMPLICIT language – not language that does not refer to anything outside the situational setting. But what exactly does one mean by 'implicit' then? This brings us to another slippage which is again fairly common in ordinary use.

5.3.1 *The feature 'implicit': the coupling of situation, meaning and wording*

It is a fact that the term 'context dependent' is treated as pretty close in meaning to the term 'implicit' in the SRU literature; even a quick reading would confirm this claim. A problem arises here because in ordinary language 'implicit' and IMPLIED are treated as more or less synonymous. However, in using language to describe language, words do undergo some change in their meaning – sometimes quite a significant one; so at the cost of being tedious, it pays to be clear about what meaning is being ascribed to the terms in a given L of a horizontal knowledge structure[45]: they are defined in a particular way because of the work of description they have to do.

These remarks are relevant to the semantic value of *implicit* and *implied* in the L we are using: 'implicit' is a term used to refer to the PRESUPPOSING member of a COHESIVE TIE, as for example 'she' in 'she wasn't well'. Here 'she' is an 'implicit' cohesive device in the sense that the listener/reader needs some mediating information to identify the ultimate referent: the term presupposes a more specific meaning which is assumed to be accessible either from within the text or from the text's MSS. Suppose one had heard someone saying 'Susan did not attend any meetings; she wasn't well', then all things being equal 'Susan' would be treated as the PRESUPPOSED member of the tie: the implicit word 'she' would be seen as referring to the same entity as the one to which 'Susan' refers. By contrast, the term IMPLIED does not relate to any single item/expression in the text; rather something implied is something understood/inferred on the basis of (substantial) parts of a text (Hasan 2009b) or the entire text, as in literature (Hasan 1985a). For example, two implications to be drawn from the previous message complex would be that Susan has some occupation and so is subject to certain obligations. Or take the message 'Susan resigned yesterday' which among other things, implies that 'Susan' had until recently held a job, so she is an adult, but there was no item in the above clause complex which *referred* to adult(hood) or even to a job (further discussion, e.g., the semantic description of 'man' in chapter 6, this volume). Explicitly voicing something that was implied goes beyond single referents. Further, it is difficult to imagine any text, even one consisting of just one major message as entirely free of implications: the overt resolution of the inference(s) of one message will most probably carry some new inferences. When language is described as TACIT as it is in extract (i) above, it is being said that its interpretation depends on being able to understand the implications of what is said. This is not a feature of only everyday discourse: the nature of language is such that, typically all speakers have to leave something unsaid, on the assumption that it will be 'filled in' by the listeners. We will return to this point later in this section (see 5.4 as well as in section 6).

5.3.2 *Context dependent/independent v. implicit/explicit*

We have paid close attention to the contrast between these two pairs of terms because their explication is critical to the discussion of context dependent/independent language. If 'context dependent' means the same as 'implicit', it is important to understand the full significance of the term 'implicit', and its opposite EXPLICIT. Implicit language is not language whose referents are necessarily to be found in the situational setting. In fact, one could refer *mostly* to the entities, processes and their attributes present in the MSS of the discourse *without being implicit in any way*, as for example in the clause: 'I see two girls eating chocolate ice-cream'. Every single item in that clause refers to something that has to be present in the situational setting. However, none can be described as an implicit device, or as a presupposing (potentially cohesive) item, and speakers of English would be able to interpret the meaning of the clause without recourse to its situational setting – and in this respect, the utterance is 'context independent'; the only thing speakers need to make the desired interpretation is the knowledge of the language. *From this view point, this mini-text is context independent.*

It seems, then, as if another way for construing context independent discourse has been revealed; the first, described above (section 5.2.2), was to refer to hardly any entities, processes, their attributes that form part of the situational setting of the text as in a recount; the second example presented above ('two girls eating ice-cream') ignores relation to situational setting and permits the claim that a text may refer to parts of the existing MSS and *yet be context independent* provided it uses lexicogrammatical patterns whose semantic value is maximally explicit. We will now add a third way of being explicit: to do this, return to the earlier example, viz., 'Susan did not attend any meetings; she wasn't well' – an example which shows clearly that *the choice of implicit patterns, per se,* does not necessarily make the language implicit. In this example, the implicit item 'she' by its cohesive relation to 'Susan' allows the listener/reader to access the more specific meaning: in simple terms, 'she' and 'Susan' mean the same thing. Compare this with 'And they went and saw several yesterday but he didn't fancy any of them.' The reason it is difficult to understand 'who saw what and who didn't fancy what' has less to do with the fact that there are many implicit patterns in this clause complex; the reason it is difficult to interpret is that it lacks a CO-TEXT by reference to which it can be made explicit. Suppose it was preceded by 'Jenny wanted to buy a cat for Andy', then as the popular expression has it, everything would fall into place. What this example suggests is that it is not the use of implicit devices as such that matters, it is the quality and consistency of continuity that counts: *if this continuity is mediated via textual cohesive relations (i.e., it is* ENDOPHORIC*), the text will make sense to reader/listener without any text-external information.* We conclude that dependence on or independence from 'context' (meaning thereby *situation*) will itself depend on how cohesively and/or explicitly language has been used.

5.3.3 *Context dependence, situation and language*

So if there are so many ways in which discourse may be rendered context independent, then what can be validly stated about context dependent discourse? The answer can be stated clearly as follows: if the arguments above are accepted then *context dependence is a potential feature to the extent that the text fails to maintain textual continuity by means of text internal cohesive relations*, i.e., in other words, in texts with 'context' dependent language the continuity creating relations are EXOPHORIC not ENDOPHORIC (Halliday and Hasan 1976, 1985; Martin 1992). It is also important to state clearly that 'context dependent' does not equal 'not interpretable': the text may contain many implicit devices whose semantic value is not fully mediated text-internally. This, however, does not mean that *all* listeners/readers would find such a text difficult/impossible to understand. As they say 'conditions apply' for turning lexicogrammatical devices into the usable currency of meaning. The conditions on how far one is able to make sense of what is being said may be listed as follows:

(i) Context dependent texts are understood without difficulty by anyone who is 'keyed into its situational setting', to the extent that the majority of the text's implicit devices can be interpreted by reference to the make up of the MSS (i.e., continuity is created by the use of EXOPHORIC COHESIVE RELATIONS).

(ii) In addition, all things being equal, discourse within a specific speech fellowship has presumption of familiarity with the MSS of the majority of its social practices, which means that daily face to face discourse within the bounds of speech fellowships is overwhelmingly free of problems in interpretation.

(iii) When such discourse is DISPLACED/DISEMBEDDED, i.e., separated from the MSS of production, and received by addressees in a different situational setting as when transcribed, then to the extent that the text assumes access to knowledge on the basis of text-external situations, and to the extent that the listener/reader is unfamiliar with the social practices in the speaker's speech fellowship, to that extent its interpretation will call for special expertise for 'reading'.

In view of the perspective taken here, there is an important difference between 'implicit' and 'tacit': in theory, it is possible to produce a text that is either entirely implicit or entirely explicit, though in practice, naturally occurring texts hardly ever reach these extreme states. By contrast, it is not possible to construct even an example 'text' consisting of even one message that is free of implied meaning: the normal natural use of language is 'tacit', in the sense in which that word has been defined above. It arises from the make up of the semiotic system of language: the meanings of the wordings used imply more than what is 'openly said'. Or to put it another way, inferred meanings are as much a part of the semantics of language as what is sometimes called 'literal meaning'.

5.3.3 *Context dependence/independence: some conclusions*

We would like to highlight three points that emerge from the above discussion of context dependence/independence in a discourse: first, there is a systematic relationship between context dependence/independence and the features of implicitness and explicitness, respectively; second, whichever pair of features we consider, they represent points on a scale, not a yes/no relation; third, the significance of these features varies with respect to the relation of the listener/reader to the speaker and the social practices which activate the discourse.

To take the first point first, whatever discourse is context (i.e., situation) independent is also necessarily largely explicit; whatever is context (i.e., situation) dependent is largely implicit to all but a certain specifiable group of readers/listeners (c.f., (i - iii) above). The features 'context independent/dependent' focus on the relation of the situation to the discourse, whereas the features 'explicit/implicit' focus on the way that the lexicogrammatical resources are deployed. If the above views are accepted, greater importance is attached to the way language is deployed than how the discourse and the situational setting are related: all the referents, whether things, qualities or states of affairs, may be in the situational setting but if the relations of continuity are endophoric, the discourse would be explicit not implicit; it would therefore be context independent rather than context dependent.

Horizontal discourse is not made up of implicit expressions only; if it had been, no one would have acquired any understanding of their social universe through it; there would have been no commonsense knowledge. Its meanings are sufficiently accessible either largely endophorically or primarily exophorically either because the discourse was 'oral', which is to say the interactants were co-present, and/or because interactants belonged to the same speech fellowship. Vertical discourse is not free of implicit references either, not even the best example of scientific achievement, or perhaps one should say, especially *not* the best achievements, since the implicit cohesive devices are a means of creating relations of identity and similarity, both being essential to maintaining continuity. What can be stated is that its implicit devices are textually 'explicated' – the sources for making them explicit are overwhelmingly text-internal. To the extent that our distinction between situational setting (MSS) and relevant context is valid, it may be useful to refer to the pair as 'situation dependent/situation independent' instead of using 'context dependent/context independent'. The former labels have the merit of actually 'saying' what the terms have always meant in Bernstein's writing.

Turning now from the situational relations to the linguistic ones, it is necessary to recognize both *what is possible in principle*, and also *what happens normally/ 'by default'*, i.e., what presents itself to the listener's/reader's senses in the majority of the actual instances of discourse. It is, of course, possible for some mini texts to be entirely explicit just as it is possible to find overwhelmingly implicit discourse. However, it is only under some very special social situation,[46] or in some medical condition e.g., forms of brain pathology perhaps, that natural talk might display extreme explicitness/implicitness; normal discourse consisting of more than even a couple of clauses, hardly ever shows such consistent occurrence of extremes as found in 'I see two girls eating chocolate ice-cream' (highly explicit) or 'those boys playing with it over there did that' (highly implicit). Concocting such lone message examples is, of course, possible but it is jolly difficult to find a natural text with nothing but explicit or implicit ways of signifying. It seems best, therefore, to respect the scalar quality of the terms explicit/implicit, by treating them as endpoints on a continuum, with the majority of language use 'bunching' around the mid-point rather than exemplifying the extremes (for the discussion of a cline of implicitness, Hasan 1984a; for a cline of situational dependency Cloran 1994, 1999b).

Finally, to claim that the language of some discourse such as those between mothers and children presented in Hasan (2009b) are fairly implicit is not to say that therefore they cannot be interpreted. If this had been the case, the discourses would have had to be discontinued before going far, which hardly ever happened. Points (ii) and (iii) above (section 5.2.4) explain why a fair degree of unresolved implicitness can be tolerated between interactants so long as the SOCIAL DISTANCE between them is not maximal, and the social practice to which the discourse is related is familiar to the listener/reader. Similarly a fair degree of explicitness such as found in Maxwell's Elementary Treatise (1881) is, in itself, neither a guarantee that it would be understood by all, nor necessarily a problem for all readers, though it will prove so for some. This would suggest that the difficulties of comprehension do not inhere *only* in Maxwell's discourse: if there is such difficulty it primarily inheres in the reader's relation to the kind of discourse. The important issues seem to be: (a) how does this relation differ from that of those readers who are able to understand, and (b) what are the properties of the Maxwell discourse with which the non-comprehending reader lacks familiarity?

This discussion draws attention to a curious fact: we pointed out above that context independence/disembeddedness is considered an important concept in the discourses of educational knowledge. But if 'context independence' implies a high degree of textual explicitness, there arises an important question: why would such disembeddedness make the text less easy for the learner, as is normally assumed? (We could raise the same question using the term 'semantic gravity'.) Where exactly does the problem lie, since it definitely does not lie in the explicitness of making meanings? This is a critical question which needs to be raised if we are to understand the exact nature of the linguistic problem which stands in the way of the successful transmission of educational knowledge. Without a clear understanding of this problem, all programmes which attempt to alleviate the supposed effects of a text's context independence are, in fact, groping in the dark.

5.4 Forms of knowledge and forms of discourse

In the above discussion of the pair of over-arching concepts, we have attempted to bring into focus many of the features used by Bernstein to characterize the two forms of discourse. Had there been more time and space, such close reading of the remaining linguistic features would have proved useful. Here we draw attention to a few additional issues. Bernstein has coupled forms of discourse with forms of knowledge: forms of knowledge function as criteria for the recognition of 'forms' of discourse (158). This of course assumes that it is possible to offer reliable recognition criteria which would enable us to distinguish the different kinds of knowledges from each other. This raises some interesting questions.

5.4.1 *Horizontal discourse and horizontal knowledge structures*

One might ask in the above context if it is possible to offer any explicit recognition criteria for commonsense knowledge. This is not just a pedantic issue: that we all know what is meant by the expression 'commonsense knowledge' does not absolve us from attempting to search for recognition criteria or from seeking an explanatory description any more than our 'knowledge of noise' (as lay 'knowers') absolves the scientist from finding an explanatory description of what the term 'noise' means in his theory – which in the end is what permits the scientist to talk of 'white noise' without leading to the kinds of problem that would arise if the common understanding of 'noise' as a word of ordinary language is taken to be the same as the theoretical concept of the term 'noise'. Terminology is not all there is to a theory, but its clear understanding is certainly critical to the interpretation of elements of the theory.

To continue with another issue of terminology: it has seemed to us that the use of the word 'horizontal' to refer to both a specific form of knowledge structure and of (a contrasting form of) discourse is somewhat problematic. Even if we begin by accepting Bernstein's view – which we have already questioned (section 4) – that the critical feature of HD is its segmental organization, the 'segmentation' of the discourse of the horizontal knowledge structures has very little in common with segmentation of commonsense knowledge. For example, each of these HOKS in any one discipline represents some kind of 'instead of' relation to the others rather than of 'also' as in commonsense knowledge: following Bernstein, segmental discourse would be about tying your shoelaces, *and* about washing hands before touching food, *and* about how to talk to granny *and* so on and on, i.e., just a collection. By contrast, all instances of HOKS in, say, linguistics are about language: they may not cover exactly the same expanse, but the general principle is that they must be concerned with some explication of the concept of language. Seen in this light, the distinct Languages of a particular HOKS are more like a number of alternative theoretical systems each focussing on the same object of enquiry from distinct perspectives. By his account, while Bernstein's horizontal discourse appears to be a collection of (segments of) discourse each associated with some specific kind of social practices, each horizontal knowledge structure (in a domain of knowledge) is in principle attempting to do the same thing from a rather different perspective, which is analogous to many cultures having different forms of commonsense knowledge.

Horizontal discourse and horizontal knowledge structures are said to have another 'feature' in common, namely, their 'volatility'. It has been somewhat difficult to fully appreciate the significance of the term 'volatile' as applied to discourse or knowledge in Bernstein's theory. If this word is used with the same semantic value as in ordinary language (not theorized, not part of a language of description), then to us neither knowledge nor discourse appear volatile – or putting it positively, the meanings of both possess a good deal of tenacity. To say that horizontal discourse is a means of transmitting commonsense knowledge is to say that the semantic value of horizontal discourse survives in the form of that knowledge: it is the meanings of such discourse that may be said to construe commonsense knowledge. It is true that the details of this knowledge will vary systematically across the distinct speech fellowships. If this makes commonsense knowledge volatile then it would be difficult to come across anything in the culture that is not volatile.

Admittedly, in comparison with HIKS, the theoretical vocabulary of HOKS tends to be subject to quicker changes; in this sense, perhaps, the lexicon of HOKS may be considered comparatively volatile. But what is it that is changing? This too is an important consideration. Take, for example, the referents of some of this 'volatile' lexicon: what are the ways in which the referents of 'primary socialization' differ substantively from those of 'local pedagogy'? We accept that difference in perspective, point of view, coding orientation, ideology – and perhaps other near synonyms – have ruled the instances of the horizontal knowledge structures over the ages, but, all the same, often the changes have been only skin deep: they have been more like changing fashions of clothing, the result of following a trend, rather than arguing a position.

The quality of tacitness, i.e., working on the basis of what is implied rather than what is said in as many words, is not unique either to horizontal discourse or to vertical, nor can it be ascribed to the horizontal knowledge structures, implying that the hierarchical knowledge structures are free of this quality (for discussion section 6). We hasten to add there may be differences but if so, the question is perhaps going to be: how coherent are the implications in different forms of discourses which realize different forms of knowledges when seen in relation to what is already there 'in black and white', i.e., in 'words and structures'? To our knowledge, linguists researching in the SFL framework have not raised this question about the various knowledge genres which they have successfully analysed for what is said, but such an enquiry could lead us to understand how the tacitness of commonsense discourse/knowledge differs from that of structured horizontal knowledge and how the latter differs from tacitness in hierarchical knowledge structures.

5.4.2 *Varieties of vertical discourse and forms of knowledge*

We could of course say that a form or category of knowledge is recognized as such and so on the basis of its lexicogrammatical features; in that case, however, the description of linguistic features could not remain at the level of situational setting; it would have to be much more focussed on context and semantics which would imply attention to the lexicogrammatical selections. In this context consider, for example, vertical discourse, to which correspond two distinct forms of knowledge.

We would agree that at a primary degree of delicacy the language of both hierarchical and horizontal knowledge structures may be said to be alike, particularly when seen in comparison with mundane everyday non-specialist discourse. The language used in both the hierarchical and the horizontal knowledge structures is specialized and relatively explicit as Bernstein points out. Thinking of their ontogenesis, we add that both forms of discourse have to be learnt not on the mother's knees but deliberately under the pedagogue's keenly evaluative eyes. Despite these similarities, it would be quite surprising if there were *no* linguistic differences between the two forms of discourses that construe two distinct kinds (forms?) of knowledge structures. If nothing else, the referents would differ in one general respect: those pertaining to the hierarchical knowledge structures concern material physical phenomena; those pertaining to the majority of the horizontal knowledge structures would concern social and semiotic values. Since the procedures of the two kinds of knowledge structures differ, certain kinds of activities are more likely to occur in one than the other; this in turn will have led to linguistic differences to which attention has been drawn by a good deal of research in genre-based examination of such disciplines as history, geography and science (e.g., Eggins *et al.* 1993; Halliday and Martin 1993; Martin 1993; van Leeuwen and Humphrey 1996). Equally important is a closer examination of the various disciplines from the point of view of their register potential.

It is notable that Bernstein (1999) seldom refers to the language of horizontal knowledge structures as any kind of 'theory/theoretical discourse'. The many instances of HOKS are simply a series of Languages. This appears surprising; Bernstein's own theory of the social has launched concepts such as coding orientation, pedagogic device, recontextualizing agencies and so on. These describe phenomena in the universe of social experience; they are as much a product of theorization as Heizenberg's 'uncertainty principle' or Einstein's 'relativity theorem', or more recently 'dark matter' and 'dark energy'. So both hierarchical and horizontal knowledge structures exist as transmissible theories despite some differences: the phenomena the social sciences describe are far more difficult to 'ascertain' than the atom. One would expect that the kind of discourse which facilitates their transmission would vary. If so, what linguistic features might be identified as pertaining to these two forms of discourse, other than the fact that in the former there is only one theoretical position (see section 6, on this perception of theories describing physical phenomena) and in the latter there are many? A good deal of work needs to be done on several fronts, including the linguistic and the sociological, to show both what is in common to the language of the two kinds of structured knowledges and what differentiates them. Here the extension of the work already done by SFL linguists under the leadership of Halliday (2004a) and Halliday and Martin (1993) would be highly relevant.

5.4.3 *Register variation and vertical discourse*

In comparing the concepts of text types and discourse (Section 4.1 – 4.2.1), we suggested that 'discourse' is a relatively under-described category. We pointed out also (section 3) that forms of knowledge as presented here pertain to knowledge already produced: it is this knowledge and the discourse that construes it that is 'subject to pedagogic transformations' (157). The processes of recontextualization transform the discourse of produced knowledges; our aim is to focus briefly only on those transformations of the recontextualized discourses of the produced knowledge which take place as a result of the *process* of knowledge, e.g., the processes of presenting knowledge, of ensuring through revisions and rehearsals the internalization of knowledge on the part of the learners, as well as providing feedback in preparation for the final evaluation of learning. These are pedagogic actions inherent to official pedagogy; equally important are those actions which must be undertaken by the learners, e.g., participating in the process of revision by responding, producing essays, conducting lab experiments, and so on. The form of discourse will systematically vary to some extent in response to the variation in the pedagogic action. Apart from the 'transformation' of the discourse in this respect, there will also occur linguistic variation correlating with variation in the mode of discourse: reading, discussion, responding to specific questions, each displays systematic variation in their linguistic make up according to whether the interaction is spoken or written (Halliday 1985b).

Important as each of these correlates of linguistic variation in the transmission and 'acquisition' of knowledge are, the variation that is most notable in the discourse of knowledge is the longitudinal one: introduction to certain segments of knowledge – whether from the domains of the hierarchical knowledge structures or from that of the horizontal ones – will, in the early stages of education, concern such topics as, say, electricity, nature of magnetic force, food chain, rain cycle, blood flow in human bodies, volcanic eruptions, earthquakes, and so on and so forth. Concepts relevant to such areas of structured recontextualized knowledge begin to be presented at the early stages of education, say, from the age of 11 or so (corresponding to the upper primary stages in Australia), continuing right into to the tertiary initiation, say, around the age of 18 or 19. This is a good investment of time – from something like 7 to 8 years of a pupils life – during which many of these concepts will have been repeatedly brought to the pupils' attention, but each time the 'forms of discourse' would vary compared with the forms experienced previously: this variation too is systematic – it corresponds to the pedagogic system's concept of 'pupil readiness' based on certain ascribed features such as age (also known as 'maturity') and others imagined to have been achieved by virtue of the evaluation processes.

If some knowledge is somehow being transmitted, internalized, being appropriated by at least some pupils, the question that interests us here is: what is the status of these early to late forms of knowledging discourse?

Is any variety of discourse about, for example, the workings of magnetic force, the solar system, and so on, to be seen as pertaining to hierarchical knowledge structure? If yes, do they display the features of vertical discourse? If yes, what specific features of the vertical discourse survive over this long trajectory? To our mind, a detailed analysis and understanding of the ontogenesis of knowledge and the transformations of discourse types over the long trajectory of the pupils' life most probably constitute a necessary element of teacher education. Such understanding is clearly relevant to the teacher's actions in the classroom. And, most probably these issues are relevant to the sociology of education as well, on the assumption that in the final analysis, the system underlying such practices must relate to the concerns of that discipline. We agree with Bernstein that the theory of the structuring of pedagogic discourse must not be reduced to an account of the pathology of pedagogic practices, but it is difficult to see how a socially responsible sociology of education can *ignore* the genesis of that pathology. After all, it seems that many manifestations of this pathology could be taken as arising from the *absence* of (attention to) a viable theory of the sociology of education; they are thus an argument for further developments in a sociology of pedagogy such as introduced by Bernstein. It is only on this reading that Bernstein's comments on the centrality of education to democracy and to communal well-being may be interpreted the way they need to be (cf., Introduction in Bernstein 2000).

6 On kinds of structured knowledge

In this section we examine the two faces of knowledge – unstructured i.e., Bernstein's 'segmental' commonsense knowledge, and the vertical knowledge structures (which we have argued are segmental, section 4). The majority of the section concerns vertical i.e., structured forms of knowledge, and within that the emphasis will be on hierarchical knowledge structures. We briefly summarize here our understanding of the relation between the terms of the first major division as presented in the 'essay'. So far as the 'essay' is concerned, a case seems to be created for the strong separation of the two primary terms – unstructured/structured knowledge. Space does not permit a full discussion, but we would reiterate our suggestion (section 4) that the relations of these two terms are best reinterpreted in light of the history of knowledge. Commonsense, learnt through the experiences of life and accumulated as folklore, communal habits of mind, and belief systems – some would call it IDEOLOGIES – become the foundation of those discourses that we know as some of the scientific disciplines of today (Lloyd 1999; Grant 2007). Not only that, but also some of the prejudices were imported by famous Greek scholars from everyday beliefs into the scientific discussions of 'Medical treatments and biological theories in the fifth and fourth centuries B.C.' about 'The female sex' (Lloyd 1999: Part II). These prejudices still cast their shadows: the female form, considered inferior to the male at that time, continues to be treated as inferior – not in *correct political speak*, of course, but certainly in other ways that matter perhaps more, e.g., substantially lower wages,[47] and control over opportunities which might attract power to the females. To achieve those social goods, females must adopt the male modes of behaviour: the principle is retained, the external form may deceptively point to Margaret Thatcher, Indira Gandhi, Golda Meir, and others.

The strong boundary whereby commonsense knowledge has its own formless form and its own horizontal discourse, which appears as if non-present in the processes of structured knowledge, does not appear tenable. We may not have stated in black and white, but we have clearly implied that something very much like horizontal discourse – accessible to those as yet untutored in 'the language of science' – must be recruited in initiating pupils into the discourses of what (if they are successful) will become the basis for their 'vertical discourse and vertical knowledge' (see section 5.4.3). If there is an argument that early experience of such discourses related elsewhere (e.g., Hasan 1984c, 2000, 2001, 2009b; Cloran 1994, 1999a, 1999b; Williams 1995, 2001) has no bearing on the formation of orientation towards such discourse, then we suggest that argument needs to be cited and discussed. The theme of a logical relation between unstructured and structured knowledge and the weakness of the boundaries between the hierarchical and horizontal knowledge structures will run almost as a prosody throughout the remainder of this discussion.

6.1 On the nature and methods of hierarchical knowledge structures

In considering the actual developments of hierarchical knowledge structure using physics as a paradigm, we will need to take into account other relevant instances of enquiry. Our emphasis is on the anomaly, pointed out by Bernstein: why is hierarchical knowledge structure (HIKS) so different from horizontal knowledge structure (HOKS) both in humanities and in social sciences? We will explore this question by investigating the methods 'specific' to HIKS, certain aspects of the ontogenesis of hierarchical knowledge, its evolution, and the role of kinds of discourse in these processes. So what are the methods imputed to, or most associated with HIKS? In making generalizations here, we draw particularly on the work of such scholars as Toulmin (especially 1972), Lloyd (2002), and Whitaker (2006).

While it is widely agreed that many forms of enquiry have the characteristics of a 'rational enterprise', which could motivate the ascription of the disciplinary title of 'science' – as for example with life sciences, health sciences, social sciences and neuroscience – it is not very clear exactly what characteristics, or ensemble of techniques, produce 'science' and hierarchical knowledge structures. Popper (1972) emphasized falsifiability, along with conjectures and refutations, but falsification – like other suggested criteria of the scientific – cannot be applied uniformly across the 'segmental' subdivisions in physics (consider e.g., 'dark matter'). The points that tend to persist, however, in accounts of science and its development, centre on experimental practices that produce 'observables', honouring empiricism based on reports of the senses. Bernstein's essay makes consistent reference to the empirical dimension, though he does not elaborate on its direct connection to HIKS. Similarly, codification – the property of making delimitable predictions – is also emphasized by Bernstein (cf. 'strong grammar' e.g., p. 165), as by other commentators on the evolution of science. We arrive at the following generalizations about physics, not out of step, we believe, with the drift of Bernstein's argument (1999: 167-168). Physics, as a paradigm case of HIKS, is characterized by:

(i) predictions which typically apply both to individual cases as well as to groups of such instances (note: this is because population-based or statistical predictions without case by case predictability are a hallmark of some HOKS like sociology); and
(ii) axiomatic codifications of the relations between the core concepts, since these turn some of the argumentation into a form of 'exo-somatic' calculus i.e., codification through the application of symbolic tools that are not embodied in the knower (cf. Popper's world 3).

In addition to these points, in order to offer a coherent and historically based account of physics, we need to raise the following issues: first, how useful is a polarization of specialized 'epistemic' knowledge and broad experience-based knowledge? For instance, this polarization tends to diminish the crucial roles of technical skills – the 'techne' of Classical Greek (Roochnik 1998). This class of embodied skill is not just significant for technologies, but in Classical Greece encompassed trainings as different as shipbuilding and medicine. Today, it would still include surgery, and, more recently, perhaps aspects of computing. Bernstein addresses this issue briefly (168), placing crafts under 'Vertical Discourse: HOKS; Weak Grammar; Tacit Transmission', (i.e. preceded by modelling the task). But a sound case can be made for subsuming crafts under HIKS, since there is an accumulation of empirical outcomes and such a tradition may be transmitted *explicitly*, though perhaps the explicitness is not one of wording. In keeping with the drift of Bernstein's argument (168), such transmissions may appear only weakly aligned between different guilds or colleges within the same craft, and hence look more like HOKS. Secondly, we need to ask why there is such an emphasis on ideational meanings in the characterization of knowledge structures. There is strong evidence that interpersonal meanings, in specific personal relationships, have directed the historical course and theoretical character of much disciplinary knowledge (see section 6.8-9).

6.2 Prediction and axiomatic codification in HIKS

It is important to reiterate that conditions (i) and (ii) (see last section) do not typically apply at *any* given phase of a subject area to *all elements* of the 'objects of enquiry' in that subject. What is soluble or tractable changes as subjects are divided into more specialized disciplines or unified by the equations (axiomatic codifications) like those of Newton (1642–1727), Maxwell (1831–79), Boltzmann (1844–1906), Einstein (1879–1955). Mathematics and cognate codes in physics have supplied a form of *lingua franca*, or a 'dynamic Esperanto', by which 'things' quantifiable could be shared by a class of cognoscenti across linguistic and political boundaries (especially in combination with the influence of Latin and Greek). Mathematics changed the meaning potential of a 'diaspora' of specialists who could be defined by their ability to converse in a code which both refined what could be said about commonsense experience, and created domains of expression which were intelligible to those 'in the know' even though often seeming in conflict with common sense.

As an example of the above claims, we will briefly consider conditions (i) and (ii) (section 6.1) with respect to cosmology. For instance, if we set off from the now well accepted notion of 'black holes', we can see that they were first inferred in 1939 through condition (ii) above; and they were later 'confirmed' only by the measurable perturbations they create in other celestial bodies – hence, a version of condition (i), that is the sensible, but without direct experiment. As for experiment applied in individual cases, not just in populations, this seems only to apply to black holes by means of speculative modelling, typically a result of mathematical tools, i.e., again an aspect of condition (ii). One might conclude, then, that different scientific topics within physics – the paradigm of HIKS – vary in the extreme with respect to the characteristics said to be typical of HIKS. This is the case even though the whole subject known as 'physics' is ascribed the prestige of objective method! This variability around different elements of the objects of enquiry obscures issues around the broad typification of knowledge structures and their characteristic discourses. We suggest that the uncertainty, especially about the initial stages of the genesis of scientific thinking, is the result of the entanglement between communal patterns of intellectual and practical life (as discussed briefly in the section 6 above). Encountered in horizontal mundane discourse, the communal patterns of living are precisely what commonsense knowledge is about.

We can return, then, to why it is that experimentation and prediction are two characteristics that underpin the distinctiveness of the hierarchical knowledge structures and their evolution. Methodological strategies which promote replication maximize the possibilities for others, first to accept the demonstration (as long as it is focussed on a relevant issue) and, second, to extend the enquiry. This may seem all too obvious; but it is a remarkable for the fact that 'explanation' is arguably not a distinctive dimension of HIKS. We can have many competing and compelling construals of events (or findings), *but the opportunity to replicate the findings oneself, and to use them as a benchmark for reports against the sense and substance of a knowledge domain, make the rational method in science distinct from reasoning and intuitive insight outside of* HIKS *– and in 'pre-scientific' communities as well.* For instance, the 7000 line poem by Lucretius *De Rerum Natura* has been described as a version of reality that was only eclipsed by the science of the 20th century (Johnson 2000; Cohen 2005: 52-54). But the 'science' of Lucretius, a projection of the thinking of Epicurus and Empedocles, involved only intuitions based on observational reasoning: the atomic theory in the poem is nonetheless astonishingly contemporary, though not operational or experimental.

The central activity of scientific method appears to have been to create conditions where a causal connection is inexorable within a procedure and, therefore, apparently undeniable (see Lloyd 2002 on public debate amongst the Greeks). But this paradigm – much like 'the gold standard' of double blind, randomized trial in medicine – does not apply for many of the most important activities we now include in the subject area in which it developed. This is particularly the case in:

(a) those developments that moved away from sensory report to highly derived, abstract concepts (over which there can be multiple construals);
(b) those that are focussed on human minds, with the higher order of complexity implicated in the language/brain;
(c) many topics that depend on the specifics of evolutionary history, as emphasized by the account of genetic variation demonstrated by the work of Lewontin (1995 and 2000a).

6.3 Prestige and HIKS: power in epistemology

The institutional and social powers of HIKS are topics that require detailed historical analysis in order to differentiate epistemological motivations from extrinsic factors, for example, the relevance of physics to ballistics and warfare. The focus on experimentation and the sensory outcome of enquiry are crucial here: scientific enquiry has been tied directly to knowledge of 'the natural order' – the *physics* which impinges most directly on our survival amidst the natural elements. Beyond this there is the *metaphysics*, literally what is beyond the physics, and is closer to an existential principle. Through controlling nature, communities received a potential not previously countenanced – a measure of control over the future. Ironically, the most extreme case of this control is atomic fission, also the most extreme threat to the future of humans. In his review of the quantification of the Western perception of the world, Crosby (1997) states that the motivation for all his writing projects is his attempt to understand the success of European imperialism. We would suggest the answer lies perhaps in the natural efficacy of measurement.

6.4 'Consider the Heavens': regularity in astrology and astronomy

The contexts from which hierarchical knowledge structures have developed, as distinct from the epistemological conditions which applied in those contexts, suggest that the origins of such knowledge are diverse and, therefore, unlikely to be classifiable under the disciplinary notions which we invoke today. The diversity and anachronism involved in many accounts of knowledge development, and hence in the characterization of HIKS, can be exemplified by the subject areas of astrology and astronomy. The two traditions are set off by the potential for contrast in their names – the 'meaning or study' of the stars (astrology), and the 'naming or enumeration' of the stars (astronomy). Interpreting and reasoning about 'heavenly bodies' have been activities accessible in all communities to all humans with vision and language. The entanglement of proto-science with practical affairs in the community could not be more in evidence, and is brought out non-technically by Tillett (2002). The data were truly 'the given'; the object of enquiry truly 'that which is thrown down' before us (*ob jecta*): namely, the lights of sun, moon, and stars (including the wayward 'wanderers' – i.e., the planets). The first abstract tool for theorization devised by humans may well have been the mud-based impressions of a month of moon phases, which is both a record and a predictive model from 30,000 years ago, as presented in Figure 1. This representation follows the interpretation of Alexander Marshack, and is taken here from the work of Conkey (1996).

Figure 1: Modelling a month of moon phases [source: Conkey 1996: 341]

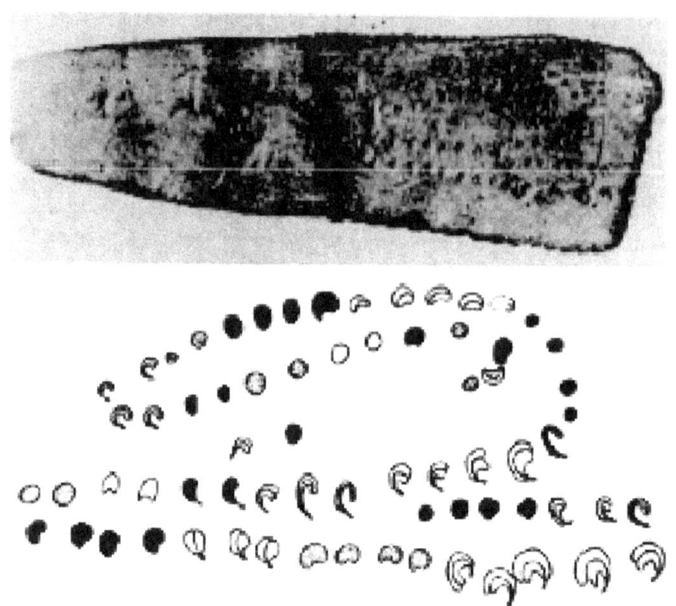

6.5 Cross cultural perspectives on HIKS

Astrology and astronomy shared the activity of systematizing the regularities of the night skies, and of diurnal changes more generally. In China, however, the activity was part of the mechanisms of state, with bureaux to ensure the power of the dynasty was not compromised by celestial events, including eclipses, comets and other such hazards, which might be taken as portents that the Emperor had lost the 'mandate of heaven'. By contrast, Greek astronomy was based around the theories of entrepreneurial masters, each competing for students and for kudos. In fact, Lloyd's depiction of the latter situation adheres closely to Bernstein's account of Horizontal Knowledge Structure, as so many Ls competing in today's social sciences!

The context of Greek learning (which dominated around the Mediterranean, even under the millennium of Roman domination) produced a diversity of competing theories, typically associated with a leading figure, but with less depth of data upon which to make predictions (see, for example, the comparisons brought out by Lloyd (2002: Ch. 2: Modalities of Prediction), while the statecraft of Chinese astrology, with anonymous public servants, produced sustained records. Greek theorists were more focussed on modelling physical relations, while the Chinese and Babylonian traditions (truly 'vertical' in their columnar records of celestial events and, therefore, of assistance to current practitioners of astronomy) seem to have been content to leave a break in the numerical records – a 'zig-zag' – rather than create an extravagant explanation (Lloyd 2002: ch 2). One could regard this as evidence for the fact that prediction was seen as more important than explanation in the institution-based astronomies of Babylon (based in the temple) and China (one form of imperial bureau), and prediction was, in considering the heavens at least, more achievable than any explanatory model.

It is useful to reflect on contemporary sciences and their potential for prediction. Social and human sciences can produce broad, rational explanations, even with strong predictions at a statistical scale – that is at the scale of a community or population. But such predictions are seen as having little reliability in relation to any single case. We might suggest in this regard that the difference is not well described by the idea of 'strong vs weak grammars' with its inherent evaluation. The differences appear to depend more on narrowing the object of enquiry and limiting complexity (typically by excluding the social mind). In the 20th century, the paradigm of HIKS, atomic physics, has had to settle for statistical, rather than instantial, predictions.

6.6 From the sensible to the heuristic

Astronomy and its history also demonstrate how much our notions of science begin in a knowledge of that which is available to the senses. This strong dependency on sensory report is illustrated by the impact of the telescope, a tool enhanced by Galileo (Henry 2008: 28ff). When Galileo can show us that the moons of Jupiter actually move around Jupiter, and not 'around' the earth, then 'natural philosophy' – what today we call 'natural science' – grows in hierarchical fashion. By increasing the power of the senses, humans have developed knowledge that must be integrated in any plausible account of nature. Again to avoid anachronism, the concept of nature itself has to be construed, typically, within a belief in supernatural design.

The new power of a mathematical language helps us to see today how the lines of 'progress' in science – those aspects, which, looking back today, we regard as central to hierarchical knowledge structures – were obscured by alternative theories, metaphysical prejudices, and the 'common sense' of the era in which they were still without an abstract formulation. The comparison between Aristotle's dynamics and the formulations of Newton (cited in Toulmin 1961: 51ff.) bring out just how incommensurable concepts can be across eras in what putatively is the same subject. Mathematical tools, essential to the arguments of Copernicus, Galileo, and then Kepler, were losing a direct connection with arguments from the senses. Concepts like mass, velocity, acceleration, force, came to be defined in terms of unreal, idealized conditions, far from sensuous experience, and intelligible only to those who could forsake common speech for precise formulas. This was in complete contrast with Aristotle's pragmatic science, which elaborated on the most typical naturally occurring cases (for example, how we might understand the forces involved in a horse pulling on a cart: Toulmin 1961). Even more abstract concepts – derived from measurements but of a more heuristic character, for example, dealing with change, not just with magnitude – characterized science from the 17th century. Newton, born in 1642, the year of Galileo's death, produced the theory of fluxions (known as 'calculus' in the parallel work of Leibniz) with strange fictions like 'infinitesimal' and 'limit'. Bishop Berkeley skilfully lampooned such notions as absurd, and less credible than anything in 'Divinity' (see Kline 1953: 283). Again, the debate around this paradigm of scientific development – the calculus – played out for 200 years, much like the haggling between theorists that Bernstein emphasizes in depicting the horizontal knowledge structure. It was not till 1821 that the sense and nonsense of calculus was clarified (by Cauchy in *Cours d'Analyse*), although the 'comedy of errors' did not even then come to a simple stop (Kline 1953: 268).

While HIKS may be marked by unifications of disparate branches of knowledge (viz. Schrodinger's application of atomic physics to biology in 1949), one needs to consider tendencies towards 'divisio': the rhetorical term for the breaking down of issues into separate theses (cf. 'divisibility', section 4.3.2). The spiritual significance of number, so characteristic of the view of the Pythagoreans, especially in the development of musical theory, reminds one of the common origins of what are today separate disciplines. Number, music, and the theory of human emotions were all part of the Greek enquiry into measure – the theory of musical modes, patterns corresponding to particular human emotions, were still influencing poets as late as Milton and Pope.[48]

Metaphysical and aesthetic assumptions can also mislead thought (Hallyn 1990), as in the belief that planetary orbits would have to be circular (i.e. given the assumed perfection of circles and spheres). Kepler removed this prejudice for the heavens. Elliptical orbits fitted the mathematical facts and the demands for prediction (Henry 2008: 28). This swept away the intricacy of cycles and epicycles in the Ptolemaic geocentric theory, which astonishes us today for its physical implausibility, and for the fact that it dominated for a whole millennium.

One needs to reiterate that the dominant world views of those figures we most associate with HIKS – e.g. Newton; Déscartes; right up to even Darwin – were fundamentally religious (even fundamentalist, by today's standards). Science and mathematics were means to the revelation of God's design in nature. Newton's writings in this regard are as copious as his 'scientific' writings. Newton did not make a boundary, a strong classification, in the way we do looking back at the value of his scientific work: in fact, it is a shock to see how many of Newton's statements give priority to his 'theological' work that today we could only rate as eccentric or bizarre (Kline 1953: 297). From a similar perspective, we can see that Déscartes' view of self-consciousness – its status as a given of being human, along with the dualism which such self-consciousness has been taken to imply – are not transferable to contemporary cognitive science and linguistics. The concepts today involve a completely different theoretical 'valeur' (in the relational perspective highlighted by Saussure's lectures 1906–13). As Toulmin argued (1972), Déscartes' views were maintained under the assumption that God had recently created the cosmos, and that humans were an even more recent conception of God's design for the world. Without the extended time of evolutionary theory (which Darwin appreciated from the geological work of Lyell), it is hard, perhaps, not to be a mind/body dualist! In view of this, invoking Déscartes' philosophy, for instance in the way that Chomsky has done (cf., Cartesian Linguistics), presents a serious danger of both misrepresenting the thinking of the past and of infantilizing the complexity of a post-evolutionary view of brains and language (cf. Toulmin 1972: 28).

6.8 Hierarchical Knowledge Structures as state and as process

The process by which human conjectures and intuitions are built up to become known as HIKS is pretty *non-linear*: there is little power of prediction between the initial conditions and the ultimate outcome of the historical process. This is despite the fact that we can experience a strong teleological impression of causal linearity, or historical 'logic', when we are looking back over those conjectures that were taken up as useful, and which were ultimately elaborated with the passing of millennia of human culture. But such an impression is an illusion, a function of assuming that the correct ideas ('ours') have survived.

The teleological impression belies the reality of developments within cultures and the diversity of contexts across cultures. Lloyd (2002: 44) warns against such teleological interpretations even with respect to the history of mathematics. The self evidence of scientific 'truths' is an index of our ignorance of the conditions of living and the strengths of thinking in cultures before our own. As cited above, Toulmin (1961: 50-61) gives a detailed case of such false historicism by comparing the Aristotelian 'paradigm' of a horse and cart, to the Newtonian account of dynamics (2,000 years later). These two treatments of putatively the same problems are, in fact, semantic inversions of each other. They are very different forms of discourse. Aristotle elaborates on concrete cases from quotidian experience; Newton's language is based on abstract and unreal conditions, by which the actual is supposedly explained! Aristotle could hardly be impressed by the commonsense of a 'body moving at uniform speed in a Euclidean straight line', free from all forces, 'even its own weight'. The 'intelligible' and virtual has become more crucial than the 'familiar' natural wisdom of observation (Toulmin 1961: 61). Nevertheless, in defence of Bernstein's emphasis on the formation of HIKS, it must be clearly stated that both these very different strategies for developing knowledge, ultimately, involve some sort of check against the world, and evidence from what is 'sensible'

There is a theoretical locus here then for Bernstein's contrast between HIKS and HOKS, but the analysis must be itself more rigorous in pursuing the threads of discourse which provided the opportunities for development in each actual case, and the theory must be finer grained in noting how, across the spectrum of topics in physics (for instance), conditions of the HIKS and HOKS can all apply in close proximity. Some topics within physics are more soluble or tractable, depending on tools and experimental practicalities. For example, in 1927, de Broglie offered a modification to quantum theory which was castigated by Heisenberg and Pauli as 'ideological' and metaphysical (Whitaker 2006: 256 and 248). A related proposal was taken up as a thought experiment by Einstein (in the EPR experiment) and in later work by Bohm (for which Bohm was accused of being a 'philosopher'!). In the 1980s the French physicist Aspect and his team showed that the thought experiment could be conducted (with the results not favouring Einstein's views). John Bell, a leading researcher with C.E.R.N., has shown that this line of enquiry needs to be kept open for future experiments, in particular because it may limit the need to appeal to the role of the observer. What is to one researcher 'philosophy' or 'ideology' becomes tractable experimental physics to another researcher or to researchers in another era.

While Bernstein makes a reference to this kind of progression – namely, when a debate between opposed theories in a HIKS evolves into experiments with empirical choices (1999: 163) – more might be made of the indeterminacies and anomalies that characterize physical theory, in particular in the areas of a supposedly established, 'standard' theory like Quantum Mechanics (=QM). With the purported 'strong grammar' of QM, which has received support from so many decades of successful predictions, the ongoing contentions around the 'meaning' of the theory create a quandary. The contentiousness of interpretation suggests there is a deeper complexity about the HIKS – HOKS opposition, ie. deeper than any general theory has yet adumbrated. Such complexity may be best pursued by a closer examination of the specific textual bases for hierarchical knowledge in particular lines of epistemological enquiry. As appeals to the senses in science are replaced by totally abstract modelling, no generalizing theory can encompass the vectors of semantic evolution involved.

6.9 HIKS and HOKS: science through human interactions

Evidence from specific scientific debates in physics suggests that the discourses around the human interactions involved were like other forms of social disputation – personalized (a form of localization); requiring tacit understanding; settled by polemic and rhetoric rather than by epistemological subtlety; and often directed by beliefs to which one is committed (ideologically) rather than to where the problem might be leading. This is hardly surprising; but it makes the bifurcation between discourse and knowledge structure very difficult to defend in any categorical way. The hierarchical character of physics is relative to the symbolic resources that are integrated to achieve its version of nature, as well as by the fact that the subject has successfully divided up nature into a series of 'segmented regions' (ironically), thus insulating the objects of enquiry in sub-fields which limit challenges that would come from dealing with a fuller range of human experience. Some of these segments produce tractable questions with soluble problems, thus promoting the profile of HIKS. But, as suggested above, others generate 'romantic' ideas that are not forced upon the scientist by experimental facts, but rather by metaphysical 'choice' (see Whitaker 2006: 201 and 256 for Bell's rebuff to uses of 'the mind of the observer' over determinism).

The separation of discourse and knowledge structures distorts the crucial dependence of knowledge on the particularities of semiotic/linguistic resources, and diminishes the role of interpersonal meaning in the directions that cultural history has taken. Bernstein raises the first of these problems – the potential for distortion in separating knowledge and discourse (1999: 166) – but he does not elaborate on this issue in his essay. Specific interpersonal factors influenced the standardization of Quantum Theory in the Copenhagen Interpretation (e.g., see Whitaker 2006 and Cassidy 1992: eg. 214-215 for the vituperation between Heisenberg and Schrodinger over the visualizability of science). The quarrels between the titans of physics, Einstein and Bohr, are astonishing for their 'horizontal discourse appearance' – it is as if the proponents of this hierarchical knowledge were living in two very different semantic frameworks when it came to the limits of the knowable in science.

When we read sciences backwards, often from the versions of key participants in the fashion of apologia, it is all too easy to miss the complexity of the linguistic or semiotic imbroglio which produced the 'science'. For example, the Roman church is lambasted for its opposition to the new science of Copernicus *et al.* concerning the stars and planetary orbits. But the crucial role of the church in the development of 'speaking naturally' (an option open to church scholars, in contrast to 'speaking theologically') was the main reason that scientific development was sustained at all in the West, and that it 'flowered' in the 12th century and in the Renaissance. Galileo's blunders with Pope Urban were a disaster for the future discourses of learning, since Urban had been well inclined to Galileo's work (cf. Grant 1996 and 2007). To take another case of historical mythologizing: the discoverer of genetic principles, Gregor Mendel, was not an isolated researcher in the simplistic way his life and experiments are typically presented, but an active researcher into animal and agrarian sciences within a network of monasteries committed to such research, somewhat like university centres today (Lewontin 2000: Ch. 3). As Toulmin notes, the history of science has suffered for too long from fables about 'George Washingtons cutting down their father's cherry tree' (1961: 48).

Niels Bohr summarized the role of physics with respect to the new forms of epistemology confronting atomic physics and the science of matter. He gave particular emphasis to the 'complementarities' which occur when the instrument of enquiry determines the nature, and limit, of what can be known:

> We are not dealing here with more or less vague analogies, but with an investigation of the conditions for the proper use of our conceptual means of expression. Such considerations not only aim at making us familiar with the novel situation in physical science, but might on account of the comparatively simple character of atomic problems be helpful in clarifying the conditions for objective description in wider fields (Bohr 1961: 2).

When semiotics is both an instrument of enquiry *and*, inevitably, a crucial dimension of the object of enquiry, we have a complexity of high degree. This is the kind of challenge Bernstein has taken up with HIKS. It is the form of complexity in which he first initiated theory in the past – over the consequences of codes/coding orientation. It is crucial to set out the 'complementarity' at issue so that the roles of language in the enquiry and as object of enquiry are made visible. Halliday's schema, from matter to meaning, prepares us for the levels of complexity that must be encompassed by theories that try to tease apart 'discourse' and 'knowledge'.

The development of a science of linguistics, as Halliday has argued (e.g. 1994b [2003]: 412) requires that we distinguish the phenomenal realms of matter, life, society and meaning; that we recognize the geometric increase in complexity with each realm; and that we accommodate to the systemic conditions that also distinguish each realm. The latter point, for instance, includes the difference between the physical realm, with its causal systems and linear equations concerning matter, and the social and semiotic realms (of culture and meaning) in which one has to analyse realizational systems. These are 'non-linear' and inextricable from the conditions of living which produced them. As Halliday's systemic functional approach demonstrates, the degree of complexity in semiosis can be 'managed' in order to achieve clarification of specific kinds: e.g. concerning the textual drift in scientific discourse; the changes over time in a grammatical system; the uniqueness of an author's strategy in literary foregrounding (albeit a strategy based on conventional linguistic patterns).

From this brief interregnum on the history of science, it seems reasonable to suggest that all sciences have moved towards such 'management of complexity' rather than to any ideal of total resolution of enquiry. As nature is renewed in its complexity, as life and society and meaning emerge from material complexity, the study of the higher order systems must integrate the complexity (the ensemble conditions) of all the systems below, and find in that complexity the relations peculiar to its own extension of the natural order. Furthermore, such systemic interrogation can only come from above, from semiotic tools. Even the simplest of material phenomena are not, then, self-evident but must be rendered semiotically.

We have to take seriously the possibility that physics and semiotics, for example, suggest that the HIKS–HOKS distinction is not inherent in forms of knowing (see also Jakobson 1973). The distinction may be more dependent on the politics of funding and warfare, and on some strategies of convenient segmentation (simplification) of enquiry in the tradition of physics; this is to say 'convenient' in relation to the resources of a specific community in a specific cultural moment. HIKS may depend on strategic limitations of enquiry – method that does not make its own explanatory limitations explicit.

The tools of natural sciences can be applied in semiotics, as long as they are applied to genuinely semiotic phenomena, or dimensions of such meaningful action. Such tools can be brought to bear not only on regularities of semantic behaviour, but also on how such regularities are distributed socially. Bernstein's semantic insights can be argued through the 'strong grammars' of method in the natural sciences; and it is from this perspective that Hasan's own investigations of Bernstein's theory (Hasan 2009b) can be evaluated.

To this end, and in considering the usefulness of the HIKS–HOKS contrast, it is helpful to consider the discussion of 'human diversity' by the leading variationist in biological sciences – Richard Lewontin (1995). The variation in living things is brought to a new level of subtlety by Lewontin's demonstrations of the role of environmental opportunity (and chance) in activating biological potential. Yet this recognition of the significance of context is just the kind of complexity so much associated with horizontal knowledge structures, namely, those in which the specifics of an organism's history will not license abstractions which neutralize contextual variables (hence Lewontin (2000): 'The **Triple** Helix. Gene, organism and environment').

A strong classification separating HIKS and HOKS may be misleading in the interpretation of the future development of knowledge. We can reflect here on 'how we construe...causation' and 'non-local' influences in quantum physics. It shows the more equivocal side of the HIKS 'strong grammar' and 'precise' representations (Dewitt: 2004: eg. 298 and 305): 'we can, at last, give a precise answer... [to the nature of this influence: Eds]...no one has the foggiest idea'.

While Bernstein's insights on HIKS and HOKS and on vertical discourse provide us with important probes of the evolution of human knowledge, a closer contact with the historical actualities of the development of Western science suggests that the kinds of contrast for which Bernstein is arguing do not get sufficient support from the historical details. The cost of the high level of abstraction may be itself too high to defend. The growth of knowledge is a more heterogeneous phenomenon than Bernstein's global view presents. At the same time, the theory allows us to have debates that would be difficult to conceive of without some such point of departure.

7 'The essay' and 'the work'

In opening his paper, Bernstein positions its enterprise by relating its origin to the entire history of the development of 'the work'. Itemizing the concerns and achievements of his theory particularly in the sphere of human learning and teaching, he points to one lack: that within this theoretical framework 'no analysis of the discourses subject to pedagogic transformation' (157) had been conducted. The 'essay' was perhaps a first step towards throwing open issues in this domain. Thus at this early point there exists a tacit assumption that the shortly to be revealed varieties of discourse will bear an important relation to Bernstein's earlier work, especially that concerned with pedagogy. And to the extent that the work he did on the nature of codes and coding orientations bears any relation to his work on pedagogy, the former too may be seen as implicated. There seems to exist some licence for inferring continuity of theoretical orientation between the essay and the work as a whole.

As we feared, for us time and space are now already over-stretched. The reader will notice repeated reference to earlier work by Bernstein offered as a source to which one might go for elaboration, clarification, and for a deepening of the issues contained here. This is indicative of the fact that the Bernstein oeuvre is not just a series of so many different topics: 'the work' is all of one piece – all concerned with the Sociology of Codes, Control and Consciousness; from local to official pedagogy, from the working of horizontal to vertical discourse, the concern is with how a biological organism becomes a particular kind of social subject, and why.

The fact that a mere 16 page article by Bernstein has led us to engage in a discussion of this length is perhaps indicative of the importance we attach to the work and the essay. However the details of how the essay on forms of knowledge and forms of discourse contribute to Bernstein's sociology of pedagogy and to his earlier work – bringing them together not as a collection but as an integrated explanatory system – must await another occasion.

Notes

1 This paper has been co-authored with David Butt. I thank him for permission to include it here. We are grateful to Karl Maton for his very helpful comments on the first part of this paper.

2 I am thinking here of such scholars as Wittgenstein, Popper, Lakatos, Medawar, Bourdieu, Habermas, Giddens and of course Bernstein himself.

3 We are aware that some colleagues distance the work on pedagogy from the earlier work on code theory; in our view instead of representing in his sociology the poignant post-modernist fragmentation of the social universe, Bernstein is an architect of a sociological theory whose internal lines of cohesion are simply breathtaking in their reach: after all he is, to our knowledge, the most eloquent and dispassionate analyst of the routes by which our so-called egalitarian system of education so successfully maintains the escalating non-egalitarian (global) society we inhabit.

4 We are indebted, nonetheless, to the work of colleagues who have reported in Sadovnik (1995), Christie (1999), Bernstein (2000), Morais, Neves, Davies and Daniels (2001), Muller, Davies and Morais (2004), Moore, Arnot, Beck and Daniels (2006), Christie and Martin (2007), and in particular to Maton (2008, 2009).

5 It is important to add that a good deal of work is continuing particularly around topics arising from the discussion of Bernstein's view on knowledge as is evident from the work cited above (note 4). So the concepts in this paper will not languish in Bernstein's absence, but it is one thing for others to comment on Bernstein and it is quite another for Bernstein to revisit his own earlier writings. The truth of this assertion is evident to any keen reader of Bernstein.

6 And sometimes fail to interpret simply because we do not possess the requisite resources for unpacking the traditions which support the sociological discourses.

7 We are referring here specifically to chapter 8 of *Pedagogy, Symbolic Control and Identity: Theory, Research, Critique*, which reproduces Bernstein 1999 with minor changes.

8 We are aware that some readers of Bernstein think of his later work concerning pedagogy as moving away from the code theory: we believe this reading is hasty and cannot be supported by Bernstein's own writings when examined with care.

9 The obvious exception to this generalization are mannerisms such as 'twitching', 'winking' and other body gestures which are potential signals for meanings but as mannerism they are just bodily acts neither 'intended' nor meaningful.

10 We use 'language' unashamedly to refer to language as is being read now – i.e. a calibrated unity of meaning, wording and sound. Other semiotic systems whether primary such as gesture, voice quality or secondary i.e., derivative, such as images, graphs etc will not concern us here, but if it does, the Thing 'language' will be used with a Qualifier as in *language of gesture*.

11 And it is relevant to add here that modern research conducted by many neurologists has come to accept the role of experience in the formation of human consciousness – a line of argument that brings language and consciousness together (for some discussion chapter 2 included here).

12 Hasan has suggested that some variety of bodily action function as the expression stratum for the elements of semiotic systems which are primary, while the secondary semiotic systems use as their expression resources that depend on some mediating instrumentality.

13 Where only numbers appear in parentheses, e.g., '(158)' here, they refer to page number(s) in Bernstein 2000.

14 What Bernstein is calling segmental knowledge has also been described sometimes as 'everyday knowledge', or as 'local knowledge' (Geertz 1973, 2000), or as 'common sense knowledge' (Bernstein 1971a). No doubt by calling it segmental knowledge, Bernstein most probably intended to draw attention to some aspect in which his segmental knowledge differs from the others. As outsiders we are unable to see what this difference might be; or what discourse in sociology will draw attention to the significance of these different labels, which seem to refer to the same thing.

15 It is notable that typically with reference to the horizontal knowledge structures, Bernstein avoids the use of the word theory, preferring 'language' instead. Discussion in section 5.4-5.4.3).

16 It is as if Bernstein is reluctant to assign these the status of theory: each knowledge structure in a horizontal knowledge structure is said to 'be' a Language, not a theory.

17 For collection/integration codes see Bernstein 1975b, 1990.

18 The situation is far from easy: for example, generative linguistics has the following varieties in succession: classical, standard, principles and parameters, and no doubt some others. Where does the counting begin, where does it end?

19 When in an actual extract enclosed in inverted commas, some material is inserted in square brackets, that material is introduced by the authors in order to clarify their understanding of the original comment.
20 Bernstein's work has in one way or another always been concerned with Codes, Control and Consciousness: these three distinctive C-concepts are fundamental to both the problem he isolates as the basic question of sociology and to his contribution to the analysis of its central elements. I understand Maton's Legitimation Code Theory (e.g., 2009) operates within the larger domain identified by Bernstein as the basic concern of 'classical Sociology'.
21 Note again that the term 'field' as in 'the field of discourse' differs in its reference from the term field as used in Bernstein (1999: 164-169).
22 Originally Halliday *et al.* (1964) called this 'dimension' the STYLE OF DISCOURSE. Because the term 'style' is often used to refer to the 'manner' i.e., the 'how' of language use, which is supposed to bear no relevance to its 'content', i.e., the 'what', Michael Gregory (1967) suggested the term 'tenor' would be better instead of style. This suggestion was accepted.
23 Exception should be made of the early Bernstein (1971c, 1975c) writings as here with focus on CODING ORIENTATION, human relationships have always acquired a prominent role.
24 A potential is best described paradigmatically as system networks; this has been well demonstrated for the level of lexicogrammar: witness, for example, the many system networks pertaining to the clause (Halliday and Matthiessen 2004). In fact, in the study of context, many scholars have been attempting paradigmatic descriptions of each of these parameters following Hasan (e.g., 1999b and earlier circulated versions) and Butt 2004 mimeo.
25 As this term is used in Bernstein 1999.
26 There could also be many linguistic interactions co-occurring in the same spatio-temporally identified location, e.g., a cocktail party, a railway carriage, and so on; but by definition the context of discourse for each specific linguistic interaction would be different (Hasan 1985c).
27 Imagine that you are discussing with a colleague the important concept of 'recontextualization' while your child is playing nearby. The latter part of the situation is an element of the MSS of the ongoing discussion which is your text in the making, and should the child suddenly make a din with some toy or other, there could be an interrupting text such as: 'Timmy, could you please go play in the other room; we are just trying to work here'. As an analyst of the process of language you have many choices in this situation: you could ignore the interruption as of no consequence, or regard it as an un-analysable segment due to the synoptic nature of text, or treat it as 'an interrupting text' that construes an element of the wider situation but does not directly form part of the relevant context of the main text which is concerned with 'informal discussion of recontextualization with a friend'. We suggest the last is the best choice, which requires the recognition of the concept of MSS. For such actual examples see Hasan 1999b; Cloran 1994, 1999a, 1999b.
28 For example, while listening to a recording of mother-child interaction when in the middle of reading a picture book to the child, the mother says 'don't torment pussy; she doesn't like her tail pulled' we learn that in the material

situation setting of that discourse there was a cat present, and that an action other than that of listening to the story was also going on.

29 What we mean by immediate material situation is the situation as perceived from the spatio-temporal location where the interaction is occurring.

30 It is not being said that there will be some specific item(s) referring to the speaker, but that his/her identity as a social being will be at least partially revealed by the 'textual attitudes'.

31 On the definition of the term 'message' see Hasan 1999b, 2009b; Cloran 1994, Williams 1995. In this sense 'message' is not the same as in Halliday 1985, 1994a, where it is used as labelling a grammatical category.

32 By saying this, we mean that it has not been explicated by placement within the structure of an articulated theory whose aim is to enable a viable description of the selected object of enquiry.

33 The reference is to the body of researches in Hasan 2009b (also accompanying CD).

34 The research conducted by Cloran (1994) and Williams (1994) in similar areas was equally as impressive, particularly considering that the scope of their research had to be limited by the procedural demands of their doctoral dissertations.

35 Though we recognize the fact that the further the history of the philogenesis of say physics, mathematics etc are pushed, the less easy it is to know 'which particular individual did what with whom'.

36 The distinction we are foregrounding here echoes that made by Halliday between 'evolved' and 'designed' institutions, though it differs from the latter in important ways without contradicting it.

37 This may well be one of the measure of the strength of an L when compared with other Ls devised for the same discipline. We assume that in hierarchical knowledge structures theories will move towards a maximally explicit formulation of all critical relations between components of the phenomenon they investigate.

38 In fact, many colleagues wondered why the team was spending so much time and energy on it; to them too it seemed the data had nothing special in it!

39 There certainly does occur conflict in the agenda set by the mother and the child – when to play in the bath with what toys, how to do so, how to eat, what to eat, and so on – but whatever the agenda and whatever the outcome, it always has some significance for the child. The thing to be learned 'has a place in the scheme of things'.

40 The non-technical paraphrase of the 'forms of' an object is its 'variety' /'shape' as also in Bernstein's use of 'forms of consciousness'. When the expression is applied to linguistically created phenomena it is taken to mean 'structure' as in the form of the novel/sonnet/lyric' or as 'expression', as in the Hjelmslevian cycle of content and expression (Hjelmslev 1961; Halliday 1992a; Hasan 1995a). It is possible that the phrase has some other meaning in sociology, but if so, we have not come across it.

41 Sound/aural images are the initial signalling device for lexicogrammatically formed meanings; the written/visual images are derived from these.

42 An excellent source of information with helpful references for every aspect of

the theory is Matthiessen (2007); the volumes of Halliday's Collected Works are a rich source of details of the theory. The brief account on which we draw here is found in Hasan (1995a, 1996a, 2010).

43 Thanks to the debate between Martin (1985, 1992) and Hasan (1995a), research on the nature of context itself has continued (Hasan 1980, 1999b; Butt 2005; Butt and Wegener 2007; and most outstandingly Cloran 1994); as a result, the relations of language and context appear to be clearer now than they were some four decades ago.

44 And let us not beat around the bush but say clearly that this communal segment contains disadvantaged exploited people with a low level of education typically at a fairly dominated level of occupation for whom life is highly likely to bring greater satisfaction by being like others in their group, than by 'doing your own things' unlike the individuated individuals of the exploiting groups. There is far less prejudice in accepting that such communal segments do exist than there is in letting them have recognition as invisible beings featuring as percentages in statistics about levels of affluence published every few years by all democratic progressive countries, with the reports quite clearly showing the gap between the two segments increasing at each such survey.

45 This problem is less severe for HIKS and it would be useful some time to ask why that should be so. We believe the reason does not lie simply in the serial nature of the Ls used in any one discipline.

46 For an interesting discussion of some cases, visit Douglas (1975).

47 Recently there was a demonstration outside Federal Parliament House in Canberra in protest against the unjust wage system according to which, even today, in many professions women are paid substantially lower wages for exactly the same work.

48 The Pythagoreans produced the first case in which human experience of qualities (in this case, harmony) were explained by natural quanta – the proportional lengths of strings.

II

Language and Literacy

5 Literacy, everyday talk and society[1] [1996]

1 Introduction

One problem with the word 'literacy' is that it is semantically saturated: in the long history of education, it has not simply meant different things to different generations, but also different things to different persons in the same generation (Luke 1988). This might be read as a sign that in the somewhat fading academic jargon of yesterday, the term is ripe for deconstruction. My paper is an attempt to do just that by enquiring into the many meanings of 'literacy' but not simply as an exercise in empty semanticization: I believe the meanings assigned to literacy are significant for what they imply. So for each interpretation it should be possible to ask: if this interpretation of literacy is accepted what would this imply about the pupils and the teachers engaged in its processes? What about the pedagogic practices relevant to the achievement of its goals? And what conceptions of learning and knowledge would this interpretation presuppose? Sociologists of education (e.g., Bernstein 1975b, 1986, 1987, 1990; Bourdieu and Passeron 1977) have argued that a close relationship exists between a society's pedagogic institutions and the principles underlying its social structure. Their theories highlight the logic following which today's pedagogic institutions functioning as the powerful arm of the state tend also to be the prime site for the reproduction and (closely watched) production of knowledge. This chapter will draw attention to similar concerns with specific reference to literacy pedagogy as perhaps the most crucial pedagogic action in today's world. Approaching literacy this way furnishes a much wider context for the literacy debate which has often appeared to be concerned only with formulating THE valid definition of literacy, with rival definitions typically tending to be couched in terms of the goals of literacy. But if the definition of literacy necessarily implicates wider social processes then the affirmation of some definition – some goal(s) – represents not a conclusion, but a beginning. The goals of literacy can hardly have a value in and of themselves: they need to be seen in the context of the wider social environment which is at once the enabling condition and the enabled product of literacy pedagogy. The multiplicity of meanings ascribed to literacy suggests that it is a multi-faceted process embracing phenomena of different kinds; the controversies raging today around literacy tend to assume that only one facet is important; the others can be safely ignored. I will suggest that this view is open to question: to understand literacy is to understand how the various facets enter into the formation of that complex whole which we call literacy.

2 Literacy: an initial exploration

The referential range of literacy is well captured by The Macquarie Dictionary which glosses it as 'the state of being literate; possession of education', claiming also that being literate is 'being able to read and write, having education'. These formulations suggest continua: being able to read/write or having education is not a simple 'yes/no' affair. At the more advanced end of the continuum is, for example, Marx, able to 'read' Hegel and to write *Das Kaiptal*, while nearer the initiate end is the 'literate' person so labelled in some countries for the purposes of literacy census on the ground of merely being able to recognize her/his name in some script. One might protest that a person just able to recognize her name is neither literate nor educated. But in making this protest, one is implicitly recommending a specific point on the continuum as the true referent of the terms, identifying the norm for being judged literate and educated. It is reasonable to ask: who ratifies the validity of this norm? Where do they derive their legitimacy from?

Quite obviously any standard of literacy is ultimately evaluative: it is a covert demand to accept a certain view point; and this inevitably raises questions about the basis of its own validity. On the other hand, this act of evaluation is more or less thrust on us: where the referential space is as elastic as with literacy, a preference for some point or other on the continuum is unavoidable. So it seems apposite to ask whether the literacy of Marx and that of the initiate are the same kind of social and cognitive facts, whether a preference for the kind of literacy demonstrated by Marx is just a matter of social prejudice, simply pandering to dominant interests of the elite. If not, what makes the two different?

An important step toward answering these questions may be taken by treating the referential indeterminacy of the term literacy as a positive starting point: literacy is not the name of some fixed state; it refers to a developmental process. This implies, in turn, that its nature can be known effectively through the practices its development enables. If literacy is an ongoing process whose present transforms into its future stages, then each of its stages should be identifiable by reference to some distinction in practices that the process of literacy at that stage enables. Let us ask then what practice is specific to the initial stage – to the very onset of literacy?

2.1 Defining the onset of literacy

Dictionaries are agreed on reading/writing as the *sine qua non* of literacy, but reading/writing are specific and complex practices; they cannot be taken as the onset of literacy itself: underlying these more complex activities there must be a simpler less specific ability. I suggest that this less specific ability is *the grasp of the principle of representation*. This ability consists in relating two qualitatively different types of phenomenon – an expression and a content – to each other so that the significance of one is understood in terms of the other. So becoming literate in the sense of being able to read/write presupposes the ability to 'see' a phenomenon as 'standing for' something other than itself; in fact the ability to relate expression and content in this way is a necessary condition for using any semiotic system whatever. From this point of view, the fundamental attribute for the onset of literacy is the ability to engage in acts of meaning: to be an initiate in literacy is to be able to make sense of a sign.

Defining the onset of literacy as the ability to make sense construes it as a variety of semiotic praxis: literate acts are acts of semiosis. This conceptualization of the basic nature of literacy is significant on several counts. First, it emphasizes the commonalities between different classes of sign, e.g., a gesture, a symptom, a picture, a painting, a sonnet, and so on. One thing these have in common is their nature as signs: as signs, their coming into being is a licence to their being interpreted while the fact that they are capable of being interpreted makes them signs. Secondly, interpretation is at once both formally and socially grounded. It is formally grounded in that a sign comes to be that sign, having that interpretation, by virtue of its relation to other signs in the system; it is socially grounded because the meaning of a sign becomes tangible for the user in the context of his/her life-situations; in other words, the relations of one sign to other signs have to be perceived as such and so by interpreters who are by definition socially positioned. Third – and related to the last point – if the interpretation of a sign relies on the user's experience of how it functions in her/his life-situations, and if even in the same community different persons' life-situations differ, it follows that their variant experience of the sign's function in the living of life will contribute to the development of a disposition for variant interpretations of what might be called the same sign from some point of view. Finally, for most of us the experience of signing involves co-interpreting signs from a number of distinct sign systems: for instance the picture of the skull and cross-bones with the legend ‘Danger! High Voltage!’ combines conventionalized pictorial and linguistic signs to create a single semiotic whole.[2] The computer screen often presents a configuration of the pictorial and the verbal. Sign interpretation is thus entirely context sensitive – it is sensitive to the context of its own system; to the users’ context of social situations; and it is sensitive to other simultaneously operating sign systems.

If these characteristics apply to all sign systems alike, then clearly the onset of literacy bears no special relation to reading/writing which are specifically language-based practices. There are other semiotic systems than just language; and they are just as amenable to interpretation. This might tempt one to conclude that the term literacy should be de-coupled from the specific semiotic system of language, that it should be construed simply as the ability to make sense. In fact this view of literacy already exists in pedagogic discourse where many scholars prefer to talk about ‘literacies’. The use of the plural underlines the assumption that literacy, at least in one of its senses,[3] consists in making sense of anything that can be/is taken as expression. There is more than a hint in the literature that it is conservative to define literacy as simply making sense of linguistic signs, as most dictionaries do; that the practice unjustifiably ‘privileges’ language; and that it is desirable – progressive? egalitarian? – to give literacy a definition that is neutral to the semiotic character of what is being interpreted. How justified are these positions?

Before we begin to answer this question, it is best to be clear that the views recounted above involve two related but somewhat different positions: (i) that the term literacy should be decoupled from any specific sign system whatever; and (ii) that literacy should be decoupled specifically from language. We will examine both these positions in turn.

2.2 Literacy as simply making sense

Typically definitions of literacy have been formulated in the context of pedagogic goals. From this point of view literacy as simply the ability to make sense raises some serious problems. For example, if this definition is accepted, then what pedagogic practices would be deemed relevant to the achievement of its goals? Indeed what precisely are these goals, and what would count as evidence for their successful achievement? What attributes would be implied as necessary to engage as teachers or pupils in the processes of developing such literacy? Attempts to answer these questions highlight the problems in conceptualizing literacy as simply concerned with sense-making without relating the process of sense-making to some specific semiotic system: it appears impossible to devise any pedagogic program around the notion. Literacy so defined is unteachable in any known or imaginable schooling context.

Part of the problem is of course that while for purposes of analysis one might dissociate the act of interpretation from that which is being interpreted, in actual practice this is about as impossible as 'languaging' without using grammar! Note also that there exists the term semiosis to refer to this analytically isolated process of interpretation, but the idea that there can actually occur any process of semiosis dissociated from any semiotic system(s) whatever is simply nonsense. The semantic structure underlying terms such as interpretation, making sense, semiosis etc. is inherently relational implying a duality; the terms refer to processes which relate two phenomena – the meaning and the expressions – to each other. One cannot just make sense; one must make sense of some type of sign. And since signs are sensitive to the context of their own system, a specific sign cannot be interpreted independently of the system to which it pertains. Literacy as the ability to make sense in dissociation from specific sign systems is thus an incoherent concept; interpretation has to be anchored in some signing modality or other. Hence the need for a modifier for example in expressions such as 'media literacy', 'map literacy', and so on.

This does not mean that we have to abandon our claim about the nature of the onset of literacy; we have already seen that to think of literacy as founded on the grasp of the principle of interpretation reveals the sign based nature of this process allowing us to deduce certain important characteristics of the process (cf. section 2.1 above). But to say that the onset of literacy consists in the grasp of the principle of representation is to simply claim that the process of literacy, whatever its specific evolving character, cannot proceed without this ability which is thus its necessary condition. By contrast, conceptualizing the entire gamut of the process of literacy as simply the ability to interpret is to be highly reductive, elevating the necessary condition to the status of a sufficient one! This is problematic not least because the nature of literacy is not static. And if literacy is an ongoing process, then its onset must be differentiated in some critical way from its more evolved stages. The conclusion seems inevitable that literacy cannot be taken to refer to just the ability to interpret; the term cannot be meaningfully decoupled from specific semiotic system(s). But does this necessarily mean the term should be coupled, as it has traditionally been, with language?

2.3 Literacy as language-based semiosis

My brief response to this question is to say that in the last resort the issue is purely terminological since the character and role of language in human life is such that irrespective of what name is given to its development, it will always have an important position in both pedagogic and everyday contexts: reference to it will need to be made. It is certainly true that language is only one among many semiotic systems and that in some important ways the various sign systems are alike (see section 2.1 above); this however does not mean that they are identical in all respects. For example they differ considerably in their potentiality. The potentiality of a sign system can be estimated by reference to how far the system impinges on the significant life-situations of a community; the more it does so, the higher its potentiality.

A sign system's having a higher potential is not inherently a *moral good* of any kind; however, borrowing the jargon of economics *à la* Bourdieu, one might claim that a sign system with a higher potential will have higher investment returns for those who can appropriate it; by the same token, those who cannot, face a liability. So it seems reasonable to argue that control over a sign system with a higher potential is relatively more important, and there is no virtue in treating all sign systems on an equal footing. Besides, no matter how successfully one mouths the jargon of revolutionary discourse, the issue is not that the various sign systems – or even the various disciplines – must be treated impartially; the issue worthy of revolution, if one is really keen on bringing one about, is rather that the users of the sign systems must enjoy an equal opportunity for appropriating higher potential sign systems! The term 'privileged' is often used in educational discourse almost as an emotion laden war cry. But to say that some semiotic system, e.g. language, is being privileged at the cost of others simply because it receives greater attention reveals a lack of analytic acuity; there is no attempt in such declarations to engage with the variability in the efficacy of the various sign systems in the life of the community. One can hardly deny that compared to most sign systems, language has an exceedingly high potential; its investment value is bound to be a good deal higher as by its very nature it will always impinge more on the production and maintenance of social life whether in its ESOTERIC or its MUNDANE manifestation. We need no deep theoretical insight to establish that neither of these manifestations of human social life can come about in the absence of language. Moreover, contrary to popular belief, the rise of multi-media has further strengthened the position of language as a hidden accomplice in many crucial social processes. The more reluctant we are to recognize overtly the importance of language, the more dangerous it can be as a tool of domination, both inside and outside pedagogic contexts.

These considerations suggest that if the term literacy is decoupled from language, then a language-based interpretive praxis will still resurface under some other name,[4] still holding an important position in the pedagogic context: language is just too powerful a means of control to be ignored or set aside in the prime controlling environment of pedagogic action. True that none of the above arguments necessarily force us to actually retain the traditional coupling of literacy with language, but it is also obvious that such a coupling will have to be recognized under some name or other; there seems to be no advantage whatever in re-semanticizing literacy and coining another term to take its place! In my view what would be helpful is to recognize the conventional reference of the term, without accepting conventional views about language. So this debate might be concluded by saying that literacy develops into a specific kind of semiosis; its specificity resides in the fact that this kind of semiosis uses language as its resource. While the onset of literacy is an undifferentiated stage which calls for a non-specific ability, entry into literacy processes has a relatively more specific character: it is this which differentiates the unqualified term literacy from such coined phrases as 'computer literacy', 'map literacy', and so on.[5] This perspective returns us to the traditional dictionary definition of literacy but with some significant differences: unlike the dictionary, we conceptualize the onset of literacy as an inherently variable semiotic process without restricting it to reading and writing.

3 Learning literacy, teaching literacy

Literacy in the sense of using language to mean has two simultaneous lines of development. In the first place, literacy in the sense of linguistic semiosis develops in the context of mundane or quotidian activities. The child's learning of language is taken for granted. Or to be more precise, the fact is treated as completely unremarkable that by a certain maturational stage every normal child will have begun to speak to those around it; what draws attention to itself is rather the absence of this semiotic development. Moving from the physiologically mediated, pre-semiotic behaviour (Trevarthen 1974b; Trevarthen and Hubley 1977) to the individual based protolinguistic stage, the child finally enters the language of its immediate community – its mother tongue (Halliday 1975a; Painter 1984). And although technically this completes what is known as 'language acquisition', the process of learning how to mean is in actual fact a life-long one. Ways of interacting with differentiated others, of engaging in varied processes continue to be learned in the course of the daily living of life for a long time to come. Obviously, this quotidian development of literacy in the sense of growing prowess in semiosis by language is shaped to a very large extent by the learners' life-situations, i.e., by their social positioning; and the mode of semiotic engagement in this line of development tends to be the spoken word. The learners' daily living of life might or might not also introduce them to the mysteries of the world of print. Increasingly, in the Western world at least all segments of the society are 'exposed' to print, and it seems reasonable to believe that in the natural line of literacy development most members of the society come to have at least a passive acquaintance with writing. However, not all members of the community will naturally develop 'command' of all forms of written and/or spoken discourse, and there will be definitely some segment which will not engage in meaning by writing along their natural line of literacy development.

Alongside this 'natural' quotidian line of literacy development is a second, exotic or specialized one: this is *the* literacy development as it is conceptualized in the official pedagogic contexts. And while in all societies known to us this line of literacy development both chronologically postdates and logically relies on the gains from the quotidian one, it is this second line of literacy development that is the more socially effective, the more politically salient, in the sense that those whose literacy development successfully follows this route are, all else being equal, also very likely to be socially advantageously located. This line of literacy development also happens to be the one that is much closer to the dictionary's view of literacy. It is here that the spoken mode must be less valued and writing must be elevated to a higher status.[6] The everyday modes of interaction are underrated; the specialized ones are given prestige.

There are some important points of contrast between these two lines of literacy development. In terms of Vygotsky's notion of 'intellectualization' (Vygotsky 1978; Hasan 1992c, 1995b), it is possible to recognize two levels of intellectualization of language: one, a speaking subject's self-conscious view of what language is like, and the other, an unself-conscious 'feel' for language. It is the latter that is in fact more important in giving shape and character to the speaking subject's actual semiotic practices, whereas the former is typically first produced in lay discourses *about* language. In the quotidian line of development, the unself-conscious feel for language is dialectically engaged with the speaking subject's social life, shaping and being shaped by it. In the exotic, i.e., specialized or pedagogic, line of development, it is the self-conscious view of language that has supremacy, which is to say the view of language here is not that by which we live as socio-semiotically active creatures, but rather one which is in many respects a counterfeit. Typically underlying this line of literacy development is a conception of language far removed from language as social semiotic practice; and typically the goals of exotic literacy development are consciously set, while in the quotidian line of development there is hardly any awareness of goals: there is simply social action, successful or otherwise. Further, both the view of language and the consciously designed goals for pedagogic literacy development derive from needs that are not necessarily felt to be needs by all the learning subjects, whereas logically in the quotidian line of development this disjunction just cannot occur. Finally, the goals set for the pedagogic literacy development are objectively better suited for, and familiar to, some section(s) of the community, thus perpetuating the inequalities of social positioning through the workings of the pedagogic system.

It is in the uneasy co-existence of these two lines of literacy development that the secret of the complexity of the notion of literacy lies: this is where we must look to trace the origin of our problems. Literacy in the sense of untutored quotidian language development without the intervention of official pedagogy is already complex enough, simply because speaking is itself a social act of immense consequence; literacy in the sense of language development following the image of language which is self-consciously conceptualized by largely linguistically uninformed pedagogues compounds the complexity even further. In the following sections, for lack of space, I shall directly approach the various conceptions of literacy in the pedagogic context, referring to the mundane line of literacy development only occasionally.

3.1 Teaching literacy[7]

The dictionaries firmly define literacy as the ability to read and write. This formulation gives pride of place in the activities of literacy to the grasp of the correspondence of the marks on the paper – what is known in linguistics as the ORTHOGRAPHIC SYSTEM – to the sounds or THE PHONOLOGICAL SYSTEM that enable contact with the words of a language. This particular cycle of EXPRESSION-CONTENT – what written marks signify what sounds – is, however, a later development both in the history of individuals and in that of the human race (Goody 1968; Goody and Watt 1972; Halliday 1985b). So whoever begins learning to read and/or write must already have been using some language as a resource for making meanings by speaking, and there are some languages of the world which, as the popular phrase puts it, have still not been 'reduced' to writing. With literacy defined as the use of the linguistic system for making sense of signs, control over the orthography-phonology correspondence is not a necessary part of being 'literate', since meanings can be made without the use of orthography.[8] Indeed, some scholars (e.g., Basso 1980) have argued that the invention of orthography adds nothing to the acts of meaning making; that all it does is to shift the making of meaning from one channel, the phonic-acoustic, to another, the graphic-visual. Others (e.g., Goody 1977; Olson 1977) have suggested, explicitly or implicitly, that the invention of orthography has been a significant step in the evolution of humanity. Clearly this controversy is important (for a discussion of the relevant issues see Halliday 1985b, 1996b).

3.2 Recognition literacy

It is no secret that the correspondence between orthography and phonology forms the major thrust of literacy teaching in many schools. Most of us have gone through the 'bat, pat, hat, mat' stage in our schooling; most of us remember the wise words 'dot your i's and cross your t's'. Such injunctions are designed to teach us how orthography and phonology in calibration act as the expression of the lexical items 'bat, pat, hat, mat', and how to form letters the right way so the appearance of, say, 'tame' is not confused with that of 'lame', etc. Though much has been written against the limiting nature of this conception of literacy development which focuses on teaching sound-shape correspondence, and which is known in the trade as the CODING approach, it remains alive and well in many schools even today. A remarkable thing about this entire process is that in the intensity of the focus on expression – what the shape looks like, what sound it represents – the issue of meaning can and often does get ignored (Kress 1982; Wells 1987). In coding literacy the more complex forms of meaning-making by language remain alien to the developmental program. This exaggerated focus on expression leads to a fragmentation of linguistic facts. Thus words are grouped and brought to the pupils' attention not on the basis of the words' meaning potential but because of their sound-shape correspondences either because this correspondence is regular (cf., 'bat, pat') or because it is irregular (cf., 'shun, ocean, nation, commission'). Language as a mode of social action is ignored; language as inventory of forms has precedence. So pupils may be asked to 'turn' active sentences into passive; to cite tense conjugation of verbs, e.g., catch, latch, shoot, loot; to find a substitute for some word. I will refer to this entire spectrum as RECOGNITION LITERACY.

Underlying this kind of pedagogic literacy development program is a conception of language far removed from language as social semiotic practice. This is not to claim that the kinds of relation which form the centre of attention in recognition literacy are unnecessary for the development of the ability to make linguistic meanings in writing; on the contrary, these relations constitute important means for expressing meaning. The problem is not that recognition literacy is concerned with script, or grammatical features, or lexical paraphrases; clearly these are nonexpendable elements of a language. The problem is simply that, in the absence of an approach to language which sees it as a mode of social action, the nature and function of these aspects of language is badly conceived, and worse still, these unfounded conceptions have often become the very end of literacy teaching in the pedagogic context. Most text books are witness to the focus on the isolated sentence, the recognition of paradigm memberships, and so on. It is not surprising then that the pupil's progress is usually measured precisely in terms of these 'skills' – how good the pupil is at giving the definition of the parts of speech, of spelling trick words, conjugating verbs with exceptional patterns, the list goes on and on. Note, however, that the popular idea of what literacy is all about is very close to this letter-sound-word correspondence: when politicians, ministers of education, and newspapers talk about the forever declining standards of literacy, they very often have in mind the spelling and punctuation conventions, the fairly obvious features of linguistic form, e.g., for English, such features as the concord between subject and finite verb, tense sequence in hypotactic clause complexes, the contrast between *that* and *which* in the defining relative clause etc. They have hardly any idea of grammar as a resource for meaning (Halliday 1976a, 1994a).

What expertise would a teacher need in order to be able to teach the elements of recognition literacy? It is easy to underestimate the degree of expertise required for the purpose, provided the teaching is to be done with understanding. The relations between the patterns of language are not transparent: for example, the principles underlying the calibration of orthography and phonology in English are very complex (Albrow 1972); and the same is true of the lexicogrammar and semantics (Halliday 1994a; Matthiessen 1995). The teacher needs this expertise to understand the nature of that which she is teaching, but she seldom possesses such understanding. The irony lies in the fact that if she did possess this expertise, then it is highly likely that she would also recognize the futility of attempting to develop literacy the ways popular in many schools. Since this understanding is more often lacking than not, the so-called rules of spelling, punctuation, and grammar that the teacher teaches are often rules by fiat: someone has set up those standards, and the teacher is supposed to inculcate them in her pupils. This implies she has to be willing to accept certain 'facts' without seeking explanations. Obviously, when these features of recognition literacy are stated overtly, very few would admit to supporting it. Yet the surprising fact remains that it is the most persistent form of teaching literacy.[9]

The learning done by the pupils in recognition literacy can be discussed at least on two levels. Assuming that the teaching is successful, the pupils will learn to recognize the correspondences that form the centre of such pedagogic action. This is the manifest level of learning. At a deeper level, the pupils also learn the value of conformity. Recognition literacy has limited ways of answering a 'why' question. So if you ask: why does the letter 'b' represent the sound /b/; why is the subject typically in concord with the finite verb in the English language; why and where can 'why' substitute 'what is the reason that', these questions can only be answered either by appealing to tradition: this is just how we do it, or by a superficial appeal to the properties of language: this is what this language is like. Aspects of language thus appear to be either blind tradition or entirely unmotivated form – a view that is accepted even by some linguists. We know that the norms of language children are taught in school are precisely those which conform to the practices of a certain segment of the society. But since, according to recognition literacy, linguistic choice is arbitrary, the social motivations for the choice of a particular variety as the favoured one in the pedagogic environment cannot be effectively highlighted. Standards of correctness are simply given, to be accepted not to be questioned. At a deeper level of learning, then, the underlying message of this approach is to go on doing what others have been doing, to regard language as not socially motivated, and perhaps to conclude that at least some systems of knowledge are not open to questioning. By presenting language as pure form, recognition literacy creates an ideology of language as plastic and powerless. As pure form, language only has the power to reflect pre-existing meanings passively, just as a mirror might reflect passively without playing any active part in the creation and maintenance of that which it reflects. This is very far from the role language actually plays in the mundane sphere of our lives where much of our social universe is created and maintained with the complicity of language. A good amount of disquiet about the teaching of literacy can be attributed precisely to what the pupils are learning in learning recognition literacy. But just as the lay perception of literacy is very close to recognition literacy, so also popular ideas about the nature of language itself are in agreement with the ideas about language that underlie this view of literacy. And it is not simply the proverbial layman who shares this emasculated picture of language which underlies recognition literacy. Talk to academics, and you will find that irrespective of their intellectual prowess in some field of learning or other, they too are very likely to echo precisely the same view. This is not surprising since most of us have been schooled in recognition literacy, which remains the most popular pedagogic perspective even today.[10]

The persistence of recognition literacy might make one think that it must be enabling in some significant way, or else why invest so many resources, so much energy and time into it? But the fact of the matter is that recognition literacy persists thanks to ill-informed politicians in search of power and equally misinformed but opinionated educators who believe that simply because being tutored by life they can use language to mean, therefore they know all about the nature of language. For the hours of schooling we put into this futile mode of developing literacy, the return is pathetic. Certainly, many of us who have been taught a second language largely by methods akin to recognition literacy have been dismayed to find that after years of such learning, we are not able to use that language for exchanging meanings. It is one thing to turn an active sentence into a passive as a formal exercise, it is quite another to know where to use the one or the other. When this same pedagogic method is applied – as it is very often – to the development of the pupils' mother tongue, this creates a peculiar situation. On the one hand, it contributes very little if anything to the actual development of the pupils' ability to use language effectively to mean; on the other, thanks to the quotidian line of literacy development, this fact remains largely invisible because at least some pupils' abilities to use language develop in the 'right' direction anyway. On the other hand, there are pupils whose natural literacy development does not converge with the direction required by the pedagogic context. For example, they are not able to answer comprehension questions or to write reports or essays satisfactorily. In these cases the responsibility for the failure can be laid at the pupil's door: after all, the other pupils are doing well with the same 'teaching', aren't they? It is no secret that the pupils whose natural development diverges from the pedagogic standards typically belong to the disadvantaged classes of the community. The construction of a specific section of the community as willing failures despite 'good teaching' is a strong reason for disquiet with the teaching of recognition literacy in schools.

Logically, the ideals of recognition literacy demand pupils who are not likely to ask questions, who are willing to follow wherever authority in the guise of the teacher leads them; they have to be pupils who do not expect their educational knowledge of language to have any direct relevance to what they do with language in the living of their life. To use Bernstein's descriptions these pupils have to be 'flexible and conformist'. So recognition literacy would flourish best in societies that are authoritarian, with a routinization of conduct, or at least where the nature of educational knowledge is non-negotiable. How is it, then, that recognition literacy can be still found in practice in the so-called progressive societies? There are at least three reasons for this. First, progressive societies, despite their proclamations, are authoritarian, and possess hidden mechanisms for the preservation of the power of authority. Secondly, the cost of implementing recognition literacy is substantially low. It is low both in terms of what it costs to appear to be teaching literacy and also in terms of who it is that suffers from such teaching. Those who suffer most, particularly when recognition literacy is applied to mother tongue teaching-learning contexts, come from the disadvantaged groups in a community; their voice is not the voice of authority, and it is not represented in the schooling systems. Finally, an equally important reason for the perpetuation of recognition literacy is the ideology of language it perpetuates. When it comes to ideas about language, we are caught in something of a catch-22 situation. Generally, thanks to being schooled in recognition literacy, we tend to misrecognize the nature of language, failing to appreciate its character as a social semiotic; so when it comes to designing language curricula, then given our mistaken views of language, it is not surprising that our creations leave much to be desired. We give recognition literacy in schools to get back recognition literacy in the curriculum, to perpetuate the misrecognition of language by being schooled in recognition literacy! This cycle recycles itself. It should, however, be obvious that if literacy counts as the ability to use language for making meanings, then recognition literacy does not really meet that ideal. The disquiet against literacy teaching practices in schools should not be attributed to 'the privileging of language', as some scholars put it. It would be nearer the mark to attribute it to common ignorance about language.

3.3 Literacy and language use

This discussion of recognition literacy has emphasized that if literacy is seen as linguistic semiosis, then the ability to read and write which dictionaries cite as the quality of being literate cannot be equated simply with the pairing of certain visual shapes with certain sounds, and being educated cannot be synonymous with knowing the conjugations of weak and strong verbs. What more is needed then to make reading and writing semiotic acts, and how does it – whatever that 'it' is – contribute to being educated? To answer these questions, let us focus on that aspect of language which is largely ignored by recognition literacy.

What is missing from recognition literacy is any concern with those processes that lie at the centre of the actual use of language. When these processes are taken into account, the focus is shifted from fragmentary language to contextualized language. I am using the term contextualized language to draw attention to two types of contexts that are central to any language use: one is the VERBAL CONTEXT of the on-going talk, and the other is the SITUATIONAL CONTEXT. I have already suggested (section 2.1) that a sign can take on meaning only in the context of other signs, and that signing always occurs in some context of social situation. Language in use is no exception. It does not come in a fragmented form as words, phrases, sentences arranged in lists according to some formal or semantic feature; it comes as texts relevant to some social situation. This means it has both the property of TEXTURE and of STRUCTURE. The sayings that the speakers produce typically bear some relevance to what else has been or is about to be said; at the same time, the way that a talk progresses as a whole displays the speakers' awareness of the relevance of the occasion of talk to that talk (Halliday and Hasan 1976, 1985). This quality of DOUBLE RELEVANCE is such a typical feature of linguistic acts of meaning that where this feature is absent, the absence is taken as an indication of some kind of pathology. So, if literacy is a variety of semiosis that consists in linguistic acts of meaning, and linguistic acts of meaning entail the production of contextualized language, then an important part of literacy development should be the development of that discursive ability, which teaches how to engage in discourses displaying this double relevance.

Scholars are agreed that in the very early stages of the development of their language, children's language use does not display this double relevance. Speakers are not born with discursive ability any more than they are born with the rules of grammar; the emergence of such discursive ability is a developmental phenomenon, which begins sometime after the proto-linguistic stage (Halliday 1973a, 1975a; Bruner 1975; Dore 1977; McTear 1985; Painter 1984). As the child approaches the end of the transition which heralds entry into the mother tongue, the contribution of the social experience of talk comes to play a more decisive part (Halliday 1976a; Andersen 1986; Painter 1989). Through their interactions with others in their environment, children naturally develop double relevance. They learn that signs relate to signs, and the act of signing as a whole relates to what one uses signing for. This is not to say that children know consciously about either kind of relevance, about what it consists in; it is simply to say that they know how to 'act relevant' in using their language.

But doesn't this way of looking at literacy development dismiss the need for the pedagogy of literacy in the sense of development of discursive ability? Since discursive ability develops 'naturally' through the use of language for meaning making in social contexts, it follows that, pedagogy or no pedagogy, as speaking social beings we will have this ability. In fact, even the kindergarten learners come to school already with considerable discursive ability. Why do we need literacy development programs to teach them this same thing? The answer to these questions is implied in my discussion of the natural, quotidian line of literacy development. The naturally developed literacy of social subjects will be socio-culturally specific: different segments of a society will be literate in different ways, depending on what variety of language they use, what for, and who with. As a modality of meaning making, language is riven by diversity precisely because it is so deeply implicated in creating social boundaries: men do not speak as women do; old people do not speak as young do; city-dwellers do not speak as people in the villages do; and certainly members from different socio-economic strata speak differently. This being the case, children from different segments of the society come to school speaking differently: their literacy development will take different forms. Because this literacy is the product of the natural line of development, their voice will be the voice of their own immediate group, their own speech fellowship (Firth 1957).

3.3.1 *Language as social action and linguistic variation*

In formal linguistics, speaking differently has been treated as simply some difference in expression (Labov 1972; Trudgill 1978); so members of a community are said to speak different social dialects with different accents. This is a limited view of what it means to speak differently as other forms of variation exist which implicate meanings, not simply expression (Hasan 2009b). Consider first the notion of REGISTER VARIATION (Halliday *et al.* 1964), or speech variety (Hymes 1972). This difference has to do with the fact that people will talk differently about the same thing depending on who they are talking to, *a propos* of performing what social activity, and what shape their semiotic contact with the other takes. Take, as an example, talk about the water cycle. A teacher engaged in the social activity of presenting information about the water cycle to a class of nine-year-olds will talk differently from one who is addressing a high school class in performing the same activity, and, compared to both these, another teacher doing the same thing with a class of university students will talk differently yet again. Then again the same teachers will talk differently to the same learners depending on whether they are presenting information or revising already presented information. For example, a presentation lesson is likely to be more monologic, even though spoken, while by comparison the revision lesson would tend to be dialogic. Consider yet another vector of differentiation. Suppose that we have a chapter in a textbook, which presents information about the water cycle. We might think of this as the written analogue to the spoken presentation lesson. Here again we will find that the written presentation lesson i.e., the textbook chapter, will differ according to which group of learners it is written for.

These points have been demonstrated by Cross in an interesting study (1991). So given the same subject matter, teachers will talk differently depending on what activity is going on – presentation or revision; who they are addressing – young school children or university students; and whether the same activity is being carried out by speaking or writing – lesson to present information or chapter to do the same. This shows that variation in register is motivated by variation in social action, in speaker-addressee relations, and also by variation in the controls on the progression of this interaction. These contextual factors are relevant to both what overall structure the interaction will have, and what meanings and wordings will appear in the texts. The structure of a presentation lesson will be different from that of a revision one; the structure of a presentation lesson addressed to university students will be different from that addressed to the nine-year-old pupils; and a spoken presentation lesson will have a different structure from that which it would have when presented as a chapter. The forms of discourse, i.e., the meanings we mean and the wordings with which we make these meanings, thus differ from one social process to another, and the double relevance that I spoke of as the defining characteristic of discursive ability has its genesis in this relation between the social contexts and the linguistic meanings typically associated with them (Halliday and Hasan 1976, 1985; Hasan 1995a).

One very important fact to recognize about register variation is that not every member of a society enjoys the possibility of engaging in every kind of social activity. The limits placed on these possibilities are entirely social, even though sometimes they are presented as 'natural'. For example, take cooking: in Pakistan, only women engage in this activity, unless it is performed as a professional activity, carrying substantial cash in return for labour, when it is typically performed by men; bathing children, feeding and dressing them, domestic cleaning, chores around the house are typically women's activities, whether as paid labour or as mistress of the house; the pursuit of professions such as driving taxis, trains, other vehicles or acting as mechanics, gas pump attendants etc., are men's activities; playing chess, bridge etc. is typically a male (upper) middle class activity; only women of the highest social class may engage in these activities. Similarly certain sorts of relationship are enjoyed by some but not by others. On the Indo-Pakistani sub-continent, relations between males and females are typically conceptualized in terms of kinship. A woman is someone's wife, mother, daughter, daughter-in-law, sister etc. Up to quite recently, being just 'good colleagues' was not recognized as a legitimate relation between a man and a woman. What all this means is that the registers prevalent in a society as a whole are not 'available' in the normal course of living to every speaker in that society: people engage in different social processes depending on their 'place' in society; in fact, this is partially how their place in society is recognized (try presenting a budget speech without 'being' the federal treasurer; try being a federal treasurer without being able to make a budget speech!). Register variation needs to be seen from two perspectives in the present context: first, the use of language varies depending on variation in social processes; and secondly, not all speakers enjoy the possibility of engaging in all social processes. It follows that pupils will come to the school with differing discursive abilities, with differing experience of participation in registers, simply because of the differences in their social positioning. Speaking in the 'voice of one's speech fellowship' refers not simply to accent and social dialect but also to the fellowship's REGISTER REPERTOIRE – what people use their language for, what social processes they engage in.

3.3.2 *Semantic variation and natural literacy development*

This brings us to the next kind of linguistic variation involving meaning. It is true that the possibility of engaging in social processes is not the same for every group in a society, but of course the groups do not differ absolutely in this respect. There will certainly be some social processes in every society that would be in common to its larger segments. For example, most people will have the experience of talking to neighbours, swapping jokes or telling stories to friends or kin, and most mothers will attempt to control their children's behaviour, or give them information about the world, and so on. But while most people might do the same thing, their ways of meaning by way of carrying out these activities could be critically different. Speakers are oriented towards different ways of saying and meaning depending on the material conditions of their social existence. It is this meaning orientation that Bernstein (1986, 1987, 1990) talks about as CODING ORIENTATION. According to him the coding orientations of the dominating classes in a society are critically different from those of the dominated ones. The sociolinguistic research at Macquarie University has shown that both in controlling their children and in giving them information, mothers of the dominating and dominated classes differed significantly from each other. There is, thus, a good deal of semantic variation across social strata; different social segments of a community develop different predispositions for meaning making, different ideological stances, so that given the same social process, they will tend to say and mean somewhat different sorts of things (Hasan 1989, 1991, 1992a, 1992b; Hasan and Cloran 1990; Cloran 1994; Williams 1995).

It is important to recognize this form of linguistic variation, which I have called SEMANTIC VARIATION as it allows us to appreciate the complexities of speaking within what might be called the same speech community: on the one hand, social groups are distinguished by having distinct register repertoires by virtue of engaging in different social processes; and, on the other, where they do engage in 'the same' social processes, there the difference in their ideological stances is still sufficient to maintain the distinction between their discursive practices. The voice of the speech fellowship the pupils bring to the classroom will, thus, represent the pupils' experience of accents, dialects, registers, seen with the eyes of an ideology that is specific to their social positioning. What this means is that the conditions of being, of doing, and of saying in a community are represented in the classroom through the make up of the learning subjects. I suggest that all these aspects of sociolinguistic variation are relevant, in different ways, to debates on literacy. It ought to be a matter of primary interest to teachers of language, that within one and the same text, within a single exchange of meaning, there may be combined different strands of socially engendered variation: that of dialect and accent, that of register, and that of the ideological perspective resulting in semantic variation.

3.4 Action literacy

If what I am saying about pupils' linguistic experiences is correct, then discursive ability is a complex concept. People don't just either have it or not; they can 'have' different degrees and different varieties of discursive abilities. True, thanks to the natural line of literacy development, pupils will come to school with some discursive abilities, and true that even if they are not schooled in literacy, they will develop *some* discursive ability. These things are not in question; what is in question is whether they will all come to school with the sort of discursive ability which will permit them to engage in the educational process with equal facility. It seems to me that here three considerations are relevant. First, the exotic specialized contexts of education are somewhat remote from the contexts of everyday living so that it is rather doubtful that the ability to engage in educational discourses could develop naturally without experience of the educational processes. Secondly, while it is true that the educational context is a specialized context for most members of a community, different social classes in the community are placed differently in this respect. Members of the dominating classes do engage more often, than do those of the dominated ones, in practices of saying and meaning which are closer in their discursive properties to educational discourses. The best way to express the nature of this closeness might be to say that there is an IDEOLOGICAL CONGRUENCE between the two. To report again from my sociolinguistic research, it appears that irrespective of who their pupils are, teachers' classroom discourses tend to be, ideologically, significantly closer to those of the middle class mothers' (Hasan 1987b, 1988, 1989): they display a similar perspective on what it means to learn, what counts as knowledge, and how knowledge should be 'produced'. And finally, turning to the schooling context, so long as we do not opt out of the educational system altogether, and so long as we hold the ideal of egalitarian education, there will be a need to teach literacy in the sense of developing pupils' discursive abilities in relation to EDUCATIONAL REGISTERS, since this is a necessary condition for 'having education', for getting to know knowledge! In fact, it would be difficult to draw a distinction between the pupils' knowledge of an academic discipline and their discursive ability to listen/read, speak/write the discourses of that discipline. Academic disciplines are after all largely a constellation of certain types of discourse, and, in the end, what counts as knowing a discipline is the ability to participate successfully in the discourses of that discipline.

Turning briefly to the question of writing and reading, to the extent that educational discourses make use of reading and writing, to that extent an essential characteristic of being educated would be the ability to use reading and writing to participate in discourses of knowledge. And to the extent that certain aspects of the creation and maintenance of knowledge depend on the invention of writing, to that extent being educated implies being able to read and write. So, we can begin to perceive a deeper truth in the dictionaries' juxtaposition of being literate and having education, and in its paraphrase of the state of being literate as being able to read and write, having education.

Now, like dictionaries, educational systems too have always recognized the close link between the development of discursive ability, and the state of being educated. This can be seen from the fact that, following on recognition literacy in schools, the very next step tends to be that of teaching pupils 'connected writing', comprehension and composition, the art of self-expression, creative writing, and the like. Whatever reservations we may have against these approaches, the fact that such pedagogies exist and have always existed is a way of acknowledging that the goal of literacy has to extend beyond the mastery of lists and paradigms; it has to go past the stage of recognition literacy to the development of an ability to use language for what Firth (1957) used to call 'the living of life'. Inspired by linguistics, several new approaches to the teaching of literacy as discursive ability have arisen over the past few decades. Let me mention here one such pedagogic approach, developed under the leadership of my colleague, J. R. Martin (1985, 1986, 1989, 1992), which has gained a great deal of momentum in educational linguistics in Australia. Known as GENRE-BASED PEDAGOGY, this approach is deeply concerned with issues in literacy teaching, as many of its representative writings show (Painter and Martin 1986; Martin, Christie and Rothery 1987; Christie 1988, 1991; and Rothery 1989 etc.). Of the various existing programs for the teaching of discursive literacy, genre-based pedagogy is, perhaps, the one that makes its assumptions and arguments most explicit. According to this approach, the goal of education should be to provide equal opportunities for all pupils to develop their discursive abilities precisely in those respects which are essential to their education. Pupils must be schooled to participate successfully in 'educational genres' because of the consequences education has for life chances in a society. Compared with the traditional approach to, say, creative writing or self-expression, genre-based pedagogy differs significantly in its arguments and in its methodology, not least because of its commitment to language as a social semiotic. But if I speak generally of pedagogies concerned with the development of discursive abilities, then these pedagogies fall within the same group. Each has the aim of enabling the pupils to do something with their language, and in this sense they are all action-oriented, though the range of genre-based pedagogy is the widest, the methodology most systematic, explicit and replicable. I will use the term ACTION LITERACY to refer to this entire spectrum of literacy pedagogy. Action literacy ranges from the more traditional practices of getting the pupils to produce some form of connected writing to the more linguistically informed text based approaches, of which genre-based pedagogy is the best example. Let us ask then what sorts of pedagogic practice are associated with the achievement of this goal.

Naturally the answer depends on how discursive ability is conceptualized. If it is thought of simply as the ability to comprehend and convey one's thoughts and feelings, to read and produce 'connected writing', then with this rather simplistic view, the teacher might draw attention to awkward expressions, comment on some part of a pupil's writing as good or bad, whether the writing was effective, and so on. Turning to actual language patterns she may teach how sentences should be put together, which expression goes better with which other, and which part of a passage was 'saying' what, etc. The students could be set such tasks as to write a story, summarize some given text (fragment), answer questions which require understanding some part of some prescribed written material, express their views on some situation or other. As to teacher expertise, most of this instruction could be carried out on an *ad hoc* basis, without any awareness of what social factors are critical to the production of discourse, and – much worse – without any understanding of what part the patterns of language play and why in making these socially activated meanings.

At the other end of this spectrum of literacy pedagogies – that is to say, with genre-based pedagogy – discursive ability is conceptualized as the mastery of educational genres. So in this pedagogy the teacher would try to get pupils to produce the sorts of texts which would belong to the various educational genres. And to achieve this goal, ideally she will herself need to be aware of the specific properties of these genres. She will need to know the ways in which talking science (Lemke 1990) is different from writing science (Halliday and Martin 1993), which is different from writing history (Eggins *et al.* 1993), which is again different from writing about literature. Participation in a discipline calls for discursive abilities which differ to some extent from one discipline to another. Since a crucial distinction across genres is in what Martin refers to as SCHEMATIC STRUCTURE (Martin 1985, 1989), pupils will need to know how texts in the target genres are structured. One important aim of teaching would be to develop precisely this ability in the pupils to produce well-formed texts in the genres. It follows that pupils will need to know what structural STAGES characterize the various target genres; how these stages are sequenced; and so on. A second closely related aspect of controlling the production of well-formed texts is to know those lexicogrammatical patterns which typically occur in these various stages. According to genre-based pedagogy, the teacher's task is to make these aspects of educational genres accessible to the pupils. Through these and similar teaching foci, the teacher would be able to increase her pupils' awareness of what counts as a report, and what as a description; how an instruction for carrying out an experiment differs from an essay on the evils of racism, and so on.

What can the pupils be expected to learn through the pedagogies of action literacy? Clearly, the more aware the teacher is of the theoretical underpinnings of textual production, the more effective would be her intervention in developing the pupils' discursive ability. So for example, given genre-based pedagogy, ideally the pupils will learn to produce language of the type that is required of them to succeed in the educational system. This makes it likely that at least a higher proportion of pupils will succeed in getting their educational credentials, and it would not be unreasonable to expect that the experience of participation in this kind of literacy pedagogy would also enable pupils to act more confidently with their language in other social activities than just those specific to the educational context. It is obvious, then, that the pedagogy of action literacy at its best has considerable edge over recognition literacy. Pupils' learning and their doing will be not isolated from each other, something that makes recognition literacy so ineffectual in real life situations. It is important to note, though, that in order to achieve these goals of action literacy, pupils will need to have internalized the sorts of information that form the content of recognition literacy: they will need to be able to recognize the relations between the written shape and the spoken words, and they will need to know about the lexicogrammar. But there is a crucial difference: in action literacy, all this learning will be harnessed to some act of meaning which has a significant place in the pupil's social life.

What do pupils learn at the deeper level of learning from the teaching practices associated with action literacy? Before answering this question, let me repeat that there is a world of difference between the teaching practices of the more recent linguistically informed approaches such as genre-based pedagogy and those of the traditional ones, which are devoted to teaching the reading and writing of connected prose, focusing on comprehension and composition, or on the development of 'creative', 'aesthetic', 'expressive' sensibilities. This difference is evident in how the pedagogic steps are visualized in the two types of approaches to the pedagogy of action literacy. In genre-based pedagogy these steps are explicitly identified on the basis of a conscious understanding of the target genres and of language as meaning potential (see, for example, Veel and Coffin (1996) and also Macken-Horarik (1996)). This understanding is itself based on the linguistic analyses of genres valued in the educational system. In the traditional teaching of reading and writing connected prose etc., the reliance is on 'intuitive' understanding. It is assumed without debate that because the teacher can herself read and write, therefore she is competent to teach reading and writing. But this silent assumption is false. After all, not all competent native speakers of a language are competent teachers of that language. So there are some very important differences between the two ends of the spectrum, which are classed together here purely on the ground that both are concerned with textual production, not with fragments of language.

Since the primary aim of action literacy is to teach pupils how to do certain things with their language in the ways that those things are done linguistically in the pupils' culture, this necessarily implies using existing models of discourse, whether the nature of the model is explicitly analysed or not. Pupils are provided with standards for some selected aspects of language use – how to structure discourse, how to use the lexicogrammatical resources – and their task is to produce texts the critical features of which match those of the approved models. In effect, then, pupils are being schooled to reproduce the selected discursive models, and on this basis, certain varieties of action literacy have been criticized for subscribing to social reproduction (Luke 1996). The critics claim that action literacy ends up teaching pupils to go on doing precisely what (some) others have been doing in their society, thus reproducing social structures and relations.

Again, the issues in this debate are complex, and the scope of this paper does not allow discussion of all aspects of this critique. Let me first say that I agree with the observation: there certainly is a strong reproductive element in action-based literacy of all varieties. However, I disagree with the conclusion drawn from this, namely that this necessarily renders all varieties of action literacy unfit as a pedagogic program. Let me elaborate on this comment. In the first place, I will emphasize once again the wide range of rather disparate literacy pedagogies which are included under the label action literacy. For example, the traditional comprehension-composition approaches or the self-expression, creative writing movements differ significantly from genre-based literacy which is founded on a deeper understanding of language as social semiotic; it is explicit in its methodology; and in my view it has produced some of the best language teaching resources for teachers to-date. Now it is significant that sociologists of education and proponents of critical literacy have appeared more worried by the reproductive nature of genre-based literacy; in fact hardly anyone has raised this as an issue with regard to the other forms of literacy pedagogies. Why? I believe one reason for this lies in the strengths of genre-based literacy: since its intellectual program is made explicit it permits discussion about itself in a way that the fuzz around the traditional approaches cannot. But these traditional approaches too are reproductive. Take for example the seemingly less likely candidate – the self-expression, creative writing movement. What is 'self'? How is it constituted? What steps do these teachers take to ensure that the 'self' is not a reproductive projection? In fact, criteria for creativity, excellence, accuracy, and other such 'nice' attributes cannot be defined without reference to standards set up within the society where the criteria makers live. Operating independently of socially given standards is the prerogative of the mystic or the mentally deranged (Douglas 1975).

Genre-based pedagogy, which makes its assumptions visible, and so easier to criticize, operates on the assumption that pupils' chances of success in education will be considerably enhanced if they are enabled to produce the sorts of discourse which are valued within the educational context. In this sense, this kind of literacy pedagogy could be said to be consciously aiming to be reproductive. And they seem to be right in making these assumptions: educational systems are inherently evaluative, which implies the acceptance of some standard by reference to which evaluation can be made. As teachers, most of us have some time or other refused to 'pass' an essay because it did not conform to certain discursive criteria. In other words, teachers have to, and do, operate with some ideas about what pupils' essays should be like, how reports should be produced, what counts as a précis, and so on. Teaching and the idea of successful teaching are inalienably related; so long as we are willing to operate with teaching systems of any kind whatever, we will also operate with models and standards. Typically these models and standards will come from (some section of[11]) the society to which the educational systems belong. In short, the brutal fact about the human social condition is that to live in a society is to collude to maintain at least some of the ways of being, doing and saying that are prevalent in that society; no one has yet shown us that to live in society can mean anything else, and the natural line of literacy development is largely a process of reproduction.[12] Critical literacy may be right in saying that to teach educational genres is to reproduce existing knowledge structures, but as against this there remains the much more disturbing fact that to fail to master educational genres is to almost certainly collude in the reproduction of the inequalities of the social system at the cost of precisely those whose voice is absent from the educational curricula! It may be true that educational capital is not automatically converted into economic capital: to succeed educationally may not necessarily mean moving to positions of power. But there does remain the fact that without educational success the chances for the majority of us to attain any power over the course of our lives are almost non-existent. Moreover, there is no convincing evidence to assume that in order to change a society, its members have to be innocent of the prevalent ways of being, doing, and saying; that to show the young how their society lives by language would entirely prevent them from moving towards social change; nor do I believe that there is ground for supposing that the production of the ability to act linguistically as the powerful people act in our culture will necessarily equip pupils to contribute to change (Hasan 1995b). It seems to me that the issue of reproduction has been exaggerated and that it stands in need of careful thinking.

My critique of genre-based literacy, which I repeat is so far the only literacy pedagogy worthy of serious attention in the entire range of action literacy, is rather different: I believe that the introduction of planned, consciously designed change requires the ability to analyse, reflect and judge the underlying motivations for those actions. I believe also that while much of education consists in reproduction/recontextualization of knowledge (see n. 11) the endpoint of education has to be the production of new knowledge. So an important question is whether in learning discursive ability through genre-based pedagogy, one is also learning the ability to analyse, and to challenge the desirability of the prevalent ways of being, doing and saying. To my knowledge, in the range of pedagogic practices that are associated with genre-based literacy, there is no explicit element designed to encourage such reflection.[13] The implied underlying message of this pedagogy is conformism, a respect for convention which is not required to be tempered by analytical reflection. In this respect, there is not much to choose between recognition literacy and action literacy: both encourage conformism; the difference is that recognition literacy does not enable discursive action, whereas action literacy equips pupils to act with their language, and that within the gamut of action literacy, genre-based literacy is to be preferred because of its superior methodology.

3.5 Literacy and knowledge

Following discursive conventions – talking the way that others in our society talk – is the norm of social life; it is what we mean, in large part, by the expression 'socially adapted' or 'well adjusted'. The great strength of action literacy, and particularly of genre-based literacy is that it introduces pupils to certain norms of discourse and of knowledge. But paradoxically this is also the source of the weakness of action literacy. Since the norms of language and knowledge are both filtered through the educational system itself, if the learning of these norms was treated as the ultimate goal of literacy, we would naturally inherit whatever shortcomings there may be in the educational norms. This applies inevitably to all pedagogies of the type I have referred to as action literacy. For example, if we take the self-expression variety of action literacy, a pupil may be asked to write his reactions to a poem, but to be approved by the teacher, his reactions have to be written in the ways in which one is supposed to write one's reactions about poems in the school system; and, interestingly, even the reactions have to be reactions of a certain category; so it won't do at all to just write 'I didn't like that poem because it was a load of rubbish', even if this represents the pupil's honest conscious apprehension of his reaction. As a second example, take genre-based pedagogy as a notable example of a linguistically inspired case of action literacy. Unlike the self-expression variety of pedagogy, it recognizes its aims. Its acknowledged aim is to teach pupils the norms for reading, writing, and speaking about some sort of educational knowledge, but these norms are naturally norms recognized and upheld as norms for doing those same things within the schooling context. There is, then, a certain circularity about the enterprise. Discourse norms that, for example, genre-based literacy teaches are the norms of what is considered good discourse in the educational environment; the norms of knowledge it teaches are norms of what counts as knowledge within the educational context. If this reasoning is correct, then, we end up teaching literacy for schooling, creating the literate subject in the image of the existing standards of education. It could be argued then that it is an instrument for the perpetuation of the standards of the existing educational system, and one might go on to argue that if the ideal goal of teaching is to enable pupils to produce new knowledge, not just replicate the existing knowledge, then genre-based literacy falls short of this ideal.

How is it that using the norms of the educational system puts us into this quandary? After all, education is popularly thought to be a means for the transmission of knowledge and cultural values, which are supposed to lead to social progress. If that is so, then why criticize genre-based literacy for perpetuating the norms of education? And how is it that following these norms fails to enable pupils to produce rather than reproduce knowledge? Sociologists of educational knowledge have argued that school knowledge is typically knowledge that is produced elsewhere; it is relocated into the curricula; and the standards of the educational system simply demand a degree of the mastery of this already produced knowledge as a sign of educational success. So school knowledge comes to have norms largely by treating knowledge as a finished product – something that has been created in the past by some other producers. But when it comes to the process of producing knowledge, the situation is qualitatively different. Here the existing knowledge is simply the point of departure for the creation of something significantly different from it; the very idea of right knowledge has to be viewed with caution, if not with suspicion, for the essential nature of knowledge in this context is to change within a framework of seeming stability. Its changing nature becomes evident only when viewed from a time-distance. At one time in our knowledge, the earth was flat, not round; there was no evolution of species: the human species grew as a result of the first female's foibles; sickness had no physical basis: it was the work of the devil; and so on. That in these respects our knowledge is different now shows that we were able to reflect, to analyse and to challenge that which was taken to be true in nature though it was true only by convention. In making this reflection, this analysis, and this challenge, the discursive conventions too must have had to change from those which had appeared natural for talking about the earth, about creation, or the creator. And in as much as acts of reflection, of analysis, and of challenge call into question systems of belief that are naturally accepted, they also call on speakers to speak un-naturally, to use un-natural locutions, un-natural collocations. I am arguing, then, that both the norms of knowledge and of discourse change, and they change together; that like knowledge, the essential nature of language is to change within a framework of seeming stability. This similarity is not accidental: the possibilities of knowledge and the potentiality of human language cannot be understood in isolation from each other. Discourse and knowledge go hand in hand. It so happens then that while in the schooling system the norms of knowledge and of discourse are treated as stable and fixed, outside this system, both the ways of using language and of construing knowledge continue to evolve with the result that the norms for both are subject to change.

But should teachers be concerned about the evolution of knowledge and if so, why? Scholars have argued for some time now that the evolution of knowledge is a highly significant process in human history because it serves a function very much like the function of the bodily evolution in animals. In both cases, the function is to enable the species to survive (Vygotsky 1978; Popper 1972). To quote the philosopher, Popper,

> Animal evolution proceeds largely … by the modification of organs… or the emergence of new organs … Human evolution proceeds largely by developing new organs outside our bodies or persons: 'exo-somatically' as biologists call it…man, instead of growing better eyes and ears, grows spectacles, microscopes, telescopes, telephones, and hearing aids… (Popper 1972: 238).

The close link between the exo-somatic evolution of human beings and the growth of knowledge is quite obvious. It is the evolution of knowledge that allows us to produce the technical aids that Popper talks about as exo-somatic organs. With this argument, the production of knowledge becomes a condition of human survival. Popper goes on to suggest that as human beings we experience three orders of phenomena. First, we know the world of physical states; secondly, there is the world of mental states; and thirdly, there is the world of objective contents of thought. The last of these, known as Popper's World 3, is what some might describe as COMMUNAL HERITAGE OF KNOWLEDGE, what is fashionably referred to today as the 'cultural capital'. Popper believes that this World 3 exists independent of specific individuals; it is autonomous. For example, the theory of relativity remains an element of this world, irrespective of whether or not Einstein is still alive. The elements of this world, described in general terms, are theoretical systems, problem situations, the state of critical arguments and of discussion. This World 3 develops as a result of individuals interacting with the elements of World 3. I prefer to put it another way: *knowledge evolves through reflection and analysis of the elements of communal knowledge in relation to social life*. The elements of World 3 – that is to say, our communal knowledge heritage – are thus resources for the creation of further knowledge because they carry a certain set of implications. These implications are objectively there; whether we recognize them or not, they exist. From this point of view, it is immaterial that it was Einstein who produced the theory of relativity; what matters is that the germs of the theory were already there in the implications of the existing theoretical systems, the problems they gave rise to, and their close analysis. For knowledge to evolve, what we need is someone – anyone – to perceive the problem(s), to develop the implications; this implies a search for explanations, raising how-questions and why-questions, using existing knowledge only as a point of departure, not as the end of intellectual journey. Vygotsky (1978) would add that these abilities develop within society, and to this extent knowledge depends on a society which allows such mental activities.

3.6 Reflection literacy

It follows from these views, that if we are actively interested in the evolution of knowledge, then we cannot take for granted the certainty of facts simply on the ground that those facts have generally been treated as facts; nor can we treat the prevalent ways of saying and meaning as utterly binding on us simply because these happen to be the accepted ways of doing things with our language. Neither the norms of knowledge nor those of discourse can be treated as stable, arrested at some point in time; change is the only abiding condition for human existence. This puts emphasis on a qualitatively different aspect of discursive ability than that which underlies pedagogies of action literacy. Participation in the production of knowledge will call for an ability to use language to reflect, to enquire, and to analyse, which is the necessary basis for challenging what are seen as facts. So, if our aim is to enable pupils to produce knowledge, then we would need a view of literacy designed to develop these faculties. This literacy will necessarily prioritize reflection, enquiry and analysis. For this reason I refer to it as REFLECTION LITERACY. Reflection literacy should not be confused with critical literacy. The notion nearest to reflection literacy is Wells' idea of epistemic literacy.[14]

At this point two important questions arise: is reflection literacy teachable and even if it is, is it necessary? Taking the first question first, I do believe that reflection literacy is teachable. After all, we have somehow succeeded in keeping the evolution of knowledge going. So unless we believe in born theoreticians, born scientists, sociologists etc., we would have to grant that some variety of reflection literacy is not only teachable but must be being taught at some level of education to permit the production of knowledge rather than allowing just its replication. And while it is true that normally the students' contribution to knowledge production occurs at a fairly late stage in the educational system, it must also be true that the orientations that assist them in this task must begin to develop long before the event. I would suggest that the sorts of perspectives typically needed for knowledge production are taught throughout schooling – and perhaps earlier than that – but they are taught invisibly. In analysing the language of the classroom in a picture reading session in the first year of schooling in some suburban schools in Australia, I found (Hasan 1987b, 2004, also Chapter 7 here) that as early as the very first year of schooling, teachers already insisted on objective evidence; they rejected answers that were not explicitly supported by some evidence in the picture. They also rejected conclusions that were not logical; to be received with approval, conclusions had to be implicational in their reasoning; and the responses which the teachers favoured highly were those presented as universal generalizations. Of course it is these discursive features which are primarily relevant to the sort of knowledge production that Popper values so highly. But it must be pointed out that this invisible pedagogy would have meaning only for some pupils, not for all; the pupils for whom it would have meaning are those who are familiar with this voice as the voice of their own speech fellowship. They would be able to log in, as it were, because the code is their code. My research has shown also that these ways of meaning are typical of the mothers of the dominating classes in the Australian society; they do not represent the voice of the dominated classes (Hasan 1988, 1989, 1991, 1992a). To say that the pedagogy was invisible is to say that the teachers themselves are not aware of what they are doing; this being the case, they would find it difficult to employ such pedagogy systematically in such a way as to develop reflection literacy in all pupils, irrespective of their naturally developed voice. So far as the teaching of reflection literacy is concerned, we really do not have many alternatives: either we have to teach reflection literacy so as to develop the potential of all pupils to participate in the production of knowledge, or we should abandon claims that our educational system is egalitarian and leads to progress.

The answer to the second question is already implicit in this discussion. It is often thought that the ability to reflect and to enquire is a divine gift; some have it, others don't. But the very concept of native intelligence is problematic. We have no clear idea of the range of intelligence levels enjoyed by infants at birth, and whatever that range may be it is not sufficient for the living of life without further development which inevitably occurs in and by social interaction. The development of higher mental functions that we think of as guided by intelligence is essentially fashioned by the living of life in society, and this means that it is guided by semiotic interacts of one kind or another, but largely of linguistic semiosis (Vygotsky 1962, 1978; Halliday 1975a, 1979b; Donaldson 1978; Bernstein 1971c, 1987; Hasan 1988, 1992b; Painter 1996). What is specifically relevant to reflection literacy is semantic orientation (see section 3.3.2) since it is speakers' orientation to meaning, their ideological stance that underlies their disposition to make enquiries, analyses and challenges of one kind or another. An important feature of language is that as a meaning making resource it is not dedicated to any specific purpose. In theory, it can be used by any one of us to conform or to question. But, in practice, because all members of a community do not occupy identical social positions, their naturally developed MEANING MAKING DISPOSITIONS – their semantic orientations – are not identical, and it cannot be assumed that along the natural line of literacy development, everyone in a community will naturally come to possess the disposition to enquire, to analyse and to challenge in ways that are considered necessary for the production of knowledge (Hasan 1992c, 1995b). If literacy is what education is about, and education is supposed to be truly egalitarian, and if the aim of education is to enable participation in the production of knowledge – and not just its reproduction – then it follows that we would need to develop in all pupils the ability to reflect, to enquire, to analyse and to challenge.

But what sorts of teaching-learning practices are implied by this view of literacy? To put a question to a text – to ask why the said is being said, what it implies, and on what grounds – calls for a much deeper understanding of language as a resource for meaning. So the teacher will need to sensitize pupils to not simply the overall schematic structure of the text, which is just one aspect of discursive ability; she would also be concerned to show what alternative ways there are of saying the 'same thing'. The point is that one can never say exactly the same thing using a different wording; so in fact, the teacher will need to make pupils aware of the sorts of difference in meaning that may arise from putting it one way as opposed to another. If it is true, as I claimed earlier, that within the same text is interwoven evidence of the various sorts of linguistic variation, then there are many ways in which a text can be read. This does not mean that meaning is in the reader, as the post-modernist sentiment has it (Rosenau 1991: 25ff.); rather it means that our perceptions of meaning are coloured by our point of view, and our point of view – in as much as it is capable of being studied and taken into account – is related to who we are, socially speaking (Hasan 2004, 2008). To say that a community has many voices is to say that there are experiences of saying and meaning which differ from one social group to the next; this includes the possibility that the way a locution is evaluated in one segment of the community might be critically different from that in another. So it becomes important to ask whose point of view does the writing represent, whose point of view is implied in which reading? It is from this kind of deeper understanding of what 'the' text means that we can move to explanation questions. For example, pupils would not simply note the way a text is structured, but they would also ask why it is structured in the way it is; if the structure were to be changed, what would change, for whom and at what price? They would not simply observe whose voice(s) underlie messages of what category, they would also ask why these voices and these messages go together, what (potentially relevant) voices are absent and why. This is indeed to question the very norms of discourse. Just as the teacher will need a good deal of expertise and understanding of language as a meaning potential in order to be able to help develop this kind of discursive perspective in her pupils, so also she will need to be deeply familiar with the nature of the disciplines she is to discuss with her class: what issues does it problematize? What methods for the resolution of such problems were employed in the past and what today? What counts as a fact and why? What sort of evidence upholds the status of a fact as fact?

Schooling in reflection literacy is, then, literacy for educating to produce knowledge. If the pedagogy is successful, it should ideally produce in the pupils a disposition to distrust doxic knowledge, i.e. knowledge whose sole authority is the authority of someone in authority. Since the history of a discipline is also the history of how it has changed, this pedagogy should create a perspective which refuses to consider the accepted ways of doing things in a culture as beyond questioning. So, apart from questioning the norms of discourse and of knowledge, a literacy of this kind would seek to examine the norms of education itself. For example, why do systems of education always insist on using the standard dialect? Why is educational success distributed in a society the way it is? Why does the production of knowledge get appropriated by a particular segment of the society? Why is knowledge conceptualized as it is? In what sense do the accepted western notions of the evolution of knowledge represent progress? How should we understand the term progress when it comes to the survival of humanity? Indeed, how should we understand the term survival? In what sense can we talk about the evolution of knowledge contributing to the progress and survival of humanity in an environment where both are linked to the idea of competing successfully against some other? We might justifiably expect that such literate pupils might be able to question the wisdom of the short-sighted goals that we have embraced the world over. They might indeed be able to ask what we have lost by gaining control over the environment, while ignoring all notions of self-control, by construing knowledge as a competitive enterprise, while failing to acknowledge the centrality of the other in our very survival as human beings. A literacy that can turn back upon the very systems that perpetuate the literacy teaching practices in a society is indeed worth striving for. If and when literacy and education stand in this relation, then we shall indeed be justified in paraphrasing 'literate' as 'educated', and 'educated' as 'displaying qualities of culture or learning'.

4. Literacy, talk, and society

We have travelled a good distance in this paper from 'bat, pat, hat, mat', from weak and strong verbs, from paraphrases, from schematic structures, and the like, taking on board the point of their pedagogic relevance. Perhaps the paper has given some indication of how the uneasy co-existence of the two lines of literacy development in essentially non-egalitarian societies contribute to the complexities of literacy pedagogy. This perspective draws attention to the close links between literacy, everyday talk and society. The voice of the speech fellowship that the child brings to the school is the voice developed in everyday talk. So far as the exotic pedagogic line of literacy development is concerned, the one thing that can always be taken for granted is that all children will have had experience of ordinary everyday talk. There will be many, of course, who will also have had the additional experience of having been read to or of acquaintance with print. But when and where parents enter into discussions with their children (Cloran 1994), or how they tend to read with them vary from one social segment to another (Williams 1990, 1995); and unlike the experience of everyday talk, these features of the experience of talk cannot be taken for granted as universally possessing the same qualities: research shows systematic variation across society in these respects. For example, do we know what goes on in these respects in some small remote villages of Uzbekistan, or of the interior of Australia, or in the remote north of Pakistan? The answer to this is not always available, but what we do know is that there too parents and the immediate meaning group – those who form the core of the child's speech fellowship – talk to the child, and it is this experience that gives the child his voice. Just because it is certain that every child will come to school with the voice of his/her speech fellowship, it is also certain that the educational system will encounter sociolinguistic variation in the many ways in which voices can vary. It is equally important that the ordinary everyday talk occurs in the course of some social action, that it is really the semiotic aspect of those social processes. The implications of the varying experience of social processes that pupils bring to the pedagogic context needs urgent attention not only in the teaching of literacy but in all pedagogic activity. A serious source of disquiet with literacy teaching practices is precisely that the educational systems deal with this variability by simply ignoring it – by raising one voice as the only legitimate voice, and that voice happens to be the voice of the dominating segments of the society. If education represents a social resource, then this resource is appropriated with the greatest ease by those same social classes which also control the society's material resources, thus making the strength of their control that much more formidable.

It should not surprise us that literacy poses so many issues. Literacy in the sense of making meaning by language imports the most socially sensitive signing system, namely language, into the educational arena. Language is not a mirror that just reflects social inequalities and hierarchies which exist in our society, mocking our claims of egalitarianism. Language is in fact actively involved in the creation and maintenance of social inequalities, because human social systems cannot be made without language. Here is cause enough for problems, especially when we know whose linguistic norms are the silently endorsed norms in the educational system. But this problem is made worse by a misrecognition of the nature of language. People typically think of language as passive, a clothing for meanings and ideas which are external to it. This popular but false idea about language prevents us from raising important questions. The inability of teachers to understand the nature of language as a powerful social instrument does not, indeed cannot, help them in any way to recognize, much less to respect, the many voices in their classroom or reflect on the social genesis of those voices; teachers that are so ill-equipped to reflect on language cannot be expected to scrutinize the 'rationality' of the choice of norms and standards which they inculcate. Keeping teachers of literacy uninformed about the close relation between development of language, everyday talk, learning, and society, in fact, plays into the hands of the dominating segments of society, whose ideologies remain the ideologies of education. Thus the cry against privileging language raised by some proponents of critical literacy is ironically an aid to the domination they profess to abhor rather than a release from it!

5 Concluding remarks: the many faces of literacy

In opening this paper I suggested that literacy is a many-faceted process. Identifying the onset of literacy as semiosis, I located it topologically in the same domain as any other semiotic practice with which it shares many critical attributes. I went on to claim that its specific and decisive character consists in being language based semiosis. If it is desirable to extend the use of the term literacy, as in 'media literacy' etc., this does not appear to be a serious problem worthy of much deliberation. The fact worth emphasizing is that language based semiosis under whatever name will occupy a central position in any discussion of education. We can, if we choose, turn language classes into sites for the discussion of wider social issues, for raising pupils' consciousness about any pressing social problems. The choice is not between bringing such issues to the students' attention OR developing understanding of language as a powerful social semiotic. Both need to be done, and a more relevant question is: what is the best way to do both? Those who argue against focus on language, on the explication of its internal character, on the power of lexicogrammar to construe reality, or on the efficacy of discursive knowledge speak from a less than adequate understanding of the role of language in the living and shaping of social life. Whatever else literacy pedagogy needs to be, one thing it cannot avoid is to help pupils to 'intellectualize' in the Vygotskian sense of the term[15] the nature of language. Learning about nature and structure of language is not an expendable educational activity.

I have talked about the three facets of literacy, each being presented in a rather idealized form, as if each existed or was able to exist on its own. This is of course not true. What is true is that different educational systems, different institutions attach different degrees of importance to these facets. Each facet has its own focus. Recognition literacy is concerned primarily with language as expression; action literacy focuses on language as expression and content in relation to social processes, while reflection literacy is concerned with the reflexive capacities of language when it functions as meta-discourse; in this capacity, it analyses both the nature of expression and of content by relating both to the exchange of meanings among socially positioned speakers in the living of life in society. Different as these three perspectives on literacy are, they are nonetheless logically related to each other. To see this we need to analytically separate what the various facets focus on as the material for teaching and how they actually do it. It is the former that is important for my claim of the inter-relatedness of the three facets of literacy developed here. Let me elaborate this point.

I have suggested earlier that the pedagogy of action literacy presupposes the sorts of understanding about language that form the content of recognition literacy. I will ignore once again the comprehension-composition and self-expressive, creative pedagogies on the ground that from the point of view of understanding language as a social semiotic system such pedagogies are deplorably inadequate. Consider, however, genre-based literacy: to talk about the structure of a text is to talk about what meanings construe its various elements/stages, and to talk about the meanings is to talk about the lexicogrammar that will construe those meanings, with the implication that an awareness of lexicogrammar as functionally focussed on the construal of meanings is important. But meaning and lexicogrammar is the most abstract part of language (Hasan 1995a); what impinges on the human senses is the manifestation of these categories in phonic and/or orthographic form. Thus the phonology-orthography correspondence to lexis and grammar is an essential part of the understanding of language. The success of genre based literacy – and there is no doubt that it is successful at teaching language – resides in the fact that it has appropriated these aspects of recognition literacy harnessing them to language in use in social contexts as viewed by systemic functional linguistics. A similar relation can be shown to exist between reflection literacy and genre-based literacy. If for example we wish to understand why politicians toss language education around like a football in the field of political gains, if we wish to ask why sociology only pays lip-service to language, if we want to ask why literary scholars sidetrack issues of language when the universe of literary art is anchored to our intelligence purely by the mediation of linguistic meaning, if we wish to understand how critical literacy can be a program for literacy development without a viable basis in an understanding of the workings of language, if we wonder how and why women have colluded in the processes of their own oppression, then we will need to be able to read and read with understanding the many discourses that reveal the principles underlying these positions. We will need to become familiar with how 'they do it' – how they put these perspectives across, what justifications they offer, from whose perspective. It means being sensitive to discursive strategies. Reflection presupposes understanding; and understanding someone's point of view is synonymous with understanding their discourse.

Let me make it quite clear, though, that I am not talking about a temporal ordering here: I am not saying that genre-based literacy must be taught from A to Z – whatever that might mean – before reflection literacy can begin, or that recognition literacy has to be taught before genre-based literacy. It is possible to pursue all three perspectives within reason during one and the same teaching stage. So the issue is not of temporal sequence but of logical implication. In the natural line of literacy development, patterns of language are learned in discourse: genre-based literacy must logically presuppose the development of patterns of language. Its program from this point of view is successful to the extent that learning about discourse is also learning about 'how language does it'. Similarly, the pedagogy of reflection literacy depends on being able to analyse the existing discourses of knowledge from the point of view of what they present as the norms of discourse and of knowledge. It is in understanding discourse as discourse that the critical faculty will develop. Logically it is impossible to achieve this goal without bringing in the sorts of understanding that are essential to the creation of texts. So these three facets of literacy are related by logical inclusion: reflection literacy includes a well informed variety of action literacy such as genre-based literacy, and the latter includes recognition literacy; the reverse is, however, not true.

This has a practical implication: in theory there exists a possible choice of perspective in the teaching of literacy, but because of this inclusion relation, the choice can only proceed in one direction. One may be limited to recognition literacy without action literacy, or to action literacy without reflection literacy, but if reflection literacy is to be developed, this will necessarily involve insights that form a linguistically well-informed variety of action literacy such as Martin's genre pedagogy framework, and that in turn will entail the pedagogy of the semantico-formal working of language. The cry of back to basics does a good deal of harm, because those who utter this war-cry often do not really know what they want and why. But perhaps my account of the logical relations between the three facets of literacy clarifies why knowing about language is important. It is important only if and in as much as it contributes to a conscious understanding of the resources of one's language for acting with it. The ability to act with language is important because it contributes to our ability to analyse those same acts. What we need to avoid is the danger of ending up by focussing only on formal structures of language without relating them to their social functions, i.e. getting locked into recognition literacy, as the resting point without moving to action; similarly, I would not wish to end up with focus on action literacy without moving to include reflection. I have tried to point out how each of these resting points will have different consequences in terms of the kind of social world it will help to produce. Literacy is not simply a semantically saturated term; what it refers to is a socially powerful process, which can be used in different ways, some perhaps more beneficial to a society in general, some to only some persons in it!

Notes

1 This is a revised version of a plenary paper presented at the 5th Anniversary Symposium of the Society of Pakistani English Language Teachers (SPELT), held in Karachi, 4 July 1989. My thanks are due to the organizers of the SPELT Symposium for release of the manuscript for publication here.

2 See van Leeuwen and Humphrey (1996) for a discussion of how graphic signs such as maps and pictures co-operate with the linguistic materials in a geography text.

3 There are at least two other senses in which the term 'literacies' is used. The plural is used to show that being literate in any one educational discipline (or discipline cluster) differs from being literate in some other(s). In this sense, one might talk about, say, 'science literacy', 'social science literacy', and so on. Secondly, the plural is used to show that different segments of the society are literate in different ways, depending upon the point of view they bring to the 'reading'. In this sense, one might talk about 'feminist literacy', 'dominant literacy', and so on.

4 For a discussion of this point see also Halliday 1996b.

5 Note the close analogy with language. The unqualified use of this word means natural human language; its use can be extended as in 'sign language', 'body language', 'computer language', and so on.

6 From this point of view Derrida's diatribe against the 'privileging' of speech by linguists is a curious twist that calls for a re-assessment.

7 My thanks are due to Jennifer Hammond (University of Technology, Sydney) with whose help I developed many of the ideas presented in this and subsequent subsections, specifically those concerning the pedagogies specific to each of the three perspectives on literacy development.

8 We note once again the tension between the mundane line of literacy development and the exotic, pedagogic one.

9 Often it is argued that we neither have the time nor the resources (cf. Terry Threadgold, personal communication) for familiarizing teachers with the relevant aspects of language such as its nature, its form, its function all of which are, of course, interdependent. It is worthy of reflection though that neither time nor resources are allocated to the pedagogic system by an act of nature; they are the expression of our commitment to the so-called 'egalitarian education' and need to be scrutinized, even though such scrutiny is very much less dramatic in its impact on audience than certain forms of rhetoric.

10 A couple of years ago a national Australian newspaper proudly announced the emergence of yet another 'innovative' literacy program 'developed at Baltimore's John Hopkins University' which some Australian researchers in the Education Department of a prestigious university were hoping to use so as to 'help poor or deprived children' in this country. The accompanying photograph showed a blackboard with the following 'meaningful utterances': *I am Pam. See the map, Pam. Sam is on the mat. Pat Sam.* (Sydney Morning Herald, 11 September, 1993). And no doubt more advanced and innovative literacy programs have been introduced since, which are, in effect, not very different from *bat, pat, hat, mat* variety of recognition literacy. This type of 'language-based' literacy development is a cause for worry, not because it privileges language but because it privileges ignorance of language, hiding the true nature and power of language.

11 One may of course question, as sociologists of education have done, the inequity of choosing the point of view of a particular section of society. Criticizing the educational system for being monopolized by the 'ruling classes' is, however,

a somewhat different issue from criticizing it for 'reproducing' knowledge and/or social relations, for it could be argued that education is largely nothing but reproduction under a different name. In this sense to oppose reproduction in education altogether is to imply the need for the replacement of education by some other institution, whatever that may be. If this is the position taken by critical literacy, then there is as yet very scant indication of any viable alternative or of any strategy by which the alternative could be achieved.

12 See for example the results of sociolinguisitc research Hasan 2009b; Cloran 1994; Williams 1995.

13 Attention should be drawn to the fact that genre-based literacy is not a static package. It has shown a good deal of responsiveness to its critique by colleagues and more recently elements are being introduced in this form of pedagogy to overcome the shortcomings, e.g., Macken-Horarik 1996.

14 Although Hammond and I developed our system of literacy classification on which my account here is based (with some revision) independently of Wells (1987), it is interesting to note that Wells recognizes four levels of literacy which cover approximately the same space as the three perspectives presented in this paper. He refers to his first level of literacy as *performative literacy*. I prefer the term *recognition literacy* because it is a clear reminder of what this literacy pedagogy is about: it helps us recognize a language pattern as a pattern of a specific kind. Besides, all literacy involves performance of some kind, but not all literacy requires focus on recognition of isolated patterns. My term *action literacy* covers approximately the same area as Wells' *functional* and *informational literacy*. Wells distinguishes between these two as *literacy in interpersonal communication* and in *communication of knowledge*, respectively. The basis for this distinction is not very obvious to me: from my point of view all discursive language is both interpersonal and informational, though the distinction between everyday genres and educational knowledge genres does appear valid. If this is the distinction, then in the spectrum covered by my *action literacy*, genre-based pedagogy is nearest *informational literacy*. Finally, my term *reflection literacy* is quite close to Wells' notion of *epistemic literacy*, which according to him provides *ways of acting upon and transforming knowledge*.

15 By 'intellectualization' Vygotsky (1962, 1978) meant the process of making a concept one's own in such a way that a person becomes able to recall it at will, use it in conjunction with other appropriated concepts, see it as part of some system(s) of ideas – make it pliable.

6 Globalization, literacy and ideology [2003]

1 Introduction

My theme is global, but to me the primary attraction of this occasion[1] is very personal: this celebration to honour Braj Kachru offers me an opportunity to express my affection and admiration for him. I met Braj all those years ago in Edinburgh of the 60s. He was engaged in his PhD; I was a mere novice; but with the characteristic Kachru urbanity, I was made welcome in his circle. To be with Braj then was to be at home while abroad; for me at that time there could have been no better gift. My admiration for Braj's intellectual achievements grew with a better understanding of his chosen field. Early in the Edinburgh days, my disdain for the assumptions underlying the discourses of ESL/EFL industry was perhaps equal to Braj's own: in fact, the intensity of my feelings moved me completely out of that discipline. Braj Kachru, with his vision and his deeper analysis, redefined the very meaning of what it is to learn English as it gets transplanted in foreign lands by some historical accident; he deconstructed the notion of English itself, finding a pantheon of Englishes where there had been a single Queen's English. With the same intellectual integrity which helped him maintain his convictions about the functional nature of language – an unwelcome foreign perspective for the American scene of mid-60s linguistics – he bent his energies to securing recognition for the many Englishes in their own right. Perhaps, in what I am about to say, there might be heard an echo of Braj's idea of the re-semanticization of a language, though in my case the context for the re-semanticization is not so much national as it is international: in my presentation, the process of re-semanticization is fired by the processes of globalization and driven by an ideology that has polarized the much advertised unity of our so-called global village. Globalization has aroused mixed reactions: some regard it as a blessing, others are convinced it is the old game of domination played under a new name. We need to understand the nature of the semantic processes that support this contradictory reading, particularly since the resolution of this contradiction does not lie in a simplistic choice between truth and falsehood. Rather, what we are witnessing is the deployment of language in a struggle to control the very picture of reality. Whatever the outcome, one thing seems certain: to understand how globalization might affect our lives, we will need a form of literacy that goes beyond simple interpretation to reflection on the social significance of acts of meaning. It has to be a literacy with the potential of enabling one to decide whose meanings are voiced in which acts of semiosis and for whose benefit. A word, then, on globalization itself.

2 Globalization – an old phenomenon, or new?

Much has been written on globalization by way of tracing its history (Hopkins 2002), describing its essential character (Ong 1999), revealing its insidious penetration of cultures (Tomlinson 1999), its relation to human exploitation from early colonization right through to the 'free trade' of today (Ellwood 2002), and by way of extolling its power to generate wealth and to help the poor of the world. The view prevails that the intense interconnections of today's globalization represent the coming of age of MacLuhan's 'global village'. From this perspective, the successful spanning of material and semiotic distances by air-ways and ether-waves has simply multiplied the linkages which had begun almost invisibly several decades ago. All that is different today from those early days of globalization, in this view, is the intensification of these long existing interconnections and dependencies across the globe, which now tie distant destinies together even more closely than ever before. As to what has been globalized McGrew's (1992) list offers a typical answer: 'nowadays, goods, capital, people, knowledge, images, crime, pollutants, drugs, fashions and beliefs all readily flow across territorial boundaries'. The haphazard order of entries in McGrew's list is iconic of the absence of any evident principle for selection: the implicit message is that today anything and everything is globalized.

2.1 The underlying principle of globalization

I do not outright reject the relevance of these perspectives, but the narrative as it stands appears incomplete. It is reasonable to demand that an adequate 'globalization theory' should be able to explain the specific thrust of globalization as experienced today – the hostile reactions it is arousing in certain sections of the world community, the control on the initiation and the direction of its flow, and the underlying principle for selecting what will be globalized, for it is simply not the case that everything is open to globalization: as advertisements offering discount goods often warn, *conditions apply*. Strange as it may seem, I suggest that this underlying principle is implicit in the history of the word 'globalization'. In view of the wide acceptance of what Emmer (2003) calls 'the myth of early globalization', it comes as a surprise that the word 'globalization' is a relatively recent entry in the reputed English dictionaries of the world: it appears as if hardly any one used the word much before the 1990s. Take Collins COBUILD Dictionary of the English Language as a reliable source, since it is based on a huge 'flow through' corpus of contemporary English in daily use. Its first edition, appearing as late as 1987, makes no mention of the words 'globalize'/'globalization'. Of course the long established word 'global' is there, but 'globalization' is a newcomer on the scene. Here is part of what COBUILD Dictionary (1987: 167) had to say about 'global': 'global /gləubəl/ means **1** concerning or including the whole world ... **2** involving or relating to all the aspects of a situation...'.

Following the logic of English grammar, the verb 'globalize' may have been derived from the adjective to refer to the process(es) of making global had there been a need to do so. The next derivational step would yield the noun globalization, which by the same logic would mean 'the processes of globalizing'; 'the state or condition achieved by the process(es) of globalizing'. In other words, thanks to the logic of English form, a place had already been staked out for 'globalize'/'globalization' in the lexical potential of English, but this potential was not actualized right up to the end of the last century: the lexical items had no entry even in the 2nd edition of Collins COBUILD published in 1995. Significantly, the entries first appear in the 3rd edition dated 2001, as if heralding a new age. If 'globalize'/'globalization' first appear as dictionary entries in the year 2001, it appears safe to assume that they were already in use in the early to mid-90s, though as yet too much of a new arrival to gain sufficient weight for inclusion in the 1995 second edition. It seems reasonable to ask: what exactly happened post-1987 to bring the words 'globalize'/'globalization' increasingly into use? Systemic functional linguistics (=SFL) postulates that the secret of the activation of a linguistic meaning-wording conjunction is best sought in the context of culture. And a look into the cultural contexts of the Western nations in the late 1980s and the early 1990s reveals events significant enough to exercise the kind of semantic pressure (Butt 1985) which would activate new meanings: and true enough, major cultural changes, nothing short of dramatic, crystallized in the year 1989. A year of memorable happenings, it brought us Tiananmen Square in Beijing; hard upon which followed the dissolution of the communist regime in United Soviet Republic of Russia; and finally there was the fall of the Berlin Wall.

These events were widely seen as heralding the final vindication of capitalism: it had out-stayed the seemingly unstoppable success of communism.

Not surprisingly, the event was widely taken to 'prove' that capitalism had deserved to win. Coming at a decisive moment, the supremacy of capitalism has, without doubt, deeply affected the material and semiotic basis of our culture, bringing new markets, and new and cheaper resources for production, as well as a new moral basis for interpersonal relations. It was only logical to wish to globalize the capitalist ways which had proved successful in managing the production and distribution of goods and services. The greater spread of free trade is simply indicative of the principle underlying today's globalization; the need for expansion inheres in the system itself, as Collini (2000) remarked: 'capitalism requires global expansion; anything less is just a pause for breath'. In the political climate of the world symbolized by the year 1989, what could be more natural than the wish to carry the fruits of our victory to every corner of the world? These features of contemporary globalization are duly acknowledged in Collins COBUILD English Dictionary for Advanced Learners (2001: 665):

> **globalize** /gloubəlaiz/ (**globalizes, globalizing, globalized**)
> V-ERG when industry **globalizes or is globalized**, companies from one country link with companies from another country in order to do business with them *One way to lower costs will be to forge alliances with foreign companies or to expand internationally through appropriate takeovers – in short, 'to globalize'.*
> V- n **globalization** /gloubəlaizei *ʃən/ Trends toward the globalization of industry have dramatically affected food production in California.*

'Lower costs of production', 'international expansion of companies', 'appropriate takeovers' – these are the processes that 'in short' stand for the process known as 'to globalize'; and they are rather different from establishing the silk route along mountains and valleys or sailing the ocean in the *Cutty Sark* with sacks of tea and spice. The harmless sounding expression 'companies from one country link with companies from another country' somehow suggests the privilege is open to all – it is just a matter of choice; we will see below that this is not really the case. Speaking from the point of view of cultural context and of the usage of the Inner Circle English, the phenomenon we refer to as globablization is a post-1989 happening, which is not to claim that global trade, global media, global fashion, global pollution did not exist before. They did, but there was an important difference: before the 1990s they were not guided by quite so strident a faith in the virtues of 'free market fundamentalism' (Hobsbawm 1999: 69) as they are today. Of course, history had been slowly leading up to this climax; but then history always does that for every 'new' development, and in this sense there is nothing new under the sun. As Hobsbawm (1999: 61) observes, 'Globalization is not the product of a single action, like switching on a light or starting a car engine. It is a historical process that has undoubtedly speeded up enormously in the last ten years…'. What I am claiming here is that the speeding up of the historical process in this case has been accelerated by a large-scale acceptance of the staying power of capitalism. Globalization proclaims the virtue of this system. It has the potential of leading those countries which subscribe to it towards freedom, progress, democracy.

One may, therefore, justifiably paraphrase 'globalization' as the world-wide promulgation of principles and practices governed by an ideology of capitalism, an interpretation which captures the specific nature of today's globalization. We will globalize anything and everything, be it the Givenchi see-through tops or the demure harem trousers, music or mustard gas, fashion or GM food, our self-serving compassion or our dramatic devotion to democracy: the only condition is that, in the final analysis, the private monopoly of profit should remain protected in its incremental march. This is the underlying logic of McGrew's haphazard list. The history of the emergence of the words 'globalize'/'globalization' offers a remarkable insight into the fundamental principle which governs the various forms of globalizing practices, as well as the patterns of protest, and of contestation. In fact, what first drew my attention to globalization was how the English language was being mis/used in this confrontation.

2.2 Capitalizing on Capitalism

In this 'win-win' situation, there were very soon signs of growing dissatisfaction: language seemed to play a game the rules of which proved difficult to figure out. Starting with the first active protest against the underlying principle of globalization in Seattle during the WTO's Millennium Round of Trade Talks in December 1999, there have been protests at every gathering of active globalizing agencies. But it was in the early protests, especially the one in Seattle, that the 'tower of babel' effect seemed most striking. A fascinating quality of this discourse was that the meaning of apparently familiar expressions seemed to take on a protean quality, as if the semiotic currency had been deregulated to float to its true value by the forces of free market in speech. The protesters were protesting against the WTO as heartless exploiters of poor nations. However, WTO's publicity materials claimed that its policy was governed by a deep commitment to help underdeveloped countries, and by an unequivocal concern for the poor. International trade liberalization, non-discrimination and sustainable development were presented as the professed policies of this organization. These claims were corroborated by responsible citizens of the world. Mike Moore, the then Secretary General of WTO, declared with serious conviction: 'to those who argue that we should stop our work, I say: tell it to the poor, to the marginalized around the world, who are looking to us to help them' (*The Australian*, 2 December, 1999). Clare Short, as Britain's International Development Secretary, hailed globalization in a turn of the century policy document as a means of improving living standards in poor countries and hoped fervently that the protesters will not 'derail' this process. Kofi Annan, the UN Secretary General, counted 'faster growth, higher living standards, new opportunities' (*The News*, 15 December, 1999) amongst the benefits of globalization, especially for countries in need of help. Interpreting these statements in the 'ordinary' way, one would agree with the WTO spokesmen – and usually they are men! – that the protesters were either misinformed or mischievous trouble-makers, if not both. But the sympathizers of the protesters seemed to side with them: they told a different story. John Madeley (2000), author of *Big Business, Poor People* (1999), pointed out:

> The principle of non-discrimination is embodied in the 1993 Uruguay round agreement on trade related investment measures. It means that developing countries cannot give special treatment to their domestic companies. Neither can they insist that foreign companies use local labour... To many civil society groups *the principle of non-discrimination is unjust* – anti-democratic, because it threatens laws drawn up by democratically elected governments, and anti-economic development, because it ties the hands of poor countries, making development policy subservient to trade policy. The WTO's *'free trade' philosophy effectively reduces the freedom* of governments to buy locally produced materials or to use local labour (Italics introduced, *RH*).

Reflecting on the free, liberal and non-discriminatory practices of the WTO, Eduardo Galeano, the Uruguayan historian, commented that 'The problem with the specialised division of labour between nations is that some nations specialise in winning and others in losing.' Other sympathizers, such as Kevin Watkins, a policy adviser at Oxfam, explained that this happened so regularly because 'the winners specialise in fixing the rules to ensure that the losers stay where they are'. Listening to the sympathizers, one begins to appreciate why the protesters oppose the brand of egalitarian and liberal offers made by agents of globalization as harmful to poor countries: it is their view that the locutions and actions of organizations such as the WTO and the IMF are irreconcilable with each other. Their critique is further supported by reports of huge rises in corporate profits, while the gap between the rich and the poor continues to widen. For example, according to a report from the *Financial Times*, also cited by Hertz (2001), General Motors' annual revenue in the year 2000 was almost equal to the combined GDP of eight countries, namely, Chad, Nicaragua, Namibia, Kenya, Sri Lanka, Uruguay, New Zealand and Ireland – significantly, none of these countries has any real power to take decisions which might alter the rules governing globalization practices; they must all participate in the process but on terms fixed by others with an eye to their own profit, as is logical in a capitalist world!

3 A globalized language

The contradictory reading of intentions and actions by the contesting parties might tempt one to treat the matter as a simple choice between truth and falsehood. This, however, cannot be the case, if for no other reasons than that the 'falsehoods' appear so transparent they could hardly be attempts at a consciously and carefully crafted lie. What is happening is not so much the distortion of reality, but very probably a semiotic struggle to promulgate a definition of reality where, speaking metaphorically, the distinction between black and white is wiped out. Whatever the case, when the claims of the two sides in this confrontation are examined, then at least from the perspective of a conventional reading of English, what emerges is simply a series of oxymorons:

non-discrimination	is	discriminatory
free trade philosophy	reduces	freedom
liberalization of trade	imposes	constraints
non-discrimination	is	anti-democratic

In normal use of English, i.e., with conventional wording-meaning couplings, each of the above assertions is likely to be perceived as SELF-CONTRADICTORY. As a semiotic system, the internal make up of language is completely impartial to ethical matters: despite warnings from philosophers, languages neither tell the truth, nor do they lie. They simply express whatever the speaker is capable of wanting to express, and more to the point neither truth makes language sound 'better' nor do lies disturb the normal formal functioning of language: to succeed as a lie, the lie has to 'look' pretty much like a truth. But there is one discursive feature – namely that of self-contradiction – that does interfere with the efficient working of linguistic form. This may be because self-contradiction clearly interferes with what Saussure called a sign's ASSOCIATIVE BONDS: it seems to throw into doubt those *in absentia* relations of a sign which, though materially absent from the syntagm, are nonetheless active in its process of meaning construal. For this reason self-contradictory speech is received with reserve: the listener will often 'look around' to find an interpretation which will allow the 'rational', i.e., conventional interpretation or one that suggests deliberate effort at creating a 'new'/'secret' language. If all such efforts fail, self-contradictory discourse is highly likely to be treated as indicative of some kind of pathological condition in the speaker.

The deliberate creation of a variety of language by a sub-section of the wider speech community is a well recognized sociolinguistic phenomenon. Such 'new' varieties are not necessarily crafted to display 'artistic creativity' as for example with the symbolist poets or the dada-ists; the newness may be motivated by a desire for 'secrecy'. The latter situation is well recorded by Mallik (1972) who reported on the variety of language spoken in the underworld of West Bengal by the criminal community and the prisoners. In discussing this underworld sociolect, Halliday (1976c) coined the term 'anti-language' – perhaps because it goes against the accepted conventions of the communal language. This anti-language is a variety that construes a parallel reality, turning the wider community's usage upside down. How was this effect achieved? The strategy they used has been referred to as the device of RE-LEXIFICATION: for referring to old concepts, the speakers of anti-language created new words sometime by applying certain principles to the original ones or by replacing them by a semantically related item. Thus the outer world's /dʊkan/, meaning 'shop' becomes /kʊdan/ in the parallel world of the prison; the Arabic word /xəlas/ meaning 'end' replaces the word /xun/, meaning 'blood/murder'; the English word 'ḍəbal-ḍekar' (double-decker), borrowed in many Indian languages, is metaphorically turned into 'a plump woman'.

Something of a similar kind seems to be going on in the language devised for dealings in the globalized market. But there are important differences between the two variety types: first, the variety of English used by the chieftains of globalized industry and trade – let me call it GLIB-SPEAK for ease of reference – is not spoken by disadvantaged members of the under-world as is Mallik's; the speakers of this glib-speak are 'on top of the world' in more than one sense. We have here a variety devised by the executive cadre of corporate concerns, whose benign organizations produce what, from the point of view of the disadvantaged countries, in fact, turns out to be a contradiction in terms at the level of meaning. Secondly, while a modification of meaning is being attempted in both varieties, in glib-speak, the method goes beyond re-lexification which as we saw above relies on phonological reversal, or by the introduction of borrowings; even straight lexical metaphors do not seem to be employed in the variety we are calling glib-speak. Words such as 'equality, 'freedom', 'liberalization', 'non-discrimination' acquire a meaning that turns the semantics of ordinary English upside down: for words long familiar to the ordinary speakers of English, the globalizing variety of English is offering new concepts, which are friendly to those fully familiar with the ideology of capitalism but deadly for the newcomers in the field. The conflict is ideological in glib-speak just as much as it is in Mallik's West Bengal anti-language, but without the overt formal features specific to the latter. There is, however, clear evidence of a 'liberal' use of re-semanticization: in the end, in both cases, language is simply pressed into service to do what it always does, i.e., to act as a resource for speakers' acts of meaning. This invites closer attention: how is re-semanticization effected in glib-speak?

3.1 The re-semanticization potential for glib-speak

It is my understanding that in different world Englishes the specific patterns of re-semanticization are activated by elements in the designs of the host cultures – elements that are in fact applicable to the wider community at large. By contrast, re-semanticization in glib-speak only respects boundaries set by power and control on material wealth: it is a variety devised by and useful to the captains of industry in advanced, progressive democracies. If the meanings of long-established linguistic patterns are being 'hijacked' in order to disarm objections by those to whom the locution is addressed and whose interests are at risk, the interesting question is: what properties of language allow the systematic production of such devices? Naturally, for any pattern of language to be voiced, we need a sentient speaker with percepts, beliefs, intentions and what-not, but whatever these beliefs or intentions might be, language itself has to have the potentiality of being used in ways that permit the possibility of 're-writing' large segments of its own semantic potential without easy 'detection' by the ordinary speakers of the language. And this is done not through a slow process of change as happens naturally from one historical language-stage to the next, which forms the subject of enquiry for experts studying historical linguistic change, but through an intensity of use within a short period of time by those who can enforce their will within a particular specialized sphere. By way of attempting an exploration of these processes, let me first examine certain general properties and patterns that will be found in all languages and that appear open to use in ways that could lead to some variety of re-semanticization. In the following section I will identify three specific ways of bringing about semantic camouflage, for this is what glib-speak seems to be out to achieve. If the focus is on meaning then clearly the levels of language most relevant to the discussion will be those of lexicogrammar and semantics.

3.2 Language as a resource for exploitation

One such pattern has its basis in a widely recognized phenomenon, albeit under different names; this is the contrast between 'purr' and 'snarl' words as illustrated in a two member (rather improbable!) clause complex, such as '(i) my children are *lively*; (ii) your children are *unruly*'. The lexical item highlighted in (i) is a 'purr' word, conveying a positive evaluation; that in (ii) is a 'snarl' word; it creates a negative evaluation. But what is it that is being evaluated? In this particular case, we might note the curious fact that pretty much the same state of affairs might be being referred to with the difference that in one case the implied actors are 'my children' and in the other they are 'your children'. With the use of the purr word in (i) 'my children' *look good*: they are 'lively' and being lively is regarded generally in the community as a good quality; by contrast, your children *look bad* having been described as 'unruly' which is rather an undesirable quality. And yet in actual fact, what they may have been doing is being 'very active'/'making a lot of noise'/'creating a hullabaloo' – call it what you will, but note that here, too, evaluation is occurring; the three descriptions of the states of affairs move increasingly towards the less desirable end! In other words, the judgmental nature of human language is something that cannot be avoided: language usually refers to human ways of being, doing, thinking and feeling, as it does also to human attributes; and as yet we have not come across a community that does not automatically 'judge' these phenomena by reference to the standards prevalent in the community. Using the concept of metafunctions as theorized in SFL we might describe the two clauses as same/similar experientially, but differing markedly in terms of the interpersonal. At the level of context, the tenor of discourse is different for the two utterances in that the speaker's evaluation of the state of affairs, specifically with reference to the subject of the clause is markedly different.

The reason for starting with the well known device, which will be referred to here as INHERENT EVALUATION,[2] is to point to the familiar but highly effective resource every language has: languages are not simply a mechanism for referring to things and events. Along with their potential for the construal of experiential meanings, they are all *at the same time* also a resource for the creation of human relations, whereby we establish, maintain and alter our relations to our addressee, we express our likes, dislikes, our attitudes to those we are interacting with as well as other persons, things and events we may be talking about; we may indicate our estimates of possibility, probability, obligation, and so on. Inherent evaluation is just one of the linguistic patterns pertaining to the interpersonal metafunction.

Turn now to a second pattern of language – this time beginning with the semantics of the lexical items. Consider an ordinary clause such as *Mona's husband is not a man*. Interpreted literally, it would be self-contradictory. It will therefore call attention to itself. In the absence of evidence to the contrary, listeners typically operate on the default assumption that speakers are neither pathological nor willing creators of nonsense; they will, therefore, look for some other explanations. On the evidence of sensi-ble information they know the speaker is not denying Mona's husband the properties of being animate, *Homo sapiens*, adult, male. This leaves those properties which are conventionally associated with being a member of a category so defined, which may be stated roughly as those of being 'humane', 'brave', 'fair', 'civil', 'possessing judgment', and so on. We may, in fact, make a general claim: (with the possible exception of the QUALIA) all lexical items are a composite realization of a configuration of semantic features which can be analysed as pertaining to two distinct parts. First, a lexical item realizes semantic elements that are INHERENT to the category in that they are in some sense demonstrable such as for the item *man* the elements 'animate', '*Homo sapiens*', 'adult', 'male'; and secondly, the item will also realize a set of features that are INFERENTIALLY DERIVED from each of the inherent features. Thus from the feature 'animate' may be inferred automotive mobility and mutability – i.e., the quality of being subject to change as in the processes of birth, growth, death. From '*Homo sapiens*' can be inferred intelligence, humanity, non-brutishness i.e., civility, fairness among other qualities; and so on for the remaining semantic features of the first group. Traditional linguistics has recognized these two groups of semantic features, as DENOTATIVE and CONNOTATIVE meaning, respectively. With its partiality to experiential phenomena, it has treated denotative meaning as the 'real stuff'; after all these are the features that 'define' the category: they are sensi-ble. By contrast, connotative meaning has received less attention: derived properties, they tend to be just intelligi-ble. These meanings are said to be based in individuals' experience, and so, less stable across the community. I hope to show that this view lacks logical/empirical foundation, even though it is hallowed by tradition.

Be that as it may, the point to be emphasized here is that the lexical items in all languages possess a property one might refer to as INHERENT SEMANTIC ELASTICITY. This arises from the two part grouping of the semantic features as discussed above. For most language users, the inherent/denotative elements of meaning are highly likely to be at the conscious level of awareness; the others, i.e., inferred/connotative ones are likely to remain relatively submerged. This, however, does not imply that such meanings are irrelevant or unimportant, simply that when it comes to recording their meaning in dictionaries, it is the former that are given pride of place; the others, some times but not always, get a mention. They *will* float into users' conscious awareness as soon as their applicability is challenged as for example in

Mona's husband is not a man or *last night it rained heavily so the garden is dry today*. Based on the associative bonds, (discussion, section 3), these submerged elements of meaning are 'cryptotypic' (Whorf 1956): their significance is brought to consciousness when their reactance is called into question: to challenge reactance is indeed equal to denying 'unquestionable' reality. The apparent fluidity of meanings brought to consciousness in actual acts of saying is a resource which offers speakers a choice of truncating or extending the meaning of (some part of) an utterance. Naturally the choice between which semantic features will be offered to the hearers' consciousness is not accidental: it too serves the interests of the speaker, governed by their 'natural' ways of thinking, i.e., by their ideology.

A third, equally familiar pattern of human language is the sense relation called HYPONYMY, whereby a more general class is related to two or more subclasses, each of which is more specific than the general class. The former – the more general class – is traditionally known as SUPERORDINATE, while the others – the more specific classes – are known as the SUBORDINATE/HYPONYM categories. The set of semantic features underlying a hyponym is more extensive than those of its superordinate: in fact the former includes *all* features of the latter. A good deal has been written (e.g., Kress and Hodge 1979) on the ideologically sensitive potentiality of the passive voice to withhold information when it suits the speaker. It is clear that with their relatively more general meanings, the superordinate items too are a good device for 'withholding' information. For lack of time and space, I will not be able to return to this pattern in more detail, but let me present a quick example, provided recently by the Australian Chief Superintendent of Police who, prior to a contentious meeting of the globalizers, announced that 'normal measures for crowd control will be employed' if the protesting crowd refused to 'disperse on advice'. The formulation 'normal measures for crowd control' does away with such repugnant facts as the use of batons, tear-gas, rubber bullets and arrests, while creating a spurious sense of comfortable normality. The restoration of order is normally a comforting thing unless we know that in creating such 'order' there might be 'collateral damage' in the shape of wounded and/or dead bodies. Here, then, is another means by which the speaker can control the listener's access to information to suit his/her own purposes. The three patterns I have brought to attention are clearly not the only ones which can serve speakers' ideological purposes. If language is viewed as a system of multiple systems of choices, then, in a manner of speaking, all its use has to be seen as ideological: in the final analysis, the actual choice, albeit unconscious, lies with speakers, who 'in the nature of things' are socially positioned and thus ideology-specific; their inclination towards this choice or that is a matter of their *habitus*, their mode(s) of orientation to experience. I limit myself to these three patterns, because they seem particularly revealing in the analysis of the variety of globalizing English which I am calling glib-speak.

3.3 Subverting evaluation

Let me turn first to inherent evaluation: it clearly depends on a grading along the continuum of desirability. In the examples offered, I have already identified its two endpoints: the POSITIVE, e.g., celebration, victory, applause, praise and so on; and the NEGATIVE, e.g., murder, deception, loss, denigration, and so on. Between these endpoints is the median position, call it NEUTRAL, e.g., activity, organization, group, and so on, which are relatively free of affective reaction. I have deliberately used nouns as examples, since it has been often taken for granted that only certain kinds of adjectives can function evaluatively. In fact, evaluative gradability is a parameter applicable to all lexical items; they after all refer to things, events, circumstances, which, in their turn, are commonly seen by the members of a speech community as either good, or bad or neither.

It is important to conceptualize inherent evaluation as a continuum with a median point which, in a manner of speaking, is neutral. For this neutrality can be exploited by certain structural means: for example, the neutrality of reaction is compromised/modified when/if the neutral items are in close collocation with items attracting decidedly positive or negative evaluation, as illustrated by the following examples:

POSITIVE	NEUTRAL	NEGATIVE
helper	group	terrorist
charity	organization	incendiary
supportive	activities	obstructive
free	trade	restrictive

Most members of the community would welcome a helper group (or a group willing to help); hardly any would be delighted at the prospect of being visited by a terrorist group (or a group engaged in terrorism): let me refer to this as the device of AFFECTIVE COLOURING, whereby the referent of the neutral item acquires a desirable or undesirable face. Items from the two endpoints of the continuum of desirability will typically not be placed in close colligation (Firth 1957) e.g., in a modifier-head structure, though after Iraq *benevolent bombing* should, perhaps, be conceded as a distinct possibility: benevolent is positive while bombing is decidedly negative. The liberal interpretation that items such as 'liberal'/'liberalize' have received in glib-speak illustrates the usefulness of affective colouring. The reason that the mention of liberal/liberalization has aroused such feelings of bitter disillusionment have to do with the reversal of meaning which ends up appearing to give with one hand while taking away with the other. To appreciate this claim, we must first examine the meanings of liberal that lie at the level of conscious awareness, and are enshrined in dictionaries, e.g., in the Collins COBUILD entries (1987: 833):

> **liberal** /libərəl/, **liberals**. **1** liberal is used to describe **1.1** a person or institution that is tolerant of different kinds of behaviour or opinions. ...**1.2** a person who is moderate in their political beliefs, favouring gradual social progress by the changing of laws, rather than by revolution... **1.3** a person who is in favour of people having a lot of political freedom or a system which allows a lot of it...
>
> ....
>
> **liberalize** /liəbərəlaiz/, ... When a country or government **liberalizes** its laws or its attitudes, it makes them less strict and allows people more freedom in their actions. EG ... *a move to liberalize the state abortion laws...*

The elements that seem to be important to the meaning of liberal are freedom, tolerance, and moderation. The adjective *liberal* definitely expresses a positive evaluation, and so, logically, the semantic features realized by the item (and its derivatives) would also be commonly perceived as positive by most speakers. A cryptotypic element of the meaning of liberal/liberalization is the inference of generosity, sensitivity to the need of the other; instead of being focussed on the speaker's own benefit, to be liberal is to be other-oriented. This is why it would be odd to hear someone say *I made a liberal demand*: a demand by its nature is for the benefit of the demander, not for that of the demandee! Thus, at a deeper level of consciousness, I would take the semantic feature 'other-oriented' as relevant to the meaning of liberal (and its derivatives). In glib-speak, and so in reports on it, the item liberalization typically collocates most often with trade (about 33%) or trade-related items such as market, economic, business (about 40%). Now the meaning of trade is markedly different from liberal/liberalize etc., as the delicate grammar of typical trading activities such as buying, selling, lending and borrowing shows (Hasan 1985a). In the reciprocal processes of trade, each participant must guard his/her own interests – an age-old principle recognized even in the custom of barter; in other words, trade is precisely the converse of liberal so far as its cryptotypic semantic feature other-oriented is concerned.

From the point of view of the addressee, who of course does not have the benefit of such analysis, the colligation of 'liberal' and 'trade' through its affective colouring makes trade appear more desirable, *precisely because liberal trade promises to be other-oriented*: the ordinary use of the English language does not prepare the listener to interpret this as trade for the benefit of the speaker. But the inventors of this expression are corporate commercial bodies: in their ideology, trade is worth engaging in only if it is to one's own advantage. Naturally then *there has to be a semantic reversal whereby the cryptotypic feature other-oriented comes to be replaced by its converse, i.e., ego-oriented*: liberal trade effectively becomes trade for the benefit of the initiators of globalization. As Watkins said 'the winners specialise in fixing the rules to ensure that the losers stay where they are'. Through bitter experience, disadvantaged countries, which have experienced the 'liberalization of trade', know that when WTO talks of liberal trade, what this means is 'trade organised for the benefit of the successful capitalist countries'; any advantage that comes to the disadvantaged workers of poorer countries is incidental. Klemperer (2002: 16) in his discussion of the changes to the German language during the Nazis period thoughtfully observes that 'if someone replaces the words "heroic" and "virtuous" by the word "fanatical" for long enough, he (*sic*!) will come to believe that a fanatic really is a virtuous hero'. True enough, but people such as Klemperer who actually suffered from this semantic reversal could hardly have subscribed to that belief, even if they had no means of protesting, even if they had a sense that language was being used as an instrument of oppression! This powerful effect is achieved through a subtle exploitation of the potential offered by inherent evaluation and by inherent elasticity of meaning. A decade ago, following the views of dominant linguistics, Bourdieu (1992: 39) had remarked that whereas denotation, enshrined in the dictionary, represents the 'official meaning' of a word, 'connotation refers to the singularity of the individual experiences…' However, I suggest that what makes semantic reversal so powerful a strategy is the communal agreement about a word's connotation: it is the reversal of a connotative (cryptotypic) meaning in the use of 'liberal' that has aroused the angry sense of betrayal in the community of the poorer countries.

The anti-language of Mallik's underworld speakers does not appear to use the strategy of semantic reversal; what is used is phonological reversal, and a skilful melange of borrowing and metaphorical signification. The cultural context in which this variety is embedded helps to explain the pressures for the production of such patterns: as Halliday (1976c) suggests, the language of the wider community and that of the one which inhabited the underworld formed two parallel orders of reality. Dialogue between the two is certainly not sought by the underworld; the devices of phonological reversal, borrowing with a special sense and metaphorical reference all render their variety of language relatively 'opaque' to the outside community, which is how the speakers liked it. The cultural context of glib-speak is remarkably different. Far from the exclusion of others, what is essential to the users of glib-speak is to use other members of the community as a resource for their profit-making activities by invoking the familiar to create an impression of normality while at the same time playing on wordings and meanings in a manner that offers the opportunity for profit making. Unlike Mallik's subjects, the speakers of glib-speak do not seek to protect/create an alternative reality; far from it, they seek to have reality defined on their own terms by playing/preying on familiar words, in ways that help secure their economic goals. In this sense, if an anti-language is a variety for the exclusion of the other, glib-speak is a variety for creating false consciousness in the other, which should remind one of Karl Marx's (1985) views on ideology.

3.4 Exploiting semantic elasticity, restricting the meaning of democracy

It is not simply the connotative/cryptotypic meaning that can be exploited for defining reality in ways that are friendly to the speaker's ideological stance. Denotative meanings too can be subverted by constraining the defining semantic features. To illustrate this let us take the word 'democracy', and its derivatives, since the liberalizers of trade and commerce are also dedicated to the cause of democracy, and a significant first order collocate of democracy is free trade/market/commerce, not to speak of freedom itself, which is appreciably different from 'freedom' as used in the context of global trade. While the mention of the word might remind some of us of its famous description as 'the government of the people, by the people, for the people', a reliable dictionary such as Collins COBUILD, bases its judgment on what is perceived as the views prevalent in the community as judged by normal natural usage. Here is an extract from the dictionary entries for 'democracy'/'democratic' (375):

> **democracy** /dimɒkrəsi/, **democracies. 1. democracy** is **1.1** a system of government in which people choose their rulers by voting for them in election…
> **1.2** a system of running organizations, businesses, groups etc., in which each member is entitled to vote and participate in management decisions…
> **2** A **democracy** is a country in which the people choose their government by voting for it…
> **democrat** /dimɒkræt/, **democrats. 1** A **democrat** is…
> **democratic** /dimɒkrætIk/. **1** A country, government, or political system that is **democratic** has representatives who are elected by the people…

> **2** Something that is **democratic** is based on the idea that everyone should have equal rights and should be involved in making important decisions...

In this short extract, the words choice/choose, vote/elect occur more than half a dozen times. This might imply that the primary defining element of the meaning of democracy is 'people's right to choose'. Elections and voting are treated as orderly ways of effecting choice, and in our daily experience a 'democratic' government is one that has been voted in by the people. However, we are also told by the dictionary that 'something that is democratic is based on the idea that everyone should have equal rights and should be involved in making important decisions'. There are, thus, other elements to the meaning of this word: the right to elect a representative governing body; to participate in decision making; equal rights for justice, education, health care, and systems of belief; freedom from coercion; right to personal dignity; right to property and no doubt some more such things. Given the confusion that surrounds the use of the terms denotation and connotation (Lyons 1977), it is not easy to say which of these elements of the meaning of democracy are to be treated as decidedly denotative, which connotative. But what is quite clear is the fact that due to the inherent elasticity of meaning, speakers have the ability to choose as they wish. In the hands of the powerful, this is a powerful strategy for the classification and re-classification of common categories of experience; even a communally recognized primary meaning such as the right to elect a representative government can be, and has been, subverted.

To give an actual example of how in glib-speak, democracy changes its semantic colour like a chameleon, let us recall an event in October 1999, when the ruling Prime Minister of Pakistan, Nawaz Sharif, was toppled by his own Chief of Army Staff General Parvez Musharraf. The democracies of the world, from the west to the east, were outraged, because a democracy had been replaced by a military regime. But was Nawaz Sharif's government democratic? The answer depends on what semantic elements may be considered inherent to democracy. The source of the answer might be either how some particular segment of the world community uses this word, or one might visit the opinions of those who had a direct experience of how Nawaz Sharif's democratic regime actually worked in their life. I offer below some of the reactions reported by reliable sources.

> *This is the face of a man who betrayed his own people*
> [A caption under Sharif's photo pinned to a tree in Bani Gala, Pakistan]

> *He (i.e. Sharif) destroyed our house; now God has destroyed him. We're happy he's gone!*
> [Comment by a Saidpur Pakistani whose house was demolished because it had appeared as an eyesore on Sharif's route to the capital: reported *New York Times* October 99 http://www.nytimes.com/library/world/asia/103099pakistan-coup.html].

> *you bribe people, it works: you don't, it doesn't.*
> *for the people there is no democracy: who comes, who goes makes no difference to us*
> [anonymous comments by Pakistanis on how democracy works in the country]

For its breach of democracy, Pakistan was promptly punished by sanctions from the many progressive countries of the world, who, nonetheless, find it morally sound to go on trading with Burma. Perhaps, one should concede that even a semblance of democracy is better even under generals as in Burma than a military coup d'état, or foreign occupation by force. But Sharif's democracy was strictly speaking a democracy in an entirely attenuated sense of the word. Certainly there had been elections; votes had been cast, but the majority of voters had very little idea of the significance of their votes, and it is by no means certain that the voting was by free choice: if media reports from the country are to be credited, threats and bribes were used. As the comments on the occasion of his political demise show, there had been no general participation by ordinary people in decision making, no right to equality, no right to personal dignity, not even safety. It is worth noting that amongst the outraged nations, the US, which claims to be the first democracy of the world, was equally, if not more, incensed. This was in late 1999; but things were to change dramatically in a short span of two years after 9/11. In late 2001 the sanctions were lifted and Musharraf became an important part of the Alliance against Terrorism; so far as democracy is concerned, the internal political situation of Pakistan was practically the same as it was in October 1999. What should we say democracy meant at the moment of forging this alliance? Recent regime change to bring democracy and freedom to Iraq through continued military presence and violence shows quite clearly that the term democracy is used in the context of Iraq's freedom simply because of the term's positive evaluation; if at this moment Iraq is conceded to be a 'democracy', then certainly the element of free choice can no longer be thought crucial to the meaning of democracy, even by those who approve of this formulation. Thus there does not appear to be any linguistic strategy at work in connection with democracy, except that of ignoring the communal usage or altering it unilaterally to suit the convenience of those agencies that have been active in the globalization of the world.

3.4 Locution, action, and democracy as people participation

So far we have discussed the primary element of the meaning of democracy, namely people's right to free choice of a representative governing body. Let us turn briefly now to consider who it is that the chosen representatives serve and who has the privilege of participation in decision making. The dictionary talks blithely of people 'being entitled to vote and participate in…decision [making]' and that 'everyone should have equal rights and should be involved in making important decisions'. But perhaps as the popular saying goes sometimes actions speak louder than the words. On people participation, we turn for an example to the first democracy of the world, the United States of America. The well known journalist Martin Kettle (2001) reports in the 'Washington Diary' that:

> …'Conservation may be a sign of personal virtue, but it is not a sufficient basis for a sound, comprehensive energy policy,' Cheney said in Toronto. 'The aim here is efficiency, not austerity…'.
>
> Environmental groups claim that they have been shut out of the energy review. Cheney quite simply refuses to discuss his ideas with them. By contrast, the views of industry moguls and insiders are given long and lavish attention…
>
> Cheney's report will not only advocate drilling in Alaska [National Wild Life Refuge]. It is also being pressed to loosen restrictions in parts of the Montana Rockies, as well as to extend offshore drilling. The coal industry will get a boost too, and the report will endorse the building of the first new nuclear power plants in the US since the Three Mile Island accident in 1979.

A closer examination of the brief quote from Cheney reveals the powerful exploitation of 'connotative' meaning and communal evaluation in glib-speak. Note the contrasts: conservation clearly cannot be reviled; but if there is a contest between it and sound comprehensive energy policy, then the latter wins hands down in a world dominated by capitalist modes of production and distribution. Energy is the lifeline of everything the capitalist enterprise stands for; a 'sound policy' to manage its continued flow is anytime much more important than any 'personal virtue,' which stands no chance whatever in comparison with 'national interest', for which read 'the corporate sector's interest'. From the experiential point of view, 'austerity' is not an antonym of 'efficiency'; but, interpersonally, the two terms are located at the opposite end of the desirability continuum. Austerity is undesirable: hardly anyone is likely to welcome it. Similarly, anyone who knows the English language – no matter which variety of world Englishes it is – would welcome efficiency: it is a desirable thing to have. Thus the two terms are directly opposed; or, technically, they are interpersonal antonyms. Brief as the quoted Cheney utterance is, thanks to the property of inherent evaluation, it says in no unclear terms: 'listener! if you are being rational, you will side with me'. But this view of rational behaviour is not as unquestionable as Cheney makes it out, and this becomes clear as we move further into Kettle's report. We learn that austerity has something to do with placing restraint on practices that contribute to environmental degradation; what it means in this context is the adoption of measures that might safeguard the long-term survival of the world, rather than the short-term profiteering by interested groups, the prime principle of the capitalist systems.

But there is more to the report: we are told of environmental groups' claim that 'they have been shut out of the energy review; Cheney 'refuses to discuss his ideas with them. By contrast, the views of industry moguls and insiders are given long and lavish attention'. So we gather that in the first democracy of the world there is certainly consultation and participation in decision making, but not by 'people' in general. A shift has occurred in the reference of the word 'people'. The common expectation is that this word will refer to any member of the community in question: but the reality is different. There is certainly participation in decision making but there is also exclusion as the report points out: thus, for 'people' read 'government approved sub-section of people'. Why should this be so? What determines which sub-section will be consulted and who will have the privilege of participating in decision making? Perhaps the following snippet from the World section of *South China Morning Post* reported on 19 May 2001 (p. 15) is relevant:

> US energy companies lavishly financed Republican political campaigns last year, according to watchdog groups.
>
> Oil and gas companies gave Republican politicians US$25.5 million…, almost four times as much as they gave Democrats, according to figures obtained by the Centre for Responsive Politics. The electricity industry gave almost US$450,000 to President George W. Bush, seven times what they gave his Democrat opponent, Al Gore. The coal industry gave Mr Bush over US$100,000 and the nuclear power industry over US$290,000.

> Common Cause, another watchdog group, revealed electric utilities contributed US$10.1 million to the two major parties.

This reminds us of the protestors' complaint that the words of the powerful authorities active in globalization are irreconcilable with their actions. The way the word people is interpreted in action is quite different from the general understanding of the word: only those qualify as people with the right to participate in decision making who hold their purse strings open for the candidates during election time. So, what does it means to say 'people's right to choose'? Are all the people really choosing by voting in an election or is a certain choice being thrust on them by the machination of those who favour that particular choice, because it is in their interest? The manipulation of meaning, which seems to be the hallmark of glib-speak, provides its own silent answer. MacIntyre (1999: 122) sums up the cultural milieu of today's globalized world:

> Ours is a political culture deeply fractured by fundamental moral disagreements. It is also a political culture whose public rhetoric is well designed to disguise and to conceal the extent of that disagreement by invoking an idiom of consensus with regard to values. In order to function effectively that rhetoric must be able to make use of sentences that both command widespread assent and yet which are at the same time available for the expression of sets of very different and incompatible moral judgements. Thereby an illusion is created of agreement in valuing such virtues as courage, generosity and justice, while at the same time disguising the range of alternative and conflicting conceptions of such virtues…

4 Globalization and education

In recent years there has been much debate about the relations of globalization and culture. It is suggested that the complexity of the culture and of globalization cannot be understood simply by examining 'production, circulation and consumption' important though they may be (Tomlinson 1999). However, the analysis of the characteristics of glib-speak shows how deeply and widely the principles of capitalist management penetrate the many aspects of our social existence, which at first glance appear to be quite independent of economic considerations. There is little reason to doubt that as time goes on, 'the blind mole that is capitalism' will, in the words of Collini (2000) 'burrow deeper into the texture of life. It knows no other way.' From fashion to education, from freedom to modes of self-assessment, the capitalist philosophy regulating the march of globalization will continue to shape our existence. In fact higher education has already received an ultimatum (Oblinger 1999), as the extract from Becket's (1999) review indicates:

> It is high time, says Oblinger, that academic communities started to concentrate on teaching the skills, attitudes and personal attributes that business requires. Students should be taught 'to understand the unwritten rules of the corporate culture'. The Regius Professor of Lithuanian Mythology must make way for the Bill Gates Professor of Massive Profits…
>
> But what if academics refuse to allow business to dictate the curriculum? Then, opines Oblinger grimly, they face a bleak future. 'To get a sympathetic ear from legislators, higher education will need strong advocacy from the business community, an ally it is unlikely to win unless it has put itself through the same sort of streamlining and re-engineering that the business community has.'

This prophesy has partly come true: corporate business, as symbolized by Nike, has already shown that it will exercise control on how educational institutions conduct themselves: note, Nike withdrew its huge grants to universities whose student groups had participated in protests against work conditions for off-shore labour. 'We are not going to give a blank check to dictate our business', its chief executive declared. If students are committed to fight for workers' rights in ways that impinge adversely on the production policy of corporate businesses, damaging their profit margin, they would have to be politically very naive to go on expecting generous grants from them. In the ethos of 'compassionate capitalism', this stands to reason: it is a demonstration of non-discrimination and fair business practice; no one should expect something for nothing!

4.1 Literacy in a globalized world

This brings me to the final movement of my paper, namely the role of literacy education in the 'brave new world' fashioned by globalization. There are, of course, different understandings of the word literacy, inspired by ideas about what constitutes education. Thus, literacy education may be simply seen as teaching students how the sounds and letters of a language calibrate; how to convert a message (fragment) from the visual modality to the aural one, and vice versa. This is the oldest interpretation in official pedagogic sites all over the world, and elsewhere (Hasan 1996b; Chapter 5 here) I have called it RECOGNITION LITERACY: persons with this expertise might 'read out' an instruction; the degree of comprehension might leave much to be desired. It is a form of literacy that flourishes where, as Bernstein (1975a) put it, curriculum is governed by 'collection code': language is simply an item in the list of disciplines. A (historically) second interpretation of the term became popular in the second half of the last century, particularly in the more affluent industrialized countries, call it ACTION LITERACY. It is a form favoured in educational systems governed by Bernstein's 'integration code': the boundaries between subjects are seen here as permeable. 'Language across the curriculum' is an expression of this approach. It includes such impressive sounding goals as 'self-expression', and display of sensibility, as well as the much better theorized discourse on the ability to produce texts in genres that are educationally valued, so as to maximize chances of educational success (Martin 1986). This latter form of literacy, known as genre-based pedagogy, aims to enable pupils to 'write to mean' (Painter and Martin 1986). Whether it is the former, vaguer self-expression or the latter highly explicit genre-based pedagogy, in both cases the goal is conformity to an already established pattern. Following logically the dictates of action literacy, education must, in this era of globalization, teach its pupils to become fluent in glib-speak, to package their ideas in the preferred mode so as to maximize the chances of success in profits. Action literacy is certainly a considerable advance on recognition literacy, and educating pupils to understand how things are done in their culture by using language is a necessary part of education; nonetheless, we also need to go beyond it, to what for want of a better term I have called REFLECTION LITERACY. This form presupposes the expertise of both forms of literacy discussed above, but at the same time it aims to create in the pupil an understanding of reading and writing as bearers of deep social significance, not simply as a vehicle for information but as a potent instrument of social formation of personalities: it is a form of literacy that would go beyond simple interpretation to reflection on how the 'same' words can be made to construe different meanings and what is the social significance of such semantic construals. The interpretations of extracts presented and discussed in this chapter are one example of how the successful teaching of reflection literacy would lead to a deeper understanding of the messages encountered in any mode. The implication is that reflection literacy moves from comprehension into enquiry: the literate person should be able to interrogate the wording and the meaning of any utterance – why these words, what meanings are ascribed to them, how do they differ from the use of the word elsewhere, what do they achieve by the way they are used, contributing to whose loss and to whose benefit? In my view literacy of this kind will enable the listeners of varieties such as glib-speak to understand where the elected democracy of one's country might be taking one, how much comfort our so-called progress has brought to humanity, and what the underlying principles of our admirable civilization happen to be. From the point of view of reflection literacy, education is not simply a system for the transmission of a certain quota of information packaged within named disciplines; it should aim at enabling one to live as a human being deserving of the term *Homo sapiens*.

4.2 Concluding remarks

Much has been written about the power of language from the point of view of world Englishes e.g., Kachru (1986), Thumboo (1986), Kandiah (2001), Rahim (1986), to mention but a few. Throughout this paper, I too have emphasized the power of language, but perhaps by this phrase I mean something slightly different. For me, this power resides simply in the flexible design of language as system whereby it meets most if not each and every demand of the speaker. However, one thing it is essential to remember: in itself the power of language is simply a potential; its semiotic energy requires the ideological spur of the speaker to be activated; the active principle is always the socially positioned speaker. When in the context of its world-wide expansion, we talk of English as a killer language, we put the blame where it does not belong. It is not English that is the killer, it is the ideology of the dominant speakers of English, their ways of being, thinking, doing and saying that knowingly or unknowingly kill. 'Language as power', in the words of Edwin Thumboo (1986), may be 'a truism, topic, slogan, bone of contention, premise, proposition, irritation and much else'; but one thing that language as power is not is 'wilful'. To say that the power of language is in its potential, is to say that it is capable of being used as an infinite resource (Halliday 2001); but this potential is ideologically neutral,[3] which follows logically from the fact that it has to satisfy the needs of diverse ideologies: it has neither the will to exploit, nor to support, nor does it deceive. However, the situation is different when it comes to language in use, where the language's potential is actualized by speakers in the living of life: this use is always ideological, because both the production and reception of discourse is performed by socially positioned subjects (Bernstein 1990, esp. chapter 1; Hasan 2005, esp. chapter 1). From this point of view, the wilfulness is entirely that of speakers: we alone are responsible for harnessing the language's semiotic energy in our own chosen ways. If there is guilt or blame, it does not attach to language as potential; it attaches to some section of some speakers somewhere, who are the actualizers of this potential; and it is my belief that ignorance of intention or effect is no excuse. The trick is to know through careful reflection and analysis exactly how they do it and why: reflection literacy taught with understanding appears to be something that might take us one step closer to the understanding we all need. What use is literacy if it does not enable the literate person to decide how meanings are exchanged and how they fashion the world we live in.

Notes

1 As this introduction indicates, the talk was presented to mark the retirement of Emeritus Professor Braj B. Kachru. It was delivered at the Symposium on World Englishes Today, Part I held at the University of Illinois at Urbana, 17-19 October 2002. Published in *WE: World Englishes: Symposium on Approaches to Change in American English*, Salikoko S Mufwene (guest editor), Vol 22:4. 2003.

2 See also a fuller description of evaluation under 'Appraisal' in Martin's recent work e.g., 1996.

3 I am aware that this claim could be taken as a challenge to Whorf's relativity theory. However, nothing could be further from my intentions. I believe Whorf has been seriously misread in several crucial ways. However, the elaboration of this point demands much space and time, and must await another occasion.

7 Literacy pedagogy and social change: directions from Bernstein's sociology [2007]

1 Introduction

The problem I want to explore in this paper[1] is whether the pedagogic practices of literacy in the classroom can be co-opted for bringing about social change of a specific kind, which in turn will raise questions about what change and why. The obvious sociological theory to which such issues can be usefully brought is Bernstein's – but it needs to be added that I do so not as a *sociologist manqué* but as a linguist interested in understanding society because society is the condition for the maintenance and evolution of language.

2 On Recognizing Change

The first obvious question is: why the implied declaration of need for social change? Change is, after all, an inherent condition of society, just as it is of language: both are always in flux. However, it is one thing to affirm the constancy of ongoing change; it is quite another to recognize its manifestations (or 'displays'), and yet another, to assess its impact, or to justify the need. So far as impact is concerned, the declaration of need for change is itself often a symptom of negative response to some change that has already become part of our social life. The call for change is neither because change is not occurring, nor because we as social agents have not contributed – consciously or unconsciously – to that change. The call is made because the caller has an agenda: s/he consciously desires to set in motion a specific kind of change. This in turn calls for an impartial assessment of the declared need.

Though most change in society and in language occurs through our participation in social and semiotic processes,[2] we often need a time depth[3] to 'see' change as change. In real time, we typically become aware of change after it has already set in. With deeper relation to an arena and with the ability to reflect, one might be equipped to observe a change while it is still in progress; with greater understanding of the inner character of the arena, one might assess the consequences of even an ongoing change, as Bernstein did in the arena of symbolic control in the early 1980s, when he analysed the State's 'increasing control over its own agencies of symbolic control, especially education' (1990: 154). He spelt out its 'profound implications [for pedagogy] from the primary school to the university', and from ways of learning to ways of being:

> Today led by the U.S.A. and the UK, there is a new principle guiding the latest transition of capitalism. The principles of the market and its managers are more and more the managers of the policy and practices of education. Market relevance is becoming the key orienting criterion for the selection of discourses, their relations to each other, their forms and their research ... Knowledge, after nearly a thousand years, is *divorced from inwardness and literally dehumanized* (Bernstein 2000: 86; emphasis mine).

The State-manufactured ideological conjunction of the Official Recontextualizing Field and the Pedagogic Recontextualizing Field, has meant that pedagogic practices in official pedagogic sites are undergoing a rapid change; the knower is being distanced from what is to be known; the concept of 'trainability' is fast replacing that of commitment to knowledge, separating it 'from the deep structure of the self'. As others have also observed (Apple 2002; Beck 2002), Bernstein's assessment of these market driven changes in official pedagogy was markedly negative. His last public pronouncement forcefully expresses the strength of this negative assessment, and it will probably be conceded that at the same time it calls for a constructive response to the situation:

> I am against any kind of pedagogy which leaves the self empty, and this is what I fear most of all, the emptying of the self and the role of pedagogy in such *evacuation*, and I think we have to mount a critique ... But a critique which enables us to show how pedagogic discourse works. How it's produced, how it's distributed, and...you see, its effectiveness is often assumed...we have to ask ourselves when it is effective, what are the conditions that have made it effective, and what does effectiveness actually mean with respect to what has been acquired? (Bernstein 2001: 380).

If we agree with Bernstein's assessment, then mounting a critique from a position of understanding as he advises is a necessary response to the conditions leading to the production of today's 'totally pedagogized society'. And, if we deplore the 'emptying of the self' as undesirable, and want education to play a 'crucial role in creating tomorrow's optimism from today's pessimism' (Bernstein 2000: xix), then beyond the first indispensable step of informed critique, some urgent action is also needed. My excuse for selectively recalling details of Bernstein's discourse on the formation of the 'totally pedagogized society' lies in its relevance to my call for social change through literacy pedagogy: these discourses provide not only its motivation but also suggest the direction of the change.

3 The Domination of Market Orientation and 'Schizoid' Language

To elaborate, my sense of a need for change through literacy pedagogy dates back to the last months of 1999, when media were saturated with news of the Seattle protest riots – the first public voice raised against the 'latest transition of capitalism', by now transformed into globalization. Clearly, globalization is a celebration of 'free market fundamentalism' (Hobsbawm 1999: 69), which counts as the central principle of capitalism and acts as the prime motivator of globalization. Whatever the naïve readings of the word 'globalization', the free market principle inheres in the global circulation of all goods and services, be it tourism and trade, or fashion and ethnic food, or entertainment and sports, or education and progress, or freedom and democracy (cf. Chapter 6, here).

What struck me most about the Seattle encounter was the contradiction emerging from the discourse of the protagonists. The rioters were protesting not against 'trade' but against *free* and *liberal* trade; against exercising the policy of 'non-discrimination in recruiting labour'; against 'putting poverty-stricken countries on the path to prosperity'. On the face of it, the protest appeared irrational: it went against the tenets of what the West knows as democracy. Now, everyone who knows anything about linguistics, knows about 'ungrammaticality' as a crucial concept in language description. However, it is quite easy to find a so-called ungrammatical sentence making perfect sense, but, by contrast, something natural language greatly abhors is internal contradiction: there is no way of making sense of sentences which claim or imply that non-discrimination is discriminatory, that freedom should be replaced by restrictions. If, language announces, in all seriousness, that fair is foul and foul fair, this has to be interpreted as the symptom of some pathology as it was in Shakespeare's *Macbeth*. In his account of market-dominated pedagogy, Bernstein talks about the likelihood of 'schizoid' identities, which he feared were being produced by market-oriented agencies of official pedagogy. What one was encountering in the discourse of rioters and their opponents was 'schizoid' language, created by market-oriented ideology: non-discrimination *was* discriminatory; free trade imposed restrictions. Language was being pathologized, as it had been once before in the Third Reich (Klemperer 2002).

But while the rioters were being talked of as violent and wild by the representatives of the World Trade Organization (WTO), whose meetings they had disrupted, they were quite obviously not mad hooligans. A reading of commentaries, by writers such as Madely (1999), Hertz (2001), Ellwood (2002) and others suggested that their behaviour might even be justified. So what exactly was going on?

4 Markets and Meanings

Let me not tax your patience with a detailed analysis of the linguistic features of this schizoid language,[4] but something does need to be said about the constitutive elements of this schizophrenia as they help explain why a particular kind of pedagogic action appears necessary.

First, the normal condition of a living language is variation/heterogeneity – not even an individual speaks the same variety of language all the time. From this point of view, the schizoid language, which I have called GLIB-SPEAK (Hasan 2003; Chapter 6 here), is simply a variety of English; and its speakers/propagators are identified by their extensive control on communal resources for the production and distribution of material capital. But to understand the specific nature of this variety, we need more information about its semiotic character: the principle underlying the linguistic character of glib-speak is that of RESEMANTICIZATION. A word then about the concept.

If, as Bernstein argues, the market orientation of pedagogy is separating knowledge from a knower, *glib-speak is an attempt to separate a signifier from its legitimate signified* – i.e., that signified which is treated by the speech community in general as legitimate. Glib-speak replaces the communally legitimized signified with one that is friendly to the interests and ideologies of its speakers. To be sure, the separation of a particular signifier and its associated signified is part of the natural process of change in language; but under natural conditions, it occurs slowly, often over generations and typically with wide communal participation.[5] Which explains why it is not perceived as a 'separation'; in fact, it is to be doubted whether in the natural course of normal meaning exchange, ordinary speakers are even aware of the changes happening. By contrast, in glib-speak, it would be truer to say that change is not just happening; it is being actively *manufactured*: its pace is grossly accelerated. The technical term for the deliberate and accelerated process in this case is 'resemanticization': words and their meanings are being forcibly divorced from each other, so that a new meaning may be attached to the word for the benefit of a specific set of global citizens. But how is this achieved, and what does it do by way of furthering the interests of its speakers? By way of an answer consider two strategies for resemanticization, referred to here as (1) EXPLOITING EVALUATION; and (2) SUBVERTING MEANING.[6]

The strategy of exploiting evaluation depends on the fact that the words (more accurately LEXICAL ITEMS/LEXEMES) of a language can be ordered on a continuum of desirability. We may think of the two endpoints of the cline as 'positive' (=desirable) and 'negative' (=undesirable), with the mid-point treated as (relatively) 'neutral'. This applies to all categories of lexemes/content words. The natural use of language will typically display what one might call 'internal evaluation agreement': thus it would be odd to say, 'they *praised* him for his *meanness*'; or, 'most people *enjoy* being *deceived*'. Neutral lexical words often tend to refer to general categories: examples would be 'group, neighbourhood, contract, design, plan, action', and so on; these have neither positive nor negative evaluation, and refer to a relatively less specific category of experience. When, however, a neutral word is combined with an evaluative word, the whole construction acquires the evaluative colouring of the latter – a colouring that suffuses the whole construction. Thus we may talk of 'a fair contract' or 'an unfair contract', and of 'a rough neighbourhood', or 'a good neighbourhood'. Typically such constructions are formed with an evaluative adjective as here, but this is less important than the presence of at least one clearly evaluative term in the construction, as for example in the 'liberalization of trade' where 'liberalization' is a noun with positive value. Glib-speak makes heavy use of this strategy, but with a twist, to appreciate which we need to look at the second strategy, namely, subverting meaning.

Putting it simply, the meaning of a word is the product of the relations into which a word enters, and since each word enters into a vast network of relations, word meaning is typically considerably extensive. In ordinary uses of language, only some of the meaning relations are uppermost in our consciousness, while the others are, as it were, present in their silence, and clamour for attention if the threat of internal contradiction arises. One might, thus, see the meaning of a word such as *man* as a two-part affair. The part lying on the surface of our consciousness has such elements as, say, 'animate, human, adult, male', while the second part consists of meanings inferentially related to these elements. So from 'animate' we infer such things as 'mobility' and 'mutability', i.e., subject to processes of change such as birth, growth, death; from 'human' we infer humanity, non-brutishness, i.e., civility, and fairness etc. and intelligence of a particular kind; from 'adult' we infer maturity, judgment, reasoning, and from 'male', courage, strength, and other physical attributes, such as a certain order of height and weight, among other things; a single word might thus pack a significant quantum of our ideology. Traditionally, the first grouping of semantic elements has been called DENOTATION;[7] the second, CONNOTATION; which according to Lyons consists of 'secondary implications' (1977: 278). It is the first grouping that is uppermost in speakers' consciousness, which is why when someone says, 'Susan's husband is not a man', we do not hear it as making the absurd claim that Susan's husband is a female, or a baby, or an animal or an object.[8] Rather, the utterance brings to the surface of our consciousness the implicational/connotative/inferred elements of meanings. Thus we interpret it as claiming that Susan's husband does not conduct himself as normally a man would be expected to in that speech community. One effective way of subverting meaning is to simply ignore a denotative and/or a connotative element of meaning. As an illustration, I briefly discuss the construction *liberalization of trade*.

Using a positive evaluative term in a construction introduces a *feel good* factor. The general view is that liberalization makes laws, attitudes etc. 'less strict and allows people more freedom in their actions' (COBUILD Dictionary: 833); restriction is taken to be coercive and liberalization, helpful. A connotative meaning of *liberal* is *munificent, generous*, which implies sensitivity to the needs, and attitudes of another. The direction of liberality is other-oriented; thus it is odd to say *I am being liberal to myself.* So if A initiates a liberal trade contract with B, B may legitimately infer that it would be to his/her benefit. It is thus reasonable to interpret *liberal trade* as trade oriented to the benefit of the person or institution being invited to trade. However, in actual practice, a simple subversion of meaning undercuts the positive evaluation of the semantics of *liberal trade* by simply resemanticizing *liberal* so that it turns out to mean *liberal* as in *I took a liberal/generous helping of the ice cream* – i.e., *a big helping*. A comment from Madely (2000) supports this reading:

> The principle of non-discrimination is embodied in the 1999 Uruguay agreement on trade related investment measures. It means that *developing countries cannot give special treatment to their domestic companies*. Neither can they insist that foreign companies use local labour ... To many civil society groups *the principle of non-discrimination is unjust* ... and anti-economic development, because it ties the hands of poor countries, making development policy subservient to trade policy. *The WTO's 'free trade' philosophy effectively reduces the freedom of governments* to buy locally produced materials or to use local labour (Madely, *Guardian Weekly* 2000, emphasis mine, RH).

Like middle-class maternal control, the strategies employed in glib-speak for the control of material gain are 'invisible': this is in fact an important condition of its success. My research has so far shown no other *principle* of variation in glib-speak than that of 'manipulating' word meaning. Its grammar conforms impeccably to the standard variety – at least in English, but then English, particularly its American educated variety is the language of globalization – right across the various 'genres', such as technological exposition, reports, plans or argumentation. This grammatical conformity is significant: it maintains the appearance of normality, thus rendering the manipulations of resemanticization invisible, and *that* is a necessary requirement for the successful functioning of glib-speak. Its speakers need to present themselves as benefactors, while engaged in acts of ruthless profiteering: the language they speak weaves a perfect web of lexical camouflage by exploiting evaluation and subverting meaning. No wonder the speakers of glib-speak have been so keen to strike international agreements using terms of 'liberal trade' with poverty-stricken under-educated countries for whom English is not a native language. The speakers of glib-speak can profess to be putting such populations on the path to prosperity, while the terms of the agreements, fashioned by their own agencies, are worded so that they are biased in their own favour, not those of the poor countries.

5 Is Change Really Needed?

Glib-speak is quite wide in its reach. The expressions *non-discrimination policy* or *liberal trade* are not just two isolated cases picked out from one instance of confrontation. For example, from Pakistan to Florida[9] and from Florida to Iraq, the word *democracy* has been subtly resemanticized as and when needed. All over the western world, *accountability* in State documents is no longer about responsibility to society; it is about conformity with and accommodation of the money-making enterprises and market pressures. *Career* is pretty much an obsolete concept; and the idea of *success* whether in education or in other spheres of society increasingly celebrates commodification. Everyday news must be interpreted with caution; being a native speaker is no longer enough; you need to be an insider to know who is being bolstered, who misrepresented. One of Bernstein's chief concerns was the evacuation of self in the changing totally pedagogized society (TPS). I suggest that the evacuation of self is an enormous project: it cannot be achieved by change in one single arena, be it as pervasive in its influence as official pedagogy. Language is being coerced into recategorizing experience, and language is a main means of communication, not simply of pedagogic mediation. If language becomes schizoid, then what used to be taken as an undisputed 'fact' becomes subject to doubt, or worse still it is subverted for the benefit of corporate bodies. A very important element of what we knew as 'language education' is being changed to suit the caprices of this 'new transition of capitalism', the 're-organized capitalism of the twenty-first century' (Bernstein 1990: 153).

One might ask: so what? Enormous changes have occurred before in society. Indeed one way of conceiving human history is simply as a series of related changes. For example, education itself has moved from theistic to humanistic; from the 16th–18th-centuries' concern with producing the well-rounded renaissance man, to 20th-century concern with producing specialists, invested in some minute fragment of some specific knowledge structure. In retrospect we appreciate the enormity of such changes, but while bringing about the changes, we think of it as 'marching with time'. So what is wrong in marching with time once again by substituting specialism by specializing in trainability? Isn't one's response to current changes somewhat hysterical? I believe the answer must be 'no' because of what the advent of glib-speak implies. The acceleration in the resemanticization of language cannot be ignored, if only because it is a mode of forcibly making exploitation legal *by contract and by convention*. Like cunning old Fury in the Mouse's Tale in *Alice in Wonderland*, our captains of enterprise have appointed themselves both judge and jury to condemn and dominate. Because the majority of this exploitation – you only have to examine the 'sweat trade' in China – is offshore, its effects are not insistently obvious to the private sectors of so-called developed countries. This, however, does not mean that our 'progressive' societies are safe from the effects of the legalization of exploitation: in a globalized world, like pollution, discontent too can have a world-wide effect. Collusion in providing a hospitable environment for glib-speak cannot be in the interest of humanity. But such collusion is occurring in the name of 'teaching what is usable, what opens the doors to opportunities' without also teaching how to question the uses, how to assess the long term effects of these opportunities. A substantial segment of the academic community believes that their job is to produce humans who can fit into the globalized world. To neutralize the effectiveness of glib-speak, it is necessary to unravel the web of lexical camouflage. Though the agents of symbolic control in the private sector could play a major role in this enterprise (Bernstein 1990: 133ff.), perhaps changes in literacy pedagogy would be most effective, especially if they could become the norm across the educational system. What are these planned changes, and how feasible is it to implement them?

6 Changing Literacy Pedagogy

Despite the universal nature of the pedagogic device, the instantiations of pedagogy in the classroom are often enormously varied, literacy pedagogy not excepted. Even if we were to ignore multimodal literacies (van Leeuwen and Humphrey 1996), kinds of literacies as identified by reference to some (segments of a) given culture (Street 1995), and critical literacies (Gee 1990), literacy remains a complex concept, its pedagogy less than capable of coping with the problems posed by the advent of glib-speak. Due to lack of space I reluctantly abstain from elaborating this claim, but simply present my own conception of literacy. This will enable me to locate the various manifestations of what passes as literacy pedagogy. I take literacy to be fundamentally the process of making sense by interpreting some semiotic system, whether actively or receptively. The process is thus inherently semiotic (Hasan 1996b) and clearly not restricted to language alone. However, the discussion of literacy here will concern only the semiotic system of language, because language seems to be the only system of meaning relevant to the content of glib-speak, though attractive presentation at the expression level is not unimportant. To sum up, as used here, *literacy is the process of making sense of instantiations of some language system, whether in its transmission or its reception.*

Even restricting literacy this way, there remains a good deal of latitude for variation in the interpretation of the term. For example, if the notion of sign is limited to its visual manifestation, literacy becomes a 'translation device' for converting GRAPHEMES (letters) into PHONEMES (sounds), and *vice versa.* If the notion of meaning is limited to naming or to correspondence between signs and elements of extra-linguistic reality, and/or the system of language is seen in isolation from its process in the social context, then literacy pedagogy is restricted to what I have called (Hasan 1996b; Chapter 5 this volume) RECOGNITION LITERACY: it amounts to 'barking at print'. The instructional discourse in such literacy pedagogy is focused on recognizing what written shape corresponds to what sound, what word corresponds to what meaning; little or no attention is paid to discourse as an object of study. Such literacy pedagogy is typically divorced from allied fields such as 'comprehension', 'composition', and so on. Recognition literacy is still alive and well, specially in the (always) developing (i.e., technologically/industrially backward) countries. The teaching and evaluation in recognition literacy come cheap, so despite its limitations as a resource for democracy, it is often found attractive. I would go so far as to suggest that, whatever the framing of pedagogic discourse, this variety of literacy pedagogy cannot play a constructive part in unravelling the lexical web of obfuscation woven by glib-speak. Despite this, the internalization of the relationships between the written shape and the uttered sound is fundamental to literacy pedagogy of any kind (Halliday 1985b, 1996b); and where apprenticeship to vertical knowledge structures is concerned, such internalization is entirely indispensable. However impressive non-literate societies may be, the fact remains that the two modalities of language – the written and the spoken – do display a division of labour in the kind of knowledge structures they are able to mediate (Olson 1977).

If the sign system is interpreted as a resource for the living of life, then its process in context would be treated as an essential aspect of literacy. If, in addition, linguistic meaning is seen not merely as a surrogate of language-external reality, but as a meaning-creating system, essential to shaping reality and internalizing experience (Halliday and Matthiessen 1999), then the goal of literacy pedagogy will have to go a good deal beyond that of recognition literacy: it will need to focus on various forms of social process, relating them to the context of situation in which the various text types have grown; in other words, the techniques for the production of texts in various registers/genres will become an important part of instruction. I have referred to this as ACTION LITERACY. Action literacy is performance oriented;[10] it is aimed at enabling pupils to act with their language, i.e., making sense *of* and *with* language used in some social context of living. The most extensive programme for the pedagogy of action literacy was developed by Martin (e.g., 1986) and his colleagues. Known as 'genre-based pedagogy', it turned the concept of literacy in education from an aspect of the usual instructional discourse on language to 'instruction in language across the curriculum'. Literacy as the process of making sense has, in this system, become synonymous with the displays of instructional discourse of one kind or another. Essential features of this programme have been co-opted internationally, with or without acknowledgment, in the instructional discourse of language education. Action literacy certainly appears to have the potential of being extended into a model that could de-construct glib-speak successfully, since behind it lies the powerful grammar provided by systemic functional linguistics (Halliday 1994a; Matthiessen 1995). However, despite its many strengths, genre-based literacy has been, on the one hand, selective in the genres that it chooses to bring to the students' attention – these happen to be privileged and privileging in the context of educational success; and on the other hand, the reception of discourse types had until recently been limited to identifying the structural composition, i.e., generic stages. This consumed most of the instructional programme of genre-based literacy,[11] turning it into something more akin to a technology of text production and reception without, as it were, confronting the texts (whether produced by the student, or brought from outside as exemplars) with the wider contexts of communal existence, by reference to which they receive their true social meaning. However, changes have recently occurred in the writing reading methodologies of genre-based pedagogy (Martin and Rose 2003) which pulls it a good deal closer to literacy as making sense.

It is somewhat ironic that the so-called 'literacy as social practice' approaches have tended to focus more on the individual.[12] The name of the game is self-expression; and the attainment of uniqueness is the prized goal. While lip-service is to 'meaning-making', the instructional programmes remain blithely innocent of the necessarily social basis of meaning. Like many false dichotomies which appear from time to time in humanities and social sciences, the opposition between individual and social perspective appears profitless. Nor have I come across any modes of instructional discourse associated with social and/or critical literacy which appear to actually engage with the processes of making sense by means of a semiotic system; language, it appears, has to be 'neutralized' in these approaches, because apparently it has been too privileged (Bourdieu 1992)! A social orientation to literacy pedagogy is an absolute necessity; I doubt, however, that the existing pedagogies associated with these models would succeed in an informed critique/deconstruction of glib-speak.

Hasan (1996b) proposed a literacy model she called REFLECTION LITERACY; she suggested that such a model would build on the strengths of existing literacy pedagogies, taking on board the text-and-context based aspect of action literacy, the writing/speaking distinction basic to recognition literacy, and the social concerns professed by social/critical literacies. Distinctively, and importantly, it would also include the perspective of confronting the texts with the wider contexts of communal existence, in and from which they receive their true social meaning. Glib-speak at that point was not visible since it has really flourished since the arrival of globalization (discussion in chapter 6); but it was suggested that basic to reflection literacy are the concepts of SEMANTIC ORIENTATION, and of INTERROGATION: what orders of meaning are viewed as relevant by whom as evidenced in their discursive practices. Reflection literacy is viewed as a means of facilitating the acquirers' understanding of linguistic action from the perspective of its social motivations and consequences: texts are not simply bearers of information organized and arranged in specific sequences/stages; they are not simply expressions of 'me' or of functioning simply as an instrument for attracting opportunities for material success, important as this is; they are also, and equally importantly, potent instruments of social formation. Literacy as a process of making sense should therefore take seriously the construing power of language, and this means paying attention to the meaning construing power of the lexicogrammar. The lexicogrammar of language is not simply dry stuff without any relation to the living of life: rather than presenting it as a catalogue of mind-less categories such as 'gerundives' or 'subject raising', grammar should be seen as the theory of human experience (Halliday 1994b). It is through the deep analysis of the lexicogrammatical systems of language that we can appreciate the strategic mendacity whereby 'democracy' becomes a sign with emasculated meaning used differently, but each time friendly to the interests of those who subvert its meaning (Hasan 2003).

There are three basic principles of reflection literacy: (i) the study of the meaning-making potential of language should never be divorced from literacy pedagogy: this potential is also a potential for linguistic variation; (ii) all instances of meaning making should be subject to interrogation: e.g., 'what meaning construed how', 'why' and 'why here'; and (iii) the significance of what language refers to, what meanings it makes, should never be divorced from the social context from where the pressures for meaning making arises (Butt 1985). If literacy education could go this far, it would create in the acquirer a sensitivity to the meaning-making practices of large sections of a community in the context of a number of social practices; it will make clear the centrality of meanings to the living of life in society; and it would be a productive recognition of the co-genetic relations of language and society, whereby each depends on the other for its existence. I believe that a literacy education of this kind could contribute to the formation of the kind of consciousness that is able to see 'through' the lexical webs of camouflage, whatever their origin.

7 The Pedagogic Device and Planned Change through Pedagogy

Imagine, for a moment, that everyone here agrees with the goals of reflection literacy – an outcome highly unlikely given that we trade in HORIZONTAL KNOWLEDGE STRUCTURES (Bernstein 1999, 2000) and are not going to buy just anyone else's ideas! After all, to be scholars of some consequence, each of us must have our own individual theories, never mind the tower of babble effect. But imagine that for some reason we do so. This, instead of a grand resolution, would discouragingly be only the beginning of a host of problems – problems that attend all planned change; problems that might arise with innovations from below as it encounters aspects of some specific instance of the pedagogic device.

Contemporary discourse in much of humanities shows great concern with change – witness the plethora of titles sporting the word *change*, with or without the qualifier *social* – my own included! But it is not customary to clarify what kind of change, for whose benefit, who might actually desire it, and why. Bernstein often remarked that between the language system and speech lies social structure; the same is true about an existing state of culture and some planned change. Even where the agenda of planned change has been clarified, its desirability for the majority of the community well argued, it is still a fact that the working of social structure lies between the agenda and the outcome: to strive for a particular change is probably within one's control, but what the outcome of the striving might be is not entirely so. This does not mean that change should not be contemplated, but to increase the chances of achieving the desired outcome, we must heed Bernstein's advice: *critique must be from a position of understanding; action must be in awareness of the terrain on which it has to be tried out*. So what are the conditions for making a change such as outlined above? I want to explore this question by reference to the concept of pedagogic device. But first note that the instructional discourse of reflection literacy – the way linguistic meaning enters actively into the living of life – is embedded in a regulative discourse which orients acquirers' consciousness toward the salient features of social life. In what follows below, I shall focus largely on issues in the linguistic component of the instructional discourse.

There can be no doubt that today the insulation between the arenas of production and education has been greatly weakened, nor that the 'dominant principles' of the political party of the State is blatantly market oriented. Here is a piece of advice given by the State to academics as reported on page 8 of the *Guardian Weekly*, 20-26 May, 2004:

> Academics have been urged to spend a little less time on expanding human knowledge, and more on drumming up cash for their universities' endowment funds. A government-appointed task force has said that 600m pounds (sterling) could be raised if staff adopted US-style techniques to extract donations from former students and big commercial donors.

Given this climate, it would be somewhat naïve to expect that the agents of official or pedagogic re-contextualizing fields are likely to be favourably impressed by the 'pedogogeme' of reflection literacy. The existing distributive rules of official pedagogic device in much of Europe and European-style educational systems are stacked against any such innovation.[13] If the innovation is to surface at all, it will have to do so from below, through the actual practices of literacy pedagogy.

In one respect, the situation is more promising here: the primary context of the production of the discourse at issue has been strongly supported; the 'intellectual field' of a socially aware and semiotically competent linguistics already exists which would support a literacy pedagogy of the type under consideration. In other words, primary contextualization of the field has taken place and a specialized discourse has been developed which could be taken as a resource for the pedagogy of reflection literacy. So far as the reproduction of this kind of discourse is concerned, some relevant material exists at primary, secondary and tertiary levels. Williams (2000) reports on research in the pedagogy of grammatics as a resource for meaning at the primary level of schooling. Here through instruction in the meaning-making potential of certain grammatical categories, the young school pupils were able to do 'reflective' reading of a children's story. They identified how the relations of the various participants in the story were linguistically enacted, what grammatical patterns went into creating what kind of CHARACTER DEPICTION (Hasan 1964), how a variation in the lexicogrammatical patterns would vary meanings; and what is the social significance of how the linguistically created 'persons' behave in relation to others in the story. This kind of literacy would put the acquirers well on the path of developing sensitivities to the power of language as revealed through the lexicogrammatically construed meanings of the text. The already well-devised model of genre-based pedagogy would provide a strong basis for continuing such enquiries at the secondary level, though it will be necessary to develop the stance of enquiry into the social significance of the discourses brought to the acquirers' attention. In this context the latest innovations in genre-based pedagogy by Martin in collaboration with Rose (Martin and Rose 2003) could be highly relevant. One element that still needs further attention is to bring into teacher education materials that might sensitize the teachers to the relation of semiosis to the sociopolitical organization. Similarly, the work on the analysis of verbal art (Halliday 1971; Hasan 1971, 1985a; Butt 1983, 1988; Butt and Lukin 2009; Lukin and Webster 2005), some of it written specifically for teachers' use could be employed at the tertiary level for the pedagogy of reflection literacy. A good deal of work is available on linguistic variation, providing an understanding of the relation of language to speakers' social positioning, including the work on semantic variation (Hasan 1989, 1992a, 1992c; Cloran 1989, 1994, 1999a, 1999b; Williams 1995, 2001). But there still remains the problem of the third context, which 'structures the field or subset of fields whose positions, agents, and practices are concerned with the movements of texts/practices from the primary context of discursive production to the secondary context of discursive reproduction' (Bernstein 1990: 192). For this step in recontextualization, Bernstein makes the following thoughtful comment: 'at the level of the university or equivalent institutions those who produce the new knowledge are also their own contextualizers' (Bernstein 1990: 188); thus, the prophet has to induct the priest who may then be able to address the laity. In other words any innovation in pedagogy from below has to be a boot-strapping enterprise; if academics are convinced of the value of bringing to attention a literacy that enables the acquirer to see through linguistic chicanery, they will have to act for its promotion.[14]

Changes of the kind we are witnessing do not remain encapsulated within one segment of the community: there is bound to be external pressure from parents, who want their children to 'succeed' – a success conceptualized in the short-term perspective: forms of education not directly contributing to the market-oriented conception of success too are likely to be criticized. In Australia, media often criticize the academics for 'wasting tax-payers' money' by teaching what nobody wants to know. As things stand, the higher we move in the educational scheme, the more success in examinations matters for pupils' future. Any programme of teaching which does not directly seek to enable the students to jump this hurdle is often seen as 'incompetent' and irresponsible. Further, there is the most serious issue of winning the students over so they willingly invest time and effort in learning what 'does not pay' in terms of grades: the importance of positive student identification for successful pedagogy (Singh 2001) bootstrapped innovation cannot be ignored. However, despite these problems, what favours the introduction of reflection literacy pedagogy is its status as a 'pedagogeme' in a space that, though often beset with ill-informed curricula designers and reconextualizers leading to poor education, still remains a recognized legitimate intellectual field, namely that of language education. On a positive note, there are two recent developments: one in literacy education, both linguistic and social, which favours reflection literacy; and more recently an awakening to the fact that after all There Is Such a Thing as Society (Christakis and Fowler 2009) makes one think that perhaps, all that the propagation of reflection literacy involves now is simply the visibility of the need to take the social and the semiotic perspective more seriously.

8 Concluding Remarks

I am aware many questions remain; but I hope that the need for the introduction of a literacy pedagogy which enables students to reflect on their own experiences of discourse will be granted. I am not against pedagogy which assists resistance to bias in education against class, gender, ethnicity, skin colour, but all of these phenomena are elements of, and attain their value in, specific kinds of social structures. To see these specific problems as part of the larger picture, and ultimately pertaining to the field of production, could prove beneficial. Moss has remarked recently (2002: 557):

> Within the academic community there is a considerable degree of disquiet over the loss of autonomy that the new pedagogic concordat

> represents. This is almost always told as a story of deep loss, without always owning up to the real strengths and weaknesses of what went before. But the new pedagogic economy produces new affordances as well as constraints.

I do not question that the current changes in the educational system, almost despite themselves, might have got something right. But broadening the context of Moss' remark from visible/invisible, competence/performance pedagogy, the issue would seem somewhat different. A British Marxist remarked in the 1940s: the problem for capitalist educational authorities is how to educate their citizens so that they can read and understand the Bren gun manual, but not the Communist Manifesto. By contrast, our hope has to be that the capitalist world never succeeds in resolving this problem. There is something very wrong with a system of education, no matter what its affordances, that on the one hand pays such close and almost invariably ill-informed attention to details of how students should be educated by laying down rules about skills, tests, principles of assessments and the like, and on the other, persuades its employees that a literacy pedagogy of the type being recommended here is subversive or reactionary, and that the job of the educator is to turn the educational institutions into a profit making purveyor of pre-packaged knowledge.[15] And there is something very wrong with a literacy pedagogy which does not cultivate in the acquirer the basic function of learning, namely to interrogate, rather than remain a docile recipient of information. Educational systems can never be divorced from society, but all things being equal, to obtain the socially most desirable outcome, the classification between education and production needs to be balanced. If this classification is very strong, it could encourage the 'ivory tower' syndrome with academics pursuing their own agendas irrespective of what problems the external community's conditions of living happen to give rise to; such education becomes a state within a state, catering to a parasitic elitism. But equally, if the classification is very weak, as is happening now, the ability to question the official agencies and the agents of production might be severely threatened, because the external pressures might translate themselves into internal ones. If this happens, then we are dangerously close to some form of fundamentalism, and I doubt that the fundamentalism of capitalism is any more palatable than that of religion. Reflection literacy will certainly not be an antidote to all social problems; what makes it desirable is its treatment of discourse as discourse needs to be treated, i.e., dialogic. Above all, it enables the literate to see through the hypocrisy of the progressive and the civilized.

Notes

1. This chapter first appeared in R. Moore, M. Arnot, J. Beck and H. Daniels (eds), *Knowledge, Power and Educational Reform: Applying the Sociology of Basil Bernstein* (London: Taylor and Francis, 2007). References to publications have been updated and some new endnotes have been introduced.
2. The relationship between social and semiotic processes is not one of simple co-occurrence but of mutual reliance: social processes typically need semiotic action, and all semiotic actions have their roots in some social action (Hasan 2005, 2009b).
3. See Halliday 1992b on 'time depth' in relation to language change and the *langue parole* dialectic.
4. For the discussion of some features, Hasan 2003.
5. Bourdieu's (1992) account of how linguistic meanings get shaped appears suspect. Precipitate meaning disjunction is typically an indication of violent ideological change.
6. For discussion, Hasan 2003.
7. '...by the denotation of a lexeme...will be meant the relationship that holds between that lexeme and persons, things, properties, processes and activities external to the language system' Lyons (1977: 207).
8. Such interpretations would involve internal contradiction since the denotative meaning of *man* is included in the meaning of *husband.*
9. I refer to the managed first election of George W. Bush as President of the most powerful 'democracy' in the world.
10. Pupils are judged by textual performance, but a successful pedagogy of modes of performance must create competence in the learner.
11. For exception and imaginative attention to lexicogrammar, see early Rothery 1989.
12. See Moss (2002) for a description of one such case.
13. After a seminar at an Eastern university on this topic, a colleague criticized the 'shockingly subversive' tone of the presentation, adding indignantly: 'here am I fund-raising for my university and there you go giving me such advice!' In her contribution at the 3rd Bernstein Symposium, Moss, not convinced that the present pedagogic climate permits resistance, expressed serious doubts that such 'utopian' changes would be possible. I would say it is relevant to ask: did the Nazis permit resistance?
14. Recent publication by Nicholas Christakis and James Fowler (2009) emphasizes the need today for such a change in the pedagogic programme.
15. Bourdieu's (1992) suggestion that denotation is *official*, connotation personal/individual appears unjustified. The possibility of communication demands social recognition for both denotative and connotative meanings. The success of glib-speak depends on shared connotations.

III

Mother Tongue and Other Tongue

8 Socialization and cross-cultural education [1976]

1 Introduction

The aim of this paper is to explore the relationship between socialization and cross-cultural education, with particular reference to the Indo-Pakistani Sub-continent and England. There is a difficulty in talking of the global culture of a whole community: it necessarily implies an ignoring of the sub-cultural differences. Although this restricts the discussion to a general level, such general discussion may be justifiable on the assumption that the sub-cultures of a given culture are more closely related to each other at least at some of the levels of analysis than they are to other cultures. Thus the culture of the Chinese Muslim community – the Uighers – might differ in some respects from other Chinese sub-cultures, nonetheless it would be closer to the global Chinese culture than it would be to the culture of Indo-Pakistani Muslim community, which in turn is more readily relatable to the sub-continental culture as a whole than to the Arab, Turkish or Egyptian ones.[1]

2 Cross-cultural education

By 'cross-cultural education' I refer primarily to the situation where an individual from one culture migrates temporarily to another culture in order to acquire some academic qualification. Undoubtedly, the term is capable of a much wider interpretation: it could, for example be employed to refer to the situation, common in ex-colonies, where the content of knowledge originating from and specific to the colonizing cultures are included within the curriculum. However, the problems that may arise from this later situation differ qualitatively from those typical of the former. So, the Indo-Pakistani student, learning, say, Newtonian physics in some Indo-Pakistani situation is, in a very real sense, not exposed to a set of problems which this same student would face when learning the same body of material as a student at a British University. The cultural origin and identity of the content of knowledge, although important, would appear to be not as important in this situation as the symbolic factors inhering in the culturally distinct systems of education.

It is quite clear that moving from one culture to another would involve greater or lesser problem of personal adjustment, e.g., in food habits, physical living conditions, and in day to day interaction with other human beings. Relevant as these problems are to the total well-being of the foreign student, I am not primarily concerned here with these, as they seem to me to impinge only indirectly on the main problem of successful completion of the educational process itself. Instead, I would like to concentrate upon those factors which most probably affect the foreign student's educational achievements more directly.

2.1 Foreign student in a foreign land: practical problems

In examining these factors, I would like to make a distinction between those which relate to the mechanics of the educational process and those which relate to the social meanings of the educational system. Both in the formulation of the problem facing a foreign student and in remedies sought for resolving them, it would appear that more attention is paid to the former type – the ones that relate to the mechanics of the educational process. So, for example, the problems and remedies tend to centre around the 'medium' of education, or around the explicit 'content' of knowledge 'to be transmitted' to the student. So in effect we simply ask, (a) does the foreign student have sufficient mastery of the language through which knowledge is to be transmitted, and (b) does the foreign student understand – is he at that 'state of readiness' where he could be expected to understand – the subject matter of what he is about to be taught? The statement of requirements formulated in terms of prior knowledge which permit the admission of a foreign student to a specific course can be seen as an effort to cope with the problems arising from content. On the other hand, dilemmas arise from the fact that medium and content are inextricably intertwined. This is especially the case in the domain of social sciences and humanities, for here every element of content is typically transmitted solely verbally, and the evaluation of the student's achievement is based upon his verbal presentation of knowledge, which through this verbal presentation becomes available for examination.

The big boom in the business of teaching English as a foreign language is an offshoot of the mechanical problems in cross-cultural education. Because of this inalienably close relationship between the medium and the content, and their relevance to successfully passing the hurdle of examination, the formulation of the problem and their solutions tend to centre round the question of medium. Nor can this emphasis be brushed aside lightly: there can be no doubt that both the sufficient mastery of the medium and the readiness to absorb the concepts relevant to a content area are necessary conditions for educational success. Nonetheless, there are at least three considerations which suggest that a rethinking of this attitude may be necessary. First, although groups of foreign students with different degrees of mastery of English language arrive at the English universities every year, it is yet to be empirically established that there is a clear positive correlation between educational success of a group and the extent of the group's mastery of English. On observation, I doubt if it is true that more Turkish or Thai students fail at the various English universities than the Indo-Pakistani ones, though due to an accident of history, there is good reason to believe that the latter group may be credited with possessing 'better English'. Secondly, although in the context of cross-cultural education, the problem of medium and content may possess certain characteristics that are peculiar to it alone, it is still true that the problem of the relationship of medium and content has to be considered in the context of native speakers of English as well: in other words, the mastery of language is not a sufficient condition for mastery over content of some area of knowledge. In most educational systems, the examinations function like a traffic control mechanism: if you pass, a green light flashes to let you go ahead; in other words, you are judged ready to cope with the medium and content pertaining to the next stage. Because successive steps within a particular stage of the educational system are pretty continuous, we tend to assume that judgements formed on the basis of examination results are indicative of the true situation. However, this assumption is not always proved correct, as can be seen quite clearly at major stages of transition from say primary to secondary or from secondary to university education in England. Third, the emphasis on the mechanical aspects of cross-cultural education has had the effect of pushing into the background some problems of a different kind, which are at least as serious if not more so. These are the problems that relate to the social meanings of the educational systems.

There no doubt exist some important reasons for this preoccupation with the mechanical aspects of cross-cultural education. It is clear that the problems arising with reference to these are relatively more tangible; for them some kind of solution appears to be available without apparently bringing in any changes to the social meanings of the educational system. These are for the most part problems of the type that the educational systems have to cope with as a matter of course in the education of the native students, anyway. No matter how vague the concepts behind phrases such as 'sufficient mastery of the medium' and 'state of readiness for some content of knowledge', it can be safely assumed that some mode or other of measuring both will be feasible, while remaining safely within the established framework for evaluation. No matter what the difficulties in the successful teaching of proficiency in medium or in devising exercises for increasing the conceptual abilities of the student, the explicit practices of the educational systems have rested on the assumption that both these goals are achievable. The success of the modes of coping with these problems can also be assessed by remaining within the educational framework. Further, despite the inherent bond between medium and content, for assessment the two can be dissociated to a certain extent, as in the practices of some university teachers who ignore grammatical errors, inept lexical selection, poor spelling, even poor organization of the content etc., so long as the content of the students offering is reasonably clear and capable of being seen as cogent. For obvious reasons such dissociation is easier in 'hard sciences', especially where the presentation of content might call on statements of formulae, or on tightly regulated descriptions of experiments, and so on. Such possibilities of 'coping' with practical problems lends them a 'tangible' shape. There is nothing 'airy fairy' about them: the problems represent an area where one knows – or at least one assumes one knows – exactly where one is; one knows also what is to be done; and to what extent the doing has a likelihood of being successful.

2.2 The social meanings of the educational system

By contrast, problems of the second kind, those which arise in cross-cultural education as a result of differences in the social meanings between the two educational systems in contact appear far more intangible, especially since it is by no means obvious that those who are active players in the educational systems have any explicit realization of these meanings. Moreover, at least at the moment, there appears very little that can be done to solve these problems while still remaining within the established guidelines of the educational institutions. Here not only do we seem not to know where we are, we also appear to lack ideas about what can be done, or how the success of the doing is to be assessed.

A natural question arises at this point: what does one mean by talking about 'the social meanings of the educational systems'? Is this some more technical jargon to refer to the fact that educational processes vary in some visible, manifest ways from one society to another? I would suggest that this is not the case. It is obvious that there exist some manifest differences in the educational processes across cultures – for example, in the size of the class, the allocation of time to certain subjects, the nature of accepted/approved pedagogical practices and modalities, and criteria for evaluation. These manifest differences meet the eye, as the audible noise of language meets the ear. But just as in language there is more than meets the ear, so also in the educational processes there is more than meets the eye: in both cases the manifest is representationally related to something that underlies it, and this motivating force for both is to be sought at the level of meaning. Without pressing the analogy too far, the manifest level in both cases can be studied systematically and accurately only if it is related to the level that Hsu (1971b) has called the level of 'content', i.e., the social meaning. I shall avoid using Hsu's term 'content' here for fear that it may be confused with the term 'content' in 'content knowledge'.[2] The point worth emphasizing is that the analysis of a social institution is no less a 'quest for meaning' than the analysis of language (Whorf 1956; Firth 1957).

2.3 Social meaning and the systems of language and culture

A newcomer to the field of sociology and anthropology is struck by the fact that often a particular social institution is isolated for intensive study, but just as often, little or no effort is made to relate this analysis to the society as a whole. In such analyses, each institution can be seen as having a set of functions and a structural shape specific to it, but the question of how and at what level of abstraction one such institution can be related to the other institutions in the same system is seldom explored in any detail. Such atomistic studies of social institutions are, of course, interesting in their own right, but it could not be claimed that they contribute materially towards the statement of any principles, which account for the coherence of a society or its culture. In a series of thought-provoking publications, Hsu (1963, 1971a, 1971b) has criticized the practice of analysing the kinship system as a self-sufficient whole with little regard to how it relates to the rest of the culture, while Douglas has shown (1972) that manifestly varied social phenomena can be seen as governed by a single powerful abstract principle. The rationale for approaching the study of social institutions in this integrative manner is to be found in the very nature and definition of culture. If culture is a 'design for living' (Kluckhohn and Kelly 1945), it would seem to follow that the individual elements of the design would relate to each other in some specific ways. The principles contributing to the unity of the design are likely to be pervasive, so that at the deepest level of analysis a largely homogeneous set of principles may be found to run through the diverse social institutions, like a theme running through a musical composition.

It may be instructive at this point to turn to Whorf's hypotheses, since these were made with specific reference to a very much more self-contained, easily delimited symbolic system than that of culture. As I see it, Whorf was not concerned with the individual elements in the total inventory of the atoms of meaning in a human language; rather, his primary concern was with characteristic modes of meaning. In linguistics Whorf stands out as an exception in that he concentrated on the organizational principles at the semantic level, rather than on the atomistic semantic components themselves. This is what explains the necessity for his emphatically repeated statements that the characteristic mode of meaning cannot be studied by examining individual encoding devices in isolation from each other, be they paradigms, single lexical items, or any one syntactic system of agnates. Attempts at testing Whorf's hypothesis by reference to any isolated patterns of the latter type (e.g., in Brown and Lenneberg 1954; Fishman 1972a), whatever they may prove or disprove, still remain irrelevant to this essential part of the Whorfian hypothesis, namely that the universe of meaning for each language is organized along certain dominant principles which pervade many patterns of distinct morphological types. What Whorf tried to do with reference to meanings in language is what scholars such as Hsu, Douglas and Bernstein, according to my reading of their work, are attempting to do in the domain of largely non-verbal, social meanings which make up some culture. The gist of what has been said above may be summed up in one sentence: a given culture is essentially a symbolic system where every element holds together with other elements. It may well be true that in the symbolic system known as 'culture', this characteristic is less pronounced than it is in the symbolic system of language; nonetheless, culture is not a conglomerate of isolated institutions bearing only accidental spatio-temporal or practical-functional relationship to each other (Hoijer 1948). Whatever else might or might not be universally true of culture, this much certainly seems to be true: there is method in the madness of each culture. The apparently irreconcilable aspects of a culture may not necessarily prove the absence of method: they may only indicate an analysis that needs to proceed further in depth.

3 The meaning of educational system in the life of a culture

From the above point of view, it would follow that at the deeper levels of analysis, the social institution of education must be seen as related to the culture: it forms an important part of the total design of living in a society. Logically then, the system of education can be seen as an expression of some dominant principle(s) within the given culture. For the purposes of this paper, I shall follow closely (my own interpretation of) Bernstein's account of the symbolic relationship between the educational system and the society within which it is embedded. In his *Classification and Framing of Educational Knowledge*, Bernstein (1971a) concentrates on two aspects of education: (i) the curriculum and (ii) the pedagogy in terms of two parameters, that of classification and that of framing. 'In all educational institutions there is a formal punctuation of time into periods' (p. 203): each period is set aside to some given 'content'. One way of examining the content is to ask: how clear is the boundary between the various kinds of contents – is it clear-cut or is it blurred? This forms one basis for the CLASSIFICATION of knowledge. When the boundary between contents is clear-cut the relationship between them is 'closed'; when the boundary is relatively open or blurred, this relationship is 'open'. By reference to this parameter, Bernstein sets up two types of curriculum: (i) the COLLECTION TYPE, where the boundary between contents is clear-cut and closed; and (ii) the integrated type where the boundary is relatively blurred and/or open. The classification of knowledge is said to be STRONG in the first type of curriculum, and WEAK in the second. Classification of knowledge in the educational system thus makes contact with curriculum type and content relations.

By contrast, the FRAMING of educational knowledge makes contact with pedagogy. According to Bernstein (1971a: 205–206):

> Frame refers to the range of options available to the teacher and taught in the control of what is transmitted and received in the context of the pedagogical relationship. Strong framing entails reduced options; weak framing entails a range of options. This frame refers to the degree of control teachers and pupils possess over the selection, organization and pacing of knowledge transmitted and received in the context of the pedagogical relationship.

Questions regarding framing can, then, be examined from two angles: (i) the degree of discretion allowed to the students by the teacher in the pedagogic relationship, and (ii) the degree of discretion allowed to the teacher by the boundary maintainer of the educational system. Where both the classification and framing of educational knowledge are strong, there, typically, a hierarchic relationship permeates the entire process: the student has reduced discretion vis-à-vis the teacher, and the teacher has reduced discretion vis-à-vis the boundary maintainers. In such educational systems, if it is true that the student is not free to intervene in the selection, organization and pacing of knowledge to be received, then it is equally true that the teacher himself is largely not free to make decisions about what is to be taught when, in what order, and what content is to be brought face to face with what other content. It is pertinent to add that the greater the centralization of control in the processes of education, the more likely it is that constraints will be placed both on the teacher and the taught.

The actual classification and framing of educational knowledge in any given culture is not likely to run anomalous to the culture as a whole. It has to be granted that several dominant cultural principles or mores might operate simultaneously to determine the actual shape of the educational system; nonetheless, it should be possible to make some generalizations about certain characteristics of a culture on the basis of the type of classification and framing that we might find in the educational system embedded in that culture. It is in this light that I interpret Bernstein's comment: 'where classification is strong, the boundaries between the different contents... [are] sharply drawn ... [this] presupposes strong boundary maintainers' (p. 206). One of the functions of clear-cut, unblurred boundaries is to create 'a strong sense of membership [in a community, RH] and so a specific identity' (ibid.). If this type of analysis is applied to the Indo-Pakistani educational systems, we would find that the predictions of Bernstein's hypotheses are more than fulfilled.

3.1 One dominant principle of the Indo-Pakistani cultures: classification

Whatever the diversities of the sub-continental cultures, scholars are agreed at least about one attribute: the sub-continental cultures jealously guard the ascribed communal boundaries between segregates. The existence of strong boundaries – i.e., strong classification in social institutions of one kind or another – is not to be disputed; in fact I would suggest that this strong boundary maintenance is a dominant principle which has a pervasive effect on phenomena with variously manifested shapes. So the boundaries may be those of caste, or determined by sex, or by age, by kinship or by occupation: one thing that is common to all is that they are regarded as – or, it may be more accurate to say that they are affectively responded to, rather than explicitly, intellectually analysed as – sacrosanct and irrevocable. Not surprisingly, in the classification of educational knowledge, the typical pattern is that of collection type: the contents of the curriculum are well-insulated from each other. Nor does this tendency show any significant variation along the spectrum of the various recognized stages in the educational process: this is the type of curriculum that continues from primary through secondary to the university level. So at the university level, for graduate courses there are well established content-constellations that can be picked up as a package by a graduating student. Any effort to choose three 'subjects' (content areas), one each from three distinct packages (which would naturally make up the required number of subjects for a graduate degree course), is more likely to be frustrated than not. The boundary is of course strongest between those contents which are classified under the general label of 'hard sciences'

– subjects dealing with physical sciences – and those which are regarded as belonging to social sciences or fine arts. I would be surprised if there existed a single university on the Sub-continent where the combination of chemistry, painting and art history would be allowed as a legitimate 'graduate course', though, it could be argued that this package makes at least as good sense as English literature, education and world history – one of the pre-packaged course-constellations acceptable to most universities. At the level of practice, it is the 'timetable problems' that are blamed for restrictions on course combinations, but is there any need to point out that, unlike mountains, timetables do not exist? Like most educational conventions, they are created by us; they are cultural artifacts; as such their construction is guided by some perception of what 'should' be allowed to co-occur with what. So a cultural principle, some idea of what is relevant controls the construction of timetables, as it does that of many other cultural artifacts, with possibly very different manifest shapes.

I should hasten to add that I am not implying that the Indo-Pakistani educational system is the only one, or that it is exceptional in possessing, the collection-type curriculum. The strength/weakness of the classification of knowledge is quite obviously relative. In comparing the English educational system with that in the US and some European countries, Bernstein found that the English system possessed the strongest classification; but I have no doubt that if it were compared with the classification of knowledge in the Indo-Pakistani educational systems, the latter would prove substantially stronger than the English one.

3.2 One dominant principle of the Indo-Pakistani cultures: framing

Let me turn now to the second element of the educational institution, namely the framing of knowledge. Bernstein (1971a: 206) has pointed out that 'strong frames reduce the power of the pupil over what, when and how he receives knowledge and increases the teacher's power in the pedagogical relationship'. It does not seem too fanciful to suggest that the ancient sub-continental concept of the 'guru' epitomizes just such a relationship. Commenting on the relationship of the guru and the disciple – the sub-continent's historical antecedent of the teacher and the taught – Hsu (1963) has remarked on the 'affect' that accumulates round this relationship. To Hsu this relationship appears to be characterized by such strong affective ties that he is inclined to believe it might be a stronger tie than any associated with any kinship dyadic relation in the whole culture. One may disagree with Hsu's rating of this dyadic relationship between the guru and the disciple – and certainly evidence could be found in the behaviour of the present-day generation especially those belonging to the middle-class families that would throw doubt on Hsu's strong claim – yet there appears to be no doubt that taken in their specific context, even today, the two dyads – parent-child and teacher-pupil – closely match each other in the affect that accumulates around them. The characteristics of the parent-child relationship in the familial context bear close resemblance to the teacher-pupil relationship in the educational context. A father remains a father, to whom one always owes respect and obedience, irrespective of how much authority one's own achieved status might have bestowed upon one in all other spheres of life; a teacher remains a teacher, to whom one always owes respect and obedience no matter how much one's own acquired knowledge might have outstripped the teacher's. It is pertinent to point out that although the ancient guru-disciple relationship can be taken as the historical antecedent of the present-day teacher-pupil relationship, there are some significant differences between the two. The ancient guru was in a very privileged position: he maintained total control over what knowledge should be transmitted to his disciples, when and how; in addition, unlike the modern teacher, he himself was not subject to control by any authority whatsoever. The supremacy of the guru was absolute. There are scores of ancient tales in the culture that tell us that the guru's authority in the domain of the transmission of knowledge was not open to question – there was no external constraint on it, much less any challenge. I believe that two of the most important factors contributing to this highly privileged position of the guru were the comparatively weak boundary between religion and education and the absence of centralized control over the process of education.

An examination of the present-day sub-continental educational system would reveal several manifest characteristics which all point to the exceptionally strong framing of knowledge. In as much as there is a strong centralized control of the educational process today, this has had the effect that the teacher does not possess as much discretion vis-à-vis the secular authorities as the guru did. However, within those limits imposed upon the teacher by strong classification and centralization of control, the teacher possesses a great deal of discretion vis-à-vis the students. Although the teacher is constrained to a certain extent both by external control over the nature of the curriculum and the strict requirements of evaluation, it is still the case that within these limits not only does the teacher decide what is to be learnt when and how, but his word is also the final one within the domain of his content. Typically at no stage within the educational process is the possibility granted that a student may question, much less disagree with, the teachers' views. Thus even in the instruction of the so-called creative arts, a teacher is likely to insist on the careful imitation of a model provided by him, rather than allow the student to explore on his own. And again the character of the framing does not change much with the different stages in the educational process: the practices just described could be just as common at the university stage as they are at the secondary or even primary ones. If the beginner is expected to draw 'from' a model that has been drawn by the teacher himself, the middle school student draws from 'model books' provided by the teacher; and even at the university level, the teacher of fine arts will insist on the student following certain conventions, say in pigment or in contours, which must be followed without variaition by all members of the class. There certainly will be found exceptions, especially at the university level; but the exceptions only highlight the norm – they cannot be used for the general characterization of the system of education as such.

This kind of pedagogic relationship typically restricts – or at least fails to encourage – exploration, initiative, and independence; it emphasizes a largely unquestioning acceptance by placing a higher premium on conformity. Another interesting phenomenon is the absence of any kind of explicit or implicit grouping of students in the class. It is generally recognized that the grouping of students within a class often varies according to how much interest they have in some particular contents as opposed to others, and also by reference to what ability or adaptability they possess in one area or another. Such grouping naturally implies treating the students as the point of departure in the organization of the instructional process, which is not in step with the dominant pedagogic relationship. Hence, streaming, whatever its faults or virtues, has never appeared as an important factor in the sub-continental educational system. If we accept Bernstein's hypothesis that the 'stronger the classification and framing of knowledge, the more the educational knowledge tends to be hierarchical and ritualized, the student seen as ignorant, with little status and few rights' (p. 214), then the Indo-Pakistani system would be an example par excellence of such a practice.

Another aspect of framing also appears relevant to our discussion. Bernstein refers to educational knowledge as '*uncommonsense knowledge*… freed from the particular and the local'; this contrasts with the 'everyday community knowledge of the pupil, his family and the peer group' which is referred to as *commonsense knowledge* (p. 215). One pertinent question is the strength of the boundary between these two kinds of knowledge – the experiential community-based commonsense knowledge as opposed to the specialized uncommonsense knowledge of the educational system. How much of the outside – that which is part of the student's real life experience – can be brought into the classroom in the context of the pedagogical relationship? Typically, where both the classification and framing of educational knowledge are strong, this implies a clear-cut boundary between the uncommonsense knowledge of the school and the everyday commonsense knowledge of the community to which the teacher and the taught belong. Bernstein (1971a: 222) takes the view that,

> Such insulation creates areas of privacy. For, in as much as the community based experience is irrelevant to the pedagogical frame, those aspects of the self informed by such experience are also irrelevant. These areas of privacy reduce the penetration of the socializing process, for it is possible to distance oneself from it [i.e., the entire process of education. RH].

That such strong classification and framing of knowledge exists in the Indo-Pakistani educational system would be apparent to anyone who examined it with objectivity and understanding. I shall attempt later to relate the serious consequences of this situation to the problems they give rise to in cross-cultural education.

3.3 Life in the community where the teacher and the taught live

When the analysis of the Indo-Pakistani educational system is presented as it is here – and it must be emphasized that the above account is not exhaustive of every situation; it is simply a general characterization of the situation overwhelmingly found on the Sub-continent – many would be inclined to conclude pityingly: here is a restrictive, narrow and inefficient system, having very little to recommend it. Such evaluations appear to me beside the point. My purpose in presenting this account of the educational system was not to evaluate positively or negatively; rather, my chief concern has been to locate the educational system in the culture in which it is embedded by showing how the system is in keeping with some dominant principles pervasive in the culture. With this end in view we might take a look at another major socializing agency: the family. In approaching the analysis from this angle, a fact that forces itself upon one's attention is how closely the symbolic meanings of the educational system correspond to those of socialization in the family. As patterns of socialization vary radically from one social class to another – class here being defined by reference to caste, and/or economic status, and/or the educational status of the parents – I shall concentrate mainly on the patterns of socialization in middle-class families. Such families seldom belong to the lowest caste. Typically the male parents in such families, especially in the urban areas, tend to have had the 'benefit' of formal education up to at least the first university degree. A mother would normally be literate, though she may not possess a university degree, and in some cases may not have been exposed to formal education – though this is less likely if the mother's own family of origin resided in urban areas.

Usually the father is the bread-winner, either through institutional employment and/or through private holdings.

It has been remarked by several scholars that the early upbringing of the Indo-Pakistani child is more permissive compared to that of his Western counterpart (Mandelbaum 1970; Strodtbeck 1971). This agrees well with the culture's image of the child as a helpless, socially unformed being who cannot be held responsible for his own actions. To be sure, up to a certain point in the life of the child, such a concept of the child's role must be universally shared among humans. The reason for emphasizing this particular characteristic in the present context is to draw attention to the comparatively much longer period of time that a person is assigned such a role. It would not be difficult to substantiate the assertion that the role of an individual needing guidance and care continues well into adolescence and even early adulthood vis-à-vis certain members of the family. With the child's physical maturity, the emphasis moves on to the personal and social aspects of his self, so that a person's friendships, his marriage, his choice of profession, his modes of interaction with certain sections of the community, are not his personal affair: they are subject to guidance and control from his adults – especially his parents. I should add that this is one of the few aspects of socialization in family which seems to be undergoing a change at the present moment;[3] yet even where total discretion may be allowed to an individual, this is often accompanied by a feeling of bitterness and personal failure on the part of the adult – particularly his parents.

In the early stages of the child's life – say the first three or four years – the main interaction for purposes of control is most frequently with the mother (as in Western families) though the father and other adults might intervene. The patterns of control are normally non-verbal – e.g., a child meddling with something he should not is picked up and held close in the arms of the mother (or grandmother) without anything said about the activity that incited this response. In the culture that mother is regarded as 'competent' and 'fortunate' who can control her children by a look in her eye or by a mere expression on her face. It follows that elaborate explanations in terms of cause and effect are not frequent, though threats and verbal or non-verbal bribes are quite common. When rationales are offered, the basis is the 'code of conduct' appropriate to a particular sex – 'boys don't do that' – or a particular age group – 'only grown up people are allowed to do that' – or in terms of age-relation – 'you don't talk like that to your elder sister'. The form of interaction amongst the adults of the house provides the child with a ready-made model for interpersonal social relationships. Although in the last fifty years or so, especially in urban areas, most families can be said to consist physically of just the parents and their children, it would be an oversimplification to think of such a unit as parallel to the Western nuclear family (Mandelbaum 1970). Whatever its physical shape and size, the family in the Indo-Pakistani Sub-continent stays firmly moored to this day to the 'joint family system': the ties between the parents and the children and between the siblings are close indeed, leading to frequent interactions in varied contexts. Even though not all close relatives may live under the same roof and eat from the same kitchen, they recognize the rights and obligations of other members of their – often huge – joint family as if the members all lived together. Thus the child has enough occasions to observe in the interactions of the adults how such ascribed boundaries as those of sex, age, age relation, status, ethnicities and religion etc. are played out in actual patterns of interaction. A child would no more expect to hear his mother answer back or argue with his grandmother than he would expect himself to be able to answer back or argue with his own mother. His father is no more likely to raise his voice in speaking to his elder brother than the child himself is likely to be allowed to disregard the superior status of his own elder brother. While the authority of the mother is diffused – because the mother's mother or the father's mother have an equal right to control the child in every area in which the mother may – in this very pattern of diffusion of maternal authority, the 'inevitable' nature of hierarchically controlled exercise of authority is made real for the child. These clear-cut, unblurred boundaries set up by reference to the ascribed attributes of sex, age and kinship relation 'create a strong sense of membership, and so a specific identity'. For arriving at his identity as a cultural and social being, these close ties in the extended family are most important, although even today the relationship with the supernatural and the guru may be just as important as suggested by Hsu (1963). But when we explore the bases of these last two relations we find that the dominant principle in the guru relationship conforms to that of hierarchical boundary maintenance, while the relationship to the supernatural is a function of the everyday community-based commonsense knowledge. There is no exaggeration in the suggestion that in establishing this relationship, the educational system does not play any important initial part. If we accept Hsu's mode of examining the individual as a cultural social being, then in the psychological homeostasis of the Indo-Pakistani child, it is the immediate group – the family – that plays the crucial role of determining what affects will belong to his most intimate layer, the one that determines his 'human constant'[4] (1971b). The strong framing in the Indo-Pakistani educational system between commonsense community-based knowledge and the uncommonsense school knowledge, thus leaves the Indo-Pakistani child untouched. Unlike the West, here it is not the educational system which plays a crucial role in determining his 'human substance'; the fundamental base of his identity as a social and cultural being is complete, independently of the school and the wider peer group. By conforming to the dominant principle of familial socialization, the educational system rather reinforces this sense of identity, seldom creating any new affects which can compete with the affects already created by socialization in the family.

I want to say a few words now on another context of socialization in the family: the instructional context (Bernstein 1971c), including within it also 'play'. Despite the educational status of his parents, typically the child's instruction is a matter for the school and the teacher. Indo-Pakistani parents seldom interfere with the workings of the school; in the majority of cases, especially past the kindergarten stage – which is in any event available to a very limited section of the population – the only contact that the parents have with the educational institution is economic – the paying of fees, fines and dues and the receiving of progress reports, including examination results, which up to the secondary stage are addressed typically directly to the parents. If a student is found weak at some subject, a recommendation might be made by the school for extra tuition; and typically this means the hiring of a private instructor to coach the student for a set number of hours. Even this spatial proximity of the teacher – the special instructor – does not necessarily lead to any but the most perfunctory interaction. The teacher may be entertained as a guest either at the end or the beginning of the lesson, but normally there would be little discussion of the child's special educational problems or the mode of coping with them. In conformity with this pattern of maintaining a relatively clear boundary between the child's educational knowledge and home life, we find that the instructional context at home revolves around skills that are not likely to be relevant to what goes on in school. Studies of American Indian children have indicated that in some cultures instruction inside the family is predominantly implicit: the characteristic mode of learning is 'visual' and 'physical' (John 1972; Dumont 1972; Philips 1972). The same could be said about the Indo-Pakistani culture. It is, then, not surprising that play is unstructured and usually not subject to guidance; nor is it surprising that there is a clear-cut boundary between play and instruction. Play is not seen as representing a potential for increasing that type of knowledge which is the sole monopoly of the educational institutions. Nonetheless it would be wrong to suppose that play is not exploited for teaching other orders of relevance, and what is interesting here is the fact that it is used as a vehicle for reinforcing boundaries which are emphasized in the context of control. Thus after a certain age some kind of play might be frowned upon, depending on the sex of the player – girls obviously do not play football nor do boys play at building doll's houses; at a certain age, play with members of the other sex is discouraged; and except in the practical context of helping the mother, the playing of older children with younger ones is seen as an almost total failure in upbringing. The role boundaries are no less delineated here by reference to the ascribed attributes of sex, age and hierarchy than they are in the context of control.

It is irrelevant what our personal evaluation of such patterns of socialization in the family and the educational institutions as discussed above may be, the fact remains that at a deeper level the socialization in the two social sites is essentially congruent: it gives little or no rise to tension. Significantly the rate of truancy and other forms of delinquency are lower compared to the West – and perhaps were lower still a couple of decades ago.[5] I doubt if this could be attributed to the Pakistani child's great love of learning: to me it seems the main reason for this lies in the essential continuity of symbolic behaviour in the two major systems of socialization. The strong classification and framing of educational knowledge does not make 'unreasonable' demands on the Pakistani child in his orientation to objects and persons. The symbolic meanings of one system of socialization do not threaten or questions the symbolic meanings of the other one; rather they reinforce each other, feeding into the maintenance of value systems and beliefs that are deeply meaningful to a person. From the point of view of Hsu's hypotheses (1971b), these deeply meaningful beliefs and values belong to the most intimate layer of human being, providing him with a sense of his own identity. Through these correspondences, the Indo-Pakistani educational system is rendered 'safe' so far as cultural change is concerned.

3.4 Cross-cultural education and socialization

With this rather sketchy account of the relationship between the familial socialization and the educational system, I would like to return to the specific problem of the Indo-Pakistani student at, for example, an English University. In the latter too, the classification of education is strong though only by comparison with some other Western-style educational systems (Bernstein 1971c: 208); it appears to be remarkably weaker in comparison with the sub-continental educational systems. A much greater difference is to be noticed in the area of the framing of educational knowledge: especially when the university-level education is compared, the framing is much weaker in the English universities. The amount of discretion allowed to the student in England is much greater; and to the extent that the classification of knowledge is weaker, there is a greater degree of emphasis in English universities on 'ways of knowing' than on just 'the state of knowledge'. The weight of the entire pattern of socialization on the Indo-Pakistani Sub-continent runs counter to the increased discretion for the student, and commitment to ways of knowing. The security of a specific identity which is so carefully, though unconsciously, built into the familial and educational socialization in the latter social environment is challenged by the symbolic significance of the reduced insulation between content areas and by the blurring of boundaries between the teacher and the taught. In discussion with colleagues in England, two reactions to the situation are mentioned frequently: colleagues engaged in teaching the Indo-Pakistsani students feel that a good deal of 'mothering' is required to help the student succeed; and they are often puzzled by the unevenness of the students' performance, who can produce a meticulous first-rate summary of the publications as and when required, but flounder if asked to examine the same material critically or in comparison with another approach. It seems to me that this is as 'it should be': the former is an exercise in which the student is at home, since it is a fairly characteristic form of learning in educational systems with strong classification and framing of knowledge; the latter form of exercise is as foreign to them as fish and mashed potatoes!

Talking to the serious students, one gets the impression that the Indo-Pakistani student devotes much more time to his studies than his English counterpart; despite this he is barely able to 'keep up' with the latter. The effect of the greater discretion allowed to the sub-continental student in the new educational environment – especially in the content area of social sciences – is often overtly expressed by an uncertainty about what is actually required of him in performance and often even in uncertainty as to what has to be taken as relevant material for preparation. They will often complain that the subject is too wide, so there is too much to be learned. Both complaints indicate a mechanical and somewhat quantitative approach: as the focus is on reading and taking down meticulous notes on the read material, it is not surprising that the problem of speed of reading often comes up in discussion as a major hurdle. It is possibly true that within the context under focus the Indo-Pakistani student reads more slowly than the English one, but I would be surprised if this were true of their reading of ordinary popular fiction. If there is no crucial difference in the latter environment, then clearly it is not the mechanical act of reading English *per se* which is responsible for the slow reading pace in educational content. At this point it may appear that the Indo-Pakistani student is perhaps less able to 'receive the content'. Judgement on this issue would depend upon how one approaches the question of 'content' itself. As I pointed out earlier, a 'good' Indo-Pakistani student is just as good at summarizing the contents of an article/chapter as his English counterpart. The difference between the two is most noticeable in two areas: the English student is likely to do better (i) when it comes to stating the bases of a certain hypothesis; and also (ii) where the student needs to explore the implications of some hypothesis – what extrapolations can be made from it, where the hypothesis is 'heading'. This would seem to be suggestive of a difference in the orientation to the entire question of what is considered 'content' – or the 'object of knowledge'; and it is best not to confuse this with 'assimilating the gist of the content'. The real problem is not so much in how to read and how to understand – i.e., how to decode the message at a literal level – it is, rather, the problem of figuring out how and why one should proceed in which direction, given that the meaning of the message is as it has been understood. The difficulties arise from not being able to find out – or orient oneself to – ways of knowing, rather than from collecting bits of given information.

It would seem then that at a very deep level, cross-cultural education of the type under discussion becomes a process of the redefinition of the identity of the Indo-Pakistani student. The English educational system at the university level questions those dominant principles which formed the foundation of the formation of his self as a cultural being. It is significant that in the last half century there has been a growth in the production of literary fiction, which centres around the theme of alienation, where the alienated person is no other than our successful Indo-Pakistani student freshly returned from abroad after years of sojourn in England. It is tempting to ask whether there is a cultural awareness – though unconscious – that to be a successful scholar in Britain, the Indo-Pakistani student must radically change as person. It is also interesting to note that the problems which arise for the alienated character in the world created in fiction are just this which relate to the 'self-defining boundaries' such as those of hierarchy, sex, age and religion in the native culture.

Summary

1. Following Bernstein, I have argued that educational systems are intricately related to the culture in which they are embedded;
2. I have attempted to show that socialization through the family and the educational institutions on the Sub-continent creates a particular sense of 'identity';
3. I have argued that this identity is challenged when the student is brought into the English educational system at the university level and that a conflict arises due to many intangible problems in cross-cultural education;
4. I have argued that whereas the mechanical problems arising from the educational process are better understood by the educators, and perhaps better solved, there is so far no evidence to suggest that the problems arising from the deep symbolic differences between the two distinct educational systems have been understood, leave aside solved.

5. In my interpretation I have relied heavily on the work of Bernstein and that of Hsu. I accept total responsibility for my interpretation of their work.

Notes

1 I doubt if this is true to the same extent today [RH 2008].
2 See Chapter 10 in this volume.
3 Since this paper was first published some 35 years ago, there has been considerable change in respect of many aspects of socialization in Pakistan. Especially in the westernized upper middle classes, youngsters now have probably as much freedom of choice and perhaps even less regard to indigenous traditions as typical in the Western world. But there is no exaggeration perhaps in saying that this has created definitely distinct sub-cultures whereby the non-westernized segment of the society continues much in the same manner. In fact with greater emphasis on indigenous traditions whether seen as arising from religion or as simply 'the way we live here' many pernicious traditions which were on the wane, such as control on women's freedom of choice or 'honour killing' have been revived. It is important to recognize also that 'non-westernized' is not synonymous with 'poor' and/or 'illiterate'.
4 For the concepts used in this discussion, see chapter 9 in this volume.
5 Some indication of the state of education in Pakistan today may be found by consulting chapters 2 and 11 in this volume. Quite apart from what is lacking in the design of the curricula, there remains the serious problem of over-crowded classrooms, lack of the provision of proper education for teachers and in-service training.

9 Some sociological considerations in second language teaching [1978]

1 Introduction

This paper[1] makes an attempt to bring together ideas from different disciplines, ideas which are relevant to teaching in general, and therefore to second language teaching as well. The different disciplines I have in mind are those of psychological anthropology, social anthropology and sociology of education. There are hypotheses in all these disciplines that seem to raise interesting questions regarding some of our widely accepted assumptions in second language teaching.

First of all, though, a clarification of terms is needed. I have used the term 'second language' in my title. In recent literature, a distinction is made between a 'foreign language' and a 'second language'; hence the different qualifications of ESLT and EFLT.[2] The important difference seems to be that the second language has a more permanent and dynamic status within the learners' speech community: it is a language that has been adopted, whether in accordance with a consciously devised plan or not, as a part of the community's linguistic repertoire. A foreign language, on the other hand, does not have such a stable or prominent position. However, in my title, I have not used *second language* in this narrower, more technical sense. Rather, I am referring to a whole range of non-mother-tongue languages, the learning of which requires the intervention of formal instruction. This logically subsumes second language in its narrower sense, while leaving the possibility open that languages may have differing degrees of foreignness about them for members of different strata, even within the same macro community. An appropriate example would be the status of English in Pakistan.

2 Teaching: a brief comment

As in the teaching of anything else, so also in the teaching of language, I suggest we need to start from the three primary terms: someone who teaches, i.e., a teacher, someone who is taught, i.e., the student; and something that is taught, i.e., the subject matter, which in the present case is a second language. I suggest that the precepts and practices in the domain of second language teaching appear to bestow a status of mutual autonomy to these three primary terms, a practice which appears to be open to question. This autonomy can reveals itself in treating each of these terms as having an independent life. I would suggest that often such a position is implied in practice although in theory it may be readily granted as not viable. For example, we subscribe to such a view when we experience the feeling that if only the relevant language could be better analysed, the teaching would be more successful; or, if teachers were more resourceful, we could achieve better results; finally – and often in despair – if only the students would pay attention! Let me not give the impression that the availability of better understood material, of better trained teachers, and of more highly motivated students is irrelevant to the achievement of better results; rather, the contrary is true. But there lies a danger in such dissociation of terms: instead of treating teaching as a multi-faceted process, one may be easily beguiled into thinking that the problems of language teaching could be resolved at a fell swoop by concentrating on any one vector. It is in the light of such unarticulated assumptions that we should try to understand the disillusionment of the language teacher[3] who has enthusiastically embraced modern linguistics as the sure means of achieving that elusive goal – proficiency in a second language teaching.

2.1 Teaching as an integrated process

Luckily, recent years have seen a growing realization of the inadequacy of the above view which had trusted simple solutions for complex problems: many theoretical approaches reject now the autonomy of single vectors without reservation. Rather, the attempt is to produce frameworks in which the interaction of the three terms is adequately displayed. It is somewhat ironic, though, that this very attempt has indirectly created a position which encourages the second form of autonomy; the framework is so self-coherent as to create the illusion that it represents an essentially autonomous system. I suggest that this is no less an illusion than the belief in achieving success through attention to one single vector relevant to the process of teaching. It may be useful in this perspective to present a framework which provides some indication of the interdependence of the three primary terms, their interconnections maximally displayed. Figure 1 aims to do just that.

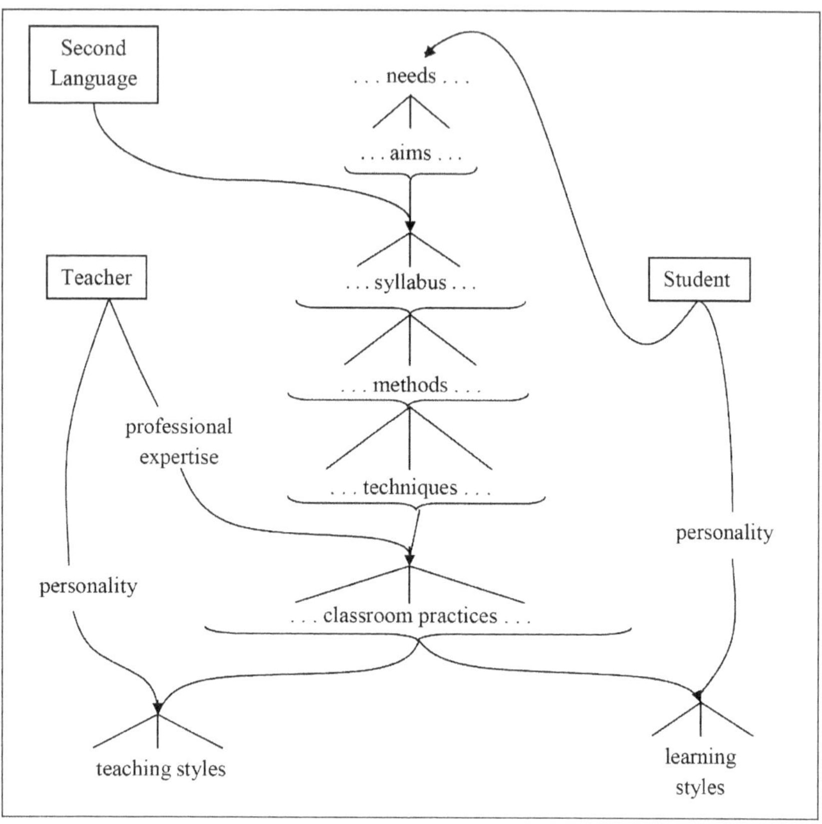

Figure 1: The process of teaching a second language: an integrated model

In Figure 1, the three primary terms are enclosed in rectangles; they enter into the diagram at different stages. However, from *needs* to *teaching* and *learning styles*, there is an unbroken set of connecting lines. There is no need to spell out the obvious fact that the three primary terms are brought together into one self-coherent whole by the single simple fact of the process of teaching. The students' NEEDS generate the range of AIMS, which, in an ideal second language teaching programme, should be taken into account in setting up the SYLLABUS. However, at the same time, the structure of the syllabus will be affected by the subject matter – *the view of a second language as a system which enables meaning making*. Thus, the syllabus for learning a 'dead language' will hopefully be different from that for learning English as a second language. The factors so far considered will give rise to a set of METHODS; some methods are more appropriate for some aims and syllabi, some for others. But at the same time the possibility is granted that for the same aim and the same syllabus, one may still evolve a different range of distinct methods. Each method is capable of generating a range of TECHNIQUES. These techniques are however not manifested except through the teacher's professional expertise; what comes across as CLASSROOM PRACTICES is, then, techniques conditioned by the teacher's own range of professional abilities. But given the same degree of professional expertise and the same set of techniques, the TEACHING STYLES can still vary. The factor responsible for the variation is the teacher's PERSONALITY; what is essentially the same classroom practice can, for example, be qualitatively distinct from one classroom to another depending upon, say, the difference in the teacher's charisma. This is not the end of the story. Teaching styles do not exist in a vacuum; by themselves they cannot be seen as the end of the teaching process. There is a necessary corresponding term: the LEARNING STYLES, which in their turn are presented as the outcome of the interaction between the classroom practices and the student's personality.

3 Teaching in society

The diagram, then, shows the interdependence of the three primary terms sufficiently to eliminate the possibility of their dissociation from each other. The logic of the interdependence between the terms arises from the logic of the process of teaching. As I pointed out before, the self-coherence of a system such as is displayed by this diagram can mislead one into thinking that the system possesses autonomy simply by virtue of being self-coherent. Just to demonstrate how mistaken such an impression would be, one needs to ask simply: where would this highly unified process of teaching take place? The perfunctory bow to the life of the community made by the recognition of needs is not even half the story: one may simply ask whose needs, and who administers to those needs. It is only an academic myth that what goes on in the school can be seen as a well-insulated area, which is not permeated by the communal living of life.

Take for example the question of personality. The Western view of personality – and I do not mean just the commonsense folk view but also fairly elaborate systems for the description of personality – is, to say the least, somewhat romantic. Here personality is seen as a germinating plant or a bud which will bloom into a flower despite the climate, despite the soil, all by itself; it is something miraculous that grows without needing to relate to anything in which it may be embedded. To many of us, the suggestion that an individual's personality may in fact be the function of the culture in which he is socialized is an anathema. To be sure, the structure of human personality may be conditioned by forces you may not be aware of; but this does not necessarily argue that such forces are inevitably intra-organic; a large part of what we are is a response to where we are, what kind of relations are possible for us, and what kind of views appear reasonable to our community.

3.1 Personality in society

The question of the relationship between culture and personality has always been a controversial one, perhaps because one tends to approach the extremes. As Hsu (1971b) points out: 'If everyone acts as individuated individuals, no society is possible. If every one acts in complete conformity with the others, there will be no difference between human beings and bees. Human ways of life are obviously somewhere in between these extremes.' I will have a few words to say on the question of striking a sane balance between the two extremes at a further point. Here I want to present an argument which raises serious doubts as to the autonomy of the framework presented in Figure 1.

To the extent that human personality may be seen as a construct of the culture in which it is embedded, it is valid to suggest that the range of teaching styles may, in the last analysis, be conditioned by the shape of the culture. And this would be all the more likely if it turns out to be the fact that educational practices within the community are also directly affected by the operative designs for living, a phrase that I take to be synonymous with culture. The self-sufficiency of the framework in Figure 1 would then be only an academic fiction, useful as a stage in the analysis of the total phenomena relevant to teaching; it could, however, not be passed off as the ultimate synthesis, as the successful model of what really goes on in the business of teaching and learning, much less as a representation of the forces that govern the myriad interactions which make up the body of classroom practices.

To avoid the difficulties that arise from the use of the term 'personality', I will follow Hsu in side-stepping the term to begin with; further, I will give a rather condensed account of Hsu's notion of how 'man lives as a social and cultural being' (Figure 2 below): what constitutes the 'central substance' of such a 'cultural being'.

PSYCHOSOCIAL HOMEOSTASIS

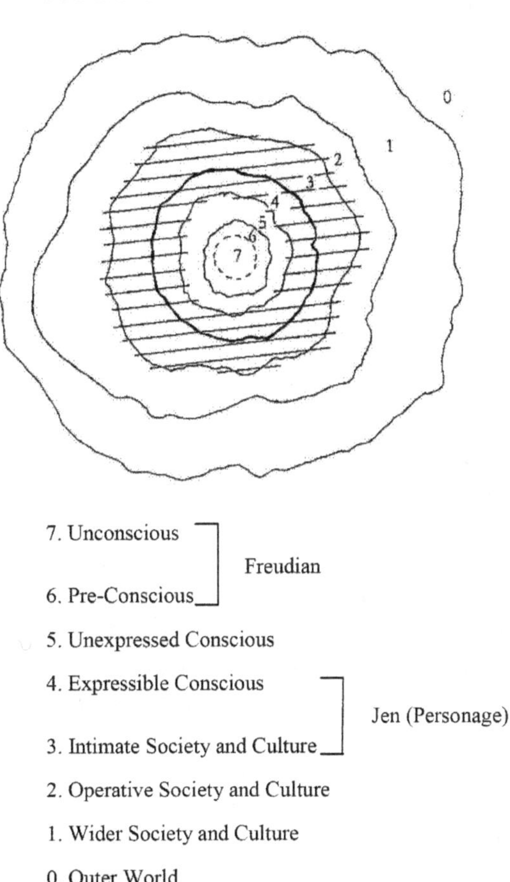

Figure 2: Psychosociogram of man (source: Hsu 1971c)

In Figure 2, 'the elements of human existence', represented as concentric layers, exhaust the social universe human beings can internalize. Here the shaded area is most relevant to our discussion, because it is in this shaded area that the HUMAN CONSTANT resides. According to Hsu, this shaded area is 'the central substance of man as a social and cultural being. It is the human constant, within which every human individual tends to maintain a satisfactory level of psychic and interpersonal equilibrium, in the same sense that every physical organism tends to maintain a uniform and beneficial physiological stability within and between its parts'. Hsu refers to the process in the human constant as PSYCHOSOCIAL HOMEOSTASIS. According to Hsu, the shaded area covering layers three and four is of particular interest to the present discussion. But what is special about these two layers? Why are they important? Hsu answers as follows: 'The hallmark of layer four is that its contents not only can be easily communicated to others but also understood and responded to by others without great difficulty'. This communicability is, however, more or less restricted to members of the same society. As for the *contents* of layer four, Hsu points out that

> On a personal level, this layer includes trivial matters such as table manners and important rules such as who should mate with whom. On a national level, it includes the meaning of patriotism, freedom, filial piety, or chastity of women, ideas about keeping black people 'in their place', ideals such as devotion to the emperor, or fears of ghosts, witchcraft, or communism.

By contrast, the hallmark of layer three is 'a high degree of affect'. This layer 'contains' human beings with whom the individual stands in an intimate relationship: they are the individual's significant alter, to use a term from Talcott Parsons. The layer contains also such cultural usages, attitudes, and artefacts to which the individual responds with affect. What forms part of this layer is a matter of personal feeling rather than usefulness. This contrasts with the second layer, which is inhabited by usages, attitudes etc. according to their usefulness rather than the individual's affects towards them. The possibility exists that what appears as the same social 'object' from one point of view may be differently categorized in different communities, so that depending on the individual's culture, the same human relationship or material substance may be in layer two or in layer three.

3.2 Human constant and social relationship

If with Hsu we accept that the human constant resides primarily on layers three and four, then it follows that the cultural value systems and social relationships recognized in a community play an important part in the psychosocial homeostasis of human beings. Taking on board the generally accepted premise that specific cultural value systems are transmitted through the range of social relations, these relationships – what they are, what they mean – are critically important in any discussion of the structuring of human personality, and there is no need to argue that the theory of roles is crucial to any theory of social relations. We, thus, move from a discussion of the structuring of personality to an examination of the significance of role relations.

Here again Hsu (1968, 1971b, 1971c) offers some interesting insights. He insists that role relationships are not free to take any direction at random within a cultural community; instead, they follow a direction set by a communally dominant [role] dyad. The DOMINANT DYAD functions as a model for other role relations in the community, so that the characteristic attributes of the dominant dyadic relation are also reflected, in their own way, in other role relations within that community. An acceptance of these views implies that there will be an asymmetry between ideas concerning teacher–student role relationship in the industrialized West and those current in the so-called 'developing countries'. Personal experience has taught me that the rights and obligations of a teacher as conceived of by an Indo-Pakistani student even today[4] are qualitatively different from those entertained by his Western counterpart (Hasan, Chapter 4 this volume).

This is an important point in itself, but what makes Hsu's theory of the dominant dyad, when seen in conjunction with his theory of the human constant, so significant for the present discussion, is the far-reaching set of implications for our conception of reality, if one may be allowed to use such a 'large expression'. The fact that the dominant dyad in the Western (type of) communities is the peer-role relation has a bearing on many aspects of the cultural designs of living. Thus the urge for individuation, the high regard for record-achievers, the value attached to originality and the emphasis on personal achievement as well the need to justify one's existence, are some cultural traits that, according to Hsu (1971a, c), arise from the insecurity inherent in the dominant role dyad in the Western cultures. It is not simply that the teacher-student relationship varies in different cultures; it is also that the personality the teacher and the student bring into the classroom is, however imperfectly, a reflection of the culture within which the two have been socialized.[5] The ramifications of such a stance have the power to at once highlight the similarities and dissimilarities between the teaching of English to the migrant Pakistani in England or Australia and the teaching of English to the Pakistani in Pakistan (i) by a Pakistani or (ii) by a foreigner – perhaps with the 'qualification' of only being a native English speaker.

3.3 Is the cultural context of teaching really important?

This debate cannot be pursued here. So returning to the main arguments, note that it is usually at this point one encounters cries of disagreement. As I said before, it goes against the grain in us to accept that culture can have such serious effects. And while one might ignore the objections expressed at the level of personal chagrin, one has to take more seriously objections expressed by 'experts' couched in terms carrying the weight of a theory. Here is an example from Hargreaves (1975): 'There is not enough substance to the social role to give a detailed guide to the actor's behaviour in specific interactional situations... The role provides a loose prescriptive framework within which the actor must to a large degree make up the lines and the action as he goes along.'

I hope that I do not misread Hargreaves in pointing out that the making up of lines and actions as one goes along is being seen by him as essentially a free enterprise. There is reason to doubt this view. If the typical behaviour of two individuals carrying approximately the same role differs over a range of similar social practices across cultures, this does not mean that variation is random, not constrained by social factors that could be identified. This view is supported by Douglas (1971), who offers a framework designed to provide an account of precisely such non-random variability in human behaviour.

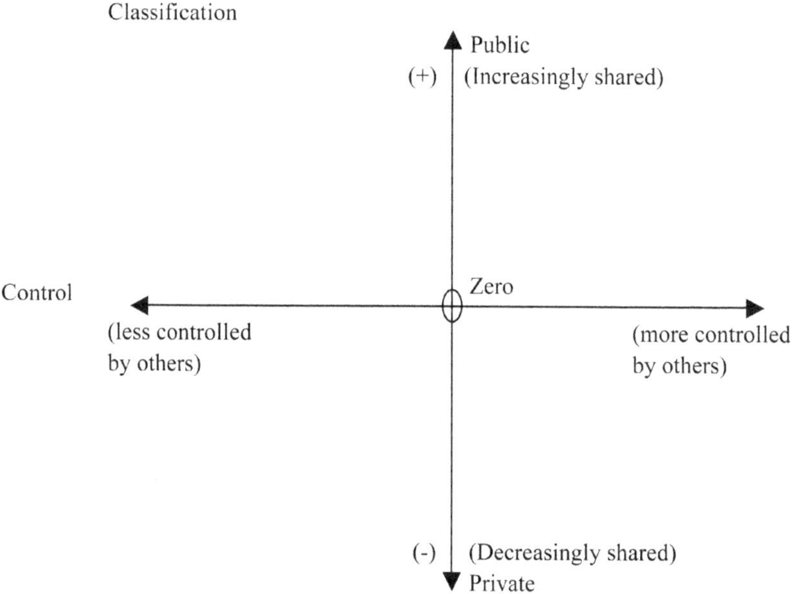

Figure 3: Classification and control (Source: Douglas 1971)

In Figure 3, Douglas presents the variables, applicable universally to all communities/sub-communities irrespective of their politico-economic status. The horizontal line here is 'the line of personal pressure'; on this line 'zero' represents complete freedom. In moving to the right on this axis, one is increasingly bonded – pressured – by others; and in moving to the left, one puts others increasingly in bond, i.e, one pressures others. The zero point where one neither pressures nor is pressured is rarely arrived at: the examples of this category, according to Douglas, are hermits and recluses, and even their stay at this point may be a fairly transitory one! The vertical line is the line of classification of elements of belief systems. At the top the classification is public, i.e., moving up from the zero point, the classification is 'increasingly shared'; moving down from the zero point it is private, i.e., 'decreasingly shared'. If below the zero is originality, the end point of the line below the zero is madness, which is the ultimate condition of aloneness: the madman's universe is populated by entities which are not recognized by others as meaningful; they have no socially acknowledged status. Cultures – and people living within cultures – vary as to which quadrant they may be said to inhabit habitually. But if I do not misunderstand Douglas, the cultural space within which humanity is allowed movement – therefore variation – is exhausted by the primary quadrants in Figure 3. It is not too fanciful to suggest that a person in social interaction is like a token sentence: the uniqueness of both is conditioned – i.e., constrained – by their respective grammars. Just as there is no sentence in a language that does not answer to some principle of that language's grammar, so also there is no person in social interaction who is totally free to 'make up the lines and actions as he goes along'. It will take me too far afield to attempt an answer to the question: what makes a culture occupy one position in the diagram rather than another? But note in passing that Bernstein's theory of codes is at least one effort to answer this question.

4 On the culturally embedded activity of teaching

The positions I have presented here are derived from theories that pertain to the fields of social psychology and anthropology that may be summed up as follows:

(i) the nucleus of personality for man as a social animal develops in cultural environment;
(ii) role relations possess attributes which go beyond the pragmatics of situation and relate to the basic culture-organizing notions;
(iii) variation in human behaviour is largely referable to one's relation to others in the culture.

In light of these conclusions, how well does Figure 1 portray the culturally created nature of the teacher-student relationship? How far does it alert us to the fact that teaching is overwhelmingly an activity governed by cultural designs of living? The answer is obvious: there is a tremendous degree of oversimplification in that framework. It is not sufficient to recognize that students have needs – which, by the by, are relatable to their life in the community anyway – or that the teacher and the students are possessors of personalities, which give rise to different styles of teaching and learning. Rather, there is need to place the entire teaching process in its wider and sociological perspective. This is so because analysis reveals that the teaching process is not free of the culture in which it takes place; to quote Bernstein (1975a) the fact is that 'How a society selects, classifies, distributes, transmits and evaluates the educational knowledge it considers to be public, reflects both the distribution of power and the principles of social control.' In what follows, I shall selectively present some parts of Bernstein's hypotheses from 'The classification and framing of educational knowledge' (1975a). I consider these to be primarily relevant to the present discussion.

4.1 The classification of educational knowledge

CLASSIFICATION concerns the relationship of the disciplines – the contents – included in the curriculum. If these are seen as having fairly well-defined boundaries with little or no blurring, the curriculum would be seen as a COLLECTION type. In such curricula, the contents stand in a closed relation to each other: each discipline is relatively insulated from the others. By contrast the concerns of the curriculum may be seen as interrelated, with boundaries that are not clearly defined, so that a certain degree of blurring is possible. A curriculum such as this, where the various content areas do not go their separate ways, is called an INTEGRATED type: in such curricula, the contents stand in an open relation to each other. I shall refrain here from discussing the various permutations of the two types of curricula; let me rather point out simply the obvious fact that from OPEN to CLOSED content relation and from integrated to collection type curricula there exists a cline. The end-points of this cline are the theoretical possibilities of the purest form of integrated and collection curricula. However, in practice variation from this pure form is to be encountered more often.

What controls the variation on this axis? It would appear that, in the last analysis, variation is relatable to certain characteristics of the social structure, within which the curriculum may be embedded. Collection type is likely to exist in communities where the principles of classification for the belief system are increasingly public and where relatively greater control is exercised on the individual by others in the community. Communities in which collection type curricula find favour are comparatively more authoritarian, with clearly defined hierarchies, where the greater emphasis is on consensus. In terms of Figure 3, such communities would occupy the top right of the quadrant. By contrast the integrated type would be increasingly favoured by communities which occupy the bottom left of the quadrant: here greater individuation and greater freedom is accorded to the individual. On this basis, one could pretty safely put forward the suggestion that the integrated type of curriculum is more likely to be popular among the members of the upper middle classes in industrialized communities such as found in the West. By contrast, the weight of the cultural pattern on the Indo-Pakistani continent[6] would lead one to expect that collection-type curricula would prevail more widely (Hasan 1976, Chapter 8 in this volume).

4.2 The framing of educational knowledge

According to Bernstein 1975a, FRAMING is concerned with 'the pedagogical relationship of the teacher and the taught' and 'the boundary between what may be transmitted in this pedagogical relationship'. Bernstein goes on to add, 'framing refers to the degree of control teacher and taught possess over the selection, organization, pacing and timing of the knowledge transmitted and received in the pedagogical relationship'.

Framing is said to be STRONG where there is a tighter control over the teacher and the taught, and where the boundary is drawn sharply between the un-commonsense knowledge, i.e., the knowledge that is pedagogically transmitted as an official element of the curriculum, and commonsense knowledge, i.e., knowledge that the students bring to the classroom from their family, neighbourhood and peers. Framing is said to be WEAK where the boundary between the pedagogically transmitted knowledge and the everyday community knowledge is blurred, and greater discretion is allowed to the teacher and the student. Again, the occurrence of the purely strong and the purely weak framing may be seen as theoretically possible: these are the endpoints of a continuum along which will be ranged the framing practices of the educational system in the various communities of the world. This variation in framing is related to the community's social structure: strong frames are most likely to be found in communities that might occupy the top right corner in Figure 3, while weak frames have an increasing probability of occurring in communities occupying the bottom left corner. Following the line of argument so far, the framing of knowledge in the Indo-Pakistani subcontinent should be strong (Hasan 1976, Chapter 8 this volume).

4.3 Some implications of sociological analysis

If we take these arguments seriously, it would follow that the place of the second language in the syllabus is not a matter that can be decided entirely by professional expertise – whether in the person of the consultant linguist or that of the experienced second language teacher, or even the psycholinguist. The place of a second language in a curriculum cannot be viably determined by a consideration of what makes language learning easier *in some absolute sense*; rather, the matter would need to be decided by reference to the learner and the role of the said second language in the learner's community. I should like to see an analysis of the underlying philosophy that supports the teaching of English for Special Purposes (ESP) along these lines: what is a 'special purpose' for some learner in one community is not necessarily 'special purpose' in another. A tentative suggestion is that the approach may be an indirect outcome of strong framing of educational knowledge in countries where we find it necessary to teach English as a second language. In those communities where English as a second language is simply a 'content' which firmly belongs in the domain of un-commonsense knowledge and as such is clearly set apart from the community's day to day life, both the relation of English to other educational content in the curriculum and the selection of what constitutes 'teaching English' might well encourage a move towards ESP. To put it simply in such communities the student only needs to know English for special purposes! *English for Special Purposes makes perfect sense in the light of social considerations so long as the social is the learner's social not the distant foreign specialists*'; at the same time, this way of looking at the need for ESP seems to highlight the problems a teacher is likely to encounter when embarked upon teaching English for Special Purposes in communities where the subject is, at best, superimposed due to historical-political reasons, and, at worst, remains alien to the majority of the population.[7] Such a perspective on ESP frees us from the often felt need to produce an 'impressive' series of 'real academic' reasons for preferring it as a superior approach to language teaching. To me it seems that the superiority of the method lies precisely in its sensitivity to the social factors, not in the principles of pedagogy or in the nature of the language being taught.

Implicit in the arguments presented here is the stance that there are principles of coherence within cultures; that, for example, institutions within a social community cannot be defined, organized, or taken to operate without reference to such principles (Douglas 1970, 1971, 1972; Geertz 1973; Bernstein 1971c, 1975a; Hasan 1976, 1984a). The teaching of the second language cannot be an exception. If anything, it is a much more sensitive area because of its role in human lives. Language is not simply a mediator of reality; it is also a weapon to create, destroy, upgrade and discredit. These latter, more intimate functions of language appear to pose more of a real threat where a second language is concerned. Without wishing to dramatize the situation, to me it seems that the largest barrier against second language learning arises from feelings of fear or hostility (no matter how vaguely sensed) to the target language. In this respect, the picture of language teaching as presented in Figure 1 is rather misleading. It focuses attention on that part of 'reality' which is easy to manage: change the classroom set up; give more hours to teaching English; use the audio-visual method; excite student interest; change the teacher; introduce the situational approach; simplify the material; and a host of other such solutions. Let me say very clearly that I am not claiming these things will never make any difference to the quality of learning, but the difference they make will be significant only if there is the right social context for the enterprise. Often the suggested changes cannot be brought forth; often they change their character while being brought forth.

5 The need for a sociologically informed review of second language teaching

If I so insistently criticize the view of the autonomy of the process of teaching, it is because it has proved so wasteful. There is no evidence to support the idea that the 'correct, advanced, humane' attitude on the part of the teacher will change the character of the educational system, as implied by Postman and Weingartner (1972); there is, however, good reason to suggest that the forms of consciousness, i.e., the habits of meaning and minding, that become possible to humans are influenced to a large extent by the social context within which the human beings have their existence. It is this latter proposition that I have examined here from different angles. There does exist some proof (Sharp *et al.* 1975) that the overtly held 'advanced progressive' attitudes on the part of the teacher do not necessarily solve the teaching problems as was expected. Between the intention of the individual and its execution within an institution, there stand serious social issues. Examination suggests that the extent to which pressure is exercised on individuals does vary from culture to culture. Equally how much effect a possible breakaway variation will have on changing the existing shape of things is by no means evident: what is needed is to examine some well thought out course of action that can be argued for and perhaps be widely adopted. The least we can do is to view the teaching of a second language carefully and soberly from the many aspects relevant to it. To give the impression, for example, that one could make an appreciable difference to the teaching of English in Pakistan simply by having progressive intentions, or by introducing audio-visual methods, or by jumping onto the latest bandwagon, is not simply grievously misleading; misleading as the belief is, it is really its irresponsibility that is more tragic: it can, and often does, lead to a wastage of resources that such countries can ill afford. Above all, it is quite obviously wrong to give the impression to the newly recruited, hopeful and enthusiastic teacher that if only they were good enough, dedicated enough, revolutionary enough, the sky would be the limit. Equally, there is no justification for pushing the weight of blame on the student. In many cases the students too are caught up in the workings of a system, in the after-effects of a series of events: the forces are much more powerful than the individual, be it the teacher or the taught (for example, discussion in Chapter 1). These forces are often diffuse so that trying to predict what leads to what – what is cause, what effect – in second language teaching is pretty much like trying to figure out the propelling impulse behind that last wave that broke by the seashore. It may be easier to see that which is tangible and visible to the eye; but in the business of teaching the real concern should be with the underlying forces: they need to be understood if we are to act on them successfully.

I want to emphasize that my message is not negative. I am emphatically not saying: give up all research in linguistics; go back to earlier methods of teaching; don't bother about the structure of the syllabus; about classroom practices; and many other such things because nothing makes a big enough difference. What I am insisting upon is the as yet not well recognized important factor relevant to the practice of teaching and learning, namely, the social context of this activity. I am arguing in favour of paying attention to all such concerns – every aspect of the teaching–learning situation needs to be understood in relation to all the others; without this holistic approach success will prove elusive. It is important that before making recommendations about the second language teaching situation, we should have a clear view of how the learners' community functions as a social structure, what place the second language has in it, and what that means for successful teaching. For example, if the second language is a means of access to technical expertise/advanced specialization, how is this fact in itself valued by the members of the community? Taking Pakistan as an actual example, so far as this aim is concerned, the role of English can be regarded as crucial; for historical reasons neither Chinese, nor Russian, nor any other European language could be treated as a viable alternative. Seen in the absolute, the need for learning English should be fairly pressing. However, the aim of acquiring high-level technical expertise or advanced specialization itself does not have a high priority, except amongst the members of a particular higher stratum. By contrast, if English had been a means of creating solidarity amongst members of small localized groups, had it been held in positive affect by people – as Persian and Arabic were some 200 years ago – half the problems that beset the teaching of English in Pakistan today would not make themselves felt; indeed the select sub-community of Pakistanis for whom English has this very function learn the language fairly well. Given the social structure of Pakistan, its educational system, the bases of interpersonal relationships and their central position of importance in daily life, it should be fairly obvious to all of us that the programme of teaching English will encounter serious problems notwithstanding the value of the language for purely technical knowledge and for advanced academic specialization. But every year the country spends huge sums of money in a futile attempt to achieve this elusive goal of 'universal proficiency' in English. It seems to me socially irresponsible for experts in the teaching of English as second language to support the impression – even by an act of omission – that, in a situation such as I have described, money spent on importing expertise, expensive audio-visual aids, or the introduction of sixteen syntactic trees instead of six, or other such 'remedies', is likely to make a significant difference to Pakistani lives.[8] It is equally irresponsible to give the impression to the trainee teacher that the *real* problems of second language teaching can be solved here by analysing the system of that language – though understanding about language is indispensable for being able to teach it; it is short-sighted to claim that understanding a generalized psychology of learning will lead to success – even though understanding about learning is important; and it is naïve to expect that following the principles and methods of an a-social pedagogy will bring educational success. It is a sad accident of modern academia that the concerns of human life have had to be segregated from each other in the name of specialization: we do not need emphasis on *or* in teaching and learning; what we want is *and*. The separation of specific areas in the human sciences might have allowed us to gain depth of understanding in different disciplines such as psychology, sociology, linguistics, and education. And this has to be applauded. But knowledge of any kind is created for human consumption, and human beings live a unified life in which action, interaction, understanding, learning and knowledge all work together: one's psychology is not set apart from one's culture; language is a part of human life, not an autonomous structure; needs are not determined by reference to a neat little area – the avowed aims human beings cherish and those which they are constrained to accept as their goal in practice might not always be identical. It appears essential that those who influence the teaching of second languages must begin to take human communities more seriously.

It is not only native languages that need a community within which they may live and thrive; a second language too needs a community of users for successfully retaining its functions in the learners' community. And the cultural patterns of the community in which the learners of a second language live will continue to decide the fate of teaching and learning a second language – *unless experts in the second language teaching trade strive to understand the learners' culture well enough to intervene intelligently.*

Notes

1 This paper was presented at the University of Newcastle in 1976 on the occasion of the first conference of the Applied Linguistics Association of Australia, which was established under the leadership of Professor Ross Steele (Sydney University) that year. Most of these notes have been added by the author in an effort to briefly relate the issues to today's world.

2 Today the terms TESOL and TEFL are more frequently used though it is not very clear whether the distinction between these categories is clearly maintained everywhere.

3 The Genre Based Pedagogy movement led by J. R. Martin (Sydney University) was yet to emerge, but having emerged it has clearly demonstrated how much progress can be made in improving teaching practices simply by introducing a functionally informed focus on teaching materials alone. This, however, does not mean that attention to the student or the teacher is less necessary. In fact, a great deal of the success of this movement lies also in the dedication of Martin and colleagues who worked with teachers and organized in-service teaching sessions to create in the teachers a greater understanding of what they were teaching.

4 Thirty years later, this observation remains largely true. In 2003 at a conference I received the traditional Indian bow to my feet from a student, though it should be added that the conventions of the progressive West do also reveal themselves – especially in the behaviour of the very young – but naturally this change is so far limited to those who have had some contact with the progressive West where age has a different social meaning.

5 The term socialization, and its scatter, are no longer acceptable in sociological discourse: the term is out of fashion. We could in conformity with academic fashions replace the verbal group 'have been socialized' with 'have grown up'. That is to say, there is no problem in using this other term instead so long as we do not imagine that growing up happens outside social environment, and that environment plays no part in the patterns of growth.

6 With India joining the industrialized club, it is possible that the situation will change, but at least at present, I would still expect to find collection code as the default preference there as well.

7 It is an interesting question whether the advent of the globalization of English in the last quarter century makes the knowledge of English imperative for every human being.

8 I understand that thanks to SPELT, Pakistan has made significant gains in the teaching of English and some of my predictions have proved wrong: globalization and above all the need to have access to media has created a greater urge for learning English, which is even today a language to be taught universally in all Pakistani schools; however, it is very doubtful to me that the conditions of Pakistani everyday life have improved.

10 Learning to function with the other tongue: A systemic functional perspective on second language teaching [1994]

1 Introduction

As a domain of academic enterprise, applied linguistics has had more than its fair share of approaches. Each new approach is presented as *the* solution to some major problem encountered in its practice; each approach promises to shore up its theoretical foundations. But the remark that Harold E. Palmer, one of the earliest pioneers in the field, made nearly a century ago still appears apposite: 'Evidence of various kinds shows that this subject has not attained the scientific stage, but is so far in the experimental or empirical stage' (Palmer 1917: 1). To remedy the situation, he recommended greater focus on language, believing that inquiry into its nature 'must necessarily be of interest to method-writers, to teachers, and to students' (Palmer 1917: 3); and a countless number of applied linguists have rightly embraced this view – we say 'rightly' because it seems reasonable to hope that an understanding of what language is like would help in deciding what to do about teaching it efficiently. We grant also that when Palmer was expressing these views, our understanding of the true nature of language was not very deep. But if the strident claims made by today's dominant paradigms of linguistics are to be believed, by now the many marvellous *revolutions* in linguistics ought to have remedied this situation. We ought to have *the* true insights into the nature of language. Clearly this has not happened, for applied linguistics still continues in ferment. It is still in search of that which it is supposed to be already applying, and there seems to be a constant uncertainty about what constitutes its centre of gravity.

To us it seems that the fundamental issues of applied linguistics have remained problematic because linguistic revolutions have not delivered what they promised. The conception of language which has emerged from these so-called revolutions and which applied linguistics has typically chosen to work with calls for revision because it fails to do justice to the complex issues that have to be addressed in doing applied linguistics. Consider, for example, three concepts crucial to the field – teaching, learning and language – each of which is highly complex, and this complexity is even further compounded by the relations of these concepts to each other: one cannot teach or learn without (some sort of) language since *semiosis* – that is, making and exchanging meaning through the mediation of semiotic systems – is an essential ingredient in all acts of teaching and learning. Nor can one *language* without teaching and learning: semiosis – the exchange of meaning – logically entails both teaching and learning. To hold this view is to claim that not all teaching and learning is necessarily intentional, deliberate and self-conscious. But the deliberate pedagogy of the classroom and the unself-conscious instructions of life situations must confront each other at some point in the history of the same individual. These two experiences need not be in agreement: thus, one might assist an orientation, which might, in fact, run counter to that encouraged by the other. It could, thus, come about that what one learns from participating in a pedagogic speech event is not necessarily what someone consciously set out to teach. This must happen regularly in actual fact, otherwise the system of education would not be so haunted by failures. When we add to this already complex situation the necessity of having to language in order to teach someone how to language with 'the other tongue', we meet a situation the complexity of which is not paralleled by any other academic enterprise (Halliday 1991: 22).

Assuming that these complex factors influence the practices of applied linguistics, what the field needs as its foundation is not a model of language as an autonomous system which is taken to evolve in isolation from human, i.e., social interaction. Nor can it thrive on a physicalistic theory of mental development where cognition is equated simply with some human biological equipment whose growth follows a preordained path laid out once for all by nature (Piaget 1960, 1973; Brown 1973; Krashen 1987), as if the individual's interactive history played no part in the process.[1] Such models of language and of human cognition fail to accommodate the complex relations between teaching, learning, and language, since the origin of this complexity is social rather than biological. We, therefore, agree with Candlin (1991: vi) that what applied linguistics needs is a thoroughgoing 'social theoretical basis for its principles and its activities'. But it needs to be recognized also that this 'social theoretical basis' is not an *optional extra* to be added to *linguistics proper*. Rather, it is an essential requirement for a competent model of language that it should successfully model the genuinely many-faceted character of language, which is at once physical, biological, social, and semiotic (Halliday 1996a). However, over the years, linguists have shown considerable disdain for the social basis of language, excluding it from their models despite evidence of the inadequacy of descriptions in ignoring this integral characteristic of language.

It is the basic concern of this paper[2] to develop these claims. Accordingly, we shall need to show what it means to give a thoroughgoing social theoretical basis to language, a question we begin to address in section 2. By way of answers, we shall highlight in sections 3 and 4 what language as a system looks like when it is given a functional basis as in systemic functional linguistics (henceforth, SFL) which adopts precisely this perspective. The SFL model claims that to treat the social aspect as integral to language is to accept FUNCTIONALITY as the underlying principle of the system of language (sections 2 through to 4). The terms 'function', 'functional', 'functionality' and other derivatives are used differently in different linguistic models. In sections 2.2–3.1, we shall clarify how the term LINGUISTIC FUNCTIONALISM is conceptualized in the SFL model. This discussion will lead us in section 4 to consider a closely related question: what does language – its system and process – look like when seen in a functional perspective? Consideration of these issues allows us to ask whether such a model of language is capable of providing a viable social theoretical basis for the discipline of applied linguistics. This is obviously a large question: we limit its scope by focusing in sections 5 and 6 on certain selected aspects of teaching and learning another tongue. Taking ESL as an example, section 5 of the paper will place it in the wider context of the living of life by raising some *macro issues*, which concern questions of wider relevance: How is the activity of teaching and learning ESL valued in a given cultural system? Who are the learners of ESL, and how are they socially positioned by engaging in its practices? In general, applied linguistics has treated ESL pedagogic practices as if they occur in socio-politically neutral contexts. Using the insights of a socially informed theory of language, we will argue that ESL has an essentially politico-economic nature, and like all pedagogic activities, its decisions participate in the politico-economic history of the community in question (Phillipson 1990; Tollefson 1991).

In section 6, we shall turn to a *micro issue* which will be concerned with a question relevant to the narrower context of the ESL classroom: what insights into the lexicogrammatical description of language could a socially based model, such as SFL, provide to the teacher? Using the SFL description of a small fragment of English grammar, we hope to show how this model treats wording as a resource for meaning. The paper will close with a brief general review of the importance of a discussion of this type in the context of comparative perspective on pedagogic grammars.[3]

2 Functionalism: the social theoretical basis of language

Let us begin by considering the SFL claim that 'to treat social aspect as integral to language is to accept functionalism as the underlying principle of the system of language'. We need to clarify what such a claim means, and the first step in this clarification is to explain what we mean by functionalism.

2.1 Language use and language function

In one sense of the term 'function', scarcely any one would deny the functional nature of language: this is the sense 'which defines language as a form of communication' (Leech 1983: 48), seeing it simply as a *useful* tool for bringing about speakers' purposes. This view makes the expression 'functions of language' synonymous with 'uses of language'. The usefulness of language is certainly an element of functionalism, but a simple affirmation of this kind is not to be confused with a functional theory. In fact, no theory is needed for such an affirmation; the claim could be based on empirical observations alone: making such a claim does not depend on an explicit understanding of the *internal* nature of language. So it follows that where functionalism consists *simply* in claiming the usefulness of language and/or in identifying the uses of language, it will fail to explain many important facts about the system of language. To take a simple example, this approach to functionalism has no way of determining what, if any, functions are universal to human languages, and why. It is just possible that an observation of *ways of speaking* prevalent in a community (Hymes 1986: 58) might enable one to draw an inventory of that community's typical language functions, specifying 'who says what to whom and when' (with apologies to Fishman 1972b: 244). Language function in this sense of the term is known as REGISTER in SFL (Halliday *et al.* 1964; Halliday 1974a, 1977, 1991; Halliday and Hasan 1985; Hasan 1973, 1995a), and it is a well-known fact that register repertoires are not identical across communities (Hymes 1968; Gumperz 1971; Fishman 1972a; Frake 1986).

Moreover, since, in principle, there is no natural principle governing the array of the uses of language, these repertories are necessarily open-ended. It follows that old uses can discontinue, and new uses can be added (Halliday 1973a, 1974a). And variant inventories of the kind, if compared, will show that functions of languages in this sense of the term are *not* universal. Consider another problem in this view of functionalism: granted that language is useful, as the view claims, what accounts for the fact that it is able to meet speakers' needs for bringing about their myriad purposes? That language actually does so is, clearly, a fact of a different order from the fact that it has the POTENTIAL for doing so. And it is valid to ask: how do we explain the fact that human language universally enjoys this potential, when the register repertoire of languages is so variable? Linguistic functionalism interpreted as simply the usefulness of language is unable to answer these and other important questions because it is *not* a *theory* of language: it has nothing to say about language as a system. It bows to the empirically validated existence of PAROLE – the use of language in the living of life – but has no way of relating it to the theoretical entity LANGUE.

2.2 Concept: metafunction

We are suggesting that where a theory treats the social aspect as integral to language, it would not be limited to just pointing out the social uses of languages; it would also be committed to showing how the social uses of language relate to the internal system of language. Such a functional theory will aim to describe how parole permeates langue, and how langue enables parole[4] – in short, how the two co-exist in a dialectic relation, both being maintained and altered by the mutually responsive workings of each other. For a theory to be functional in this sense, the concept of *function* needs to be more abstract than function equated with specific language use. It is only when functions are identified at a higher level of abstraction that they can be recognized as essential to *all* uses of language, and it is only when they are recognized as essential to *all* uses of language, becoming a property of the entire linguistic social process as such, that they can be viewed as integral to the system of language, serving to explain the nature of its internal structure by relation to its social uses. Because the term 'function' has been used in different senses (see discussion in Leech 1983; also Dirven and Fried 1987), to avoid confusion we shall use the term METAFUNCTION to refer to the more abstract functions as postulated in SFL.

2.2.1 *The interpersonal metafunction*

In the SF model, three metafunctions are considered necessary for an adequate description of language: (1) INTERPERSONAL, (2) TEXTUAL, and (3) IDEATIONAL. Since detailed discussions of these are available (e.g., see Halliday 1970a, 1973a, 1975a, 1977, 1979a; Martin 1984, 1991, 1992; Matthiessen 1990, 1992), only a brief account of each is provided here. Let's take first the INTERPERSONAL METAFUNCTION: Human language acts as a potential for the expression of speakers' subjectivity – their assessment of probability, obligation and commitment; their attitudes to and evaluations of the world they live in. Further, engaging in *any* use of language implies that speakers must assume some speech roles, thus by implication, allocating speech roles to their addressees. For example, by asking a question, a speaker places the addressee in the position of the one who is expected to respond. This is not to claim that the addressee is *forced* to respond; simply that given this situation whatever the addressee does thereafter, its interpretation will be coloured by the fact that the addressee had been positioned as a respondent. To say that speakers are able to do such 'things with words' (Austin 1962) is to say that language has an interpersonal metafunction. This metafunction in SFL subsumes what Bühler referred to as EXPRESSIVE and CONATIVE functions of speech, but (*contra* Leech 1983) it goes beyond primitive notions of exclaiming and signalling, just as it goes beyond the speech act theorist's concept of illocutionary force.

2.2.2 *The textual metafunction*

Turn now to the TEXTUAL METAFUNCTION of language. In *any* social use of language, interactants indicate what can be taken as given, what is new, what is the speaker's point of departure, whether further verbal action is anticipated, how the various parts of the discourse relate to each other, what degree of specificity is needed to get the message across (e.g., whether one can get by with 'don't leave them there' or needs to say something like 'John, when you bring back my books, don't leave them in my mail-box'), whether information is presented as retrievable from what has already been *said* (e.g., the expression 'such relevancies' and 'such meanings' as used in the next sentence), whether more information is to follow in the on-going discourse (as indicated by the use of 'first' in 'take first the interpersonal metafunction' in the last section), and so on. Every language has the formal resources for creating such relevancies, and that aspect of a language's meaning potential which enables the speakers to mean such meanings is known in SFL as the textual metafunction of language.

2.2.3 *The ideational metafunction*

The third metafunction – the IDEATIONAL – is comprised of two closely related aspects of language: the *experiential* and the *logical.* The EXPERIENTIAL METAFUNCTION of language is the resource speakers draw on to construe their experience of the world – both the outside world of physical phenomena and the inside world of feelings, beliefs and reflection: this is closest to what Bühler called 'the referential function' of language. Human language acts as a resource for the construal of classes of things (e.g., 'magnolia, linguistics, time'), qualities (e.g., 'pretty, pink, good'), and quantities (e.g., 'some, many, two, four'), and also of events, happenings and goings-on (e.g., 'doing, happening, being, saying, thinking', and so on) which in turn entail or allow certain participants and circumstances. But in such construals of experience, speakers do not simply focus on things and events as isolated phenomena; they use the resources of their language to create complex categories such as *three dark purple magnolias*, where a complex class characterized by certain qualities and quantity is 'construed'; similarly, the single events and happenings are seen in combination, producing complex events, happenings, and so on, as in 'it rains whenever I decide to go out for a long walk'. The LOGICAL METAFUNCTION is the potential of language concerned with the construal of such complex things and events. It is a resource for creating such relations as those of sub-classification ('an A *sort of B*'; or 'a B that *has an* A'), addition ('A *and* B'), variation ('A *or* B'), concurrence ('A *while* B'), condition ('*if* A [*then*] B'), report ('say that A'), idea ('think that A'), and so on.

2.3 Use, function and metafunction compared

It is clear from this account that METAFUNCTIONS are abstract properties of language which cannot be confused with functions in the sense of some social use or act. The concept of metafunctions in the SF model is more abstract than the functions of language in pragmatic functionalism (such as in Leech 1983), or even in Prague School Linguistics (Davidse 1987). And they are certainly far more abstract than are functions in the proposals of Wilkins (1976) or in the Council of Europe's concept of the 'functional-notional syllabus' (van Ek 1976), all of which are based on an interpretation of function as what language is being used for. The difference in the conceptualization of function and metafunction has certain logical consequences. Consider how functions in the sense of uses have to be mutually exclusive. If we say, for example, that a speaker is using language to give a sports commentary, we cannot say, without self-contradiction, that at the same time the same speaker is using language to give a sermon: the speaker typically engages in this use *or* that, *not both*. This kind of mutual exclusion is impossible in the abstract interpretation of the term: no matter who says what to whom and when, speakers cannot use the ideational metafunction exclusively on one occasion, the interpersonal the next time, and the textual metafunction in yet another use. Quite obviously, interpersonal meanings such as adoption and allocation of speech roles are not limited to any *one specific* speech variety; equally, no matter what the social use of language, speakers will need to invoke categories of their experience – i.e., they will need to refer to things and events and so on; and in all communication, they will attempt to maintain discursive relevancies. This is the reasoning that underlies the SFL claims: (1) that all metafunctions have to be operative simultaneously on all occasions of language use; (2) that each is needed for describing the properties of language use and language system; and (3) that although linguists have typically prioritized the ideational metafunction, all three are equally integral to language. At this point a questions arises: if metafunctions are not to be interpreted as social uses of language, then how do they relate to the social basis of the system of language? We shall answer this question in two parts: first, what is the social basis of metafunctions? And second, what justification is there for claiming that the social basis is integral to the system of language?

3 The social basis of linguistic metafunctionality

In a very real sense, the metafunctions are abstractions based on an analysis of the social situation within which language use is embedded. We will refer to the social occasion of talk by the technical term CONTEXT OF SITUATION. Context of situation is not the same thing as MATERIAL SITUATIONAL SETTING (Hasan 1973); the latter refers to all of what surrounds the speakers, including both external phenomena and the speakers' internal states, here and now, in the moment of speaking. Instead, context of situation is that part of the speakers' environment – both external and internal – which is *invariably* illuminated by the language in use. In other words, cases of language in use will always bear testimony to the nature of the relevant context of situation. As participants in a speech event on any one occasion of talk, we are aware of many factors that exercise pressure on our acts of communication, and no two occasions of talk can be said to be identical at this degree of detail. If we are to create a framework for the analysis of the social occasion of talk, it is necessary to invoke more abstract categories rather than to focus on the actually occurring factors that instantiate those categories. The notion of context of situation is concerned with identifying precisely such general categories which are *always active* in exercising pressures on our acts of communication, shaping every discourse in any speech variety whatever. According to the SFL model, no matter what speech variety/register is considered, the aspects of the social environment invariably highlighted by the language of the discourse can be assigned to one or the other of the following categories: (1) the SOCIAL RELATIONS between the participants of the discourse; (2) the nature of the SOCIAL ACTION, that is, what is being achieved in and by the process pertinent to discourse; and (3) the SOCIAL CONTACT which concerns management of the interaction as a social event (e.g., whether the activity is achieved by face to face interaction involving dialogue or whether other channels of contact are operative and these factors impinge on semiotic activity). These three categories have been traditionally referred to in the

SFL model as TENOR, FIELD, and MODE OF DISCOURSE, respectively (Halliday *et al.* 1964; Halliday 1974a; Hasan 1973), and together they constitute the schematic construct known as 'context of situation'. We are claiming, then, that these three social parameters are *always* active in the production and comprehension of any discourse; and in support of this claim we are citing the fact that it is factors of these three categories that are *always* illuminated by that language in use whose instantiation counts as (part of some) text. In other words, what creates our concept of the context of situation is the *ongoing evidence from language in use:* it is in the nature of language to construe context, and it is in the nature of social contexts that they are knowable only through semiosis.

This is how the metafunctions enter into the picture: the SFL model claims (Halliday 1973a, 1977; Martin 1991; Halliday and Hasan 1985; Hasan 1995a) that language as a resource for meaning is metafunctionally specialized with respect to the three contextual categories identified above. There is a division of labour so that *typically*[5] one distinct metafunction e.g., the interpersonal serves to express one distinct contextual parameter, e.g., tenor. The pairing of the linguistic metafunctions and the parameters of context is as shown in Figure 1.

Semiotic Structure of Situation		**Functional components of language**
Field (type of social action)	associated with	ideational metafunction
tenor (social relations)	" "	interpersonal metafunction
mode (verbal action and contact)	" "	textual metafunction

Figure 1: Context and linguistic metafunctions: realizational tendencies (after Halliday 1977)

According to the SFL model, there is a logical basis for the relation postulated between a particular contextual parameter and a specific metafunction. Taking the metafunctions to refer to aspects of language as a potential for meaning, the claim is that each metafunction is an aspect of the meaning potential of language which is particularly relevant to the construal of that specific contextual category. To elaborate on this statement we will use as example, the contextual parameter of tenor of discourse and its relation to the interpersonal metafunction.

As a contextual parameter, tenor of discourse refers to the social relations between the interactants engaged in the discourse, while the interpersonal metafunction is that aspect of language as meaning potential which is concerned with such phenomena as speech role allocation, speakers' judgements of obligations and possibilities, and their evaluations of relevant phenomena, and so on. It is meanings of this kind that construe the situational parameter we have called tenor, but it is not the entire story. The relationship between this metafunction and tenor has to be viewed from two complementary perspectives. The first perspective concerns the listener's point of view. When a speaker means a certain set of interpersonal meanings, this choice of meanings as made available through wording will construe for the listener a certain social relation between the participants. For example, on hearing A give a direct command to B, a listener will construe their relation as A most probably having greater discretion than B unless there is *good reason* (see Halliday 1976b: 216) for construing the relation in another way. The second perspective relates to the speaker. It is *his* perception of a certain social relation with his addressee that activates a specific set of interpersonal meanings. For example, wanting to get his boss to do something for him, A as the speaker will most probably not give a direct command to B (if B happens to be his boss!); his perception of his social relation with B will incline him to choose some other way of asking him/her to do something. The two perspectives of construal-activation are described here in terms of specific speech events, but of course they apply longitudinally as well. For example, human social relationships are (typically, if not always) the artefact of interaction: even the mother-child relation, cited often as the most 'instinctive', requires *mothering* as an essential condition for its creation. Human social relations are cumulatively, and therefore gradually created, maintained and changed through semiotic interacts, particularly through the interpersonal meanings of linguistic semiosis. At the same time, even the most elementary social interaction in any community has a history of assumptions and expectations and this interactive history plays a part in activating the choice of meanings in social interaction. In view of these observations, it seems reasonable to suggest that the relationship between the tenor of discourse and the interpersonal metafunction is a *natural* one: the two co-evolve; social relationships do not pre-exist acts of meaning, and acts of meaning presuppose social relationships. Similar arguments have been made with regard to the pairing of the ideational metafunction to field and of the textual metafunction to mode (Halliday 1970a, 1977, 1979a). What is the significance of these claims?

3.1 The significance of context – metafunction relationship

First, the construal-activation relation between the metafunctions and contextual parameters explains the social basis of the metafunctions. Language has just these three metafunctions because these alone are necessary and sufficient for construing the categories of context,[6] which are themselves critical in activating the meaning choices in a speaker's use of language. Each aspect of the potential of language has evolved in response to speakers' needs to express certain sorts of meanings as they use language. Language has the potential to meet the needs of its speakers in the context of any kind of use whatever because it is through the communicative pressures of language in use that the system has evolved as it actually presents itself at any point in the history of the language: this is how parole permeates langue and langue supports parole. Language use and language system co-evolve; they are in a dialectic relation.

Secondly, if each of the metafunctions is specialized vis-à-vis some particular contextual parameter, *and* if the contextual parameters identified here are necessary and sufficient for the description of the social environment of all speech communities, then it would follow unavoidably that the three metafunctions proposed in the SFL model are universal to human language. This is entailed by the logical basis of the relationship between context and linguistic metafunctions.

Third, because of this logical relation between context and metafunctions, an adequate model of language is forced to treat language not as an autonomous system but as one that is relevant to the human social context of culture and situation. Accordingly, context has to be integral to any functional model for the description of language. In the SFL model it is treated as an essential component of the modelling of language. The technical term for referring to the components of the linguistic theory is STRATA. Simplifying somewhat, a theoretical modelling of language must invoke at least four such components: context, meaning, wording and sound. Context is the highest stratum in the *theory* of language description. The logical relation of construal-activation which links the stratum of context to language is known as REALIZATION. We will return to these terms later.

4 The design of language as a social semiotic

What are the grounds for claiming that the social basis is integral to the system of language, that language is in fact a social semiotic – i.e., a system for meaning whose foundations are located in social life? A cryptic answer would be: the claim is justified because the system of language is metafunctionally organized. If, by being related to the parameters of context, the metafunctions have a social basis, then language itself has to have a social basis provided it is true that language is metafunctionally organized. This section is concerned with elaborating some of the details of this claim.

4.1 Stratification in a functional theory

We begin by examining the organization of the strata internal to the system of language. The SFL model recognizes three strata internal to language: (1) SEMANTICS, that is, systems of meaning, where the term "meaning" is to be interpreted not simply as *cognitive/referential* meaning, as in formal linguistics, but all linguistically construed meanings; (2) LEXICOGRAMMAR, that is, systems of wording, including both grammar and lexicon; and (3) PHONOLOGY, that is, systems of sound, both segmental and supra-segmental. These three strata are internal to language in the sense that every language is a union of meaning realized by wording realized by sound. Context, by contrast, is an abstraction from social environment: it consists of aspects of the speakers' social life which are relevant to naturally occurring discourse. So context, an extra-linguistic stratum, is incorporated as the highest stratum into the *theoretical model* developed for describing language. We thus have a stratal theory of linguistic description consisting of four strata – context, semantics, lexicogrammar and phonology – but for the purposes of the present discussion the last mentioned, *phonology*, will be ignored. The four strata of the model are shown in Figure 2, where the darker boundary line separates the language-external stratum of context from the three language-internal ones.

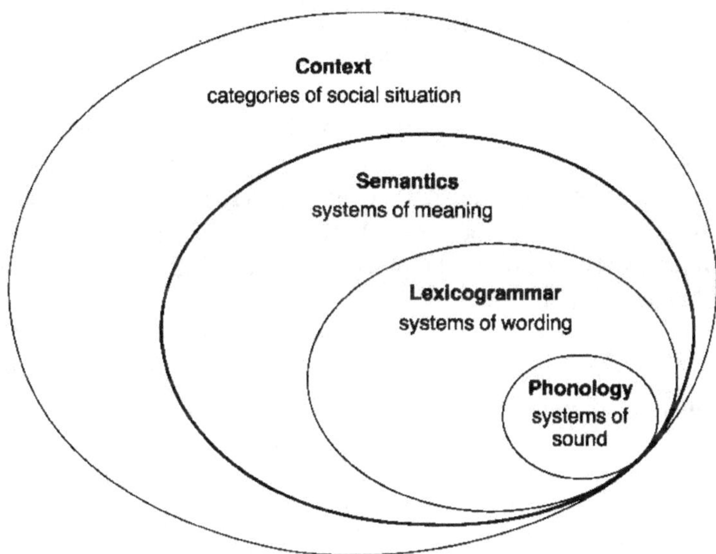

Figure 2: The four strata of the SFL model

In discussing the social basis of language, we have already drawn attention to the metafunctional specialization of language. To claim that the strata of semantics and lexicogrammar are metafunctionally organized is to say that the facts of these strata are best described by using the metafunctions as a grid for their organization. If this claim is substantiated, then it would be viable to treat the notion of metafunctions as an explanatory principle underlying the internal organization of the system, which, in turn, would imply that the social basis is integral to the system of language. In the following paragraph, we introduce the notions necessary for describing stratal organization, before attempting to substantiate the claim that the language-internal strata are metafunctionally organized.

4.2 The concept of system

The crucial concept for the organization of the internal strata of language is that of SYSTEMIC CHOICE. The term 'choice' does not refer here to deliberate acts of choosing; it simply refers to the fact that speakers are never constrained to do just one thing; whatever the environment, there exist alternatives one of which becomes operative. In this sense, the idea of choice is fundamental to the conception of language as a potential. A potential must offer choices. If by way of demanding service one always *had to* produce a direct command, then no specific significance could be attached to the given form of demanding service, and language would have to be seen simply as a set of mandatory rules which must be followed mechanically. The possibility of choice removes this mechanical determinacy, and imbues the linguistic alternatives – the terms of the system – with value. So to put it simply, a system consists of some environment that acts as the ENTRY CONDITION to a SET OF OPTIONS, such that if the entry condition is satisfied, then one, and only one, option must be chosen. The value of any one option in the system is determined by its relation to the other options available (i.e., possible) in the system at that point. Take an example from semantics (Hasan 1989, 1992b). If the entry condition ***message demanding goods/service***[7] is satisfied, then one system with the following three choices becomes available: (1) the demand may be ***exhortative*** (e.g., *tidy up your room*); or (2) it may be ***assertive*** (e.g., *you have to tidy up your room*); or (3) it may be ***consultative*** (e.g., *could you tidy up your room?*). These three options constitute one system where the value of each term is its relation to the other terms; and the system represents what speakers of English *can mean* in the environment of demanding service up to a certain point in delicacy.

The term DELICACY refers to the degree of detail in description. Delicacy of description increases as each option of a system in its turn acts as an entry condition for some other set of options. To continue with the same example (and again simplifying the picture), if the option ***assertive*** is chosen, then it becomes an entry condition to the systemic choice between the options ***desiderative*** (e.g., *I'd like you to tidy up your room*) or ***mandatory*** (e.g., *you must tidy up your room*). Here the systemic choice between ***desiderative*** or ***mandatory*** is said to DEPEND *on* the option ***assertive***: that is to say, unless the message has the semantic option assertive, there would not exist the possibility of its being either ***desiderative*** or ***mandatory***. A single entry condition can permit entry into more than one system of choices. So, given the entry condition ***message demanding goods/service***, not only do we have a system – call it system A – with the options ***exhortative*** or ***assertive*** or ***consultative*** (introduced above), but *at the same time* there exists at least one other system – call it system B – with the option ***suggestive*** or ***nonsuggestive***. Here systems A and B are said to be SIMULTANEOUS. Each of the three options in system A *must* combine with one option in system B, thus giving us finer distinctions of choices in meaning. For example, *could you tidy up your room* combines the option ***consultative*** from system A with the option ***nonsuggestive*** from system B, while *how about we tidy up your room now* combines ***consultative*** with ***suggestive***. When systems of options interlock by virtue of relations of the kinds exemplified here – that is, DEPENDENCY and SIMULTANEITY – then together they constitute a SYSTEM NETWORK.[8] Systems of options that make up one system network show 'a high degree of internal constraint: that is, of interdependence among the various options involved. The selections made by the speaker at one point tend to determine, and be determined by, the selections s/he makes at another' (Halliday 1979a: 61). An example of such 'interdependence' was presented in describing systems A and B, which must form part of the same system network. Iconic representation of such interdependencies will be found in Figures 4 and 5 (sections 6.2 and 6.4 below). By contrast, between *distinct* system networks 'there is very little constraint of this kind: little restriction on the options available and little effect on their interpretation' (Halliday 1979a: 61).

4.3 System and metafunction

The above discussion will be helpful in exploring the question at hand. We have established that a system network is an identifiable entity. If the organization of the internal strata is effected through such entities, then an examination of their underlying principle can determine whether or not the organization of the internal strata of language is metafunctional. For example, if at the semantic stratum we find one system network of options (in meaning) which typically construe the social factors relevant to tenor, another that represents meaning options that normally construe factors relevant to field, and a third system whose choices overwhelmingly construe the mode of discourse, this could be treated as evidence that the organization of the semantic stratum is metafunctional: its nature can be explained by reference to the realizational relation that logically links the system networks of meanings to the contextual categories. But is this truly the case?

When the set of semantic choices available to speakers of English are represented as system networks (Halliday 1973b; Hasan 1989, 1991, 1992a; Hasan and Cloran 1990), it appears that the options at the semantic stratum can be represented as four system networks, and each of these networks does represent the options relevant to one specific metafunction. The typical situation is that one network represents choices in meaning pertaining to the interpersonal metafunction; a second represents those pertaining to the experiential one; a third, to the logical; and a fourth represents the textual choices in meaning. *Within* each system network there is a 'high degree of internal constraint', whereas *between* the system networks 'there is very little constraint'. So choices from the interpersonal system network – for example, those which pertain to taking up and allocating speech roles (e.g., ***demanding*** or ***giving***) – 'show a high degree of internal constraint': from the system of speech function, it is not possible to choose both ***give*** and ***demand***, and/or both ***information*** and ***goods/services*** at one and the same time; only one term from each pair can combine. This is because all four terms form part of the same network, and their choice is internally constrained. However, any one of these terms can combine freely with any term of the experiential system as shown below.

1a: I have left him in there.	1b: Shall I leave him in there?
2a: I realized my mistake.	2b: Why didn't I realize my mistake?
3a: I was a baby then.	3b: Was I a baby then?

This is possible because the experiential system network has a distinct metafunctional identity, and across such metafunctionally specialized system networks the constraint is minimal. So the choice of process can vary independently of the choices made from the interpersonal system network. For example, any giving or demanding of information can combine with almost any process type, whether it is material action as in 1a and 1b, or mental cognition as in 2a and 2b, or attribution as in 3a and 3b, respectively.

The organization of the semantic stratum reveals, then, that each metafunction has a system network 'dedicated to it'. These distinct system networks are *not alternatives*; making choices from one system network does not preclude making choices from the others. On the contrary, it is *impos-*

sible to describe the semantic properties – the meaning structure – of a message completely without considering the message as the *instantiation* of choices from all system networks. This is in keeping with the view that, unlike functions in the sense of register/language use, metafunctions are not mutually exclusive. Speakers do not choose from among the various metafunctions; and (*contra* Leech 1983) there is no support in the stratal organization of semantics for treating the ideational metafunction as more integral to the language system than either the interpersonal or the textual. This examination of system networks at the semantic stratum suggests that the metafunctional hypothesis will serve as a viable explanation for one fundamental aspect of its internal organization.

But, of course, the organization of semantics cannot be seen in dissociation from what speakers do with linguistic meanings or from how linguistic meanings relate to the lexicogrammar. Semantics is an interface between context and lexicogrammar. We have already discussed the construal-activation relation between the strata of context and semantics. A similar realizational relation links the internal strata of semantics and lexicogrammar. In the SFL model, linguistic meanings are treated as the artefact of lexicogrammar: if a meaning cannot be construed by the lexicogrammar of a language, then it is not a *linguistic* meaning in that language. The realizational relation between meanings and forms implies the double perspective we have mentioned before: listeners are able to construe the speakers' linguistic meanings on the basis of their lexicogrammatical choices, while the speakers' lexicogrammatical choices are activated by their choice of (context-construing) linguistic meanings. So linguistic meaning is not something that simply "mirrors" reality, whatever the term might mean; rather, linguistic meanings are an 'interface' between the extralinguistic world and the linguistic form (Hasan 1984c). If the stratum of linguistic meanings is functionally organized, as we have argued, then because of the realizational relation between the strata there exists a strong possibility that a similar organization will be found also at the lexicogrammatical stratum.

4.4 Lexicogrammar in metafunctional perspective

Halliday (1970a) claims that he arrived at the metafunctional hypothesis, in the first place, from a consideration of the internal organization of the lexicogrammatical stratum. When the lexicogrammar of a language is paradigmatically represented as system networks of options, this reveals a pattern reminiscent of the semantic stratum. Thus, restricting ourselves to the *clause* as an entry condition, we would find system networks whose underlying basis is metafunctional: each system network is specialized with respect to some metafunction. The transitivity system network specifies the options of process, participants, and circumstances. The choices from this system network construe that set of meanings which together make up our sense of what is going on, what kind of event the speakers are engaged in. Technically, transitivity options construe STATES OF AFFAIRS or put more simply 'goings-on' (some of these have been touched upon in the preceding discussion of examples 1a-3b (on page 301 this chapter); further examples, in the next paragraph). The system networks of MOOD and MODALITY construe interpersonal meanings, realizing the rhetorical strategies for stating, questioning, ordering and so on, and the speakers' assessment of probability, usuality, and their judgement about obligation, inclination and the like (for some discussion, section 6 below 'Grammar as meaningful choice in context'). The system networks of EXPANSION and PROJECTION realize logical meanings, such as *and, or, then*, and *if*, as well as RE-TEXTUALIZATION relations, such as *say that, ask if, tell someone to, think that, wonder if*, and so on. The system networks of THEME and INFORMATION FOCUS realize textual meanings. Examples of each are presented in the next paragraph, and despite this condensed account, it seems obvious that the internal organization of the lexicogrammar is best seen as having a metafunctional basis (for discussion, Halliday 1985a; Halliday and Hasan 1989; Matthiessen 1990; Martin 1991, 1992).

At the lexicogrammatical stratum, two kinds of theoretical statements need to be made: first, the paradigmatic representation of the form as a resource for making meanings, and second, the structures that instantiate the systemic choices. 'The grammatical system has...a functional input and a structural output; it provides the mechanism for different functions to be combined in one utterance' (Halliday 1973a: 36). Each clause has a structural description in respect of the system networks named above. It is not simply that the systems at the lexicogrammatical stratum are metafunctionally organized; the metafunctional organization also characterizes the structures found at this stratum.

When these structures are examined in abstract terms, a different *type* of structure is found to be associated with each distinct metafunction. The system of transitivity realizing the experiential metafunction has syntagmatic structures that are SEGMENTAL – consisting of elements 'each of which has a special and distinct significance with respect to the whole' (Halliday 1979a: 63). For example, in a clause such as *my mother gave my sister a new car on her birthday*, the significance of each element with respect to the whole is distinct: *my mother* is ACTOR of a DISPOSITIVE PROCESS *gave*, with *a new car* functioning as GOAL, *my sister* as BENEFICIARY, and *on her birthday* as TEMPORAL CIRCUMSTANCE. The systems of expansion and projection realizing the logical metafunction have syntagmatic structures that are ITERATIVE, as in *I went to Felicity's since she needed help because her baby was unwell.* Representing this string schematically as state of affairs A *since* state of affairs B *because* state of affairs C, we note that the relation of interdependency holds between the elements A, B and C, such that each has a similar significance with respect to the other two. Another example would be: *did you know that they told Mabel that they are leaving?* This may be schematically represented as A *that* B *that* C and differs markedly from the segmental structure, where each element has a different significance vis-à-vis the others.

By contrast with this, the systems of mood and modality realizing the interpersonal metafunction generate structures that are PROSODIC; so in *could we perhaps do it tomorrow?* both *could* and *perhaps* express the choice of modality. Further details of modality will be discussed in section 6. The systems of theme and information focus realizing the textual metafunction generate structures which are PERIODIC: like waves, they have peaks of prominence. Textual metafunction concerns relevancies between textual units. All single-clause exemplification of theme or information focus is a contradiction in terms, since periodicity cannot be the feature of just one unit: units in periodic relation belong to distinct clauses. Adequate natural examples tend to demand much time and space. We present here the first few lines of a familiar nursery rhyme. The original nursery rhyme stanza presented in the left column shows a consistency in the thematic peaks represented in its various clauses. This consistency is absent from a version of the same lines on the right.

Jack and Jill went up the hill	**Jack and Jill** went up the hill
Jack fell down	**down** fell Jack
and (**Jack**) broke his crown	and **his crown** broke
and **Jill** came tumbling after	and **tumbling after**, came Jill

Note that the grammar of the clauses in the two columns does not vary in any other respect than the textual. It is therefore fair to assume that what makes a difference to their status as (part of) a text is the fact that, unlike the stanza in the right column, the one in the left has a *well-formed* periodic structure in terms of theme selection. This is why it strikes one as textually better organized, while the transformed version is 'all over the place', as teachers of composition would put it. There are other methods than that of simple repetition of content in theme for creating consistency of thematic peaks. (For details, Fries 1983; Jones *et al.* 1989; Matthiessen 1990.) The relevant point is that the selection of theme, realizing the periodic structure, is neither random nor accidental.

This closes our discussion of what it means to give linguistics a social theoretical basis. We have argued that this calls for an abstract concept of (meta)functions. In fact, metafunctions are not some *thing* that can be found at some specific point in language. When we say that language is metafunctional, we mean that the underlying principle of language is functionality. This is what explains the patterns of organization at the strata of context, meaning and wording. Figure 3 presents a picture of the metafunctional specialization of these strata in summary form. It shows that linguistic metafunctions are not restricted to any one stratum of the model: They 'resonate' throughout the system and process of language.

Figure 3 (see p. 307) shows that the metafunctional principle 'orders' the facts of speakers' social environment for linguistic interaction as well as those of the strata of semantics and lexicogrammar. The latter two strata constitute the 'intelligible' plane of language and the relationship between them is *not arbitrary*: it is *natural.* This is in contrast to the *arbitrary* relation of phonology to lexicogrammar and meaning, which has been referred to as *conventional.* Phonology does not *define* the nature of a unit at the level of form or meaning. By contrast, the value of a semantic unit *is* defined by the grammar that construes it, while its signification is defined by relation to context. These three strata – context, meaning and wording – are really three perspectives on the phenomenon of human semiosis; none of the three perspectives can be ignored without distorting the description of language.

5 Contexts of learning language in functional perspective

If our arguments are accepted, then it must be conceded that language is a *relevant*, not an *autonomous*, system. In the final analysis, we know absolutely no natural language which is not responsive to the sociality of its speakers. This section explores some macro issues concerning the nature of ESL as a social activity, placing it in its wider social context to reveal some facts relevant to the activity of ESL and to the ESL learner's social positioning.

In order to determine the nature of ESL as a social activity, some important questions need to be raised: what is a second language? How does it differ from a foreign language, or indeed a first one? The difference between first and second language has been characterized as resting either on which language was learnt first (Stern 1983: 12), or on which language is 'best developed' (Stern 1983: 13). The difference between second and foreign language is generally characterized in terms of a second language being learnt where it is used in some indigenous context(s), while a foreign language is said

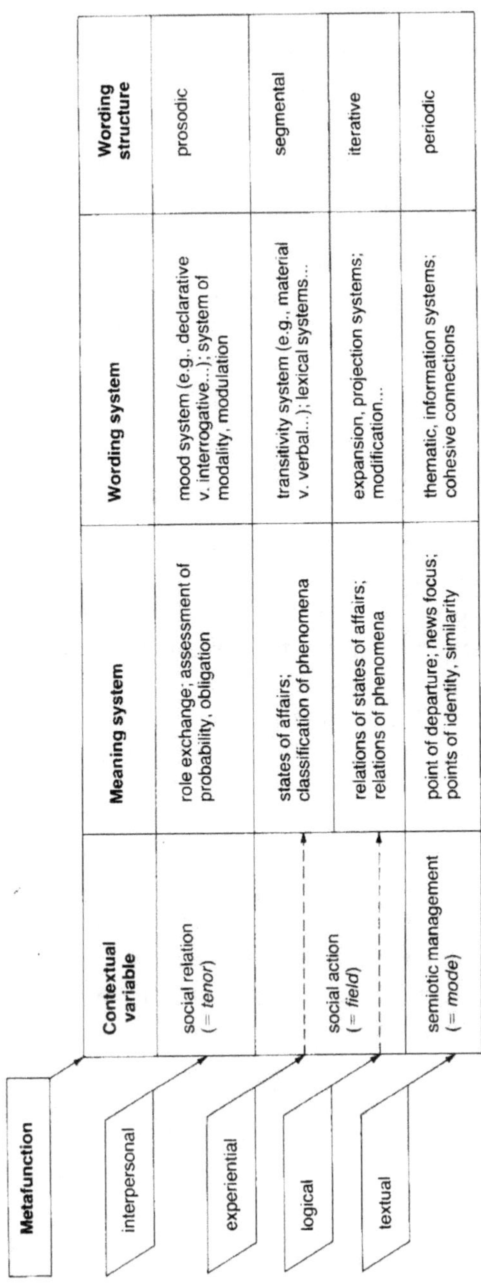

Metafunction	Contextual variable	Meaning system	Wording system	Wording structure
interpersonal	social relation (= *tenor*)	role exchange; assessment of probability, obligation	mood system (e.g., declarative v. interrogative...); system of modality, modulation	prosodic
experiential	social action (= *field*)	states of affairs; classification of phenomena	transitivity system (e.g., material v. verbal...); lexical systems...	segmental
logical		relations of states of affairs; relations of phenomena	expansion, projection systems; modification...	iterative
textual	semiotic management (= *mode*)	point of departure; news focus; points of identity, similarity	thematic, information systems; cohesive connections	periodic

Figure 3: The metafunctional specialization of the strata of context, meaning and wording

to be learnt where it does not form part of the community's register repertoire. These distinctions fail to do justice to the complex situations that arise from the phenomenon that Phillipson (1990: 4) describe as 'English rules the waves'. Thus the distinctions ignore the constantly increasing availability of international education as evidenced by the growing number of non-English-speaking–background students from emergent countries seeking higher education in developed English-speaking countries – a phenomenon that is itself motivated by politico-economic considerations. These criteria ignore also the related fact that English as the major language of international communication is increasingly employed in the management of the interpersonal politico-economic order. One consequence of these developments is that the contexts, and indeed the sequences, of learning language are becoming more complex and diverse.

5.1 Learning the mother tongue

When the activity of learning another tongue is placed in the wider social context, the critical question is not *when* or *where*, but *why* and *how*: why is this activity to be performed at all? How do learners engage with the various languages that they learn? And in the context of such discussions, a consideration of mother-tongue learning is not irrelevant. Consider its significance in the learner's life. The learning subject's self is created in the learning of a first language (Mead 1934; Wittgenstein 1953; Vygotsky 1962; Bernstein 1972; Bateson 1972; Halliday 1975a, b). Her concepts of reality, her workaday knowledge of the world, her sense of the normal are all created as the child re-creates her mother tongue with those who form her 'meaning group' (Halliday 1975a, 1979b, 1980). These important aspects of first language development have dropped out of sight because of a disproportionate emphasis on its 'untutored acquisition' and because of a narrow interpretation of what it means to learn a mother tongue. If, however, the first language development is thought of as 'learning how to mean' (Halliday 1975a), then the process of learning language cannot be dissociated from learning *through* language. Our discussion above (sections 2–4.4) has suggested that language construes speakers' sense of their social universe, implying that as the structure of language is internalized, the knowledge of the world too is internalized with it. Both kinds of internalizations share an important characteristic: both are *unanalyzed*. So the world and the language both appear entirely 'natural'. It is as difficult to question the represented world as it is to question the way one's first language represents this world. Both are aspects of a subject's *primary socialization*. We draw attention here to one very significant consequence that follows from these observations: the contexts of learning a first language are typically supportive in the sense that there is no other 'natural' reality, and the infant identifies with the speakers whose language she is now re-creating for herself (Halliday 1975a; Newson 1978; Painter 1984; Oldenburg 1986). How does this compare with the learning of another tongue?

5.2 Learning the other tongue

Taking into account the wider social contexts and their implications for the learner, the *first language* appears to be a language for the creation of self in society; it provides the learner with primary terms of reference for understanding reality. The extreme opposing case to this is a foreign language. A *foreign language* is foreign to the interests of the learner-speaker; it does not impinge directly on the daily living of life. We are not suggesting that a foreign language would be necessarily irrelevant to either the community's wider politico-economic interests or to the learner-speaker's personal advancement, simply that the processes in which the learner needs to engage in everyday living *need not call* for the use of the foreign language. There is, of course, a third, intermediate case, in which a language other than the first is used to construe at least some crucial processes of the social context, such that the processes necessarily impinge on the daily living of life for all subjects in the community, irrespective of what first language they might have learnt. Here, certain politico-economic activities which are essential to the survival of the community are symbolically construed and organized by using what is another tongue to some segment of the community. We suggest that this other tongue in question holds the status of a *second language*.

Our characterization of the first language as the creator of self and reality does not imply that the second language is passive or irrelevant in the definition of the learners' self or their construction of reality. On the contrary, our account suggests that it too must have these uses; to participate in the critical social processes for the maintenance of a full social life, the second language speaker requires a systematic use of two (or more) distinct language systems, which is tantamount to saying that aspects of the second language learners' universe are created by their second language. But these processes are not critical to the primary socialization of the speaker. Typically, the knowledge acquired in the process of learning a second language is *un-commonsense knowledge* – it is knowledge which does not have a 'natural', 'self-evident' character, forming part of the process of *secondary socialization*. It is also necessary to point out that, as the terms primary and secondary socialization imply, the creation and definition of self is a continuing process which covers a relatively longer period of life than is popularly imagined; similarly, first language development extends over a longer period of the child's life than formalist accounts of first language acquisition might lead one to believe. So, depending on changes in the speaker's social context, one and the same language may, within certain limits, have a different status at different times.

In defining the second language thus, we do not wish to reject out of hand the popular view that the learning of other languages apart from the mother tongue is a positive asset as a form of knowledge. But it would be politically naive to pretend that for a migrant in Australia the learning of an aboriginal language is just as valuable an 'asset' as the learning of Australian English! Second languages are not learned simply for love of knowledge (Tollefson 1991), even though it may be ideologically prudent to persist in this view. In fact, by its very nature, a second language is an instrument of power, because it has jurisdiction over some part of the learner-speaker's social context, and because access to a second language is seldom a natural consequence of simply living in a community. Stern appears to recognize the political power of a second language when he suggests that a second language is a non-mother tongue with an 'official status or a recognized function' (Stern 1983: 16). Because of the official status and function of the second language, its learners do not *really* have a 'free choice': to function as reasonably effective members of the community they *must* learn this language. We can, if we wish, describe the learner's refusal or agreement to learn a second language as an act of free consent, but, as Tollefson (1991: 11) points out, the desire to engage in this activity is described more accurately as 'manufactured consent', and the forces which 'manufacture' this consent are also the same ones that diminish the possibility of abstaining. It is not surprising that typically the development of a second language has to be assisted by institutional management. A large part of the dominion of applied linguistics is founded on this need for the institutional management of ESL. Our discussion suggests that ESL pedagogy cannot afford to ignore these considerations, since they must play some part in shaping the learner's motivation.

5.3 Contexts of ESL learning

This socially based definition of second language allows us to probe more deeply into what ESL might mean in different social contexts. The more specific significance of ESL as a social activity is likely to differ from one context of culture to another, since its significance is itself defined by the relation of ESL to other activities in the cultural system. To elaborate this point, let us examine two specific cultural contexts for ESL. First, there is ESL for the colonized – for example, the Indians of the first half of this century – and second, there is ESL for the migrant – for example, migrants to Australia in the second half of this century. Referring to these as CESL (colonized learners learning ESL) and MESL (migrant learners learning ESL), respectively, we will attempt to highlight some of the ways in which these two cases of ESL will differ systematically from each other because colonization and migration *create* different contexts of culture for the learners. We are not implying that SESL and MESL will each take the same form wherever they occur. The forms would respond to other elements in the wider context, but one thing is certain: a consideration of the wider cultural context will have repercussions on nearly every aspect of the ESL pedagogic situation.

In colonized India, English was the instrument of power: All functions of the state, except the very lowest, and therefore only the local ones, were typically carried out in English, the language of the ruling community. Superficially, the situation for the migrant in Australia seems to be the same, but there are important differences. It is true that in India English had a hold on the production and distribution of material wealth, and so in time it also encroached on the intellectual capital of the country, making certain forms of knowledge, reasoning and thinking obsolete; nonetheless, there still remained significant social processes to which English stayed foreign in India. With the migrant in Australia, the hold of English is supreme, and typically all except the most intimate processes of human social relations require the use of English. Where the migrant family has young children, the 'appropriate social adjustment' of these young persons to their new country can impinge even on this intimate process within the family. There is a significant difference between CESL and MESL in this respect: colonization – unless it is highly repressive, such as that of the Australian Aborigines – does not threaten the validity or the possibility of retaining one's sense of the normal. Migration, by definition, is an abandonment of the normal for the strange. And the more different the original culture of the migrant is from that of the adopted community, the truer this observation is. Thus the migrant in Australia, particularly if he is from the so-called third world, is in a situation where most things do not readily 'make sense', and are not 'self-evidently so'. The learning of a non-native tongue is one among these many strange experiences. From this point of view, the significant difference between monolinguals such as the majority of English-speaking Australians and the second language speakers in Australia is that in the case of the latter, the social universe is cleaved into two, revealing that neither is necessarily ordained by nature. For the monolingual, the universe tends to retain its self-evident naturalness, and, for reasons we have already indicated, virtually the same is true for the colonized Indian, particularly at the early stages.

In the CESL context, ESL itself is integrated into the scheme of things as a part of the same wider context, gaining a degree of normalcy by contact with the indigenous social processes. ESL was simply one of those peculiar things one did in places of learning. So, compared with the CESL situation of the Indian, the MESL situation is one of a much wider de-stabilization. Here, ESL is part of the story of encountering and trying to make sense of the strange.

5.4 ESL contexts, ESL learners and ESL pedagogy

But how does this impinge on ESL pedagogic activities as such? We suggest there are two ways this may happen: first, through the psychological consequences for the learner, and second, through implications for what ESL teaching is to achieve. Taking the first, both MESL and CESL situations are in striking contrast to the situation in first language development, where the environment is typically supportive, especially within the learner's meaning group; the world being construed by the language system is as normal as the language itself, and neither is challenged by alternative conceptions. If an intelligible world creates a supportive environment, which in turn acts as an important positive force in successful engagement in social activities, then obviously the absence of the sense of normalcy in MESL learning contexts must have some negative consequences; at the least, it would create stress of the type that the colonized Indians would not have become aware of until they arrived in the UK for higher education.

Applied linguistics has shown little interest in factors of this kind, which must affect the quality of the learner's engagement with the learning tasks. This is not because it is unconcerned with the cognitive aspects of learning: applied linguistics does engage with concepts such as 'developmental stages', 'reading readiness', 'learning sequence', and so on, which appear to involve consideration of cognition. However, in the theory underlying these concepts, cognition, intelligence and ability to learn are thought of as properties of individuals which are entirely biological, having no social basis. And so, instead of attempting to understand how, because of factors of the kind we have discussed, the MESL learner's social environment might impinge on the success of ESL teaching, applied linguistics has concentrated on 'ensuring' that the teaching materials are right, that the methodology of teaching is perfect, and that ever more sensitive instruments for evaluating language proficiency are invented, as if these were the only and all-important considerations worthy of attention. Naturally, we are not suggesting that those considerations are irrelevant, or even less important; we are arguing simply that this unconcern with the learner's social environment as a factor relevant to second language learning leaves something to be desired.

The second important reason for attempting to understand the different contexts of ESL is quite obviously its relevance to the goals of ESL teaching. This has to be based on some understanding of what the learners might be expected to achieve by using their second language. A long tradition in applied linguistics has advocated the conscious modelling of 'second language acquisition' on the first. How do the two compare when the wider social context is considered? We agree with Rutherford (1987: 5) that a first language is not learnt through 'acquiring' 'accumulated entities' one by one as isolated units of linguistic form. It is quite obvious that the first language learner learns her mother tongue in using it. The process of learning how to mean is also the process of knowing who says what to whom and when. If the second language learner is to use his language effectively, then as an important part of his language learning he too needs to know what to 'say' to whom and when. Since the notion of *register/genre* is critical in *all* language learning, it is important to understand the genesis of registers/genre learning. The first language learner's initial familiarity with (parts of) the register repertoire of her community is a 'natural' outcome of her participation in certain social activities. In this respect, the colonized Indian's situation in ESL learning is not very different from the first language learner's. In the CESL context, so long as English was being used to construe essentially indigenous contexts, the world was in its proper place; the social situations made sense; the registers, particularly of everyday contact, were familiar – as they should be in one's own culture. This is in fact what underlies the impetus for the Indianization of English (Kachru 1983). Using ESL in his own culture, the Indian learner kept using his second language to construe the culturally legitimized contexts for meaning. Under the contextual pressures that impinged on the CESL learner's language use, the system of English brought in by the rulers was RE-SEMANTICIZED. Simplifying somewhat, English English evolved into Indian English. This is not how things are in the case of the migrant. Depending upon where he comes from, what might be a social situation of one sort for the MESL learner could well be a social situation of another kind for the native English-speaking Australian; the MESL learner's participation in even everyday social processes in and by the use of English could become problematic. The cultural confrontation that the Indian learner was able to at least postpone, if not altogether avoid, is thrust upon the migrant from the very start. This mismatch between conceptions of how things are done in the two cultures is an important factor in cultural stereotyping: The differences are interpreted as aggression, pomposity, verbosity, lack of politeness, low intelligence, and so on. This highlights yet again the problematic nature of the migrant's position in the adopted country, and brings to attention a practical issue in MESL pedagogy: The desirable goal for the MESL social context demands a 'genre-based' language pedagogy (for discussions of genre-based pedagogy in the SFL framework, see Jones *et al.* 1989; Martin 1989; Rothery 1989; Christie 1991). To adjust in the adopted culture, to learn to be effective with its language, the MESL learner *needs* to feel comfortable with the adopted community's register repertoire almost from day one. This need leads us to consider another issue.

5.5 Models of English and variant contexts of ESL pedagogy

The question of model(s) is relevant to all language teaching and learning, but both 'which model' and 'how it is to be accessed' are particularly crucial questions in a second language teaching learning context. And it is important to keep in mind both kinds of teaching and learning – that which is institutionally organized, and that to which we referred as the 'unselfconscious instructions of life situations'. The models for the two are not necessarily the same; compare, for example, the 'official' pedagogic model of English in Singapore with the 'actual' model(s) from everyday life situations.

Interesting differences between CESL and MESL emerge when we consider them from this point of view. The colonized Indian lived and acted in a community comprised largely of non-native speakers of English. Whatever the 'official' model, the 'actual' model of English accessible to the majority was one 'created' and 'maintained' within India. The position for the migrant in Australia is again different. Despite the fact that a large proportion of Australians are native speakers of some language other than English, it is Australian English that is overwhelmingly the language of daily contact, particularly outside the home and outside 'ethnic' community contexts. So the model to which the MESL learner is more often 'exposed' is an 'authentic' model, perhaps much closer to the 'official' pedagogic one; this was neither true of the colonized Indian nor of the present-day Singaporean. But there is another aspect to be considered: a passive 'exposure' to language may be more relevant to the learning of phonological patterns than it would be for learning the patterns of wording and meaning. For the latter, active participation in social processes is necessary. This follows from our claim that a first language is learnt through active participation in social processes. It is salutary to ask: what are the social processes in which a MESL learner will 'naturally' participate in Australia? Clearly, the answer to this depends on the politico-economic 'meaning' of one's migrant status.

In this section we have probed the nature of second language teaching and learning in relation to its wider social context. We have argued that the 'value' of ESL is not absolute; it must differ by reference to the other terms in the cultural system. A comparison of CESL and MESL suggests that, given the typical politico-economic 'meaning of migration', MESL contexts are likely to be more stressful, both in the degree of de-stabilization which follows from 'choosing' to abandon the 'normal' in favour of the 'strange', and in the demands on the learner *if* the learner is to act as a *full* citizen. We have suggested that the stress to which migrant learners are exposed must bear some relevance to their learning activities. Conventionally, such concerns have been 'defined out' of the discipline of applied linguistics not because *objectively* they are irrelevant but because our ideology makes them appear irrelevant.

5.6 The goals and practices of ESL pedagogy

The goals and practices of ESL are predicated by the demands made on the learner. We have claimed that as with the first language, the learning of a second language too is best interpreted as learning the ability to exchange meanings in social contexts, which, given the goals of ESL, suggests GENRE-BASED PEDAGOGY as crucially relevant. Obvious as this conclusion may be, its implications for applied linguistics need to be spelt out. A pedagogy that calls for an understanding of what is meant by register/genre must take the social basis of language seriously. It could not continue with a descriptive model in which the language system is 'a-social', which somehow permits the possibility of language use in social contexts. So applied linguistics will need to theorize the relation between society, forms of talk, and the language system – the latter as a resource for bringing about those forms of talk in social contexts. This in turn means a re-conceptualization of the subject matter of ESL teaching and learning. From this point of view, success in attaining the pedagogic goals of ESL is not ensured *either* by just finding the *best* pedagogic grammar *or* by just focusing attention on meaning. It is not a choice between *either* grammar *or* meaning; *both* are equally necessary. The idea of linguistic meaning as divorced from linguistic form is problematic. In the final analysis, 'a preoccupation with meaning and an effort to cope with communication' (Prabhu 1987: 17) cannot be dissociated from how anyone knows what meanings a speaker is preoccupied with, and what it is that permits the interactants to cope with communication. If linguistic form is not just a set of labels which *name* pre-existing elements of reality; if, instead, it is what *creates* our representation of reality, then 'preoccupation with meaning' logically implies a preoccupation with linguistic form seen in relation to its use in social contexts. In making these claims, we are not implying that linguistic form must necessarily be taught overtly. This is an issue which cannot be resolved once for all.

Finally, to return to the question of models for ESL. The aim of bringing about in the ESL classroom a preoccupation with meaning so as to assist the pupil in coping with communication necessarily requires the creation of conditions in the pedagogic context which simulate the 'natural' environment for talk. Disregarding the difficulties in successful simulation, consider two other problems. First, since not *all* social occasions of talk can be simulated in the classroom, which ones should be selected, and why? Clearly, the ESL learner's place in the wider social context will be relevant in arriving at an answer to these questions. Second, the simulation of meaning exchange cannot be dissociated from encouraging the pupils to talk English the way that 'people normally talk English'. This raises the question of who 'the people' are, and what is meant by 'normal'. The answers cannot be the same for all wider social contexts. The Task-Based Approach in CESL and MESL may have the same abstract aim of focusing on meaning, but in order to be effective teaching strategies, the tasks themselves will need to be different for the different ESL situations. The CESL contexts are contexts natural to the learner; the MESL contexts need not be. And that in turn leads us to ask: what is likely to be a successful teaching strategy in the MESL context? Are there arguments for introducing contexts that are normal to the MESL learner's original culture rather than simulating those which are typical of the adopted one? In ESL, as in any pedagogic activity, the situation is highly complex. So, making absolute rules is fraught with difficulty, and the enunciation of absolute rules for classroom practices should be ruled out! It is in this spirit that we turn now to a brief discussion of grammar as a resource for meaning.

6 Grammar as meaningful choice in context

In this section we discuss the narrower question of lexicogrammatical description for ESL pedagogy. As we have attempted to establish, in a functional model the lexicogrammar is only one of the three perspectives necessary for describing language as a resource for meaning. It cannot be considered in isolation from the descriptions of context and meaning without causing distortion. The ideational, textual and interpersonal metafunctions serve to explain the internal organization of social context, meaning and lexicogrammar. The contextual factors of field, mode and tenor are linked by realization to the systemic organization of meaning and form, as depicted in Figure 3. The enterprise of teaching language implies a recognition of the need for a linguistic model which shows how the features of the social context are articulated by meaning and form working together. It follows that so long as the goal of language teaching is to enable the learner to put the language to work in social context, the teacher's primary task is to sensitize students to the lexicogrammar as the resource for meaning, and meaning as the artefact of lexicogrammatical choices in social contexts. To be effective, pedagogic grammar must break the bonds of form reaching out into meaning and social context on a systematic, not an ad hoc, basis.

6.1 A selective review of pedagogic preoccupations in ESL

Applied linguistics has certainly been concerned with context of situation, with meaning, and with form, but without making explicit the ways in which these three aspects of language description are inherently related and interdependent. This indifference to theorizing the relations of context, meaning and form has led to an underestimation of the power of language as a meaning-making system. For example, examination of the contexts of situation in which MESL occurs is common in TESOL pedagogy, and it is not confined to the functionally oriented applied linguist. However, even though much has been written on the inappropriateness of Western pedagogy to Eastern or developing countries (for example, Sarwar *et al.* 1985; Burnaby and Sun 1989; Tickoo 1990), the arguments in these critiques have tended to focus as much on the cultural contexts of learning as on the contexts of the language being taught. An examination of recent TESOL literature on methodology will reveal the reason why this critique is couched in terms of methodology rather than language content. Situational language methodology has tended to present basic structures in situations which were contrived to make propositional meanings clear without using translation; its activities had not called for social authenticity of language and were not based in the social context or the development of the text (see the description of situational language teaching in Richards and Rodgers 1986: 38).

Some changes have occurred in this approach in the last 25 years, whose justification is to be found in the models of communicative competence, which include sociolinguistic considerations, discourse and strategic competencies (Canale and Swain 1980; Bachman 1990). While these advances have helped to counteract the limitations of the concept of linguistic competence, the models of language used in such approaches have not been functional in the sense in which the term has been used in this paper. As a result, teachers still lack explanations of how language actually functions in social context. In our view, this reduces the effectiveness of their teaching strategies, since too often communicative competence is reinterpreted as mere communicative fluency. The focus on communicative fluency has been encouraged to a certain extent by the argument that natural language acquisition finds its own routes without overt instruction or intervention from the teacher (see Dulay and Burt 1973, who ask 'Should we teach children syntax?' Consider also the 'natural approach' developed by Krashen and Terrell 1983). Not surprisingly, this has sometimes encouraged teachers to virtually ignore lexicogrammar in favour of trying to devise methods for encouraging fluency – a concept which remains ill-defined. By these steps, some teaching practices have come to diverge widely from the stated aim of the communicative method of teaching, according to which 'a basic principle underlying all communicative approaches is that learners must learn not only to make grammatically correct, propositional statements about the experiential world, but must also develop the ability to use language to get things done' (Nunan 1988: 25).

Communicative language teaching has appealed to views of learning which emphasize the necessity for the learner to be actively involved in what she is learning. Task-based learning shares this impetus; and in the hands of a competent practitioner it can yield impressive results. However, tasks are often only a means of making communicative methodology more goal-centred; they do not intrinsically do anything to link language use systematically to its context. Notwithstanding the recommendation by Long and Crookes to develop pedagogic tasks which are 'systematically related to real world tasks' (quoted in Nunan 1988: 86), task-based pedagogy tends to encourage the 'assumption that the specific nature of the task and the content on which it is based are unimportant, [and] that, as long as learners are productively engaged in a task, they will be acquiring the target language' (Nunan 1988: 85). Simply because pedagogy is task based, an understanding of language is not automatically created. In task-based pedagogy, it has not been considered necessary to theorize the concept of context as an essential part of a linguistic model; so the teacher might have very little idea of the significance of what went on during a particular activity, what was learned, how and what might be done for its development. This is not calculated to facilitate teaching how to mean. As Palmer claimed (1917), an essential requirement for successful language teaching is for the teacher to know the nature of that which she is professing to teach; she should be able to understand and explain in viable terms, at least to herself, what, speaking linguistically, is going on at any one moment in her classroom. This exacting requirement is entirely realistic in terms of pedagogic needs. Whether or not lexicogrammar should be taught overtly is still an open issue in the trade. What cannot be an open issue is the need for the teacher to understand how language works – how linguistic form acts as a resource for meaning. These observations suggest two related conclusions:

1. Teachers need to be sensitive to linguistic functionality as interpreted in this paper; they need to be able to relate saying to meaning and meaning to the perception and creation of social contexts.

2. Students' learning of any element is likely to be facilitated and made more effective if the same three foci are kept in view: the properties of a formal pattern – both paradigmatic and syntagmatic ones; the semantic value(s) of that formal pattern; the context(s) in which the choice of the pattern is possible.

6.2 A brief demonstration of grammar as resource for meaning

In what follows, we first provide, in Figure 4, a small portion of the SFL lexicogrammar as an illustration of what a functional description of form looks like. This will be followed by a general discussion of a functional grammar for language pedagogy. The fragment of lexicogrammar selected for presentation here is known as MODALITY; representing the set of systemic choices up to a particular degree of delicacy in the modality system network of English, it is a part of the grammar which is realizationally related to the interpersonal metafunction. As pointed out in the section 2 (see especially section 2.2.1), this is the metafunction of language for construing the speakers' intersubjectivity, whereby social relations are created, maintained and, in time, changed. The environment, par excellence, for the workings of modality is the dialogic one. By construing the speaker's opinions and judgements, the lexicogrammar of modality can act as one sensitive indicator of interactant relationships. For this reason, it is a particularly relevant aspect of language in teaching workplace communication in the MESL contexts.

Following the principles of linguistic functionality, the terms in the system in Figure 4 are realizationally related to the stratum of semantics on the one hand, and to that of phonology/graphology on the other. Each option in the network has a consequence for meaning, and configurations of these systemic choices together characterize a lexicogrammatical entity whose 'output' is some phonological/graphological structure. We shall not be concerned with the details of the latter, but will focus on the grammatical choices and their semantic value.

Although the English language has only a handful of *items* that are conventionally thought of as modal auxiliaries, the system in Figure 4 gives some idea of the finer distinctions in their grammatical 'work'; this is why the configuration of the options in the system is able to construe such a rich array of meanings. Each such configuration identifies a lexicogrammatical *entity* whose meaning differs from all the others in some specific way. Part of the complexity of the grammar of modals lies in this *one-to-many* relation of what is popularly known as a *modal auxiliary*, as for example, the single phonological/graphological item *may*. However, this

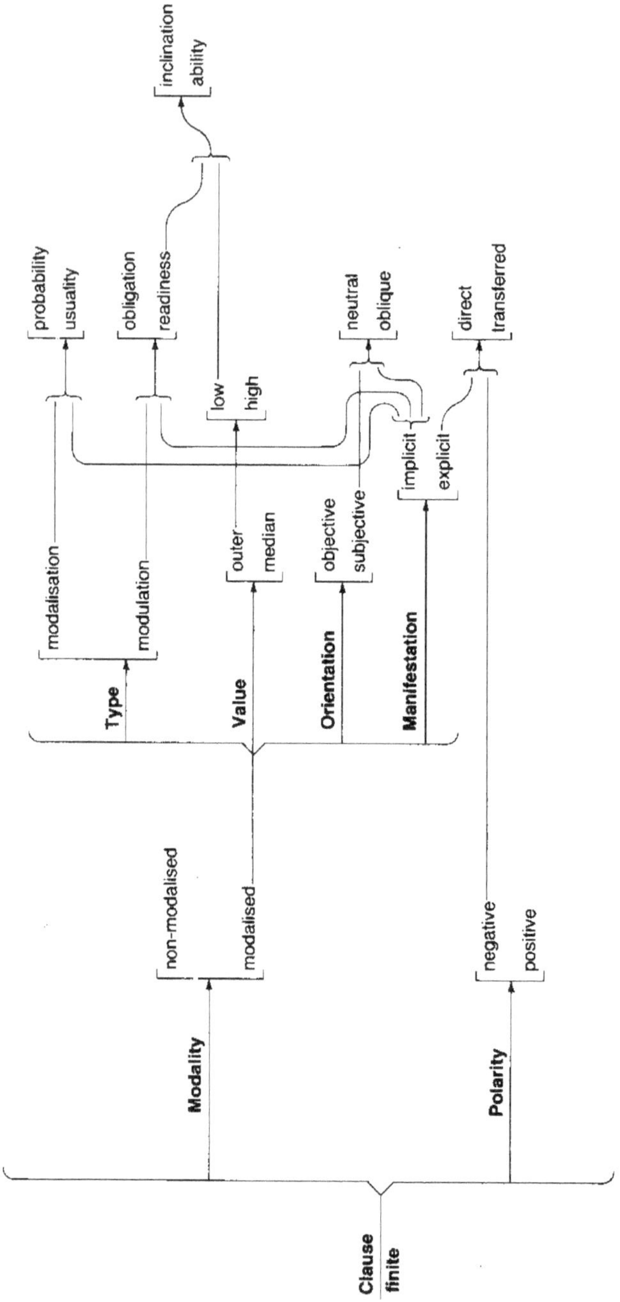

Figure 4: A simplified system network of modality in English

so-called single modal auxiliary identified phonologically is the expression of diverse grammatical entities with the multiple meanings which are construed by the varied grammatical work accomplished by it. Each modal item such as *must*, *can*, *may* does duty as the expression of more than one lexicogrammatical entity, each of which construes a distinct meaning. For example, consider the modal item *must* as used in two examples by Halliday: *she must be very careful* (where *must* is a modal with features **high obligation**) and *she must be very careless* (where *must* is a modal with features **high probability**).

It is not feasible within the scope of this paper to discuss the full set of options, their configurations, and realizations which yield well over a hundred fine distinctions of meaning. A fuller account of modality will be found in Halliday (1970b, 1982, 1985a: 85–89, 332–41). Figure 4 was produced here to give an idea of the richness that is in principle characteristic of *all languages*: as Halliday says grammar is 'the power house of language'. This does not mean that exactly the same lexicogrammatical and/or semantic choices are universally present in all languages – simply that the potential for meaning and wording is much richer than is indicated by the set of orthographic or phonological items. We will abstract a set of contrasting features from Figure 4 to discuss in some detail; but first, a few introductory comments about modality.

6.3 A few words on modality

Modality options construe 'the area of meaning that lies between yes and no – the intermediate ground between positive and negative polarity' (Halliday 1985a: 335). What this means in specific terms is explained by reference to message function, which too construes an aspect of interpersonal meaning (discussion, Section 4). In the environment of a PROPOSITION – that is, where the speaker is concerned with ***giving*** or ***demanding information*** (i.e., asserting or asking) – the area between *yes* and *no* specifies degrees of *probability* or *usuality* of some process. As an example of probability, consider *must* in *Ask Mary. She must know the answer*, where *must know* approximates *is sure to know*, while in *Ask Mary. She'll know the answer*, the group of words *'ll know* approximates *is likely to know*. The systemic options construing this area of probability-usuality are the set of choices in the modality system which is referred to as MODALIZATION, or using the philosopher's term, these are EPISTEMIC modals. In the environment of a PROPOSAL – that is, where the speaker is ***giving*** or ***demanding goods/services*** (i.e., making offers or issuing orders) – the area between *yes* and *no* specifies degrees of obligation or readiness. As an example of obligation, consider *must* in

Mary must sign the register on arrival, where *must sign* approximates *is required to sign*, while in *Mary can leave earlier on Friday*, the words *can leave* approximate *is permitted to leave*). The systemic choices here are concerned with MODULATION, or in the terminology of the philosopher, they identify what is known as DEONTIC modals. This semantic characterization of modality is based on the lexicogrammatical behaviour of the modal items in distinct grammatical environments. Figure 5 abstracts from Figure 4 the options that are relevant to **modulation** (as opposed to **modalisation**),[9] both terms acting as systemic options in figures 4 and 5, since they have the same early history.

6.4 Options in modulation: the grammar of the extent of obligation

The entry condition for the system of modality is the grammatical unit FINITE CLAUSE. We have already drawn attention to the relationship of MODALITY and POLARITY. Figure 5 shows that modality and polarity are simultaneous systems. This means that the **positive** versus **negative** distinction applies to the options **modalized** versus **non-modalized**. We shall return to polarity later. From now on, we will ignore **non-modalized**, as here our concern is only with some systemic options that depend on the option **modalized**. Figure 5 shows that four simultaneous systems of choices depend on this option, all of which are labelled for ease of reference. The system of choices called TYPE displays a choice between **modalization** and **modulation**, which has already been introduced in the last paragraph. The option **modulation** itself leads to a choice between **obligation** or **readiness**. In Figure 5, the term **readiness** is followed by an asterisk; this is to show only that the choices applicable to this term will not be discussed in this paper. In effect, the discussion is limited to the systemic options that can be co-selected with the option **obligation**. The possible configurations of the options from Figure 5 that can be co-selected with **obligation** together with their realizations are listed in Table 1.

Since **obligation** is a term in a system which is concurrent with three other systems of choices, this option may combine freely with any of the choices of those three systems. So to turn to VALUE, **obligation** may combine with the option **high**, for example, *you must wait*, or **low**, for example, *you can wait*, or **median** e.g., *you had better wait*. The choices from VALUE construe the degree of obligation. The **median** value is somewhat advisory in meaning, and at this degree of delicacy in the description *had better* could be a near-paraphrase of *should*. When the speaker's assessment of obligation is **high**, this imposes a strong requirement on the addressee; where this assessment is **low**, this leaves the addressee discretion, as in *you can wait*, which means

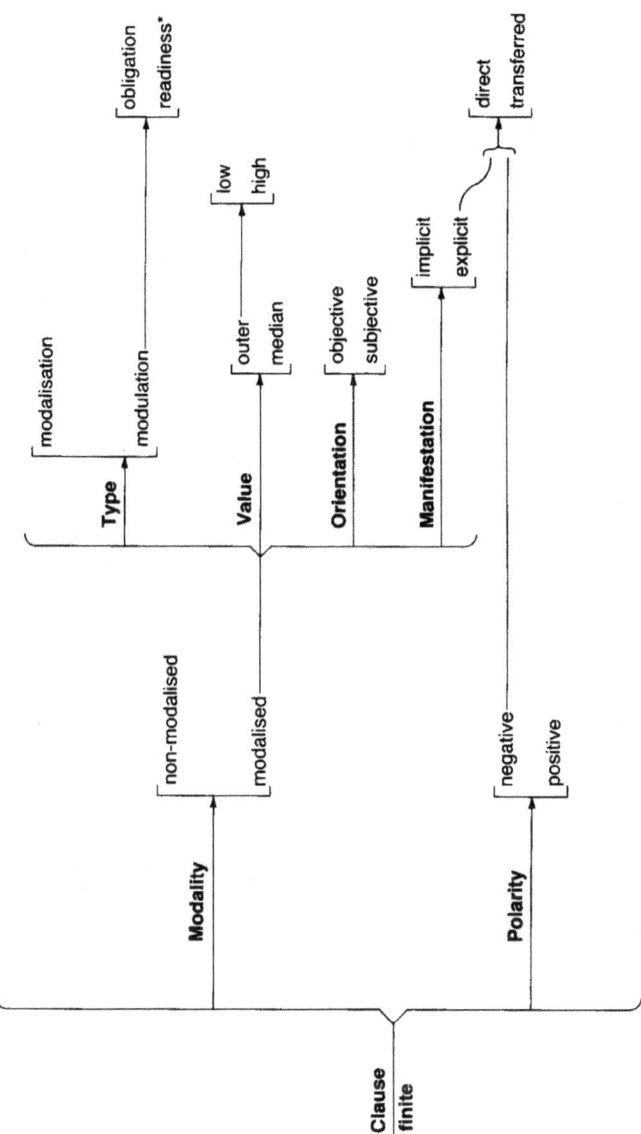

Figure 5: A fragment of modality system network in English

Systemic options in type of modulation: obligation							*Lexicogrammatical expressions*	
	Polarity	*Value*		*Orientation*	*Manifestation*		*Expression*	*Clausal example*
1.	positive	outer	:high	subjective	implicit		must/have to	you *must* leave today
2.	–[a]	–	: –	–	explicit		I insist (that you)	*I insist (that)* you leave today
3.	–	–	: –	objective	implicit		required to	you're *required to* leave today
4.	–	–	: –	–	explicit		it's necessary that	*it's necessary that* you leave today
5.	–	–	:low	subjective	implicit		can/may	you *can* leave today
6.	–	–	: –	–	explicit		I permit you to	*I permit you to* leave today
7.	–	–	: –	objective	implicit		permitted to	you're *permitted to* leave today
8.	–	–	: –	–	explicit		it's permissible	*it's permissible (for you) to* leave today
9.	–	median		subjective	implicit		should/had better	you *should* leave today
10.	–	–		–	explicit		I want you to	*I want you to* leave today
11.	–	–		objective	implicit		supposed to	you're *supposed to* leave today
12.	–	–		–	explicit		it's desirable	*it's desirable (for you) to* leave today
13.	negative	outer	:high	subjective	implicit		Must not	you *must not* leave today
14.	–	–	: –	–	Explicit	:direct[b]	i insist . . . don't	*I insist (that) you don't* leave today
15.	–	–	: –	–	–	:transfrd	I don't permit	*I don't permit*[c] *you to* leave today
16.	–	–	: –	objective	implicit		required not to	you're *required not to* leave today
17.	–	–	: –	–	explicit	:direct	it's necessary . . . don't	*it's necessary that you don't* leave today
18.	–	–	: –	–	–	:transfrd	it's not permissible can not	*it's not permissible for you to* leave today
19.	–	–	:low	subjective	implicit		can not	you *can* (if you wish) *not* leave today
20.	–	–	: –	–	explicit	:direct	I permit you not to	*I permit you not to* leave today
21.	–	–	: –	–	–	:transfrd	I don't insist	*I don't insist that you* leave today
22.	–	–	: –	objective	implicit		permitted not to	*you're permitted not to* leave today
23.	–	–	: –	–	explicit	:direct	it's permissible . . . not	*it's permissible for you not to* leave today
24.	–	–	: –	–	–	:transfrd	it's not necessary	*it's not necessary for you to* leave today
25.	–	median		subjective	implicit		should not	you *should not* leave today
26.	–	–		–	explicit	:direct	I want you not to	*I want you not to* leave today
27.	–	–		–	–	:transfrd	I don't want you to	*I don't want you to* leave today
28.	–	–		objective	implicit		supposed not to	*you're supposed not to* leave today
29.	–	–		–	explicit	:direct	It's desirable . . . not	*it's desirable for you not to* leave today
30.	–	–		–	–	:transfrd	it's not desirable	*it's not desirable for you to* leave today

Legend for Table 1:

[a] A dash in a column indicates the same option as the one in the line above in that same column. Thus in line 2, in the first column the dash means **positive**; in the second column, the dashes mean **outer:high**, and in the third, the dash stands for the option **subjective**. Only the differing choice, viz. **explicit,** is entered in the final column for systemic options. In the column labelled 'realization', at least in some cases, other items than simply those shown here can function as 'realization' of the set of selected options in question. For example, in line 2, besides 'I insist', there are other realizations such as 'I demand, I require'. These alternatives are not shown for lack of space.

[b] The networks in Figures 4 and 5 have been simplified in many ways. For example, access to the systemic choice between **direct** and **transferred** depends, in fact, only on the option **negative**, not on the conjunction of **negative** and **explicit,** as shown in the two networks. Constraining the availability of choice naturally reduces the 'output'. Without such simplifications (and omissions), Table 1 would have been much longer. Note that examples of **implicit** are provided as if the options **direct negative** have been chosen. A **transferred negative** equivalent of 16 'you are required not to leave today' (**direct**) would be 'you're not permitted to leave today' (**transferred**).

[c] Note how with **transferred negative** polarity, the values of **high** and **low** terms are reversed. For example, the equivalent of 'I insist that you don't' (**direct**) is 'I don't permit you to' (**transferred**): 'Insisting that not x' is approximately the same as 'not permitting that x'. The regularity of this reversal of values can be derived from a comparison of the examples of **direct** and **transferred** in the context of **median** (examples 29–30; 26–27) vis-à-vis those in the context of **high** (examples 14–15; 17–18) and of **low** (examples 20–21; 23–24). No reversal occurs in the context of **median**, which is the fulcrum of the modality system.

Table 1: Some selected options from figure 5 and their lexicogrammatical expressions

neither *you have to go* nor *you have to stay*. Conventionally, *you can wait* has been described as the granting of permission; allowing discretion is, clearly, an important aspect of the meaning of permission. Such discretion is not found with high obligation. This difference between low and high obligation explains why it is odd to say *you must wait, if you like* while *you can wait, if you like* is unremarkable. With high obligation the meaning is that of strong requirement, the source of which is external to the addressee – someone or some situation making it necessary that…; it is therefore contradictory to make the desired action conditional on the addressee's preference by adding *if you like*. The configuration of VALUE and TYPE options refines the distinctions in the meanings of the word 'obligation'.

The primary choices in the system labelled MANIFESTATION are **implicit** or **explicit**. When a speaker says *you must wait*, it is clear that the assessment of the addressee's obligation is high, but it is not *stated* what the source of this obligation is, that is, where it derives from. However, the speaker might indicate the same high degree of obligation *and* also a source of the obligation. Thus compare *you must wait* (**obligation; high; implicit**) with *I insist (that) you wait* (**obligation; high; explicit**). In both cases the assessment of the obligation would be ascribed to the speaker; but it is only in the second case *I insist that you wait* – that the responsibility for the imposition of the high obligation is clearly construed to lie with the speaker. The option **explicit** is realized by *I insist*. As Table 1 shows, any VALUE of **obligation** can combine with any MANIFESTATION of **obligation**.

In choosing **obligation**, there also exists a choice of ORIENTATION in the speaker's message; this may be **subjective** or **objective**. These options are significant for the construal of a meaning which is perhaps central to the interpersonal metafunction: this is the notion of responsibility. In the two examples *you must wait* and *I insist (that) you wait*, the ORIENTATION was **subjective**: that is to say, whether it was explicitly stated or not, in both cases the speaker is construed as the source of the judgment. She may, however, choose to give an **objective** ORIENTATION: that is, she may give the judgement of obligation *an appearance of being imposed from outside.* This could be **explicit** as in *it is necessary for you to wait* (**high; obligation; explicit; objective**) or it may be left **implicit** as in *you are required to wait*; both signal that there is some external pressure. The choice of the option **objective** thus construes the meaning that the assessment of obligation has an impersonal character. Holding constant the options **obligation** and **high**, Table 2 gives the four possibilities from the intersection of the last two systems.

Table 2: High Obligation

	implicit manifestation	*explicit manifestation*
subjective	you must wait	I insist you wait
objective	you're required to wait	it is necessary that you wait

Table 2 highlights an interesting fact. In most formal models, modality is something that only modal auxiliaries express: it begins with words (or lexemes). The question is: what classes do these words belong to, and what words do they combine with? In Table 2, the modal auxiliary occurs only in one clause – the word *must* in *you must wait*. In all other cases, the options of the system are realized by the Predicator of the clause, either in the content verb (e.g., *insist, required*) or in an adjective as complement to the verb *be*, e.g., *necessary.* A criticism often voiced against a grammar of this kind is that it is 'not formal', implying that therefore it is less valid. But the criticism itself is valid only under a certain conception of what the 'form of language' consists in. If form is interpreted as consisting only in the behaviour of items that can be identified purely on the phonological and/or morphological basis, clearly the description above is not formal. No similarity exists between modal auxiliaries and adjectives or predicates or projection of one clause by another. But if the form of language is thought of in more abstract terms, consisting in possible systems of relations, then other criteria become relevant, e.g., what relations a unit can enter into. It is interesting to note here that all four examples in Table 2 are subject to the same condition which applies to the clause with 'must'. We make little sense if we say: *you must wait, if you like*, nor can we use *if you like* with any of the other three clauses in Table 2. The reason in *all* cases is the same: the clauses 'have' in them the grammatical features **high obligation**. Figure 5 represents a grammar concerned with relations which do not *depend* on whether or not each of these is expressed by exactly the same phonological/graphological form in the limited sense of the term 'form'.

Let us turn now to the system of choices called POLARITY. As a term in a system that ultimately depends on **modalization**, the option **obligation** may combine with **positive** or **negative** polarity. In simple formal terms, this means nothing more than that the modal auxiliaries may or may not be followed by negation. But when negation is examined in relation to other systemic choices, an interesting difference emerges. **Negative** polarity functions differently in the environments of **high** as opposed to **median** value of **modulation**. This is illustrated by the examples in Table 3. The table is divided into two blocks, **A** and **B**, each with two columns. Block

(**A**) exemplifies the option **subjective**, and block (**B**), **objective**. The left column presents examples of **high modulation**, the right, of **median**.

Note that in the left column, where **modulation** is **high**, the meaning of **negative (1)** differs significantly from that of **negative (2)**. If the choice is **direct negative** – i.e., **negative (2)** of Table 3 – the **obligation** remains **high:** compare for example, *I insist that you don't wait* and *you're required not to wait*; in both cases the requirement is negative, but strong. By contrast, if the choice is transferred negative – i.e., **negative (1)** of Table 3 – the obligation 'switches' to low: *I don't insist that you wait* and *you're not required to wait* give discretion – you may or may not wait; you may use your personal discretion.

Table 3: Negative polarity and modal value

	high explicit modulation	**median explicit modulation**
(A)		
positive	I insist that you wait	I want you to wait
negative (1)	I don't insist that you wait	I don't want you to wait
negative (2)	I insist that you don't wait	I want you not to wait
(B)		
positive	you're required to wait	you're supposed to wait
negative (1)	you're not required to wait	you're not supposed to wait
negative (2)	you're required not to wait	you're supposed not to wait

A comparison with the right column shows that with the **median** option it makes no difference whether the **negative** is **transferred negative (1)** of Table 3 or **direct negative (2)** of Table 3. Although Table 3 does not contain any examples of **modalization**, exactly the same situation obtains there as well: with **high modalization** the choice of **transferred negative** 'switches' to **low**; with **median** it makes no difference.

6.5 Language pedagogy and grammar in a socially based linguistics

The account provided here presents the details of only a fragment of the system of modality, but it is sufficient to indicate how the SFL grammar of a language provides descriptions that probe the form for meaning. It may be useful here to draw attention to three features of a functional grammar. First, when in a stratal model, the lexicogrammatical form of a language is represented as a set of systems of choices; these systems bear relations in three different directions. They 'look upward' to the levels of semantics to determine what meanings are construed by a certain (configuration of) option(s), which naturally has a bearing on the contexts construed by those meanings. In addition, the systems also 'look downward' to the levels of phonology to determine how a (configuration of) grammatical choice(s) may be expressed as some phonological/graphological structure. Finally, the systems also 'look alongside' the same stratum to see how a (configuration of) choice(s) is actualized as a (syntagmatic/linear) structure. In other words, the grammatical description is validated not by a single reference point – morphological and/or phonological – but by reference to multiple criteria including meaning, form and phonology. The second feature of such a grammar is that its orientation is paradigmatic: it is conceptualized as choice in some environment and this brings the various options in relation to each other in a systematic way. Thus the nature of choices in modality is explained by seeing them in relation to choices of MOOD and POLARITY. Note that all three pertain to the same metafunction. The third feature is as follows: the concept of choice emphasizes the idea of language as a resource – what speakers have the potential of doing. To link the system networks at the various strata by the underlying metafunctional principle is to ensure that the description of the system of language is not divorced from the description of how it can be used for the living of life. A model which sees the lexicogrammar as a means of creating meanings, and maintains simultaneous focus on meanings and wordings, can become a powerful tool for helping the student in coping with communication by making explicit the basis on which one might ascribe to a speaker a preoccupation with some meaning. Such grammar is a useful tool for learning to function with the other tongue.

We have argued that learning language is learning how to mean and that *linguistic* meaning is construed by patterns of form. If this is so, then enabling the student to perceive what meanings are typically exchanged in what context would have to be an essential goal of any responsible pedagogy, but for reasons to which attention has been drawn, this need is even more pressing in the MESL context than elsewhere. Teaching the orthographically identified items of modal auxiliary or their morphological variants is not going to do much for a MESL learner in enabling her to see the finer shades of meaning differences, such as have been presented in Table 3. However, for the true development of language proficiency, the MESL learner does need precisely these 'shades of meaning'; this is the type of detailed semantico-grammatical insight which will enable her to be 'on the wavelength' (for discussion, Gibbons and Markwick-Smith 1992). Nowhere is the influence of tenor more apparent than in the wordings that involve modulation: power is closely linked to the right to tell others what they must do and what they can do. The MESL learner will need to be alerted to the various ways in which different shades of meaning can be construed, and this will require going beyond modal auxiliaries as items whose identification is based on purely morphological and/or phonological criteria.

We claimed (sections 3-4) that wording and meanings do not just reflect the relationships in a pre-existing context of situation; they are actually involved in the on-going negotiation of the context as a step toward its validation. It follows that in an interactional situation, speakers can effect changes in the defining parameters of their on-going context; for example, by varying the choice of certain features from the system of modality, one might indicate a shift in power relations. To exercise some degree of control over one's interactive context without in the process alienating others is clearly important for successful negotiations. And an insight into how the grammar of modality helps or hinders these processes is clearly relevant. All this suggests that lexicogrammar is far too important to be ignored by teachers, and that functional explanations are clearly so necessary that they cannot be avoided. Whether the teaching of grammar should under all conditions and for all students remain unconscious – or covert – is a separate issue. We have argued that the ESL teaching context is not the same everywhere: the length of the program, the age of the learner, her needs, her cultural and educational background, and other such issues are important (for discussion of individual differences Long and Larsen-Freeman 1991: 153–219).

One source of difficulty the teacher may encounter in teaching modulation in the MESL context needs to be mentioned. Here, the grammar of modality could be 'taught' at first as formulae in social contexts which can be put to immediate use. Establishing a firm context for the presentation of the meanings of modality will avoid the need to present overt explanations. However, as our presentation shows, the choices of modality construe the speaker's attitude either to her interlocutor or to the propositional content of her message. This makes the use of such teaching strategies a little problematic, and in this respect modulation may be more problematic than other aspects of grammar. New linguistic items are frequently presented in ESL contexts in a text, so that students can first listen or read, and then learn. If the context of situation and the text are carefully chosen and appropriate explanations are given, students can be expected to understand the different meanings of the wordings. Beyond this presentation stage, students generally become involved in communicative activities or tasks which are devised to give them practice with the 'target' structures or meanings. For example, a class might be given a moral or practical problem or game in which they are to devise possible courses of action and offer possible solutions within the 'context' which the teacher has set up. Such a teaching situation is fine for assessing and correcting many of the students' linguistic practices but the teacher often has real difficulty when it comes to the discussion of modality. Difficulties with structure formation can be easily identified, but it may be impossible for the teacher to know whether, in choosing a particular form of expression, the student has got across her intended viewpoint. The solution of directing students to assume roles and telling them what their attitudes 'must' be is not a happy one, if the teacher's aim is to promote an increased ability to express their own ideas, even though this may be a necessary stage on the route to autonomous expression.

An emphasis on receptive activities can assist in this interference with authenticity. Students could listen to dialogues and identify the relevant features of the context of situation; they could be asked to compare similar texts produced on different occasions where the language of the texts has construed field, mode and tenor which are similar in some respects but different in others. Advanced students could be asked what choices of wording and meaning construe what aspects of the context; they could be asked to make changes to the lexicogrammar to correspond with certain specified changes in field, tenor and mode. At an advanced stage, when students' ability to mean is relatively developed, they could be introduced to choices from the system in such a way as to make them aware of the differences in meaning that correspond with differences in wording. Self-critique of produced material could be an alternative activity.

We should, however, clearly state one point: system networks are highly useful for describing the relations of form but they are not suitable in the language teaching classroom for the direct presentation of points of lexicogrammar. Their primary use is as a source of information for the teachers, and only at the most advanced levels might some selected meaning contrasts be discussed when learning *about* the form of language might appear a useful activity. In the course of discussing the system network, we have pointed out that systems can be drawn to different degrees of delicacy, depending upon the detail of description required for the purpose in hand. For example, Figure 4 is more delicate than Figure 5. This means that teachers can choose to 'read' a system network at different degrees of delicacy. For example, they could simply draw attention to the manner in which **modulation** – *you must be very careful* – contrasts with **modalization** – *you must be very careless* – without going into any of the other details discussed earlier, or they can choose to build in even finer details than have been presented here. This decision about how much to teach will be made not on the basis of what there is in the system of language but on what the learners need or what their proficiency level is.

7 Concluding remarks

This chapter has traversed a large area. Perhaps less than one-fourth of it would be popularly seen as belonging in a volume concerned with pedagogic grammars. So in the closing move of this discourse, it seems appropriate to say a few words about what place we imagine a chapter such as this to have in a volume such as the present one. Why talk about the social basis of linguistic theory, when the brief is to talk about pedagogical grammar? Perhaps we owe an explanation to our readers.

In choosing the design and content of our chapter, we deliberately set out to distance ourselves from certain views about the nature of human language, about what it means to do grammar, and what the place of grammar is in language pedagogy. The central concern of this volume, if we are not mistaken, is with ways of doing grammar in the context of language pedagogy. It is commonly assumed that grammar is one area of language study that can be discussed in convenient isolation from everything else. And of course, in practical terms, we can pull out even a minute segment of grammar itself to speak about – as we ourselves have done with modality. But doing grammar brings with it a set of underlying assumptions about the nature of language, as it did in our description of modality. In some cases – for example, in our description here – these assumptions are clearly articulated; in others, they remain invisible. Certainly, every language has grammar, but the grammars that linguists do – what Halliday (1984) has referred to as *grammatics* – should not be confused with *the* grammar of some language. The grammar that scholars do – i.e., any instance of *grammatics* – is simply an attempt to represent someone's idea of what the grammar of the language being described is like. The excellence, authenticity and so on, of the grammatics of a language cannot be determined by checking how well it corresponds to the grammar that inheres in that language, since this question cannot be answered with any greater validity than the question about which language corresponds best to the *real* universe. So a criterion for judging a scholar's grammar is by reference to the underlying principles that govern his or her representation of a language's grammar, and this cannot be separated from the scholar's views on the nature of language. When we are planning to simply use a grammar – say, for pedagogical purposes – we imagine that it is possible to pull out the grammatical description on its own; nothing else need be assumed. By the design and content of our chapter, we have implied that this is a misconception: a grammar is only as usable/useful as the view of language that underlies it. These views cannot be sealed off; they spill over when the grammar is put to use. This is one argument why grammars have to be seen as part of an overall framework. It seems unrealistic to imagine that the issue of pedagogical grammars can be discussed without relating the grammar to the theory of language description.

The second reason why we cannot talk about grammar in isolation arises from a consideration of the basis for our interest in it in this volume. The choice of a grammar that might be used for teaching someone *to function with the other tongue* can hardly be dissociated from what it is that a teacher needs in order to be able to 'facilitate a learner's second language development'. But the teacher's 'needs' in teaching cannot be independent of the learner's 'needs' in learning. If the choice of a pedagogic grammar is related to teachers' needs, then it is ultimately related to the place of second language learning within the society, since learners' needs do not arise in a vacuum. So when it comes to the choice of a pedagogic grammar, from this point of view we need to ask two sets of questions: (1) what sort of grammar is needed for learning a language? What does it mean to say that someone has learnt a language, and (2) who is the second language learner? Why is the second language being learnt? Does grammar play any part in language learning/teaching? Does the grammar of a language play any part in the creation, perception, maintenance and change of the speakers' social environment? Clearly, if any grammar is at all relevant, it has to be one which forms part of a theoretical framework that coherently and systematically spans this vast area from the nature of language to how language is related to its speakers' conceptions of social reality. Once again, grammar needs to be seen in relation to 'non-grammar': the validity and value of a pedagogic grammar are not likely to be determined by examining the grammar alone.

In our paper we have traversed the area from social context to lexicogrammar. In doing this we are not implying that context, meaning or form are new concepts for applied linguistics; applied linguistics has been familiar with these terms for as long as it has existed. For example, speaking broadly, there has been interest in the 'language and culture' issue. But the accounts have lacked theoretical depth; 'the connections between the language of a culture and the culture itself have … frequently been reduced to lexification of curious objects or behaviours, or the providing of inventories of appropriate phrases whose reasons for appropriateness, sources and constitutive sociologies have remained quite opaque' (Candlin 1989: 1). It is this lack of theorization whereby context is treated as a thing apart – a scenario – within which speaking happens; speaking itself becomes a series of words and structures, and the role of lexicogrammar in the creation of meaning is attenuated. This leaves gaps between; and the gaps are filled by such notions as knowledge of the world, speakers' intentionality, beliefs and cultural conventions, leaving us wondering how the knowledge of the world comes about, how cultures come into being, and how the speakers' private intentionalities, desires and beliefs attain intersubjective objectivity so that the conversational 'other' is able to 'read them off' from the words and structures and/or the context. Bringing the discussion down to a practical level, task-based approaches, situational pedagogy, the learner-centred approach all call for a theory of language description that models the close relation between context, meaning and linguistic form. If context is defined by the meanings at risk in it, if form is seen as a resource for meaning, this permits a language-based understanding of which tasks, which situations, which texts are alike, which are different in what way, and how they can be used profitably with what kind of learner.

The teaching and learning of language cannot be equated with simply acquiring control over items. The mechanical operation of 'converting' this structure into that, of providing lexical equivalents, is within reason easy to teach; this teaching leads nowhere. Speaking meaningfully is not simply producing a structure or a set of words; it is using wording for meaning within a social context for the living of life. The choice of a pedagogic grammar has to engage with the issue of whether or not grammar is relevant to successful communication. If the answer is yes, this argues very strongly for a grammar that can be used to explain the nature of text – how and why a saying comes to mean what it does. Applied linguistics has bowed to the notion of social context, to the importance of culture, to the supremacy of discourse, to a recognition of the importance of learner's culture: these 'fashions of speaking' have risen into prominence, one at a time, and then subsided, not because the problems associated with these concepts ceased to exist but because fashions in academia changed. Forever in search of its centre of gravity, applied linguistics has focused on whatever might be the new bright idea of the decade, forever failing to grasp the complexities inherent in its enterprises. As Stern points out, 'language teaching has suffered from an overemphasis on single aspects, and…language teaching is multifaceted…the different facets should be consistent with each other' (1984: 11). The search for a pedagogic grammar is in the last resort a search for a consistent theory of language which will permit applied linguistics to address the complex issues of language pedagogy.

Notes

1 For illuminating discussions of the Piagetian approach, see Vygotsky 1962; Donaldson 1978; Doise and Mugny 1984.

2 Thanks are due to Gillian Perrett, co-author of this paper, for her permission to include it here.

3 Our thanks are due to Kristin Davidse (Catholic University, Leuven) and to Jane Torr (Macquarie University, Sydney) for help in the initial stages of this paper. We thank Bev Deriwianka, Michael Halliday, Graham Lock, Terence

Odlin, David Nunan and the anonymous referees for their helpful comments and constructive critique. The responsibility for the views expressed is entirely ours.

4 For further discussion of these issues see Hasan 2009a.

5 Attention is drawn to the term 'typically', which has caused a good deal of debate that is capitulated in Hasan 1995a.

6 For example, the various models of the interactive situation provided by Hymes (1971, 1972) can be explicated by invoking the values of the three parameters (Hasan 1995a; 1999b).

7 Terms referring to the level of semantics are shown in bold italics as in ***message demanding goods/services***.

8 For two examples of system networks from the lexicogrammatical stratum, see Figures 4 and 5 in section 6.

9 Items picked out in bold *within the text* e.g. **modal, non-modal** indicate systemic choices at the stratum of lexicogrammar.

11 English process, English tense: foreign learner, foreign teacher [1995]

1 Introduction

As the title suggests my presentation[1] is concerned with what, speaking generally, might be described as temporal expressions, or how time is construed linguistically.[2] The presentation has two foci: first, the aim is to focus on temporal expressions in English primarily because it seems likely that such a discussion might be of some use in the business of teaching and learning English as a second or foreign language (ESL/EFL). Secondly, my concern is also with certain general issues: in fact I would like to open this talk with a brief discussion about the nature of human language. Now, I have a feeling that while discussing some features of the English language would be readily recognized as relevant to the teaching and learning of ESL/EFL, the relevance of the second issue might not appear obvious. It may be useful then to begin with a few words concerning why an understanding of the nature of human language is relevant to the teaching of language, whether the language being taught is a mother tongue or an other tongue.

2 The nature of language and language learning: a brief comment

Teachers of ESL are part of an international community spread over many countries of the globe. This community has struggled in pursuit of perfecting the art, the science and the technology of teaching the target tongue, English. But despite all well meant attempts over many decades, it cannot be claimed that today we definitely know the answers to all or even the most important questions that arise in teaching English as a second language or as foreign language. Part of the reason is of course that the questions are not always those which arise just from the nature of English alone: in fact, many of the difficult questions arise when ESL comes face to face with the social realities of the learners in their native environments. These social realities are not only complex in themselves, but they tend also to be unique in some measure for each specific community. It follows that each ESL learning community has to face questions which are at least in some respects specific to that community in the sense that they are rooted in the community's unique social realities. One such social reality is the learner's mother tongue: learners in countries such as Pakistan will typically have exclusively used their mother tongue for the living of life until they encounter English in an official pedagogic environment.[3] It is important to understand why the learner's mother tongue is a significant issue in the teaching and learning of other tongue(s).

Until quite recently, linguists had argued fairly successfully that each language has its own patterns of structure, its own lexicon, its own sound system and despite certain similarities there does not exist a one-to-one correspondence between the various languages. This is not to say that there is nothing in common to all languages of the world – there certainly is; but what is in common does not concern the structure of the sentences and phrases, as the dominant model introduced in the 1950s would have it. In fact, what is universal to all human language is of a fairly general nature; it concerns the deeper characteristics of human language. For example, we can claim with confidence that the internal organization of all human languages is the same; all languages are stratified systems: thus they 'have' the strata (levels or components) of meaning (semantics), wording (grammar and lexicon) and phonology and phonetics (sounds); at each of these strata, we may identify units which are related to each other in specific ways, thus languages of the world 'have' morphemes and/or words, that make up phrases/groups, certain combinations of which go into the making of clause/simple sentence; and so on.

Again, and much more relevant to my talk today, every human language is a functional system. Thus it acts as a resource for construing its speakers' experience of the world that is around them and of the world inside them: in SFL we refer to this as the EXPERIENTIAL function of language. Human languages also enable speakers to construe relationships between different elements and aspects of their experience, for example states of affairs are related by conditions, consequences, succession and suchlike; objects have shape, size and colour – language enables the construal of these phenomena: this is the LOGICAL function of language. At the same time, human languages are a resource for construing speakers' attitudes, their points of view, their position vis-à-vis others: in other words, every language is an enactor of social relationships between speakers.

This function of language we refer to as the INTERPERSONAL function. In addition, if you consider any piece of spoken or written language used in normal, natural environments, you would note that languages also enable speakers to create relevance in their discourse – for linking up what is being said now to what has already been said, and also for showing the relationships between the saying and the context of situation in which the saying is done. Language thus enables the linking of a community's past to its present and to its future: this, according to SFL, is the TEXTUAL function of language. Human languages all over the world act as a resource for the performance of these functions – and they have always performed these functions irrespective of the level of the speech community's social, technological or political development: no language is more developed today than another in terms of the kinds of function it is able to perform for its speakers.

Human languages are able to perform these functions due to their internal organisation, more specifically by virtue of their grammar and their lexicon, or as SF linguists would put it, by virtue of their LEXICOGRAMMAR. The lexicogrammar of a language – its form – is neither god-given nor accidental: it has developed, and keeps developing, constantly under semantic pressure (Butt 1988), that is to say, under the pressures of meaning exchange which continually arise in the living of social life. At the same time, social institutions, social conventions and forms of behaviour – the essential elements of social living – are maintained and changed through the workings of language in interaction. This, in a nutshell, is the meaning of the word 'functional' in 'systemic functional linguistics'. A truly functional linguistics views language as a potential for meaning, and it relates the internal form of human language to the speakers' social contexts within which meanings develop in the first place. In this approach to language, the form of language is not a body of rules built into the brain, to be followed naturally and mechanically; it is a social resource for making meanings. There thus exists no opposition, no dichotomy, between form and function: patterns of form cannot be validly identified without reference to function(s), and functions cannot be objectively recognized without form: there is no viable formal linguistics without a basis in social-semantic functions and there can be no viable functional linguistics without a basis in lexicogrammatical form. My approach to the description of temporal expressions in English and in Urdu is guided by these principles.

The acceptance of the above perspective on language implies that it cannot be thought of as vestment – just as clothing for ideas. Instead, we need to take the suggestion seriously that our ideas about the world around us, about our relationship to others, as well as about what is really real, are formed largely through the working of communal languages, i.e., through their meaning construing lexicogrammatical resources. In learning their mother tongue, young children do not simply learn what the philosopher, J. L. Austin (1962) called the 'words and vocables' of language: they also, and more importantly, learn the nature of their world. As Halliday put it, an infant, when learning his[4] mother tongue, is in fact 'learning how to mean' (Halliday 1975a; Painter 1984, 1985). And the meanings he learns while learning his language have a special importance for him, since they become the primary substratum of his consciousness. Clearly then our mother tongue is a very intimate part of our being, claiming a special status in our affections and in the processes of our life; it has acted as the first means of our contact with humanity and with the human world, since it has been the primary mediator of what we think of as the reality surrounding us.

This way of conceptualizing the nature of human language has various implications for applied linguistics, all of them important. Here I will concern myself only with one single issue, namely the relationship between wording and meaning, between lexicogrammar and semantics. I will argue that language teachers need a deep understanding of the nature of linguistic form – not as a set of formal rules and conventions, but as a resource for making meaning. It is essentially this functional perspective that is relevant to the business of language teaching, because it can provide the most effective link between the mother tongue and the other tongue which is being learned as a second or foreign language. In approaching the relationship of meaning and wording it might be useful to keep in mind three related propositions:

(i) meaning does not 'live' in isolated patterns; it is the function of the relations of a pattern – a word, a phrase, any lexicogrammatical category – to other patterns, be they words, phrases or other categories;
(ii) the relations between the formal patterns of one language are hardly ever *the same* as those in another; and
(iii) therefore the relationship between a formal item and its meaning in one language is seldom if ever replicated in another one. A dictionary is a resource to be used with a keen understanding of this principle.

To briefly elaborate on these points: the famous British linguist, J. R. Firth, once said (1957) that a word is known by the company it keeps. This can be interpreted as a general claim that the identity and value of the formal patterns of a language – i.e., its lexical and grammatical categories – become known to us through that pattern's relationships to other patterns.

This is sometimes not fully appreciated in language teaching. Consider, for example, the many vocabulary development exercises in ESL textbooks: underlying many of them is an untenable belief that if someone has learned the dictionary equivalent of a word in English, they can use that word appropriately everywhere, as if the graphic/phonic shape of the word were a container and the word's meaning, a substance that has been poured into it to remain inside it for ever. I hope to show today that nothing could be further from truth.

To say that the relationships between the formal patterns of different languages are not identical is to say that different languages have different ways of saying and meaning. In learning the mother tongue, one learns these ways of saying and meaning so unconsciously that they become naturalized: the mother tongue's way of meaning presents itself as unquestionably '*the* right way'. So, depending on the degree of difference between the languages in question, the learners of other tongues might have to make a considerable shift from their own naturalized ways of saying and meaning to accommodate other 'strange' foreign ways which do not present themselves as unquestionably 'natural' as their own. And the teachers are likely to be able to appreciate the source of such difficulties only to the extent that they themselves are consciously aware of the differences between the two languages. In what follows I will concern myself not only with some English patterns but also with some Urdu ones,[5] in order to clarify some of the points I have raised in this section.

3 Construing time: some 'time words' in English and in Urdu

Like most linguistic meanings, temporal meanings too manifest themselves in two major ways: they appear as CONTENT WORDS – more accurately as LEXICAL ITEMS/LEXEMES – or they appear as words/morphemes which realize some GRAMMATICAL categories, sometimes called FUNCTION WORDS. Later I will try to show that these two ways of construing time work together: time is in fact construed neither entirely by the lexical items, nor entirely by the grammatical categories – neither entirely by the content words nor entirely by the function words. However, for the moment I will maintain this distinction while I first examine certain familiar lexical items referring to time in English such as, for example, *today*, *tomorrow*, *yesterday*, before turning to such grammatical categories as PRESENT, PAST and FUTURE TENSE.

Linguists (e.g., Halliday and Hasan 1976; Lyons 1977) have suggested that lexical items such as *today, yesterday* and *tomorrow* contain an element of DEIXIS. Putting it somewhat simply, to say that a word 'has' deixis is to imply that the specific meaning of such words is primarily explicated in terms of its relation to a context of situation relevant to some unique interactive event. For example, everyone knows that if someone uses the word *today*, they would typically be referring to the day on which they produced that word in their speech, and the words *tomorrow* and *yesterday* can be interpreted respectively as 'the day following the day of speaking' and 'the day preceding the day of speaking'. This relationship is illustrated in Figure 1:

'BEFORE'	====>	DAY OF SPEAKING	====>	'AFTER'
		‖ ‖ V		
day before	yesterday	today	tomorrow	day after

Figure 1: English time words

Figure 1 is linear: *yesterday* precedes *today* which precedes *tomorrow*. Time is thus presented as a ribbon, with past time, i.e., *yesterday*, 'placed' on it before the present, and the present i.e., *today*, positioned before the future, i.e., *tomorrow*. One may also add to this timeline further points extending in either direction by using in English not single words but such expressions as *day before yesterday* and *day after tomorrow*, or even phrases like *two days ago* and *in two days*. The regularity in this context in the oppositional use of *before* and *after* or *ago* and *in* is to be noted: in the context of construing time, *ago* means basically the same as *before* while the word *in* is like *after*. It is possible also to make a linear arrangement of less definite units on the time line such as, for example, *now* referring to the actual temporal location of speaking, *then* as preceding that moment, and *later* as following it. As the American linguist, Whorf (1956), pointed out English construes time as a row of beads, with each bead representing some unit of time in a sequential relation to those next to it; the unit size may vary, but their relationship to each other remains the same.

Compare the above situation with that in Urdu,[6] where we may cite the paradigm *aaj, kal, parsõ, narsõ* and *atarsõ* as referring to approximately the same temporal space as that discussed for English. Here the term *aaj* bears a close semantic resemblance to English *today*: like the English *today*, Urdu *aaj* too has DEIXIS; it refers to the day of the speaker's relevant speech production. But the close meaning approximation stops precisely at this point as Figure 2 attempts to show.

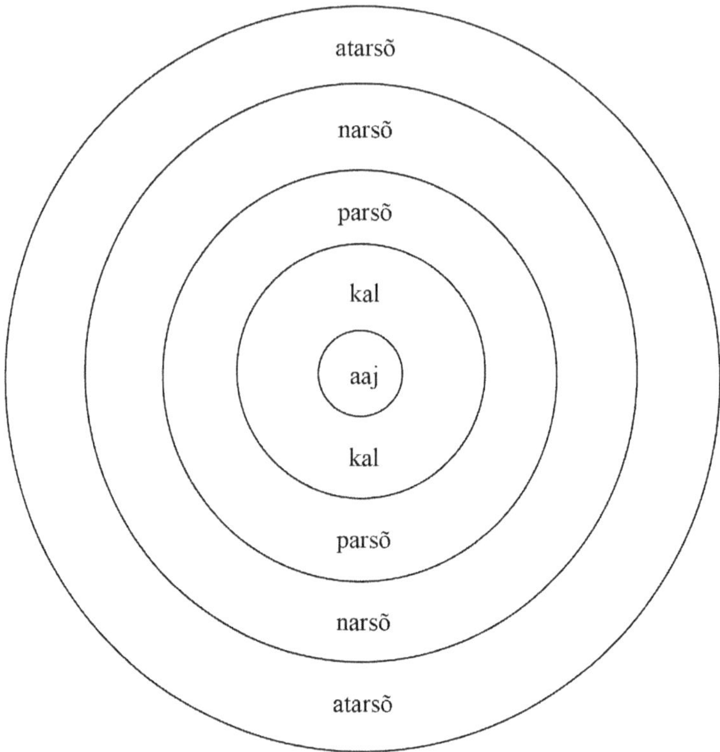

Figure 2: Time in Urdu words

Note first that while the English nominal groups *day before yesterday*, *day after tomorrow, two days ago, in two days* and so on are composite expressions that refer to distinct units of time, the members of the Urdu paradigm *aaj, kal, parsõ, narsõ,* and *atarsõ* are synthetically coded[7] lexical items, each of which will be recognized and used by speakers as a single 'content word'. Secondly, and far more important, the relationship between *aaj* and the other remaining terms of the paradigm is markedly different: the latter do not extend 'before' and 'after' *aaj* forming a row of successive units as in English; rather they ripple out from *aaj* at the centre of the circle (see Figure 2) into contiguous circles around it. *Kal* 'surrounds' *aaj*, referring to the temporal space covered by both English *yesterday* **and** *tomorrow*: it makes no distinction between the time unit prior to speaking or that following it; it simply encircles both 'before' and 'after' *aaj*, and is, thus, concerned only with the immediately contiguous point in time. *Parsõ* stands in this same relation to *kal*, referring approximately to the temporal space referred to by both *day before yesterday* and *day after tomorrow*, making no distinction whatever between time past and time to come; and this kind of relation continues right through to *atarsõ*.[8] So one way of interpreting *kal* would be to say it means one day **either** before **or** after speaking, each successive term adding a further day distance from the day of speaking. It follows that an Urdu speaker can use *kal* either with the past or with the future tense as in 1 and 1a:

1:	*maĩ ne*	*kal*	*wo*	*kitaab*	*xatm*	*kii*	
	I	yesterday	that	book	finish	did	
	I finished that book yesterday.						

1a:	*maĩ*	*kal*	*wo*	*kitaab*	*xatm*	*karũ*	*gii*
	I	tomorrow	that	book	finish	do	will
	I will finish that book tomorrow.						

Just as linearity is a pervasive feature of English time, so this concentric relation is a fairly pervasive feature of time words in Urdu. Compare the use of *abhi* in 2 and 2a: it clearly refers to a short moment before or after speech.

2:	maĩ ne	*abhi abhi*	*wo*	*kitaab*	*xatm*	*ki*	*hai*
	I	just just	that	book	finish	did	have
	I have just finished that book.						

2a:	maĩ	*abhi*	*wo*	*kitaab*	*xatm*	*karũ*	*gii*
	I	just	that	book	finish	do	will
	I will finish that book in a moment.						

Like the paradigm *aaj* through to *atarsõ* the term *abhi* too 'has' temporal deixis, but none of these terms carries a temporal directionality unlike English *yesterday, tomorrow, now, then, later*, and so on. My interest is not in making some deep philosophical point about the nature of time as such: I want to suggest simply that whatever the nature of that phenomenon we call 'time', the ordinary discourse of Urdu lexically construes time rather differently from the way that English does. Bringing it to an even simpler level, there are no dictionary equivalents in English for Urdu lexical items referring to time such as *kal, parsõ, narsõ, atarsõ, abhi*. What the Urdu-speaking learners of English have to learn is not which expression in their language is approximately the same as which in English, but rather the differences in the sensitivities of the various lexical items to their differing environments in the two different languages. The relevant question is: what critical feature of the textual environment of the word *kal* might indicate contiguity with time already sensed – i.e., the past – as opposed to time anticipated, i.e., the future? An attempt to address this question – when is *kal* past, when future – takes us to the category of TENSE.

4 Construing time: the grammatical category of tense

The examples of time expression we have considered so far draw on content words; they belong to the LEXICON. TENSE, on the other hand, is a grammatical category,[9] which in Urdu, as also in English, occurs in the VERBAL GROUP, i.e., in 'verb words' which are ordered in sequence vis-à-vis each other according to the grammatical principle(s) of the two languages. As with content words indicative of time, so with tense I will begin the discussion by a few words on English.

Every verbal group must have at least one content word, which refers to some kind of doing, or happening: this word is often called the 'main verb', and it realizes the PROCESS of the clause. Examples would be verb words such as *walk, stumble, eat, appear, talk, like, recognize, know, dream, yawn* and so on. At the same time, there is some specifiable category of word (component) in the verbal group which must be indicative of tense: words with this kind of function we call AUXILIARY verb such as *will, has, is, been.* In fact, it is misleading to give the impression that tense is always an auxiliary *word*: there are certain environments in which the tense is expressed not by some separately occurring word, but can be indicated by a word-component to which we refer as MORPHEME: this appears as part of a word, as in

3: Jamiil walk**ed** barefoot in the hot sun.
3a: The president of Pakistan pay**s** no taxes.

In the former clause the segment *–ed* in *walked* indicates the simple past tense: this is a fairly common way of indicating the simple past in English, though it is not the only one; for example, compare *lose*, and *lost*, and also *walked* v. *did not walk*. In example 3a, the segment *-s* in *pays* indicates the simple present tense; again, this is not the only way of indicating the present tense in English, but the details of this description are complex and my time is limited, so I shall simplify matters by limiting the discussion mostly to some tenses in those verbal groups (i) that are FINITE (discussion below); (ii) are part of some INDEPENDENT clause; and (iii) whose first auxiliary word/segment is not a MODAL auxiliary such as *can, may, shall, must, ought* (or related forms).

Our discussion of English lexical items referring to time has identified three significant points on the linear time scale (Figure 1): the present is identified by its relation to speech time, the past as time that preceded speech, and the future as time following the given speech event. The terms PAST, PRESENT and FUTURE are also used as the technical labels to refer to the three primary tenses recognized in most English grammars. Like the lexical temporal expressions, they too 'have' deixis. So when someone says *the boy walked very fast*, the tense 'in' the word *walked* is normally taken to indicate that the action of walking happened prior to the time of the relevant speech; it will thus be said to refer to time in the past. Compare this with *walking very fast*, where the verbal group is NON-FINITE. In this case, there is no indication of the time of walking; and no time can be assigned to the action of walking until this nonfinite verbal group can be placed in relation to a finite one, as in

4: walking barefoot in the hot sun, Jamiil burnt his feet.
5: walking barefoot in the hot sun, Jamiil might burn his feet.
6: if Jamiil walks barefoot in the hot sun, he will burn his feet.

In example 4, *burnt* is a finite verbal group; the form of the word indicates that the event happened in the past, i.e., prior to uttering this sentence: the implication is that the nonfinite verb *walking* too happened prior to speech. In the next example, the verbal group *might burn* is finite but the auxiliary *might* (formally related to the modal *may*) shows the action to be simply in the realm of possibility: the question of point in time simply does not apply, i.e. *walking barefoot* in this environment will be just a likely event, not an actual one. In 6, the time reference of present tense in *walks* is conditioned because the clause is conditional – note the adverb *if*; this suggests that the present to which reference is made by the verb is hypothetical, rather than actual. I hope this discussion shows that *primary tense deixis occurs only in finite verbal groups of the type specified above*; such deixis is not found in a non-finite verbal group or in a finite modal verbal group or in a finite verbal group occurring in a dependent (HYPOTACTIC) clause such as in 6. This is the justification for focusing here mainly on that category of finite verbal group where the choice of primary tense is free of the kind of constraints considered above. My discussion is concerned with two such tenses, SIMPLE PRESENT and PRESENT CONTINUOUS.

4.1 Time and tense in English: simple present and present continuous

There is a major difference between the lexical 'time words' such as *today, tomorrow, yesterday* and so on, and the grammatical category of tense: the referential scope of the time words is largely 'univalent': *today* must refer to the day on which the relevant speech event took place.[10] But while a default meaning may be applied to a tense, there is no such simple meaning relation between a tense and the time it may refer to: an instance of the same tense category may have different time reference depending on the lexicogrammatical environment in which it occurs. As we shall see below, this generalization holds true of the two tense categories we will be examining, viz., simple present and present continuous. First, an example of each:

7: Jamiil walks to the clinic every day.
8: Haamid is reading a book.

The verb *walks* in 7 is an instance of simple present tense, while *is reading* in 8 instantiates the present continuous (or, using SFL terminology PRESENT-IN-PRESENT) tense. Now, speakers of English know that the time reference of *walks* is not limited just to the day of speaking: Jamiil does not just walk to the clinic on the day example 7 is uttered; he walks there everyday; in other words, the clause represents a habitual activity of the actor Jamiil. The possibility of the occurrence of the adverbial *every day* in 7 validates the habituality of the action of walking to the clinic. Considered in terms of the line of temporal progression (cf. Figure 1), a habitual process covers an indefinite amount of time, which extends from before the moment of speaking – i.e., the past – up to the time of speaking – i.e., the present – and there is good reason to assume that it will also extend into time following the present – i.e., the future, unless this expectation is expressly cancelled. So the English present tense does not refer just to the 'present time' here and now, i.e., it does not refer to the moment of speech in any focussed way, or even just to the day on which the speech is uttered; in fact its time reference is fairly non-focussed, typically covering 'now, before now, and (most probably) after now'. In view of its 'habitual' and 'general' meaning, it is not surprising that the simple present tense is used in making general statements, which is indeed the default environment for its use. It helps construe either states of affairs that are 'habitual' and pertain to some particular (category of) actor(s) as for example in (7), or those that represent the so-called 'universal truths' – based in common wisdom (which need not be, and often is not true!) or in scientific 'facts' (notwithstanding the fact that these facts often get revised) – as in 9 and 10, respectively.

9: God helps those who help themselves.
10: The earth revolves round the sun.

It should be added that there is more to making general statements – or generalization, as they are generally called – than the presence of the simple present tense. In fact certain specifiable semantic qualities of both the participants of the process in the clause – i.e., the actor and the 'acted on' – as well as of the circumstances associated with the process play an important part in helping the clause to act as a generalization (for some details, Hasan 1992a; Martin 1993; Cloran 1994).

Having presented a brief view of one semantic function of the simple present tense, we move now to the present continuous tense: what is the default, i.e., prototypical time reference of the present continuous tense?

Leech (1989: 19) suggests it refers typically to 'temporary happenings'. Certainly, by contrast with the simple present tense, the reference of the present continuous tense appears to have less permanency, in the sense that the time to which it refers is of smaller duration: in the words of Halliday (1994a: 116) this tense is 'more focussed in time'; it refers to the time of an activity that is going on at the moment of speaking as in (8). And it is this feature that explains why it is possible to add quite appropriately the temporal adjunct *at this moment* to the clause in example (8) as shown in 8a:

8a: Haamid is reading a book at this moment.

Looking back at this very brief account of the two tenses – the simple present and the present continuous – curiously, neither label seems very helpful from the point of view of their potential for meaning: the so called 'continuous tense' patently lacks the kind of continuity we find in the habituality of the simple present: in fact, if anything the present continuous is bound more closely and primarily to the limits of the moment of speaking. The simple present, on the other hand, is anything but 'simple', and if by 'present' we mean the actual moment of speaking then this tense has little definite reference to that moment of time.

4.2 Time and tense: comments on default and conditioned meanings

The reference (i.e., SIGNIFICATION) of the simple present and the present continuous as discussed above concerns its DEFAULT meaning. A default meaning is the meaning a linguistic category *typically* construes: in other words, it is the interpretation that would be typically assigned to instances of this category unless there is good reason for doing something else. This is an extension of Halliday's 'good reason principle', which was first articulated in the context of the description of grammar (Halliday 1967–68); here it is being applied to the description of linguistic meaning. On the basis of my research, I would foreground the principle that default state of the categories of language – whether lexical or grammatical – is to be multivalent in their meaning, i.e., capable of construing more than one meaning – rather than to be univalent, bearing a one to one relation to meaning. This does not mean that meaning and wording are randomly related; simply that, *a viable linguistic description demands those conditions to be clearly stated which specify what meaning will be construed by what category in what environment*. I will refer to such meanings as 'conditioned': so CONDITIONED MEANINGS are meanings, construed by a lexicogrammatical category under certain clearly specifiable conditions. If any of the enumerated conditions apply, then foregoing its default meaning, a category will function as the construer of some conditioned meaning: this observation applies to both the simple as well as the continuous present tense.

Before turning to these meanings and the conditions in which they become applicable, let me put forward the hypothesis that the default and conditioned meanings might resemble each other in some ways: certain general characteristics might apply to both. So, for example, the default meaning of the present tense is much wider: as pointed out above, it is relatively 'non-focussed', referring to the past, the present (and unless otherwise indicated) also to the future. And it is noticeable that this tense also has a wider range of conditioned meanings than does the present continuous tense, which as pointed out above is 'more focussed' in its time reference. In keeping with this, and following the generalization just made, the conditioned meaning of the present continuous tense is comparatively more restricted in its range. It would seem also that the conditioned meaning is built on the possibilities inherent in the default meaning. So the default meaning of the present continuous tense appears to exclude reference to past time. The actual fact of the matter most probably is that Haamid *was* reading the book before someone 'had the licence' to say *Haamid is reading a book*; it would, however, be problematic to 'make' the present continuous tense construe reference to past time by saying either ??*Haamid is reading a book a while ago* or ??*Haamid is reading a book yesterday*. This is because the time expressions *a while ago/yesterday* uncompromisingly signify time prior to speaking.

4.3 Time and tense: the conditioned meanings of English present continuous

Difficult as it is to make present continuous tense construe time prior to the utterance, its meaning is not restricted only to 'on-going activity'. Consider examples 11a–11c below:

11a: Haamid is cooking dinner for us.
11b: Shaahid is helping me out these days.
11c: We are going to the pictures tomorrow.

Here the tense in 11a construes the default meaning: the clause will be interpreted as referring to an activity that is on-going during speech time unless there is good reason for doing otherwise. Note we can add such temporal expressions as *just now, at this moment*. In 11b the same tense is used to refer to an activity that is habitual but within a time span that is more restricted than the habituality of the present tense.

We have seen in the discussion of the simple present tense that the time for habitual activities is non-focussed: it spans past, present and future unless otherwise indicated. But there is an important difference between the construal of habitual time by the simple present tense, and by the present continuous in clauses of the type exemplified by 11b: the latter clause type must 'have' in it expressions such as *these days, now-a-days, all the time*. The function of such temporal expressions in this context is to place a restriction on the time span during which the present continuous may indicate habituality. Shaahid is doing something which extends into time prior to speaking, takes in the time of speaking within its reference and includes future time as well but all this *only within the limits of 'these days'*. And so far as the meaning of *these days* is concerned, this is indicated by the co-text. So the time reference in 11b is not like saying *she sells sea shells on the seashore*, much less like *God helps those who help themselves*; the time for Shaahid's activities may be habitual and also, technically speaking, indefinite so that it is quite close in meaning to *Shaahid* ***helps*** *me out these days*, but the extent of the time which it is allowed to signify is limited by *these days*: it is thus more focussed. The important point to note is that it is the reference to a specific time span by temporal expressions such as *these days, now-a-days, some of the time* and so on whose possibility of occurrence actually provides the necessary condition for the construal of the (conditioned) meaning to be ascribed to the continuous present tense here: in the absence of such temporal expressions the default meaning will apply. In other words, the conditioned meaning of the tense is not just *in* the tense; it is in the interaction of that tense with a specific category of lexical temporal expression(s).

In 11c, the continuous present tense will be taken to signify future time, and in doing this it will once again bear a resemblance to the simple present as we shall see in the following discussion (cf. example 13d). Here the temporal expressions such as *tomorrow* appear to make a critical difference: its presence within the same clause would seem to be significant for establishing the futurity of *are going*. But, in fact, the situation is not so simple; if a friend suddenly announces while having a quiet glass of wine with me:

12a: I am going to London

one thing is clear without any doubt: the friend is not actually engaged in going to London at the time of uttering this speech, nor is he already gone; there remains only one possibility by exclusion, and that is reference to a future act. Such almost automatic deductions from the material situational setting of the discourse are not at all uncommon (Hasan 1973): in fact we act on their basis very frequently in the use of language in everyday life. Thus on social occasions of casual chat, utterances such as the following said in the middle of a conversation would be normally construed as referring to some future action:

12b: I am doing an audition.
12c: they don't trust him; they're giving him a sack.

4.4 Time and tense: the conditioned meanings of English simple present

Let me turn now to a consideration of the simple present tense, which has many uses, leading to a complexity in its description. Here are three examples:

13a: Jaaveed Mĩããdaad bats extremely well.
13b: i: Something frightening happened yesterday
ii: I was just walking to the store
iii: when suddenly this man *comes* out of nowhere
iv: and *snatches at* my handbag
v: and I *let out* one long scream
vi: then a whole lot of things happened at once …
13c: Haniif takes a start, runs in, and bowls…
13d: I leave for London tomorrow.

In 13a, the simple present tense in *bats* refers to an activity that is usual; normal speakers of English will interpret this as claiming that this activity of batting extremely well is typical and 'habitual' of Jaaveed Mĩããdaad. In presenting similar examples earlier, it was pointed out that such habitual time reference is the prototypical, default meaning of the simple present tense.

By contrast, in examples 13b–13d the simple present tense does not construe this default meaning: in each case we have a conditioned meaning. 13b(i–vi) is an instance of recount; the simple present tense occurs in utterances 13b(iii–v), and in each case it refers not to habitual time but to time prior to the speech. In fact, it is pretty close to the default meaning of simple past tense (which has not been included for detailed discussion): note that it fits into a framing of events in the past at the start of the recount 13b(i–ii) as well as in the last utterance 13b(vi) as the sequel to letting out the scream. In popular accounts of such use of the simple present, it would be said to lend 'immediacy' to the events of the narrative, making them 'as-if' present to the senses here and now – one reason why it is sometimes referred to as the 'historic' or 'narrative' present. The conditions that enable the use of the simple past tense in this way are rather diffuse: in order for such meaning to be construed by the simple present tense, the preceding discourse must have created a frame of reference to past time – more succinctly, its status as part of some variety of narrative should be obvious. In 13b, the first two utterances perform this function: there in *Something frightening* ***happened*** *yesterday. I* ***was*** *just* ***walking*** *to the store,* the past and the past continuous tenses (highlighted in bold) have been used together with a lexical temporal expression *yesterday* which can only refer to the past.

For obvious reasons, the past tense is the typical tense for narrating events: the meaning of narrating is to linguistically re-present events that have or are supposed to have occurred in the past, and one might suppose that news reported in the papers pertains to the past in this sense. However, the simple present is quite often used with a similar narrative meaning, especially in news headlines, e.g., *US firm gets contract for incinerators (sic!) supply* (*Dawn,*[11] 15 October, p. 3), which refers to an event that has already taken place – it is certainly not habitual. This prompts the comment that perhaps the condition for the interpretation of the simple present as referring to past does not so much depend on the use of certain lexicogrammatical forms such as those highlighted with reference to 13b: it inheres in the recognition of the fact that the context of language use is one in which past events are expected to be relayed. In other words, this use of the present tense inheres in the relevant context of situation common to a family of registers dealing with the retailing of past events.

In 13c some specific actions undertaken by Haniif, a well known Pakistani cricket player, are represented by the use of the simple present tense in *takes a start, runs and bowls*. Here again the simple present does not construe habitual events: rather it refers to what is actually going on at the moment of speaking. Such use is typical of sports commentary, especially where it refers to some on-going activities of the sportsmen on the field. The use of the simple present in the environment of the register of sports commentary construes a meaning that is very close to the default meaning of the present continuous tense: the action is actually transpiring as the utterance is being uttered. Interestingly, stage directions in plays resemble sports commentary in this respect: here too the conditioned meaning of the simple present tense is typically pretty close to that of the present continuous tense. In general terms its meaning may be paraphrased as 'in close spatio-temporal contiguity to the(se) utterance(s), some specific participant is engaged in carrying out the represented processes'. Like the newspaper headlines, this conditioned meaning of the simple present is co-textually supported: the use of the simple present tense has the potential of construing this meaning in the environment of sports commentary or stage direction.[12]

In 13d, there is again a departure from the default meaning of the simple present: here the conditioned meaning is quite close to that of the simple future tense, and in this respect it resembles the conditioned meaning of the present continuous discussed above with reference to example 11c. As in the case of the present continuous construing reference to future, so also for this conditioned meaning of the simple present tense to come about, the presence of some lexical temporal expression referring to the future is required as exemplified by *tomorrow* in 13d.

This discussion of the simple present tense in English should convince us that there is not much that is simple about it. As a matter of fact the only simple thing about the simple present tense is its internal structure: there is just one tense, though it takes different forms depending on person and number – so even the formal shape of the verb is not very simple when seen with the eye of the foreign learner. There can be other complexities in tense organization within a verbal group such as PAST IN FUTURE IN PRESENT, exemplified in *he is going to have finished it* (for more detailed discussion Halliday 1976b, 1994a; Matthiessen 1995). As we see, despite the simple internal structure of the simple present tense, the pattern of its use is quite complex, construing different meanings in different contexts. To ignore such semantic multivalence of linguistic patterns is to ignore a rich resource of the meaning potential of English. And in the contexts of ESL/EFL pedagogy, a teacher's unawareness of these complexities should be cause for alarm.

4.5 Time and tense in the environment of different process types

I hope the preceding discussion has already provided substantiation for the claim that typically a formal pattern construes different meanings depending on the environment in which it occurs. As pointed out earlier this does not mean that the relationship between formal patterns and linguistic meaning is random: in the discussion of the conditioned meanings of both the present and the present continuous tenses, we have seen that the lexicogrammatical, textual and contextual environments of these tenses condition their meaning, implying that in the absence of such environments, it is the default meaning that will be construed. But the situation with regard to the meaning of these two tenses is more complex than the previous discussion has indicated: there is yet another factor that is highly relevant to the meaning these tenses are able to construe in English. This factor has to do with the type of process[13] in the clause. PROCESS is a technical term for that element of the clause which refers to some kind of event, irrespective of whether it is an event that concerns doing, saying, sensing or being. And this element is typically realized by the main lexical verb of the clause, as for example in *he is eating chocolate*, where *eat* refers to the process *he* is doing.

Now, if we return to the lexical verbs I have used in the above examples, it will be noticed that most of them realize the kind of process that in SFL would be called MATERIAL PROCESS. Since material process is a process of doing or happening, we can probe them with questions which use the verb *do* or *happen*. For example, if Mary asks John: *what do you do for a living?*, John might say *I sell fruit and vegetables*; similarly our example 13a *Jaaveed Mĩããdaad bats extremely well* is a possible response to the probe: *what does Jaaveed Mĩããdaad do really well?* Also, if some one asks: *what is Haamid doing?*, then our example 8 *Haamid is reading a book* or example 11 *Haamid is cooking dinner for us* would be perfectly appropriate answers. Similarly, in specifiable environments we can probe a material process with 'do to/with': for example *what does John do to/with the fruit and vegetable?* The response to this would elicit a material process e.g., *he sells it/he preserves it/he freezes it/he eats it* and so on. In all these cases, the simple present and the present continuous tense of the verbs functioning as Process construe their default meanings: i.e., the simple present tense construes the 'habitual' meaning, and the present continuous 'currently on-going' meaning.

4.6 Time, tense and mental process in English

But not all English clauses have material process. There are other process types that occur quite frequently: the probes used to check on the material process would naturally not apply to these other processes; further, the clauses may not display the same patterns in the construal of time by tense. Here I want to draw attention to one process type in particular. Suppose that John shows Mary a new design, to which Mary responds by saying:

14: I really like this design.

Here, clearly, it would not make any sense to interpret the simple present tense in the Process *like* as referring to a habitual activity: after all it would be odd for Mary to claim that it is her habit to like 'this *new* design', just as when someone says:

15: I think Jamiil is arriving tomorrow,

they do not mean to say that it is a habitual activity of theirs to *think* that Jamiil might be arriving the next day. And yet in neither case do we have any of those 'special conditions' described above which, I argued have to be present either directly or by implication for the default meaning of the simple present tense to give way to a conditioned meaning. So what is going on here? The fact is that lexical verbs such as *like* and *think* do not realize material process; rather they realize a process type, classified as MENTAL in SFL and that makes all the difference!

Simplifying somewhat, verbs realizing a mental process typically refer to some activity of the mind such as knowing, reacting or sensing. This process type is considerably different from the material process type. Whereas the material process type construes our experience of the goings on in the outer world – who is doing what to whom/what or what is happening to what/whom – mental processes such as *think, imagine, like, fear, hate, love, sense, see, hear* etc. refer to our acts which 'happen inside the head' though they still relate to the world outside: so they construe our internal experiences that are private to us until talked about – who thinks what, what pleases whom, or speaking more generally, who senses what phenomenon. As a general principle, English grammar and semantics distinguish the inner and outer processes rather clearly. We do not need to go into all the details of these distinctions here (for which, see discussions in Halliday 1994a; Butt *et al.* 1995; Matthiessen 1995), but what is relevant here is the fact that the choice of tense to refer to an on-going or habitual activity in the context of mental process is appreciably different from that in the context of material process. It is part of this story that the use of the present continuous tense with English mental process is highly marked: that tense can be used only in very special environments. Overwhelmingly often, in English we tend to say:

16:	(a) I like this play	*rather than*	(b) I am liking this play.
17:	(a) I know your son	*rather than*	(b) I am knowing your son.
18:	(a) I hear an odd noise	*rather than*	(b) I am hearing an odd noise.

It is clear then that in the environment of mental process, the default meaning of the simple present and present continuous tense is different from that which it is in the context of the material process. Thus examples 16a-18a refer to a time that is concurrent with some activity of sensing at the moment of speaking: in this sense the activity could be said to be 'on-going' at the moment of speaking, but at the same time it carries a greater sense of permanency than the present continuous tense does in the context of material processes. Whatever the exact time reference of the simple present tense in clauses such as 16a–18a, it is certainly different from the default meaning of both the simple present tense and the present continuous when these tenses are used with material processes. And it is equally certain that with mental process, the preferred present tense for referring to the sensing activity as 'on-going' at the moment of speaking is the simple present tense in English, not the present continuous, as shown by the above examples.

This does not mean that the latter tense is ungrammatical if used with mental process: this should be obvious from 16b–18b. After all, these clauses are not ungrammatical though they may appear odd. The fact of the matter is that the use of the present continuous with mental process construes a considerably different meaning from its default meaning in the company of the material process. This can be demonstrated by the following examples:

16c: I had seen this play before, *but this time I'm liking it better.*

17c: Working closely with your son for some time now, I feel *I am knowing him for the first time.*

18c: Remember the odd noise I was talking about? Well, *I am hearing the same odd noise again now.*

In the above italicized clauses the mental process 'has' a present continuous tense but now the clauses do not appear odd. One notable difference between these and 16b–18b is that given their environment, a change in perspective is present. In 16c, reaction to the initial encounter with the play is implicitly compared with reaction to a fresh (re-)encounter; in 17c it is suggested that better acquaintance has led to a different kind of knowing of the same person; and in 18c a past perspective is replaced by an explicitly ongoing one. To sum up, the use of the present continuous with the mental process implies a change of perspective in that instance of sensing: unless the co-text permits this interpretation, the use of the present continuous with the mental process will appear odd in English.

It will also be noted that the conditioned meanings of simple present and present continuous tenses do not appear to apply to their use with mental process. For example, unlike *we are going out to the pictures tomorrow* (11c) or *I leave for London tomorrow* (13d) we cannot say something such as 16d–e:

16d: *I am liking this play better tomorrow.
16e: *I know him tomorrow.

This unacceptability cannot be explained on the grounds that it is impossible to anticipate mental processes. Rather, their anticipation is typically presented as something in the realm of possibility/probability rather than certainty. Thus instead of the future tense auxiliary *will*, typically it is modals that are employed with anticipating mental process e.g., *I might like this play better another day when I am feeling less depressed* or *I would most probably like this painting if the colours were more definite*. Even with the use of the future tense, selection of possibility/probability expressions is quite frequent e.g. in *I will probably remember these details later when I don't really need to.*

It is obvious from this brief discussion of just two tenses in English language that in an ESL/EFL classroom, there can be no such thing as 'teaching how to use ***the*** English present tense' or '***the*** English present continuous tense': there is no ***the*** about any of the tenses – in fact any of the structural types we set apart – these tenses and others too will have different faces, depending on the environment in which they occur. What this implies is that a competent teacher will need to take these considerations into account.

5 Time and tense in Urdu

Apart from the material and the mental process types which I have briefly discussed above, English has other process types which were named above. The discussion of all these types cannot be encompassed within the scope of this presentation (for details Halliday 1994a; Butt *et al.* 1995; Eggins 1994; Gerot and Wignell 1994; Matthiessen 1995). It is time now to turn to a brief consideration of the simple present and present continuous tense in Urdu, particularly in the environment of material and mental process types. I offer this account tentatively, for indeed despite the excellent classical grammars of Urdu, I have so far not come across a functional description of the language. My assignment of Urdu verbs to material or mental process type is based on a fairly preliminary analysis. But some things seem certain: the recognition of these process types will be required in any valid grammar of Urdu; secondly, probes of the type mentioned above with reference to the English processes may be established also for Urdu. In other words, reliable recognition criteria can be established for Urdu grammatical categories, as they have been for English.

5.1 Time and tense in Urdu material process

Let me begin with the Urdu material process since it is the category that receives the greatest degree of attention in the context of teaching the verbs of any language: in ESL textbooks one would find greater focus on this process type than on the mental or verbal ones; and in generalization and description, 'rules' will be given which apply in general to the material process type, not the others. In the context of this process type, the default meaning of the two tenses in Urdu is in fact quite close to those that we have suggested above for English. Example 7 *Jamiil walks to the clinic every day* is an English clause with simple present tense and it can be idiomatically translated into Urdu with the same tense as shown in 7a:

7a:	Jamiil	har	din	daftar (ko)	paidal	jaata	hai.[14]
	Jamiil	every	day	office to	(on foot)	go	is

Jamiil walks to the office every day.

Here the simple present tense of the Urdu verbal group *jaata hai* (3rd person, masculine, singular) has the same habitual time reference as its English equivalent: this is also the default meaning of simple present tense in Urdu as exemplified by 19 which is taken from an Urdu news sheet *Hamaara Maahaul*.[15]

19	a:	Shahnaaz	ghar	maĩ	sab	se	pehle	uThti	hai
		Shahnaaz	house	in	all	of	first	wake-up	is

Shahnaaz is the first in the house to wake up.

b:	fajr	ki	namaaz	paRh	kar
	dawn	of	prayer	read	do

Having said her morning prayers,

c: dahi se makkhan nikaalti hai
yoghurt from butter extract is
(she) churns butter out of yoghurt

d: aTa guundhti hai
flour knead is
(she) makes dough

e: phir bhaĩsõ ko caara deeti hai
then buffaloes to feed give is
then (she) gives the buffaloes their feed.[16]

Shahnaaz is the first in the house to wake up. Having said her dawn prayers, she churns butter out of sour milk, makes dough and then feeds the buffaloes.

All verbal groups in this example (except that in 19b) are finite; each of these 'has' the simple present tense, and each refers to habitual time, which is obviously appropriate in the description of a routine. Each clause is a declarative, except 19b to which choice from the system of MOOD does not apply. Examples 20 and 21 are taken from two different pieces of work by the poet Saahir Ludhyaanvi. Note that 20 is an interrogative.

20: meri tasviir pe tum phuul caRhaati kiũ ho?
my picture on you flower raise why are
Why do you raise flowers in offering to my image?[17]

21a: siine ke viraã goshõ mẽ ek Thiis
breast of desolate corners in a pain
si karvaT leeti hai;
like turn take is
in the desolate corners of my heart, something like pain throbs into life;

21b: naakaam umãggẽ roti haĩ;
failed aspirations weep are;
unfulfilled desires make lament;

21c: ummiid sahaare deeti hai.
hope support give is
hope provides support.

A throbbing pain awakens in the desolate corners of my heart; unfulfilled desires lament, (while) hope offers support.

These verses are phrased in highly idiomatic Urdu, but if there are problems in translating them into English, they arise from the conventions of Urdu poetry; they have nothing to do with the meaning construed by the simple present tense. 20 and 21a-c construe habitual time, which is the default meaning of this tense in Urdu.

As in English, so also in Urdu, the present continuous tense construes 'on-going time'; so as the translation of 11 in 11a shows below, the time reference of the present continuous tense is pretty close to its original:

11a: Haamid hamaaree liiee khaana[18] paka raha hai
Haamid us for dinner cook ing is
Haamid is cooking dinner for us

Here are a few more authentic examples of the same tense from Urdu literature:

22a: xaraamã xaraamã, moattar moattar
softly softly fragrant fragrant
so softly, and with such fragrance

22b: *nasiim aa rahi hai*
breeze com- ing is
morning breeze is coming

22c: ke wo aa rahee haĩ
or s/he com- ing is
or s/he is coming.

So softly, with such fragrance, is it the cool breeze moving towards me or could it be my beloved approaching.

23a: phir ye bhi qaabilee tawajjo hai
then this too worthy-of attention is
Again this too is worthy of (our) attention

23b: ke ham – aap, maĩ – ham pakistaan ko
that we – you, I – we Pakistaan to
toRnee ki baRi koshish kər rəhe haĩ
breaking of great effort do ing are
that we – you, I – we are trying hard to break up Pakistan.

23c: is xudaa-daad pulaau ki deeG ko khaa rahee haĩ
this god-given pilaff of dish to eat ing are
(we) are eating up this god-given dish of pilaff.

23d: khaaee ja rahee haĩ
eat go ing are
(we) are continuing to gobble (it) up.

23e: hirs aur tama hameẽ paagal kar rahi haĩ
envy and greed us mad mak- ing is
envy and greed are making us crazy

23f: caaro taraf see 'maĩ' 'maĩ' ki awaazeẽ aa rahi haĩ
four ways from 'me' 'me' of shouts com ing are
from every direction, cries of 'me! me!' are coming

23g: iqtidaar ke liee ham aapas meẽ laR rahee haĩ
status for obtaining we together in fight ing are
we are fighting each other to gain status

23h: jaisee baccee khilaunee kee liee laRtee haĩ
as kids toy of for fight are
just as kids fight to get hold of a toy.

And again it is worth noting that we – that is to say, you and I – are doing our best to destroy Pakistan. (We) are eating up this god-given (gift) (as if it was) a pilaff dish – simply continuing to devour it non-stop. Excess of envy and greed is making us lose our judgement; the cry of 'me! me!' is arising from every quarter; just as kids fight for the possession of a toy, we too are fighting each other to gain control and status.[19]

24a: aap naahaq xafaa ho rahee haĩ
you unjustifiably angry be -ing are
you are getting angry without (any) reason

24b: mai to mahaz aap ki taariif kar rahi hũ
I only you of praise do -ing am
(so far as I am concerned) I am only praising you.

you are telling me off for no good reason at all; I am simply praising you .

I have deliberately used examples from registers of Urdu valued significantly differently by the speech community in Pakistan; e.g., 7a and11a are clearly examples from text books; 19a-e, is from a news-sheet presenting the picture of the 'ideal daughter of the house'; 20, and 21a-c are from the Gazals of Saahir Ludhyaanvi, 22a-c from Faiz Ahmad Faiz while the remaining two examples (23a-h and 24a-b) are from the prose of the satirist Mumtaaz Mufti – all of whom are well known figures in Urdu literature. This indicates that irrespective of the value attached to these various registers, the lexicogrammatical resources used to create linguistic meanings are basically the same in the different register types. To understand how lexico-grammatical patterns of language work in the construal of meanings in different registers is to acquire a tool for understanding the kinds of meaning exchange in a community, whether poetry or politics, jokes or jurisprudence.

5.2 Time, tense and material process in Urdu: conditioned meanings

With regard to the conditioned meanings of the two tense types in the context of Urdu material process, there is again a great deal of overlap between the two languages. The overlap is very noticeable in the case of the present continuous tense, where both habituality and futurity can be construed by this tense given the same environment as described for English. So, for example, 11b-c can be translated quite idiomatically in Urdu as shown below:

11b:	Shaahid	in dinõ	meeri	madad	kar	rahaa	hai[20]
	Shaahid	these days	my	help	do	ing	is
	Shaahid is helping me out these days.						

11c:	ham	kal	pikcar[21]	(deekhnee)	ja	rahe	haĩ
	we	tomorrow	picture	to see	go	ing	are
	we are going to the pictures tomorrow						

Here *kar rahaa hai* (3rd person, singular, masculine) and *ja rahe haĩ* (1st person, plural[22]) realize present continuous and they construe the meanings of habituality and futurity as their English counterparts do in these environments (section 4.3-4 above).

Section 4.4 identified some conditioned meanings construed by the English simple present tense, namely (i) past time in narrating stories/episodes; (ii) past time in news headlines; (iii) concurrent time in commentary; (iv) time concurrent with character action in stage direction; and (v) future time. Of these conditioned meanings, Urdu simple present tense does not appear able to construe (ii) and (iii). Beginning with (i), 25a-d exemplifies Urdu simple present construing past time in narrating:

25a:	jab	naubat	is	had	tak	aati	hai	
	when	condition	this	limit	to	arrive	is	
	when conditions get to this point							
25b:	to	wo	laRki	ghar	se	bhaag	jaati	hai
	then	that	girl	home	from	run	go	is
	then the girl runs away from home							
25c:	aur	samundar mẽ	kuud	kar				
	and	sea in	jump	do				
	and jumping into the ocean							
25d:	xudkushi	kar	leeti	hai				
	suicide	do	take	is,				
	(she) commits suicide.							

When the situation gets this tough, (then) the girl runs away from home and commits suicide by jumping into the sea.

Here 25a, b, and d have simple present tense in *aati hai, bhaag jaati hai* and *xudkushi kar leeti hai* (comes, runs away, commits suicide, all three 3rd person, singular, feminine), while 25c is a nonfinite clause; but the former would be interpreted as construing past time: the events described clearly could not be thought of as 'habitual'. However, the use of the simple present tense for construing past time in newspaper headlines does not appear at all common. For example, where in English we might find *Bus Crash Kills 60 Children*, in Urdu we would expect

26a:	bus	kee	haadse	meẽ	saaTh	baccee	mar	gae
	bus	of	accident	in	sixty	children	dead	went

sixty children have died in a bus crash.

Mar gae is simple past tense, whose default meaning is to construe past time. Another possibility is to nominalize 26a as shown below:

26b:	bus	kee	haadse	meẽ	saaTh	baccõ	ki	maut
	bus	of	accident	in	sixty	children	of	death

death of sixty children in bus crash.

Nor is the Urdu simple present tense used in the context of commentary. In English, the commentary will typically use this tense as in (13c) *Haniif takes a start, runs in and bowls…*, while in Urdu it is very likely to take the following form:

27:	Haniif aae,	vikTõ	ki	taraf	daure,	aur	geẽnd	pheeki.
	Haniif came,	wickets	of	towards	ran	and	ball	threw

Haniif came, ran towards the wicket and bowled.

Turning to the fourth conditioned meaning of the simple present in English, we find rather surprisingly in view of the above situation that the Urdu simple present too may be used for stage directions:

28:	do	sipaahi	pistaul	taanee	daaxil	hote	haĩ
	two	policemen	pistol	drawn	enter	become	are

two policemen enter with pistols drawn.

This brings us to the last conditioned meaning noted above: in English, under certain conditions, the simple present tense may construe reference to future time as in (13d) *I leave for London tomorrow*. However, in Urdu it would seem somewhat odd to say its equivalent: *maĩ kal landan jaati hũ* (I tomorrow London go am =*I go to London tomorrow*). This is particularly interesting in view of the fact that in the following example, the same clause type (29a) is not only perfectly normal but would appear to be the default choice:

29a:	maĩ	kal	wahã	jaati	hũ
	I	tomorrow	there	go	am

I go there tomorrow.

29b:	to	is	maamlee	par	abba	se	baat	karũ	gi
	then	this	matter	on	father	with	talk	do	will

then (I) will talk to my father about this matter.

I go there tomorrow, (then) I'll discuss this matter with (my) father.

Note that the second clause (29b) 'has' future tense (*karũ gi* = do-I will); this is however not a critical requirement: this same clause might have had a simple present as in *to is maamlee par abbaa see baat* ***karti hũ*** (= then I talk to my father about this matter). In either case, the tense will be interpreted as referring to future time. The environment for such use requires what is known as CLAUSE COMPLEXING in SFL. The complex may be paratactic as in 29a-b, or hypotactic as in 30a-b:

30a:	agar	kal	nasiim	see	miltii	hũ
	if	tomorrow	Nasiim	with	meet	am
	if I (do) meet Nasiim tomorrow					

30b:	to	aap	kaa	paiGaam	dee	dũ	gii
	then	you	of	message	give	give	will
	then I'll give your message to him.						

If I happen to see Nasiim I will give your message to him.

Let me close this discussion with the comment that in the context of material process type, the meanings – both default and conditioned – construed by the simple present and the present continuous tense in Urdu are fairly close to that in English. This is not to say, however, that no differences exist: the above discussion has shown points of differences as well. An explicit awareness on the part of the teacher about how certain meanings are construed in the learners' mother tongue and in the 'other' target tongue is necessary for success in a foreign or second language teaching–learning situation.

6 Time and tense in the Urdu mental process

The fairly close correspondence between English and Urdu in the use of the two tenses under discussion might lull one into thinking that it is a pretty straightforward thing to teach English time and tense to the speakers of Urdu. This illusion receives a jolt as soon as we turn attention to Urdu mental process. In this section I will briefly examine mental process in Urdu, but before embarking on this, it is important to say a few words about this process type in general.

It was pointed out earlier that mental process construes our acts of sensing. For English, Halliday (1994a) has suggested three sub-types of mental process: (i) first, PERCEPTION, where the main verb refers to physical sensing of phenomena such as happens in seeing or hearing; (ii) secondly COGNITION, where the reference is to activities calling upon such mental work as *knowing, thinking, understanding, remembering, realising*, and so on; and finally (iii) there is the REACTION type,[23] where the verb refers to activities involving emotions and feelings, such as *like, hate, fear, enjoy, please, attract, repel.*

6.1 Meaning and the definition of grammatical categories

The three sub-types of mental process have been introduced above by reference to the semantics of the relevant main (i.e., lexical) verbs. However, verb classes like other grammatical categories are not based on word meaning alone; the criteria for the recognition of the process types are lexicogrammatical. In fact, despite its apparent transparency, the expression 'word meaning' is full of problems, since 'word' itself is not an easily 'pinned down' concept particularly because it has been used so freely in many different contexts. In SFL, 'word' is treated as a lexicogrammatical unit, which 'makes up' the structure of group/phrase, and can itself be analysed as made up of one or more morphemes. The lexical meaning of a word is in fact the function of a morpheme's relations to other morphemes. These relationships do not inhere in the visible/audible shape of what we popularly think of as 'word', which is really the word's spoken or written expression. Thus the same spoken (phonological) or written (orthographic) shape of a word may stand for – to use the technical term, REALIZE – different lexical meanings, while words with very different spoken (phonological) or written (orthographic) shape may realize meanings that are pretty similar. As example, consider 'words' in the three pairs (1) *strong, powerful* (2) *pretty, beautiful* (3) *honest, upright*: they do not sound or look alike but there is a good deal in common to their meaning; on the other hand the same spoken/written form *board* has different meanings in *Board of Directors*; *we will board the door* and *it was expensive to board there*.

A lexicogrammatically identified morpheme/word functions as a 'lexical item' by virtue of the meaning it is able to construe, which meaning is never fully replicated by any other lexical item of the language in question. Potentially, then, in using the concept of 'word meaning' we face two rather different problems: first, what other words whose shape is different from, say, the word *see,* realize a meaning that in some way resembles the meaning of *see* despite having a different phonological/orthographic shape; some 'words' that come to mind are such as *perceive*, *notice*, *look, watch*, *glance*, *gaze*, and it is likely that there are some other. And, the second problem is: how do we know which meaning, i.e., which lexical item is 'meant' by say the 'word' *see.* So, for example, consider the meaning of 'see' in the following clauses:

31a: I saw the man get into his car.
31b: I see that I was wrong.
31c: I see that they're upset.

The use of *see* in 31a refers to seeing with the eye; other words one might have used are *notice* and possibly *perceive*, but not *look, watch* or *gaze*. The *see* in 31b will normally be interpreted as closer in meaning to *realize* or *understand* than to any of those listed above; in fact there may be no visible material evidence for my being wrong. By contrast, in 31c the use of the same orthographic/phonological word *see* may be capable of being interpreted the way it is in 31a or in 31b: I may see with my eyes some evidence of them being upset – for example, they may be crying – or I might simply realize (by some brain work) that they are upset.

The practical relevance of this discussion at this point is that we cannot identify mental process on the basis of a verb's orthographic or phonological shape; nor by the fact that it resembles some kind of sensing activity: we have to have criteria which do not depend on the verb by itself but which depend on the relations of the verb to other grammatical relations of the clause. We operate on the principle that if mental process is a significant pattern in the organization of the clause, then this significance will be revealed by the patterned relation(s) of the clause to some other(s), or there will be some possibilities open to such a clause which may not be 'available' to clauses with other process types. That such systemic relations exist have been suggested for English (Halliday 1994a); they may or may not be applicable to Urdu for identifying mental process – an issue that will have to be kept in mind in the following discussion.

6.2 Time and tense in Urdu perception process: present continuous

The verbs used most frequently as perception process in Urdu are *deekh-naa* (to see) and *sun-na* (to hear), though there are other 'expressions' that come very close in their meaning to each of these verbs. The majority of these are formed by the use of a noun together with such verbs as *kar-na* (to do), *rakh-na* (to place/put), *Daal-na* (to place), *dhar-na* (to put), *lagaa-na* (to apply), *aa-na* (to come), *jaa-na* (to go), to which I will refer here as SUPPORTING verb. The supporting verbs in these expressions display a complex pattern of information about mood, number, person and tense as relevant, and to gender which appears to relate to the noun in question. I will refer to verbal groups of this kind (noun + supporting verb) as composite verbal group. Table 1 shows some example of composite verbal groups which realize perception process:

Table 1: Expressions with supporting verbs for deekh-na and sun-na

Expressions resembling *deekh-na*		**expressions resembling *sun-na***	
nigaah/nazar daalna	(= to look/glance)	kaan dharna	(= to listen)
aăkh/nigaah rakhna	(= to look/watch)	kaan lagaana	(= to listen)
nazar aana	(= happen to see/glance)	sunaai deena	(= to become audible)

It will be noted that the nouns used in the above composite verbal groups bear a close semantic relationship to the function of the eye or the ear. Space does not allow a detailed description of these expressions, and most of the discussion below will make use of the prototypic verbs, viz. *deekh-na* and *sun-na.*

We noted in a previous section (4.6) that in English the use of the present continuous tense with mental process requires the special condition of change in perspective. Does the same restriction apply to Urdu for perception process with the commonly used verbs *deekh-na* (to see) and *sun-na* (to hear)? Here is one example of each:

32a:	maĩ	saRak	ke paar	ek	ajiib	ciiz	deekh	rahi	hũ
	I	road	of beyond	a	strange	thing	see	ing	am

I am seeing a strange object across the road.
(= *I see something strange across the road*)

33a:	maĩ	kuch	shor	sun	rahi	hũ
	I	some	noise	hear	ing	am

I am hearing some noise.
(= *I hear some kind of noise*)

In both these cases the reference is to an on-going activity just as it is in a material process such as *Haamid khaana paka raha hai* (= Haamid is cooking food). Unlike the English clause *I am seeing stars*, the Urdu clauses appear quite normal. However, I would suggest tentatively[24] that the favoured pattern in Urdu speakers might be more inclined to use comparable clauses of the following type:

32b:	mujhe saRak kee paar eek	ajiib ciiz	dekhaai	dee	rahi	hai
	me road of beyond a	strange thing visible		give	ing	is

across the road a strange object is becoming seen/visible.
(= *I see something strange across the road*)

33b:	mujhee	ye shor baRi deer see	sunaai	dee	rahaa	hai
	me-to	this noise big time from	heard	give	ing	is

to me this noise is being audible for a long time.
(= *I have been hearing this noise for some time*)

One thing in common to all examples presented above is the presence of the continuous tense and in each case the tense has its default meaning, construing an activity which is concurrent with the moment of speaking. In other words, unlike English, there is no difference in Urdu between perception type and material type so far as present continuous tense is concerned.

In the context of material process, it was established that both in English and in Urdu present continuous tense may construe the conditioned meaning of either habituality or futurity. Is this same potential available to the Urdu present continuous in mental process of perception as well? The answer appears to be 'yes':

34a:	in	dinõ	taare	bahot	saaf	nazar	a	rahe	haĩ
	these	days	stars	very	clean	glance	come	ing	are

these days stars are being clearly visible
(= *we see the stars very clearly these days*)

34b:	in	dinõ	aap	ki	baRi	taariifeẽ	sun	rahi	hũ
	these	days	you	of	great	praise	hear	ing	am

These days I am hearing great praise of you.
(= *I hear a good deal of your praise these days*)

35a:	maĩ	kal	ek	kheel	deekh	rahi	hũ
	we	tomorrow	a	play	see	ing	am

I am seeing a good film tomorrow.
(= *I will be seeing a good film tomorrow*).

35b:	kal	ham	un	baccõ	ki	rudaad	sun	rahee	haĩ
	tomorrow	we	those	kids	of	recount	hear	ing	are

tomorrow we are hearing those kids' experiences
(= *we'll be hearing of those kids' experiences tomorrow*).

Here 34a-b construe habituality as indicated by the choice of temporal adjunct *in dinõ* (these days) while 35a-b construe futurity as indicated by the presence of *kal* (tomorrow). We noted that with the English mental process the simple present is favoured over the present continuous. The next section will examine how the simple present features with the Urdu perception processes.

6.3 Time and tense in Urdu perception process: simple present

It seems that in Urdu, clauses with perception process can use the simple present tense, and the use of the tense will construe habitual time just as it does for the material process both in English and in Urdu. This is illustrated by 36-37:

36:	maĩ	usee	har	roz	deekhti	hũ
	I	her	every	day	see	am

I see her every day.

37:	tumhaari	sharaartõ	kee	qissee	har	din	sunti	hũ
	your	mischief	of	stories	every	day	hear	am

I hear reports of your cheeky behaviour every (single) day.

Given the default meaning of the simple present tense as habitual time, temporal expressions such as *aksar* (often), *har din/roz* (every day), *rozaana* (every day), *kabhi kabhi* (some time), *amuman* (typically) etc. can be selected appropriately with this tense whether the process refers to mental perception or to some material activity. In material clauses, Urdu present tense has the following conditioned meanings: (i) past time in narratives; (ii) concurrent time in stage direction; and (iii) future time (within a specific type of clause complex as indicated in section 5.2). Are these conditioned meanings also available to perception process in Urdu? To begin with the narrative, there seems to be no problem in construing narrative past as 38a–f show:

38a:	kaamil	ko	laahaur	gae	do-hi	din	hue	thee
	Kaamil	to	Lahore	went	two-only	days	became	were

Only two days had passed since Kaamil's going to Lahore
(= Kaamil had been gone to Lahore just two days)

38b:	tiisri	shaam	sab	TV	par	**xabreẽ sun**	**rahe**	**thee**
	third	evening all	TV	on	news	hear	ing	were

on the third evening everyone was listening to the news on TV

38c:	jab	yakaayak	xabar	aai
	when	suddenly	news	came

when suddenly there was an announcement

38d:	ke	laahaur	meẽ	bam	giraa
	that	Lahore	in	bomb	fell

that there was bombing in Lahore

38e:	Kaamil	ke	maã-baap	jaise-hi	ye	xabar	suntee	haĩ
	Kaamil	of	father-mother	as soon as	this	news	hear	are

as soon as his parents hear this news

38f:	donõ	hairaan-o-pareeshaan	laahaur	ka	raasta	pakaRtee	haĩ
	both	upset-worried	in	Lahore of	road	catch	are

very upset and worried, both of them set off for Lahore

38g:	idhar	kuch	GunDee	deekhte	haĩ
	this-way	some	scoundrels	see	are

meanwhile some loafers notice

38h:	ke	ghar	xaali	paRaa	hai
	that	house	empty	lie	is

that the house is unoccupied

Only two days had passed since Kaamil had been gone to Lahore. On the third evening everyone was watching TV news when suddenly it was announced that a bomb had exploded in Lahore. As soon as his parents hear the news, they set off, very upset and worried, on the road to Lahore. Meanwhile some loafers notice that the house is unoccupied.

The example is extensive enough to show clearly that the simple present tense with what we are treating as perception type process can construe the narrative past in the same environment as that required by the material process. 39 presents an example of the simple present used to construe time in stage direction:

39a:	Zainab	zameen	par	paRa	kot	deekhti	hai
	Zainab	floor	on	lying	coat	see	is

Zainabnotices the coat lying on the floor

39b:	aur	usee	uTha	kar	kamree	see	baahar	cali	jaati	hai
	and	it	picked	do	room	from	outside	walk	go	is

and picking it up (she) walks out of the room.

Zainab notices the coat lying on the floor, picks it up and goes out of the room.

Note that time is concurrent here with stage action just as it is in this environment in both English and Urdu with material process type. Similarly in 40a-b, simple present tense construes future time, again requiring the environment of clause complex as it does with the material process (for discussion see section 5.2):

40a:	agar	mujhe	ye	kitaab	dukaan	par	nazar	a jaati hai
	if	me-to	this	book	store	at	seen	come go is

if I happen to see this book in the shop

40b:	to	maĩ	zaruur	aap	ke	liee	xariid	lũ	gi
	then	I	certainly	you	for	use	buy	take	will

I will definitely grab (a copy) for you.

If I happen to see this book in the shop, I will definitely grab a copy for you.

The discussion in 6.2 and 6.3 leads us to two observations: (i) it would appear that unlike English, Urdu does not insist on the use of the simple present tense with the mental process of perception; and (ii) so far as tense selection is concerned, there seems to be no differences between the mental and the material process clauses in Urdu. The question naturally arises: is there any reason for differentiating between the two in Urdu? If yes, on what basis? We have already rejected the meaning of the main verb as a decisive factor for identifying process type. So what other reasons are there for recognizing the category 'perception type process'? Indeed, is there a 'mental process type' in Urdu? Avoiding a detailed discussion, let me briefly indicate three other grammatical reasons in ascending order of importance.

6.4 Is there mental process in Urdu?

First, seen from the experiential point of view, process type is the nucleus of the clause: it forms the basis for establishing what categories of THING can have the participant roles of 'DO-ER' and of 'DONE-TO' (Halliday 1994a); it helps predict the range of circumstances that might apply to a process type (Hasan 1985b, 1987a). Since mental activities are activities of sensing, the process calls for the role of SENSER – as the –ER participant: a Thing capable of sensing must 'be' conscious. The classes of Thing to be sensed – i.e. the –ED role, known as PHENOMENON – is, by contrast, wide, including Thing classes that are concrete or abstract, material or semiotic. By contrast, in material process, the Actor may be animate or inanimate, conscious or not while the Goal is limited to being material. Consider the following example:

41a: is saal qahet ne bahot logõ ko barbaad kiya
this year drought many people to destroy did
this year drought has destroyed many people

41b: *qahet ne bahot logõ ko deekha
drought many people to saw
drought saw many people

Here 41a is a normal Urdu clause but 41b is definitely odd; *qahet* is not a conscious Thing, so *deekhna*, a mental process of perception, cannot be ascribed to it. The Senser function in the Urdu examples of perception is realized by a nominal group whose Thing refers to some conscious entity (for other mental types see Table 3).

Secondly, Halliday (1994a: 116–19) has shown that the English mental processes can be represented 'as two-way processes; that is to say, we can say either *Mary liked the gift* or *the gift pleased Mary*'. So it is reasonable to ask: is such pairing also present in Urdu mental clauses? In the absence of a comprehensive SF grammar of Urdu, the statements offered below are to be taken tentatively. However, two such pairs have already been presented above (section 6.2: examples 32a and 32b which form one pair, and 33a and 33b, form the other). Here Table 2 reproduces Halliday's list of some pairs in mental process (1994a: 117; Table 5(3)). Before comparing Urdu pairs with the English ones, I provide comparable instances of Urdu mental process pairs in Table 3.

Table 2: Some English paired verbs used in two-way processes

Process: mental: reaction		Process: mental: cognition	
Like type*please* type		*like* type *please* type	
I like it	it pleases me	I forget it	it escapes me
I fear it	it frightens me	I notice it	it strikes me
I wonder at it	it amazes me	I believe it	it convinces me
I don't understand it	it puzzles me	I admire it	it impresses me
I enjoy it	it delights me	I mind it	it upsets me

Table 3: Urdu mental process: the *maĩ/mujhe* types

A: (i) *maĩ*-type: Perception	**B: (i) *mujhe*-type: Perception**
Maĩ use deekh rehi hũ *I am seeing him* Maĩ shor sunti hũ *I hear (some) noise*	Mujhe wo dikhai de raha hai *he is appearing in my vision* Mujhe shor sunai deta hai *the noise is being audible to me*
(ii) *maĩ*-type: Reaction	**(ii) *mujhe*- type: Reaction**
Maĩ use pasand karti hũ *I like him* Maĩ ye makaan pasand karti hũ *I like this house*	Mujhe wo pasand aata hai *he is likeable to me* Mujhe ye makaan pasand aata hai *this house is likeable to me*
(iii) *maĩ*-type: Cognition	**(iii) *mujhe*-type: Cognition**
Maĩ ne use yaad kiya *I remembered him* Maĩ aap ki baat samjhi hũ *I understand what you are saying*	Mujhe wo yaad aaya *he come to my mind* Mujhe aapki baat samajh (mẽ) aai *your words make sense to me*

The translation of clauses in column A of Table 3 appears quite straightforward; for clauses in column B, it is difficult to provide an idiomatic translation without better knowledge of co-text and context. The pairing here works on a principle different from that in Halliday's examples (see Table 2), and since the clause structure in column 2 of Table 3 is foreign to English, translation is pretty problematic. In unpacking what is going on in Table 2, we note each member of the pair here has a different *lexical* verb, but the principle underlying the difference remains constant from one pair to the next. This is the principle of 'converse-ness': what can function as Subject and Complement in one member of the pair will have to be reversed in the other one. Thus in the first column of Table 2, the English Subject/Senser is realized by the nominal item *I*, and Complement/Phenomenon by *it*. This arrangement is reversed with the change of the lexical verb, so that in the second column, *it* becomes Subject/Phenomenon while *me* is Complement/Sensor.

Turning to the Urdu examples in Table 3, the lexical verb of each pair remains the same, but the *form* of the verbal group changes, though, notably, the outcome of the change in the form of the verbal group is the same for the Urdu mental clause as that produced in English by the lexical change. In column 1 of Table 3, with the *maĩ*-type clauses, Senser/Subject is *maĩ* (1st person singular pronoun: form nominative) while Phenomenon/Complement is realized by a nominal group that is (= (to) him; 3rd person pronoun: accusative case). This relationship is turned around in column 2 of Table 3, which exemplifies the *mujhe*-type clause: here nominal groups such as *wo, tum, ye makaan, shor* (all 3rd person[25] pronoun; nominative case), function as Subject/Phenomenon while *mujhe* is Complement/Senser. The base form of the main verb is *dikhai dena* (literally, to become visible); this, in a manner of speaking, robs 'agentive power' from participants of the process. As I see it, in the *mujhe-type* clause the Senser has little or no volition: the activity is as unplanned and accidental as, for example, falling down. By contrast, in the *maĩ-type* clause the process *describes* the sensing done by the Senser – only co-text/context will clarify whether the act of sensing was pre-planned or non-volitional.

The *maĩ- mujhe*-type pairing is specific to the Urdu mental process clause. We do find clause types in Urdu which in some respect might look close to the *mujhe*-type, such as for example *mujhe takliif hui* (to me inconvenience happened = I was inconvenienced); but *takliif* is not a Phenomenon; rather, I would suggest tentatively it is an attribute (for discussion Hasan 1972). Nor is the *mujhe*-type clause an ordinary passive of clauses such as *mai ne us ko deekha* (I him saw = I saw him): a genuine passive of this clause actually exists, and its counterpart may be found in all process types. So passive type is neither specific to the mental process clause, nor is the form of the passive identical with the clause referred to as *mujhe*-type. Thus for the active material process clause *Haamid kitaab paRh raha hai* (cf. example 8a, section 4.1), the passive is *kitaab paRhi ja rahi hai* (book read is being = (the) book is being read); for the clause *mai ne us ko deekha* (example 1, Table 3), the passive is *wo deekha gayaa* (he seen was = he was seen). The difference between the latter and *mujhe wo dikhai diia* is quite obvious. Given the frequent use of ellipsis, the *mujhe*-type clause may occur simply as *haã, dikhai diia* (*yes, was visible*, as perhaps response to: *did you see the man*) but the potential of the clause's expansion with the appropriate functions of Senser (e.g., *mujhe*) and Phenomenon (e.g., wo) is beyond question.

The upshot of this discussion is that Urdu grammar offers two good reasons for the recognition of mental process: first, a mental process clause 'must have' a Senser and a Phenomenon; and Senser must be realized by some nominal that refers to a being with consciousness,[26] while phenomenon may be concrete or abstract, conscious or unconscious, countable or uncountable. This requirement is met by the kind of Urdu mental process clauses we have so far considered. Secondly, mental processes come in pairs: the discussion above has shown that there is a pairing pattern specific to the mental process in Urdu. It is not an exact image of the pairing found in English, but in both cases, in one member of the pair the sensing act is involuntary, and that member is the one where the Senser function is conflated with the Complement function.

According to Halliday, a third characteristic associated with mental process clauses in English is that they have the potential to project, which is to say they 'usher in' at least one clause which (i) in the case of mental process represents a thought, a percept or a reaction of the Senser and (ii) which is capable of realizing a message function such as statement, question, command, denial and other such functions. Of course more clauses may be ushered in; if so, they would be either linked to the last mentioned or in some way modify it. An example would be:

42:	mai ne	samjha	tha	ke	tu	hai	to	daraxshaa	hai	hayaat
	I	understood	had	that	you	are	then	galaxy	is	life

I had thought that since you were there life would bright as a galaxy

This line from a Faiz poem has three clauses (1) *mai ne samjha tha* (I had thought) (2) *ke tu hai* (that since you are [there]) (3) *to daraxshaa hai hayaat* (therefore life would be bright like a galaxy). Clause (1) is projecting; (2) and (3) are projected, where (2) furnishes the basis for the prediction in (3). The projecting clause here has the mental process of cognition. But this pattern of projection is open in Urdu to the other two kinds of mental clauses as well, as the following clause complexes show:

43: acaanak ham ne deekha ke hamaare saamnee ek choTi si waadii hai
suddenly we saw that us in front of a small-ish valley is
Suddenly we noticed that in front of us was a miniature valley

44: ye aise calti hai ke mujhe Dar lagtaa hai gir na paRe
she so walks is that to me fear seems is fall not might
she walks in such a way that I fear (she) might fall down

In 43 the first clause has a perception process *deekha*, which projects the second *ek choTi si waadii hai*. In 44 the second clause has the reaction process *Dar lagnaa* (fear feel) and the clause it projects is *she might fall down*. It is worth pointing out that perception and cognition process clauses are more likely to project than reaction type. Further, the possibility of projection cannot be taken as critical evidence for treating a process as mental type, since projection is also associated with verbal process and with certain kinds of attributive processes e.g., *mai bahot xush hu ke aap mere ghar aae* (I very happy am that you my house came = I am so happy you are visiting us).

6.5 English tense and English time in a foreign environment

The discussion above seems to suggest strongly that there are reasonable grounds for recognizing mental process in Urdu. SFL research on the grammar of languages other than English[27] has shown that (i) the category of mental process needs to be recognized to account for the facts of the language, even where those languages belong to families distinct from that to which English belongs; and (ii) that not surprisingly, the details of the grammar of mental processes vary from language to language. It would be surprising if Urdu alone stood out as an exception by having no mental process in its grammar or that it replicated the pattern of any other language completely. One respect in which Urdu mental clauses vary a good deal from the English ones is the use of tense. In section 6.2, I showed that the choice of tense in Urdu clauses with perception process remains the same as for material process – especially with regard to the simple present and present continuous. What seems to complicate matters further is perhaps the fact that with Urdu mental process it is not very clear in certain environments what difference it makes in Urdu to use one of these tenses as opposed to the other. Compare for example the following, where the difference in meaning, if there is some, is very subtle:

45a:	maĩ	aap ki	baat	samajhti	hũ	
	I	your	saying	understand	am	
	I understand what you are telling me					
45b:	maĩ	aap ki	baat	samajh	rahi	hũ
	I	your	saying	understand	ing	am
	I am understanding what you are telling me.					

It is my impression that perhaps 45b would be used more often than 45a, but it is not clear to me whether the tenses are truly interchangeable: scholars such as Firth would say this uncertainty only goes to show that more research is needed since they believed that a change in wording necessarily implies a change in meaning. Meanwhile, in the stereotyping of what is called 'Pakistani English', the clause *I am knowing* is as common an identifier of that dialect as *I am interesting* (instead of *it interests me*) is for some other Asian varieties of English. So far as the Urdu speaker is concerned 'I am knowing' is a good translation of *maĩ samajh rahi hũ*. Urdu after all does not differentiate between material and mental process types by tense choice.

The difference in the use of the two tenses that we have noted between English and Urdu in the context of mental process is significant. The recognition of World Englishes notwithstanding, differences of this kind – and in looking carefully at my translations the reader might note what a large list of such differences can be compiled across languages even as familiar to each other as English is to its ex-colonials – as they multiply most probably create a significant difference to the quality of meaning exchange: for, indeed, quantity does become quality quite regularly. The probability that 'small' differences here and there between Urdu and English would cause problems in efficient communication turns significantly closer to reality when we note that in the teaching of the simple present and present continuous tenses, as in the teaching of any aspect of the form of language, two principles seem to operate in the selection of materials to be taught: (i) distance the content of language teaching from the experiences of the learners' life; and (ii) avoid grammar pedagogy: it is thought to be bad both for the learner and the teacher! Let me briefly elaborate my harsh comments. The life lived by ordinary people in ordinary circumstances is full of variety, which implies that every one of us deals with different varieties of language: how much of that variety is brought into the classroom? The examination of text books favoured by the educational system of Pakistan would give a good answer to this question. Think of the two tenses that are discussed in this paper: when we come to teaching them we often restrict ourselves to the material process alone, as if activities of thinking, saying, being are unfamiliar, difficult to understand, or not likely to have any importance in the student's life: the focus remains resolutely on material processes, as if they are the ones that matter most. Even for a teacher capable of explaining phenomena of the type discussed above there is no occasion for bringing in awareness of such problems.

Teaching any language in the absence of an understanding of its grammar as a resource for meaning brings teachers and students alike to unsettling experiences. Teachers are sometimes told: all children learn their mother tongue; no one teaches them any grammar. The implication is that therefore grammar teaching is not necessary in the context of language teaching. But when children learn their mother tongue, they do this in the environments of their life through interaction with people who are close to them and who are aware of their needs and semiotic habits: speaking is an integral part of the total interactive enterprise. In the process of learning the mother tongue children internalize the grammar of their mother tongue. This process of internalization is at its most successful only where the language in the interaction flows seamlessly with the flow of the activities of life: and in this environment the focus is on meaning. For children, learning the mother tongue is learning how to mean (Halliday 1975a). Children do not learn grammar in the sense of coming to know it as a set of rules: instead, what they are doing is to say things to the best of their ability in the way that those things are said in their community – which is to say they are internalizing how wording makes meaning, and which meaning is appropriate where. For the teacher it is not enough to just internalize a grammar which is what the speakers of a language do: unlike the children learning their mother tongue, the teacher needs to be able to tell those around her in the classroom – i.e., her pupils – how to use wording so as to make meaning in such a way that the meanings are able to be understood. It is for this reason that the teacher must know the grammar, not by internalization alone, but by being able to externalize, i.e., speaking so as to show how grammar works, how the putting of words together achieves some meaning, and what difference is made to that meaning if some change in wording is brought about. Grammar is not about grammaticality; it is about elements of language functioning as a resource for meaning. This is why if someone teaches grammar in the old sense as a rule in isolation from its function in making meaning, this will turn out to be a waste of time and energy. Learning the so-called rules of grammar without relating them systematically to meaning is a waste of time; and talking about meaning without showing how you do it by putting words together is to deprive pupils of understanding; it is to deny them the power of reflection on how meanings are transacted in their community.

Teachers have perhaps not reflected enough on the curious business of teaching language – be it mother tongue or other tongue. It is worth noting that no one would be allowed to teach maths, physics, chemistry or indeed any so-called 'discipline' unless s/he has knowledge of the subject. It is only in language teaching that knowing about language is regarded with such disdain: if you are a native speaker you can walk into a class and teach your mother tongue. While the technology of language teaching grows by leaps and bounds, and feel-good phrases abound about teaching 'whole language' or the merits of the various novel methods of teaching engage attention, we pay no attention to what makes a language what it is, ignoring how and why language works in the life of its speakers – in short, we ignore its functional nature. Naturally, I am not implying that teaching technology, modern modes of assessment, daily changing methods of presentation and other aspects of language teaching should be ignored. But the fact remains: no matter how excellent our techniques of presentation, if what is presented is itself not well-founded, if it does not do justice to how language works, then the usefulness of the excellent techniques is thrown into doubt.

Appendix 1: transcription conventions

The following conventions have been used for transcribing Urdu in Roman script.

a	*as in Urdu word*	ab	*meaning*	now
aa		aaj		today
ai		hai		is
au		aur		and
bh		bhaag		run!
c		caar		four
ch		chaap		print!
d		do		two
dh		dho		wash
D		Daal		twig

Dh	Dhaak	cover
e	se	from
ee	eek	one
G	Gam	sorrow
i	is	this
ii	tiin	three
j	jaa	go!
kh	khaa	eat!
o	do	two
ph	phal	fruit
q	waqt	time
R	baRi	big (fem.)
Rh	paRh	read!
sh	shaam	evening
t	tiin	three
th	thaali	plate
T	kaaT	cut!
u	hũ	am
uu	phuul	flower
x	xuun	blood
~	haĩ	are

Notes

1 An abridged version of this chapter was published in the *SPELT Newsletter*, Vol X. No. 4 December 1995, as a record of the plenary talk presented at the 11th annual conference of the Society of Pakistani English Language Teachers (SPELT) in Karachi in 1995. This chapter has been further revised (i) to clarify the translation of certain patterns in Urdu examples for readers who are not familiar with that language; and (ii) to include the use of some descriptive and theoretical terminology developed over the years in Systemic Functional linguistics. This I had mostly avoided in my original presentation.

2 The theory used for the description presented here is Halliday's Systemic Functional Linguistics (SFL), and it is his *Introduction to Functional Grammar* (1994a) that forms the point of departure for my analysis. I alone am responsible for the details of the description of Urdu presented here.

3 There is of course a small segment of the community amongst whom English is the language used at home.

4 To avoid confusion, throughout this chapter the learner will be referred to as *he* and the teacher as *she*.

5 I choose Urdu because being a native speaker of that language I 'know' it better than any other language on the Indo-Pakistani Sub-continent, which must be taken as an adverse reflection on the educational system prevalent in the northern states of the imperial colony that was India: in a country rich

in indigenous languages, most members of my generation educated in Uttar Pradesh remained unacquainted with languages of the country other than their own mother tongue!

6 The transcription conventions for the transliteration of Urdu items are reproduced as an appendix at the end of this chapter together with examples. In numbered Urdu examples, a 'literal' i.e., word rank English translation is given first, though affixes are not identified; and an idiomatic translation is provided in the next line where, ellipsis is resolved by placing the missing words within parentheses. Note also that in the Urdu examples the proper nouns are transcribed following the Firth and Harley framework.

7 By 'synthetically coded' I mean an indivisible lexical item construing some meaning, unlike phrases such as 'day after tomorrow' where each orthographic unit has a meaning of its own and together they refer to something which is not exactly the sum of those meanings.

8 It is my perception that the items *narsõ* and *atarsõ* do not often appear in the speech of Pakistani Urdu speakers; they might be passively recognized by the older generation, especially those who migrated to Pakistan in the late 1940s.

9 This formulation encourages a *false* assumption that items of language are either lexical or grammatical. Linguistic items are both lexical and grammatical at the same time, or better still, the same item may be examined from the perspective of its lexical function and from that of grammar: these functions are complementary (Halliday 2008). This is one reason why in Systemic Functional Linguistics (SFL) we speak of lexicogrammar rather than just grammar or lexis.

10 The word may be used metonymically as in *Today, adolescents would not tolerate such restrictions*; here *today* refers to the contemporary age rather than the day of speech.

11 *Dawn* is a prominent Pakistani newspaper.

12 With hindsight, it now appears that the stage direction is register sensitive 'instruction': it can always be paraphrased as 'it is required that the named activity should occur as the speech event unfolds'. Thus consider the following in Stoppard's *Arcadia* (p. 25):

> Hannah: So he did. What a stroke of luck. (*Softening.*) Thank you, Bernard.
> (*She goes to the reading stand and opens Noake's sketch book.*)
> Look – there he is.
> (*Bernard goes to look.*)
> Bernard: Mmm.

If this suggestion is correct, then a radical departure from the function of the simple present tense will have to be recognized – namely that of the anticipated time of an imperative (Tom Stoppard, *Arcadia* (London, Faber and Faber, 1993)).

13 For a fairly detailed discussion of English process types, see Halliday 1994a; Matthiessen 1995. For advanced discussion, see Halliday 1967–68.

14 Several points need to be made here about Urdu language to explain the working of the translation in this example. (1) In English the preposition '*to*' in the locative expression *to the clinic* is obligatory; in Urdu, the presence or

absence of *ko*, the equivalent of 'to', is a matter of geographical dialect, hence the parenthesis around it; (2) Urdu has no morpheme/word rank equivalent for English *the* (for discussion Hasan 1984a); (3) the Urdu verb *jana* is not as specific in its meaning as the English verb *walk*: to walk is to use your legs, whereas *jana* can be done either by *car, taxi, gaRi,* or *pəydal*. In an idiomatic translation, it is therefore necessary to add the word *pəydal* which means 'on foot'. (4) The default condition of the Urdu verbal group is to 'agree' with the PERSON, NUMBER and GENDER of the nominal group functioning as SUBJECT. Note finally (5) the difference in the order of the groups and phrases: in English, in a declarative clause the main verbal group typically follows the Subject nominal group; in Urdu the verbal group is typically but not always the last element of the clause.

15 The English translation of the title is Our (Social) Environment.

16 The internal form of the infinitive verb in Urdu is 'Root+naa' as indicated by the following, the first five of which have been taken from example 19:

uTh+na,	to wake up/get up	*paRh+na,*	to read
nikal+na,	to take out/extract	*guundh+na*	to knead
dee+na,	to give	*jaa+na,*	to go
so+na,	to sleep	*pii+na,*	to drink

When *–ti/ta hai* is joined to the verb stem, it acts as an auxiliary verb, indicative of the simple present tense in Urdu. It is the primary auxiliary of the verbal group that is indicative of person (in example 14, 3rd person) gender (here, feminine) and number (here, singular) of the nominal group with the function of Subject. Note that Subject ellipsis is a default pattern in Urdu clauses: Subject (*Shanaaz* in 19) is here anaphorically presupposed, though cataphoric or exophoric presupposition of Subject ellipsis is also possible; its value as a cohesive device in Urdu is pretty close to pronominal reference in English. Subject ellipsis must be recognized in Urdu as this assumption forms the basis for the choice of person, number and gender concord in the clause where it occurs. And the concord of the main verb with Subject is itself obligatory in all finite clauses except those with *nee* (Hasan 1972, 1984a).

17 The language is highly idiomatic here. *Phuul caRhana* refers to a devotional ritual activity in which the devotee actually raises the offering, here flowers, moving it around the head of the image being worshipped – whether it is a picture, painting or sculpture of the worshipped being. Thus put in a 'straightforward' language, the question is: why do you worship me?

18 The English lexical items 'lunch' and 'dinner' refer to meals taken at different times of the day; in Urdu, no single lexical equivalent for these terms exists. If one wished to specify the time, the expression *rat ka khaana* for 'dinner' or *dopahar/din ka khaana* for 'lunch' would be used. However, the idiomatic translation of 'dinner' here would be just *khaana*; the time information being inferred on the basis of the moment of speaking.

19 23a-h is adapted from the original (*Talaash* by Mumtaaz Mufti. Lahore: Al-Faisal Nashran, 2006: 198).

20 The Urdu translation equivalent of the verb 'to help' is *madad* (= help) + *karna* (=to do). Many main verbs in Urdu are formed by adding an adjective or a

noun to some verbs whose only function in the verbal group is to 'carry' tense and other concord features of number, gender, and person. The most common of such verbs is *karna* (to do). Some examples: with adjective: *saaf karna* (to clean), *pareshaan karna* (to worry (someone)), *Thiik karna* (to correct); and some with noun: *harkat karna* (to act/behave/move), *shirkat karna* (to participate), *tariif karna* (to praise), *buraii karna* (to bad-mouth), etc. Other verbs, functioning in the manner of *karna* are *deena* (to give), *leena* (to take), *hona* (to be/become); *karna* has the distinction that it can be combined with the latter three, e.g., *kamra saaf kar do* (room clean do give = clean up the room).

21 The English word 'picture' has been borrowed in Urdu (pronounced as *pikcar*) and is often used instead of its Urdu equivalent *taswiir*.

22 Without more co-textual information, it is impossible to determine whether the gender is masculine or feminine, since in colloquial Urdu the form *rahe haĩ* can relate to either.

23 The term 'reaction' mental process was abandoned in Halliday 1994a, which refers to this process type as 'affection'. I prefer to use the earlier term as it is wider than affection, and is neutral in connotation.

24 This statement is based on a casual glance into a small set of Urdu writings. It would be interesting to check this initial impression by examining large Urdu corpora.

25 In fact, 3rd person is something of a red herring here; what is important is the case-shift; it is irrelevant whether the pro-noun is 1st, 2nd or 3rd person.

26 This typically implies 'human'. The word 'typically' is deliberately chosen. A clause such as *the butterfly considered the problem* is not ungrammatical; it simply makes one think of a context that belongs in the sphere of children's stories. By contrast, *Given the incentive, the chimpanzee solved the puzzle* could be a sentence from a report on primate intelligence.

27 A small selection of such references: Cafferel (1997, 2006); Li (2007); Teruya (2007).

References

Abercrombie, D. (1965) *Studies in Phonetics and Linguistics*. London: Oxford University Press.

Albrow, K. H. (1972) *The English Writing System: Notes towards a Description*. London: Longman.

Andersen, E. S. (1986) The acquisition of register variation in Anglo-American children. In B. B. Schieffelin and E. Ochs (eds) *Language Socialisation across Cultures*. London: Cambridge University Press.

Annan, K. A. (1999) Making globalization work for the poor. *The News*, 15 December.

Apple, M. W. (2002) Does education have independent power? Bernstein and the picture of relative autonomy. *British Journal of Sociology of Education* 23.4: Special Issue: *Basil Bernstein's Theory of Social Class, Educational Codes and Social Control*, 607–616.

Austin, J. L. (1962) *How to Do Things with Words: The William James Lectures Delivered at Harvard University 1955*, edited by J. O. Urmson and M. Sbisa. Oxford: Clarendon. Later editions 1975, 1980.

Bachman, L. F. (1990) *Fundamental Considerations in Language Testing*. Oxford: Oxford University Press.

Barnes, B. (1974) *Knowledge and Sociological Theory*. London: Routledge and Kegan Paul.

Basso, K. (1980) Review of Jack Goody (ed.), The Domestication of the Savage Mind. *Language in Society* 9: 72–80.

Bateson, G. (1972) *Steps to an Ecology of Mind*. New York: Ballantine.

Beck, J. (2002) The sacred and the profane in recent struggles to promote official pedagogic identities. *BJSE* 23.4: *Special Issue: Basil Bernstein's Theory of Social Class, Educational Codes and Social Control*, 617–626.

Beckett, F. (1999) Professor of large profits. *The Guardian Weekly*: Book Review, 7-13 October.

Berger, P. L. and Luckman, T. (1966) *The Social Construction of Reality*. Harmondsworth: Penguin.

Bernstein, B. (1959) A public language: some sociological implications of linguistic form. *British Journal of Sociology* XI: 311–326. Reprinted in Bernstein 1971c.

Bernstein, B. (1971a) Classification and framing of educational knowledge. In M. F. D. Young (ed.) *Knowledge and Control*. London: Collier-Macmillan. Reprinted in Bernstein 1971c.

Bernstein, B. (1971b) 'A critique of the concept of compensatory education'. In A. H. Passow (ed.) *Improving Opportunities for the Disadvantaged*. Columbia University: Teachers College Press, 1969. Reprinted in Bernstein 1971c.

Bernstein, B. (1971c) *Class, Codes and Control, Vol 1: Theoretical Studies towards a Sociology of Language*. London: Routledge and Kegan Paul.

Bernstein, B. (1972) A sociolinguistic approach to socialization: with some reference to educability. In J. J. Gumperz and D. Hymes (eds.) *Directions in Sociolinguistics: The Ethnography of Communication*. London: Blackwell.

Bernstein, B. (ed.) (1973) *Class, Codes and Control, Vol 2: Applied Studies towards the Sociology of Language*. London: Routledge and Kegan Paul.

Bernstein, B. (1975a) On the classification and framing of educational knowledge. In R. Brown (ed.) *Knowledge, Education and Cultural Change*. London: Tavistock. Reprinted in Bernstein, 1975b.

Bernstein, B. (1975b) *Class, Codes and Control, Vol 3: Towards a Theory of Educational Transmissions* (2nd edition). London: Routledge and Kegan Paul.

Bernstein, B. (1986) On pedagogic discourse. In J. G. Richardson (ed.) *Handbook of Theory and Research in the Sociology of Education*. London: Greenwood.

Bernstein, B. (1987) Elaborated and restricted codes: an overview 1958–85. In U. Ammon, N. Dittmar, and K. J. Mattheier (eds.) *Sociolinguisitcs/Soziolinguistik: An International Handbook, Vol 1*. Berlin: W. de Gruyter.

Bernstein, B. (1990) *The Structuring of Pedagogic Discourse: Class, Codes and Control, Vol 4*. London: Routledge.

Bernstein, B. (1996) *Pedagogy, Symbolic Control and Identity: Theory Research Critique*. London: Taylor & Francis.

Bernstein, B. (1999) Vertical and horizontal discourse: an essay. *British Journal of Sociology of Education* 20.2: 157–173.

Bernstein, B. (2000) *Pedagogy, Symbolic Control and Identity: Theory, Research, Critique* (Revised edition). London: Rowman & Littlefield.

Bernstein, B. (2001) Video conference with Basil Bernstein. In A. Morais, I. Neves, B. Davies and H. Daniels (eds.), *Towards a Sociology of Pedagogy: The Contribution of Basil Bernstein to Research*. New York: Peter Lang.

Bohr, N. (1961) *Atomic Physics and Human Knowledge*. Science Editions: New York.

Bolinger, D. (1975) *Aspects of Language*. New York: Harcourt Brace Jovanvich.

Bourdieu, P. (1992) *Language and Symbolic Power*. Cambridge: Polity Press.

Bourdieu, P. and Passeron J.-C. (1977) *Reproduction in Education, Society and Culture* (2nd edn). London: Sage.

Bowcher, W. (2010) The history and theoretical development of Context of Situation in Systemic Functional Linguistics. *Annual Review of Functional Linguistics*, Vol 2: 64–93.

Brown, R. (1973) *A First Language: The Early Stages*. Cambridge, MA: Harvard University Press.

Brown, R. and Lenneberg, E. H. (1954) A study in language and cognition. *Journal of Abnormal and Social Psychology* 49(3).

Bruner, J. K. (1975) The ontogenesis of speech acts. *Journal of Child Language* 2(1): 1–19.

Bullowa, M. (ed.) (1979) *Before Speech*. Cambridge: Cambridge University Press.

Burnaby, B. and Sun, Y. (1989) Chinese teachers' view of Western language teaching: context informs paradigms. *TESOL Quarterly* 23(2): 219–238.

Butt, D. (1983) Semantic drift in verbal art. *Australian Review of Applied Linguistics* 6(1): 38–48.

Butt, D. (1985) *Talking and Thinking: The Patterns of Behaviour*. Geelong: Deakin University Press.

Butt, D. (1988) Randomness, order and the latent patterning of text. In D. Birch and M. O'Toole (eds.) *Functions of Style*. London: Pinter.

Butt, D. (1989) The object of language. In R. Hasan and J. R. Martin (eds) *Language Development: Learning Language, Learning Culture*. Norwood, NJ: Ablex.

Butt, D. (2004) *Parameters of Context: On Establishing the Similarities and Differences between Social Processes*. Sydney: Macquarie University Centre for Language in Social Life (mimeo).

Butt, D. (2005) Method and imagination in Halliday's science of linguistics. In R. Hasan, C. Matthiessen and J. Webster (eds) *Continuing Discourse on Language: Functional perspectives*, Vol 1. London: Equinox.

Butt, D. G., Fahey, R., Spinks, S. and Yallop, C. (1995) *Using Functional Grammar: An Explorer's Guide*. Sydney: Macquarie University.

Butt, D. and Lukin, A. (2009) Stylistic analysis: construing aesthetic organization. In M. A. K. Halliday and J. J. Webster (eds) *Continuum Companion to Systemic Functional Linguistics*. London: Continuum.

Butt, D. G and Wegener, R. K. A. (2007) The work of concepts: context and metafunctions in the systemic functional model. In R. Hasan, C. Matthiessen and J. Webster (eds) *Continuing Discourse on Language: Functional Perspectives*, Vol 2. London: Equinox.

Cafferel, A. (1997) Models of transitivity in French: a systemic functional interpretation. In A.-M. Simon-Vandenbergen, K. Davidse and D. Noël (eds) *Reconnecting Language: Morphology and Syntax in Functional Perspective*. Amsterdam: Benjamins.

Cafferel, A. (2006) *A Systemic Functional Grammar of French: From Grammar to Discourse.* London: Continuum.

Canale, M. and Swain M. (1980) Theoretical bases of communicative approaches to second language teaching and testing. *Applied Linguistics* 1(1): 1–47.

Candlin, C. N. (1989) Language, culture and curriculum. In C. N. Candlin and T. F. McNamara (eds) *Language, Learning and Community.* Sydney: Macquarie University, NCELTR.

Candlin, C. N. (1991) Introduction. In *Planning Language, Planning Inequality: Language Policy in the Community* by J. W. Tollefson. London: Longman.

Cassidy, D. C. (1992) *Uncertainty. The life and Science of Werner Heisenberg*. New York: W. H. Freeman and Co.

Chomsky, N. (1957) *Syntactic Structures*. The Hague: Mouton & Co.

Chomsky, N. (1965) *Aspects of the Theory of Syntax*. Cambridge, MA: MIT Press.

Christakis, N. and Fowler J. (2010) *Connected: The Amazing Power of Social Networks and How They Shape Our Lives*. London: Harper Press.

Christie, F. (1988) The construction of knowledge in the primary school. In L. Gerot, J. Oldenburg, and T. van Leeuwen (eds) *Language and Socialisation: Home and School: Proceedings from the Working Conference on Language in Education*, Macquarie University 17–21 November, 1986. Sydney: Macquarie University.

Christie, F. (ed.) (1991) *Literacy in Social Processes: Papers from the Inaugural Conference of the Australian Systemic Functional Association.* Darwin: Centre for the Studies of Language in Education, Northern Territory University.

Christie, F. (1999) *Pedagogy and the Shaping of Consciousness: Linguistic and Social Processes*. London: Cassell.

Christie, F. and Martin J. R. (eds) (2007) *Language, Knowledge and Pedagogy: Functional Linguistics and Pedagogical Perspectives*. London: Continuum.

Chukovsky, K. (1971) *From Two to Five*. Berkeley: University of California Press.

Cloran, C. (1982) The Role of Language in Negotiating New Contexts.

Unpublished Dissertation, B.A. Hons, Macquarie University, Department of Linguistics.

Cloran, C. (1989) Learning through language: the social construction of gender. In R. Hasan and J. R. Martin (eds).

Cloran, C. (1994) *Rhetorical Units and Decontextualisation: An Enquiry into Some Relations of Meaning and Grammar.* Nottingham University: Department of English Studies (Monograph in Systemic Linguistics, No. 6).

Cloran, C. (1999a) Contexts for learning. In F. Christie (ed.) *Pedagogy and the Shaping of Consciousness: Linguistic and Social Processes*. London: Cassell.

Cloran, C. (1999b) Context, material situation and text. In M. Ghadessy (ed.) Amsterdam: Benjamins.

Cloran, C. (2005) The register genre debate. Paper presented at the International Systemic Functional Conference, 17–22 July; University of Sydney.

Cohen, J. and I. Stewart (1994) *The Collapse of Chaos: Discovering Simplicity in a Complex World*. London: Penguin.

Cohen, M. (2005) *Wittgenstein's Beatle and Other Thoughts Experiments*. Carlton, Vic: Blackwell.

Conkey, M. (1996) A history of the interpretation of European 'paleolithic art': magic, mythogram and metaphor for modernity. In A. Lock and C. R. Peters (eds) *A Handbook of Human Symbolic Evolution*. Oxford: Blackwell.

Cook, G. (1990) Transcribing infinity: problems of context presentation. *Journal of Pragmatics* 14.1: 1–24.

Collini, S. (2000) Is this the end of the world? *The Guardian Weekly*, 6–12 June: 11.

Cornwell, J. (2008) Game Over (a feature article on Susan Greenfield). *Good Weekend*, 12 June, 43–47.

Crosby, A. W. (1997) *The Measure of Reality: Quantification and Western Society, 1250–1600*. Cambridge: Cambridge University Press.

Cross, M. (1991) Choice in text: a systemic approach to computer modelling of variant text production. Unpublished doctoral dissertation, Department of Linguistics, Macquarie University.

Culler, J. (1976) *Saussure*. Modern Master Series. London: Fontana/Collins.

Damasio, A. (2000) *The Feeling of What Happens: Body, Emotions and the Making of Consciousness*. London: Vintage.

Davidse, K. (1987) M. A. K. Halliday's Functional Grammar and the Prague School. In R. Dirven and V. Fried (eds) *Functionalism in Linguistics*. Amsterdam: Benjamins.

Day, R. S. (1971) Systematic individual differences in information processing. *Psychology and Life 5A-5D.*

Deacon, T. (1997) *The Symbolic Species: The Co-evolution of Language and the Human Brain*. London: Penguin Books.

Dewitt, R. (2004) *Worldviews: An introduction to the History and Philosophy of Science*. Oxford: Blackwell.

Dirven, R. and Fried, V. (eds) (1987) *Functionalism in Linguistics: LLSEE 20.* Amsterdam: Benjamins.

Doise, W. and Mugny, G. (1984) *The Social Development of the Intellect.* Oxford: Pergamon Press.

Donaldson, M. (1978) *Children's Minds*. London: Fontana.

Donaldson, M. (1992) *Human Minds: An Exploration*. London: Penguin.

Dore, J. (1977) Children's illocutionary acts. In R. Freedle (ed.) *Discourse: Comprehension and Production*,. Hillsdale, NJ: Lawrence Erlbaum.

Douglas, M. (1970) *Natural Symbols*. London: Barrie & Rockcliff, The Cresset Press.

Douglas, M. (1971) In the nature of things. Inaugural Lecture, University College London. Reprinted in Douglas, 1975.

Douglas, M. (1972) Self-evidence. The Henry Myers Lecture 1972, given for the Royal Anthropological Institute. Reprinted in Douglas, 1975.

Douglas, M. (1975) *Implicit Meanings: Essays in Anthropology*. London: Routledge and Kegan Paul.

Dulay, H. and Burt, M. (1973) Should we teach children syntax? *Language Learning* 24: 245–258.

Dumont, R. V. (1972) Learning English and how to be silent: studies in Sioux and Cherokee classroom. In C. B. Cazden, V. P. John and D. Hymes (eds.) *Functions of Language in the Classroom*. New York: Columbia University Press.

Durkheim, E. (1938) *L'Evolution Pedagogique en France*. Paris: Alcan.

Durkheim, E. (1964) *The Division of Labour in Society*. Translated by G. Simpson. New York: Free Press. (1st published in French, 1893).

Edelman, G. and Mountcastle, V. B. (1978) *The Mindful Brain: Cortical Organization and the Group-Selective Theory of Higher Brain Function*. Cambridge, MA: MIT Press.

Edelman, G. (1992) *Bright Air, Brilliant Fire: On the Matter of the Mind.* New York: HarperCollins.

Edelman, G. and Tononi, G. (2000) *Consciousness: How Matter Becomes Imagination*. London: Penguin Books.

Eggins, S. (1994) *An Introduction to Systemic Functional Linguistics*. London: Pinter.

Eggins, S., Wignell, P. and Martin, J. R. (1993) The discourse of history: distancing the recoverable past. In M. Ghadessy (ed.) *Register Analysis: Theory into Practice*. London: Pinter.

Ek, J. A. van (1976) *The Threshold Level for Modern Language Learning in Schools.* London: Longman.

Ellwood, W. (2002) *The No-Nonsense Guide to Globalization.* London: Verso.

Engeström, Y., Miettinen, R. and Punamäki R.-L. (eds.) (1999) *Perspectives on Activity Theory.* Cambridge: Cambridge University Press.

Emmer, P. (2003) The myth of early globalization: the Atlantic economy. *European Review* 11.1: 37–48.

Firth, J. R. (1950) Personality and language in society. *The Sociological Review* 42(2). Reprinted in Firth, 1957. London: Oxford University Press.

Firth, J. R. (1957) *Papers in Linguistics 1934–1951.* London: Oxford University Press.

Firth, J. R. (1964) Ethnographic analysis and language with reference to Malinowski's views. In *Man and Culture: An Evaluation of the Work of Bronislaw Malinowski.* New York: Harper Row (First edition London: Routledge & Kegan Paul 1957).

Fishman, J. A. (1971) The sociology of language: an interdisciplinary social science approach to language in society. In J. A. Fishman (ed.) *Advances in Sociology of Language 1.* The Hague: Mouton.

Fishman, J. A. (1972a) *The Sociology of Language* (section viii). Rowley: Newbury House Publishers Inc.

Fishman, J. A. (1972b) *Language in Sociocultural Change*, selected and introduced by Anwar S. Dil. Stanford: Stanford University Press.

Flynn, J. (2007) *What Is Intelligence?* Cambridge: Cambridge University Press.

Frake, C. O. (1986) 'Struck by speech': the Yakan concept of litigation. In J. J. Gumperz and D. Hymes (eds) *Directions in Sociolinguistics: The Ethnography of Communication.* London: Basil Blackwell.

Fries, Peter H. (1983) On the status of theme in English: arguments from discourse. In J. S. Petofi and E. Sozer (eds) *Micro and Macro Connexity of Texts: Papers in Textlinguistics*, vol 45. Hamburg: Helmut Buske.

Gee, J. (1990) *Social Linguistics and Literacies: Ideology in Discourse.* Brighton: Falmer Press.

Geertz, C.(1973) *The Interpretation of Culture.* New York: Basic Books.

Geertz, C. (2000) *Local Knowledge: Further Essays in Interpretive Anthropology.* New York: Basic Books.

Gerot, L. and Wignell P. (1994) *Making Sense of Functional Grammar: An Introductory Work Book.* Cammeray, NSW: Antepodean Educational Enterprises.

Ghadessy, M. (ed.) (1999) *Text and Context in Functional Linguistics.* Amsterdam: Benjamins.

Gibbons, J. and Markwick-Smith, M. (1992) Exploring the use of a systemic semantic description. *IJAL*, vol. 2, no. 1: 36–50.

Gladwell, M. (2007) None of the above: what IQ doesn't tell you about race (a review of James Flynn's *What is Intelligence?*). New York, *The New Yorker*. (http://www.newyorker.com/arts/books/2007/12/17/071217crbo_gladwell).

Goody, J. (1968) *Literacy in Traditional Societies*. Cambridge: Cambridge University Press.

Goody, J. (1977) *The Domestication of the Savage Mind.* Cambridge: Cambridge University Press.

Goody, J and Watt, I. (1972) The consequences of literacy. In P. P. Giglioli (ed.) *Language and Social Context*. Harmondsworth: Penguin.

Grant, E. (1996) *The Foundations of Modern Science in the Middle Ages*. New York: Cambridge University Press.

Grant, E. (2007) *A History of Natural Philosophy: From the Ancient World to the Nineteenth Century*. New York: Cambridge University Press.

Greenfield, S. (1997) *The Human Brain: A Guided Tour*. London: Weidenfield and Nicolson.

Greenfield, S. (2000) *The Private Life of the Brain*. London: Penguin Books.

Gregory, M. (1967) Aspects of varieties differentiation. *Journal of Linguistics* 3(2): 177–98.

Gregory, M. and Carroll, S. (1978) *Language and Situation*. London: Routledge and Kegan Paul.

Gumperz, J. (1971) *Language in Social Groups: Essays by John J. Gumperz*, Collected and Introduced by A. S. Dill. Paolo Alto: Stanford University Press.

Habermas, J. (1987) *Knowledge and Human Interest*, translated by J. J. Shapiro. London: Polity Press (German Text, first published: Suhrkamp Verlag 1968).

Halliday, M. A. K. (1959) *The Language of the Chinese 'Secret History of the Mongols': Publication of the Philological Society* XVII. Oxford: Basil Blackwell.

Halliday, M. A. K. (1961) Categories of the theory of grammar. *Word* 17.3: 242–292. Reprinted in J. J. Webster (ed) (2002) *The Collected Works of M. A. K. Halliday, Vol 1: On Grammar.* London: Continuum.

Halliday, M. A. K. (1962) Linguistics and machine translation. *Zeitschrift für Phonetik, Sprachwissenschaft und Kommunikationsforschung*, 15: 1–2.

Halliday, M. A. K. (1967–68) Notes on transitivity and theme in English 1–3. *Journal of Linguistics* 3.1, 3.2, 4.2.

Halliday, M. A. K. (1969) Relevant models of language. *Educational Review*, November. Reprinted in Halliday 1973a. London: Edward Arnold.

Halliday, M. A. K. (1970a) Language Structure and Language Function. In J. Lyons (ed.) *New Horizons in Linguistics*. Harmondsworth: Penguin.

Halliday, M. A. K. (1970b) Language structure and language function as seen from a consideration of modality and mood in English. *Foundations of Language* 6(3): 322–361.

Halliday, M. A. K. (1971) Linguistic function and literary style: an enquiry into the language of William Golding. In S. Chatman (ed.) *Literary Style: A Symposium*, London: Oxford University Press.

Halliday, M. A. K. (1973a) *Explorations in the Functions of Language*. London: Arnold.

Halliday, M. A. K. (1973b) Towards a sociological semantics. In *Explorations in the Functions of Language.* London: Edward Arnold.

Halliday, M. A. K. (1973c) Foreword. In Bernstein 1973c (ed.). Reprinted in Halliday 2007b.

Halliday, M. A. K. (1974a) *Language and Social Man* (Schools Council Programme in Linguistics and Language Teaching: Papers Series II, Volume 3). London: Longman; reprinted in *Language as Social Semiotics*. London: Arnold 1976; reprinted in Halliday 2007b.

Halliday, M. A. K. (1974b) A socio-semiotic perspective on language development. *Bulletin of the School of Oriental and African Studies* 37.1: 98–118; reprinted Halliday 2003.

Halliday, M. A. K. (1974c) Social Aspects of Semantic Change. In L. Heilmann (ed.) *Proceedings of the Eleventh International Congress of Linguists*. Bologna: Il Mulino. Reprinted in Halliday 2007b.

Halliday, M. A. K. (1975a) *Learning How to Mean: Explorations in the Development of Language*. London: Edward Arnold; reprinted in Halliday 2004.

Halliday, M. A. K. (1975b) Some aspects of sociolinguistics, and also aspects of sociolinguistic research. In *Interaction between Linguistics and Mathematical Education.* Report of a Symposium sponsored by UNESCO-CEDO-ICMI, UNESCO.

Halliday, M. A. K. (1976a) Early language learning: a sociolinguistic approach. In S. A. Wurm and W. C. McCormack (eds) *Language and Man: Anthropological Issues*. The Hague: Mouton.

Halliaday, M. A. K. (1976b) *System and Function in Language*, edited by G. Kress. Oxford: Oxford University Press.

Halliday, M. A. K. (1976c) Anti-languages. *American Anthropologist* 78.3: 570–584.

Halliday, M. A. K. (1976d) The teacher taught the student English: an essay in applied linguistics. In P. A. Reich (ed.) *Second LACUS Forum 1975*. Columbia, SC: Hornbeam Press. Reprinted in Halliday, 2007a.

Halliday, M. A. K. (1977) Text as semantic choice in social context. In T. A. van Dijk and J. S. Petofi (eds) *Grammars and Descriptions*. Berlin: de

Gruyter (reprinted in *Collected Works of M. A. K. Halliday Vol 2*, edited by J. J. Webster. London: Continuum 2002).

Halliday, M. A. K. (1978) *Language as Social Semiotic*. London: Arnold.

Halliday, M. A. K. (1979a) Modes of meaning and modes of expression: types of grammatical structure, and their determination by different semantic functions. In D. J. Allerton, E. Carney and D. Holdcroft (eds) *Functions and Context in Linguistic Analysis: A Festschrift for William Haas*. Cambridge: Cambridge University Press.

Halliday, M. A. K. (1979b) One child's protolanguage. In M. Bullowa (ed.) *Before Speech: The Beginning of Interpersonal Communication*. Cambridge: Cambridge University Press.

Halliday, M. A. K. (1980) Three aspects of children's language development: learning language, learning through language, learning about language. In Y. Goodman, M. M. Hussler and D. Strickland (eds) *Oral and Written Language Development: Impact on Schools*. International Reading Association; Newark, Delaware: 1979. Reprinted in Halliday 2003.

Halliday, M. A. K. (1982) The de-automatization of grammar: from Priestley's 'An Inspector Calls'. In J. M. Anderson (ed.) *Language Form and Linguistic Variation: Papers Dedicated to Angus McIntosh*. Amsterdam: John Benjamins.

Halliday, M. A. K. (1984) On the ineffability of grammatical categories. In A. Manning, P. Martin, and K. McCalla (eds) *The Tenth LACUS Forum* 1983, 3–18. Columbia, SC: Hornbeam Press.

Halliday, M. A. K. (1985a) *Introduction to Functional Grammar.* London: Edward Arnold.

Halliday, M. A. K. (1985b) *Spoken and Written Language*. Geelong, Victoria: Deakin University Press.

Halliday, M. A. K. (1991) The notion of context in language education. In T. Le and M. McCausland (eds) *Language Education: Interaction and Development. Proceedings of the International Conference, Vietnam 1991*. Launceston: University of Tasmania. Reprinted in Ghadessy (ed) 1999; in Halliday 2007a.

Halliday, M. A. K. (1992a) How do you mean? In M. Davies and L Ravelli (eds) *Advances in Systemic Linguistics: Recent Theory and Practice*. London: Pinter.

Halliday, M. A. K. (1992b) The act of meaning. In J. E. Alatis (ed.) *Communication and Social Meaning: Georgetown University Round Table 1992*. Georgetown: Georgetown University Press.

Halliday, M. A. K. (1994a) *Introduction to Functional Grammar*, 2nd edn. London: Arnold.

Halliday, M. A. K. (1994b) On language in relation to the evolution of human consciousness. In S. Allen (eds) *Of Thoughts and Words* (Proceedings of Nobel Symposium 92: The Relations between Language and Mind). London: Imperial College Press. Reprinted in Halliday 2007a.

Halliday, M. A. K. (1996a) On grammar and grammatics. In R. Hasan, C. Cloran and D. Butt (eds) *Functional Descriptions: Theory in Practice*. Amsterdam: Benjamins. Reprinted in J. J. Webster (ed.) *The Collected Works of M. A. K. Halliday, Vol 1: On Grammar*. London: Continuum, 2002.

Halliday, M. A. K. (1996b) Literacy and linguistics: a functional perspective. In R. Hasan and G. Williams (eds) *Literacy and Society*. London: Longman. In Halliday 2007a.

Halliday, M. A. K. (2001) Is the grammar neutral? Is the grammarian neutral? In J. de Villiers and R. Stainton (eds) *Communication Linguistics, Vol 1: Papers in Honour of Michael Gregory*. Toronto: Edition deGref.

Halliday, M. A. K. (2004) *The Collected Works of M. A. K. Halliday, Vol 4: The Language of Early Childhood*, edited by J. J. Webster. London: Continuum.

Halliday, M. A. K. (2007a) *The Collected Works of M. A. K. Halliday, Vol 9: Language and Education*, edited by J. J. Webster. London: Continuum.

Halliday, M. A. K. (2007b) *The Collected Works of M. A. K. Halliday, Vol 10: Language and Society*, edited by J. J. Webster. London: Continuum.

Halliday, M. A. K. (2008) *Complementarities in Language*. Beijing: The Commercial Press.

Halliday, M. A. K., McIntosh, A. and Strevens, P. D. (1964) *Linguistic Sciences and Language Teaching*. London: Longmans.

Halliday, M. A. K. and Hasan, R. (1976) *Cohesion in English*. London: Longman.

Halliday M. A. K. and Hasan, R. (1985) *Language, Context and Text: Aspects of Language in a Social-semiotic Perspective*. Geelong, Victoria: Deakin University Press.

Halliday, M. A. K. and Martin, J. R. (1993) *Writing Science: Literacy and Discursive Power*. London: Falmer.

Halliday, M. A. K. and Matthiessen, M. I. M. (1999) *Construing Experience through Meaning*. London: Continuum.

Halliday, M. A. K. and Matthiessen, M. I. M. (2004) *An Introduction to Functional Grammar, 3rd edition* (revised by Matthiessen). London: Arnold.

Halliday, M. A. K. and Webster, J. J. (eds.) (2009) *Continuum Companion to Systemic Functional Linguistics*. London: Continuum.

Hallyn, F. (1990) *The Poetic Structure of the World: Copernicus and Kepler*, translated by D. M. Leslie. New York: Zone Books.

Hargreaves, D. H. (1975) *Interpersonal Relations and Education* (revised student edition). London: Routledge and Kegan Paul.

Hasan, R. (1964) A Linguistic Study of Comparative Features in the Style of Two Contemporary English Prose Writers. Unpublished Doctoral dissertation. Edinburgh: University of Edinburgh: Faculty of Arts.

Hasan, R. (1971) Rime and reason in literature. In S. Chatman (ed.) *Literary Style: A Symposium*. London: Oxford University Press.

Hasan, R. (1972) The verb 'be' in Urdu. In J. W. M. Verhaar (ed.) *The Verb 'BE' and Its Synonyms 5*, 1–63.

Hasan, R. (1973) Code, register and social dialect. In B. Bernstein (ed.) *Class, Codes and Control, Vol 2: Applied Studies towards the Sociology of Language.* London: Routledge and Kegan Paul. Reprinted in J. J. Webster (ed.) *The Collected Works of Ruqaiya Hasan Vol 1: Language Society and Consciousness*. London: Equinox, 2005.

Hasan, R. (1975) The place of stylistics in the study of verbal art. In H. Ringbom (ed.) *Style and Text: Studies Presented to Nils Erik Enkvist*. Stockholm: Sprakförlaget AB Skrïptor.

Hasan, R. (1976) Socialization and cross–cultural education. *Language and Education in the Third World*, issue editor: Jack Berry. *International Journal of the Sociology of Language* 8: 7–25.

Hasan, R. (1978) Text in the systemic functional model. In W. U. Dressler (ed.) *Current Trends in Text Linguistics*. Berlin: Mouton de Gruyter.

Hasan, R. (1979) On the notion of text. In J. S. Petofi (ed.) *Text v. Sentence: Basic Questions of Text Linguistics, Second Part*. Hamburg: Helmut Buske.

Hasan, R. (1981) What's going on? A dynamic view of context in language. In James E. Copeland and Philip W. Davis (eds), *The Seventh LACUS Forum 1980*. Columbia, SC: Hornbeam Press.

Hasan, R. (1983) *A Semantic System Network for the Analysis of Messages in Everyday Talk between Mothers and their Children.* Dept of Linguistics: Macquarie University, Sydney, mimeo.

Hasan, R. (1984a) Ways of saying: ways of meaning. In R. Fawcett, M. A. K. Halliday, S. Lamb and A. Makkai (eds) *Semiotics of Culture and Language*. London: Pinter. Reprinted in Hasan, 1996b.

Hasan, R. (1984b) Coherence and cohesive harmony. In J. Flood (ed.) *Understanding Reading Comprehension.* Newark, Delaware: International Reading Association.

Hasan, R. (1984c) What kind of resource is language? *Australian Review of Applied Linguistics* 7.1

Hasan, R. (1985a) *Linguistics, Language and Verbal Art*. Geelong, Victoria: Deakin University Press.

Hasan, R. (1985b) Lending and borrowing: from grammar to lexis. In J. R. Clark (ed.) *The Cultivated Australian. Beitrage zur Phonetik und Linguistik* 48.

Hasan, R. (1985c) Part B: Chapters 4–6. In Halliday and Hasan, 1985.

Hasan, R. (1986) The Ontogenesis of Ideology. In T. Threadgold, E. A. Grosz, G. Kress and M. A. K. Halliday (eds) *Semiotics, Ideology, Language.* Sydney: Sydney Association for Studies in Society and Culture. (Available from Dept of Anthropology, University of Sydney.)

Hasan, R. (1987a) The grammarian's dream: lexis as most delicate grammar. In M. A. K. Halliday and R. P. Fawcett (eds) *New Developments in Systemic Linguistics, Vol 1: Theory and Description.* London: Pinter.

Hasan, R. (1987b) Reading picture reading: invisible instruction at home and in school. Proceedings from the 13th Conference of the Australian Reading Association, Sydney [no date; no editor].

Hasan, R. (1988) Language and socialisation: home and school. In L. Gerot, J. Oldenburg and T. van Leeuwen (eds) *Language in the Processes of Socialisation.* Sydney: Macquarie University. Reprinted in R. Hasan 2009b.

Hasan, R. (1989) Semantic variation and sociolinguistics. *Australian Journal of Linguistics* 9(2): 221–276. Reprinted in Hasan 2009b.

Hasan, R. (1991) Questions as a mode of learning in everyday talk. In T. Le and M. McCausland (eds) *Language Education: Interaction and Development*,. Launceston: University of Tasmania Press. Reprinted in Hasan 2009b.

Hasan, R. (1992a) Rationality in everyday talk: from process to system. In J. Svartvik (ed.) *Directions in Corpus Linguistics, Proceedings of Nobel Symposium 82, Stockholm.* Berlin: de Gruyter. Reprinted in Hasan 2009b.

Hasan, R. (1992b) Meaning in sociolinguistic theory. In K. Bolton and H. Kwok (eds) *Sociolinguistics Today: International Perspectives.* London: Routledge. Reprinted in R. Hasan 2009b.

Hasan, R. (1992c) Speech genre, semiotic mediation and the development of higher mental functions. *Language Sciences* 14(4): 489–528. Reprinted in R. Hasan 2005.

Hasan, R. (1995a) The conception of context in text. In P. H. Fries and M. Gregory (eds) *Discourse in Society: Systemic Functional Perspectives.* Norwood, NJ: Ablex.

Hasan, R. (1995b) On social conditions for semiotic mediation: the genesis of mind in society. In A. R. Sadovnik (ed.) *Knowledge and Pedagogy: The Sociology of Basil Bernstein.* Norwood, NJ: Ablex. Reprinted in R. Hasan, 2005.

Hasan, R. (1996a) *Ways of Saying Ways of Meaning: Selected Papers of Ruqaiya Hasan*, edited by C. Cloran, D. Butt and G. Williams. London: Cassell.

Hasan, R. (1996b) Literacy, everyday talk and society. In Hasan and Williams (eds).

Hasan, R. (1996c) Semantic networks: a tool for the analysis of meaning. In Hasan 1996a.

Hasan, R. (1999a) The disempowerment game: Bourdieu and language in literacy. *Linguistics and Education* 10(1): 25–87.

Hasan, R. (1999b) Speaking with reference to context. In M. Ghadessy (ed.). Amsterdam: Benjamins.

Hasan, R. (2000) The uses of talk. In S. Sarangi and M. Coulthard (eds) *Discourse and Social Life*. London: Longman. Reprinted in R. Hasan 2005.

Hasan, R. (2001) The ontogenesis of decontextualized language: some achievements of classification and framing. In A. Morais, I. Neves, B. Davies, H. Daniels (eds) *Towards a Sociology of Pedagogy: The Contribution of Basil Bernstein to Research*. Brussels: Peter Lang.

Hasan, R. (2002) Semiotic mediation and mental development in pluralistic societies: some implications for tomorrow's schooling. In G. Wells and G. Claxton (eds) *Learning for Life in the 21st Century: Socio-cultural Perspectives on the Future of Education*. London: Blackwell. Reprinted in R. Hasan 2005.

Hasan, R. (2003) Globalization, literacy and ideology. *World Englishes* 22(4): 433–448.

Hasan, R. (2004) Reading picture reading: a study in ideology and inference. In J. Foley (ed.) *Language, Education and Discourse: Functional Approaches*. London: Continuum. Reprinted in R. Hasan 2005.

Hasan, R. (2005) *The Collected Works of Ruqaiya Hasan, Vol 1: Language, Society and Consciousness*, edited by J. J. Webster. London: Equinox.

Hasan, R. (2006) Literacy pedagogy and social change. In R. Moor, M. Arnot, J. Beck and H. Daniels (eds). London: Routledge.

Hasan, R. (2008) Modes of learning, modes of teaching: semiotic mediation and knowledge. *SPELT* 20(3): 2–19.

Hasan, R. (2009a) Wanted: a theory for integrated sociolinguistics. In R. Hasan 2009b.

Hasan, R. (2009b) *The Collected Works of Ruqaiya Hasan, Vol 2: Semantic Variation: Meaning in Society and in Sociolinguistics*, edited by J. J. Webster. London: Equinox.

Hasan, R. (2010) The meaning of 'not' is not in 'not'. In A. Mahboob and N. Knight (eds). London: Continuum.

Hasan, R. and Cloran, C. (1990) A sociolinguistic interpretation of everyday talk between mothers and children. In M. A. K. Halliday, J. Gibbon and H. Nicholas (eds) *Learning, Keeping and Using Language, Vol 1: Selected Papers from the 8th World Congress of Applied Linguistics, Sydney, 16-21 August 1987*, 67–100. Amsterdam: Benjamins. Reprinted in Hasan 2009b.

Hasan, R., Cloran, C., Williams G. and Lukin A. (2007) Semantic networks: the description of linguistic meaning in SFL. In R. Hasan, C. Mattheissen and J. J. Webster (eds). London: Continuum.

Hasan, R. and Martin, J. R. (eds) (1989) *Language Development: Learning Language, Learning Culture*. Norwood, NJ: Ablex.

Hasan, R. and Williams G. (eds) (1996) *Literacy in Society*. London: Longman.

Hasan, R., Cloran, C. and Butt, D. G. (eds) (1996) *Functional Descriptions: Theory in Practice*. Amsterdam: Benjamins.

Hasan, R., Mattheissen, C. and Webster, J. J. (eds) (2005) *Continuing Discourse on Language: A Functional Perspective, Vol 1*. London: Equinox.

Hasan, R., Mattheissen, C. and Webster, J. J. (eds) (2007) *Continuing Discourse on Language: A Functional Perspective, Vol 2*. London: Equinox.

Henry, J. (2008) *The Scientific Revolution and the Origins of Modern Science*, 3rd edn. London: Palgrave-Macmillan.

Hernstein, R. and Murray, C. (1994) *The Bell Curve: Intelligence and Class Structure in American Life*. New York: Free Press.

Hertz, N. (2001) *The Silent Take-Over: Global Capitalism and the Death of Democracy*. London: Heinemann.

Hjelmslev, L. (1961) *Prolegomena to a Theory of Language*, translated and edited by J. Whitfield. Madison: University of Wisconsin Press.

Hobsbawm, E. (1999) *The New Century*. London: Abacus.

Hopkins, A. G. (2002) *Globalization in World History*. London: Pimlico.

Hoijer, H. (1948) Linguistics and cultural change. *Language* 24: 335–345.

Hsu, F. L. K. (1963) *Clan, Caste and Club*. Princeton, NJ: D Van Norstand Co. Inc.

Hsu, F. L. K. (1968) Chinese kinship and Chinese behaviour. In Tang Tsou and Ping-ti Ho (eds), *China in Crisis*. Chicago: Chicago University Press.

Hsu, F. L. K. (1971a) Eros, affect and Tao. In F. L. K. Hsu (ed.) 1971b.

Hsu, F. L. K. (ed.) (1971b) *Kinship and Culture*. Chicago: Aldine Publishing Co.

Hsu, F. L. K. (1971c) Psychosocial homeostasis and jen: conceptual tools for advancing psychological anthropology. *American Anthropologist* 73(1): 23–44.

Hymes, D. H. (1971) Competence and performance in linguistic theory. In R. Huxley and E. Ingram (eds) *Language Acquisition: Models and Methods*. New York: Academic Press.

Hymes, D. H. (1972) On communicative competence. In J. B. Pride and J. Holmes (eds) *Sociolinguistics*. Harmondsworth: Penguin.

Hymes, D. H. (1968) The ethnography of speaking. In J. A. Fishman (ed.) *Readings in the Sociology of Language*. The Hague: Mouton.

Hymes, D. H. (1986) Models of the interaction of language and social life. In J. J. Gumperz and D. Hymes(eds) *Directions in Sociolinguistics: The Ethnography of Communication*. London: Blackwell (1st edition: 1972, New York: Holt, Rinehart & Winston).

Jakobson, R. (1973) *Main Trends in the Science of Language*. London: George Allen & Unwin.

John, V. P. (1972) Styles of learning – styles of teaching: reflections on the education of Navajo children. In C. Cazden, D. H. Hymes, and V. P. John (eds) *Functions of Language in the Classroom*. New York: Columbia University Press.

Johnson, W. R. (2000) *Lucretius and the Modern World*. Duckworth: London.

Jones, J., Gollin, S., Drury, H. and Economou, D. (1989) Systemic functional linguistics and its application to the TESOL curriculum. In R. Hasan and J. R. Martin (eds) *Language Development: Learning Language, Learning Culture. Meaning and Choice in Language: Studies for Michael Halliday*. Norwood, NJ: Ablex.

Kachru, B. B. (1983) *The Indianization of English: The English Language in India.* Delhi: Oxford University Press.

Kachru, B. B. (1986) The power and politics of English. *World Englishes* 5 (2/3): 121–140.

Kandiah, T. (2001) Whose meanings? Probing the dialects of English. In T. C. Kiong, A. Pakir, B. K. Choon and R. B. H. Goh (eds) *Ariels: Departures and Returns: Essays for Edwin Thumboo*. New York: Oxford University Press.

Kettle, M. (2001) Cheney tells US to keep on guzzling. Washington Diary, *The Guardian Weekly*, 10–16 May.

Klein, N. (2007) *The Shock Doctrine: The Rise of Disaster Capitalism*. Camberwell, Vic.: Penguin Group.

Klemperer, V. (2002) *The Language of the Third Reich*. Translated by Martin Brady. London: Continuum.

Kline, M. (1953) *Mathematics in Western Culture*. London: Oxford University Press.

Kluckhon, C. and Kelly, W. (1945) The concept of culture. In R. Linton (ed.) *The Science of Man in the World Crisis*. New York: Columbia University Press.

Korzybski, A. (1933) *Science and Sanity*. Lancaster, PA: International Non-Aristotelian Library.

Krashen, S. D. (1987) *Principles and Practice in Second Language Acquisition.* Englewood Cliffs, NJ: Prentice-Hall International.

Krashen, S. D. and Terrell, T. D. (1983) *The Natural Approach: Language Acquisition in the Classroom.* Oxford: Pergamon Press.
Kress, Gunther (1982) *Learning to Write*. London: Routledge.
Kress, G. and Hodge, R. (1979) *Language as Ideology*. London: Routledge and Kegan Paul.
Labov, W. (1966) *The Social Stratification of English in New York City*. Washington, DC: Centre for Applied Linguistics.
Labov, W. (1970) The study of language in its social context. *Studium Generale* 23: 30–87. Reprinted in Labov 1972.
Labov, W. (1972) *Sociolinguistic Patterns*. London: Blackwell.
Lave, J. (1997) What's special about experiments as contexts for thinking. In M. Cole, Y. Engestrom and O. Vasquesz (eds) *Mind, Culture and Activity*. Cambridge: Cambridge University Press.
Leech, G. N. (1983) *Principles of Pragmatics.* London: Longman.
Leech, G. N. (1989) *Meaning and the English Verb*, 2nd edition. London: Longman.
Leeuwen, T. van and Humphrey, S. (1996) On learning to look through a geographer's eye. In R. Hasan and G. Williams (eds). London: Longman.
Lenneberg, E. H. (1971) Language and cognition. In D. D. Steinberg and L. A. Jakobovits (eds) *Semantics*. London: Cambridge University Press.
Lemke, J. L. (1990) *Talking Science: Language, learning and values*. Norwood, NJ: Ablex.
Lewontin, R., Rose, S. and Kamin L. J. (1984) *Not in Your Genes: Biology, Ideology and Human Nature*. London: Random House.
Lewontin, R. (1995) *Human Diversity*. New York: Scientific American Library.
Lewontin, R. (2000a) *It Ain't Necessarily So. The Dream of the Human Genome and Other Illusions*. London: Granta Books.
Lewontin, R. (2000b) *The Triple Helix: Gene, Organism, and Environment*. Cambridge: Harvard University Press.
Li, E. S.-H. (2007) *A Systemic Functional Grammar of Chinese*. London: Continuum.
Lloyd, G. E. R. (1999) *Science, Folklore and Ideology: Studies in the Life Sciences in Ancient Greece*. London: Duckworth.
Lloyd, G. E. R. (2002) *The Ambitions of Curiosity. Understanding the World in Ancient Greece and China*. Cambridge: Cambridge University Press.
Lock, A. (1978). *Action, Gesture and Symbol: The Emergence of Language*. New York: Academic Press.
Long, M. H. and Larsen-Freeman, D. (1991) *An Introduction to the Second Language Acquisition Research.* London: Longman.
Luke, A. (1988) *Literacy, Textbooks and Ideology*. London: Falmer.

Luke, A. (1996) Genres of power? Literacy, education and the production of capital. In R. Hasan and G. Williams (eds) *Literacy in Society*. London: Longman.

Lukin, A. (2010) 'News' and 'register': a preliminary investigation. In A. Maboob and N. Knight (eds).

Lukin, A. (2010) 'News' and 'register': a preliminary investigation. In A. Mahbbob and N. K. Knight (eds) *Appliable Linguistics*. London: Continuum.

Lukin, A. and Webster, J. J. (2005) SFL and the study of literature. In Hasan, Matthiessen and Webster (eds).

Luria, A. R. (1976) *Cognitive Development: Its Cultural and Social Foundations*. Translated by M. Lopez-Morillas and L. Solotaroff, edited by M. Cole. Cambridge, MA: Harvard University Press.

Lyons, J. (1968) *Introduction to Theoretical Linguistics*. Cambridge: Cambridge University Press.

Lyons, J. (1977) *Semantics, Vol 1*. Cambridge: Cambridge University Press.

MacIntyre, A. (1999) How to seem virtuous without actually being so. In M. J. Halstead and T. H. Mclaughlin (eds.) *Education and Morality*. London: Routledge.

Macken-Horarik, M. (1996) Literacy and learning across the curriculum: towards a model of register for secondary school teachers. In R. Hasan and G. Williams (eds).

Madely, J. (1999) *Big Business, Poor People*. London: Zed Books.

Madely, J. (2000). Putting People before Principles, *Guardian Weekly*, January 6-12.

Mahboob, A. and Knight, N. (2010) (eds), *Appliable Linguistics*. London: Continuum.

Malinowski, B. (1923) The problem of meaning in primitive languages, Supplement 1. In C. K. Ogden and I. A. Richards, *The Meaning of Meaning*. London: Kegan Paul.

Malinowski, B. (1935) *Coral Gardens and Their Magic, Vol 2*. London: Allen and Unwin.

Mallik, B. (1972) *Language of the Underworld of West Bengal* (Research Series No 76). Calcutta: Sanskrit College.

Mandelbaum, D. G. (1970) *Society in India, Vols 1 and 2*. Berkeley: University of California Press.

Martin, J. R. (1984) Functional components in a grammar: a review of deployable recognition criteria. *Nottingham Linguistic Circular* 13: 35–70. Nottingham University: Department of English Studies.

Martin, J. R. (1985) Process and text: two modes of human semiosis. In J. D. Benson and W. S. Greaves (eds) *Systemic Perspectives on Dis-*

course, Vol 1: Selected Theoretical Papers, the 9th International Systemic Workshop. Norwood, NJ: Ablex.

Martin, J. R. (1986) Intervening in the process of writing development. In C. Painter and J. R. Martin (eds) *Writing to Mean: Teaching Genres across the Curriculum*. Occasional Paper No 9: Applied Linguistics Association of Australia.

Martin, J. R. (1989) *Factual Writing: Exploring and Challenging Social Reality.* London: Oxford University Press.

Martin, J. R. (1991) Intrinsic functionality: implications for contextual theory. *Social Semiotic* 1(1): 99–162.

Martin, J. R. (1992) *English Text: System and Structure*. Amsterdam: Benjamins.

Martin, J. R. (1993) Technicality and abstraction: language for the creation of specialized texts. In M. A. K. Halliday and J. R. Martin.

Martin, J. R. (1996) Evaluating disruption: symbolising theme in junior secondary narrative. In R. Hasan and G. Williams (eds).

Martin, J. R., Christie, F. and Rothery, J. (1987) Social processes in education. In I. Reid (ed.) *The Place of Genre in Learning*. Geelong, Victoria: Deakin University Press.

Martin, J. R. and Rose, D. (2003) *Working with Discourse: Meaning beyond the Clause*. London: Continuum.

Marx, K. (1985) *The German Ideology: Part One*, edited by C. J. Arthur. London: Lawrence & Wishart.

Mathesius, V. (1928) *On Linguistic Characterology with Illustrations from Modern English*. Actes de premier Congres Internationale de Linguistes a la Haye.

Maton, K. (2008) Grammars of sociology. Presented at the fifth International Basil Bernstein Symposium, 9–12 July. Cardiff University, UK.

Maton, K. (2009) Cumulative and segmented learning: exploring the role of curriculum structure in knowledge-building. *British Journal of Sociology of Education* 30(1): 43–57.

Matthiessen, C. (1990) *Metafunctional Complementarity and Resonance in Syntagmatic Organization.* Sydney: Department of Linguistics, Sydney University.

Matthiessen, C. (1992) Interpreting the textual metafunction. In M. Davis and L. Ravelli (eds) *Recent Advances in Systemic Linguistics*. London: Pinter.

Matthiessen, C. (1993) The object of study in cognitive science in relation to its construal and enactment in language. *Cultural Dynamics* VI(1-2): 187–242.

Matthiessen, C. (1995) *Lexicogrammatical Cartography*. Tokyo: International Language Sciences Publisher.

Matthiessen, C. (2007) The architecture of language according to systemic functional linguistics: developments since the 1970s. In R. Hasan, C. Matthiessen and J. J. Webster (eds).

Matthiessen, C., Teruya, K. and Lam, M. (2010) *Key Terms in Systemic Functional Linguistics*. London: Continuum.

Maxwell, J. C. (1881) *An Elementary Treatise on Electricity*. Oxford: Clarendon Press.

McGrew, A. (1992) A global society? In U. Beck, S. Hall and A. McGrew (eds).

McMurty, J. (1999) *The Cancer Stage of Capitalism*. London: Pluto Press.

McTear, M. (1985) *Children's Conversations*. London: Blackwell.

Mead, G. H. (1934) *Mind, Self and Society*, edited by C. Morris. Chicago: Chicago University Press.

Miller, D. R. and Turci, M. (eds) (2007) *Language and Verbal Art Revisited: Linguistic Approaches to the Study of Literature*. London: Equinox.

Moore, R., Arnot, M., Beck, J. and Daniels, H. (eds) (2006) *Knowledge, Power and Educational Reform: Applying the Sociology of Basil Bernstein*. London: Routledge.

Morais, A., Neves, I., Davies, B. and Daniels, H. (eds) (2001) *Towards a Sociology of Pedagogy: The Contribution of Basil Bernstein to Research*. Brussels: Peter Lang.

Moss, G. (2002) Literacy and pedagogy in flux: constructing the object of study from a Bernsteinian perspective. Special Issue: *Basil Bernstein's Theory of Social Class, Educational Codes and Social Control, BJSE* 23(4): 549–558.

Mufti, M. (2009) *Talaash*. Lahore: Al-Faisal Nashran.

Muller, J., Davies, B. and Morais, A. (2004) *Reading Bernstein, Researching Bernstein.* London: Routledge.

Newson, J. (1978) Dialogue and development. In A. Lock (ed.) *Action, Gesture, and Symbol: The Emergence of Language*. New York: Academic Press.

Nunan, D. (1988) *The Learner-Centred Curriculum.* Cambridge: Cambridge University Press.

Oblinger, D. (1999) *What Business Wants from Higher Education.* New York: American Council on Education.

Oldenburg, J. (1986) The transitional stage of a second child – 18 months to 2 years. *Australian Review of Applied Linguistics* 9(1): 123–135.

Oldenburg-Torr, J. (1997) *From Child Tongue to Mother Tongue: A Case Study of Language Development in the First Two and Half Years* (Monographs in Systemic Linguistics, No. 9). Nottingham: University of Nottingham, Department of English Studies.

O'Halloran, K. (2007) Mathematical and scientific forms of knowledge. In Christie and Martin (eds).

Olson, D. R. (1977) From utterance to text: the bias of language in speech and writing. *Harvard Educational Review* 47(3): 257–281.

Ong, A. (1999) *Flexible Citizenship: The Cultural Logics of Transnationality*. Durham: Duke University Press.

Painter, C. (1984) *Into the Mother Tongue: A Case Study in Early Language Development*. London: Pinter.

Painter, C. (1985) *Learning the Mother Tongue*. Geelong, Victoria: Deakin University.

Painter, C. (1989) Learning language: a functional view of language development. In R. Hasan and J. R. Martin (eds).

Painter, C. (1996) The development of language as a resource for thinking: a linguistic view of learning. In R. Hasan and G. Williams (eds).

Painter, C. and J. R. Martin (eds) (1986) *Writing to Mean: Teaching Genres across the Curriculum*. Occasional Paper 9, Applied Linguistics Association of Australia.

Palmer, H. E. (1917) *The Scientific Study and Teaching of Languages*. London: George G. Harrap & Co. (republished 1968. Vol. 18 in series Language and Language Learning: The Scientific Study and Teaching of Languages. David Harper [series ed.]. London: Oxford University Press).

Parsons, T. (1964) The school classroom as a social system: some of the functional in American society. In *Social Structure and Personality*. New York: Free Press.

Philips, S. U. (1972) Participant structures and communicative competence: Warm Spring children in community classroom. In C. Cazden, D. H. Hymes and V. P. John (eds) *Functions of Language in the Classroom*. New York: Columbia University Press.

Phillipson, R. (1990) *English Language Teaching and Imperialism*. Tronninge: Transcultura.

Piaget, J. (1960) *Language and Thought of the Child*. London: Routledge and Kegan Paul.

Piaget, J. (1973) *The Child's Conception of the World*. Translated by Joan Tomlinson and Andrew Tomlinson. London: Paladin.

Popper, K. R. (1972) *Objective Knowledge: An Evolutionary Approach*. Revised edition. Oxford: Oxford University Press.

Postman, N. and Weingartner, G. (1972) *Teaching as a Subversive Activity*. London: Penguin.

Poynton, C. (1984) Names as vocation: forms and functions. *Nottingham Linguistic Circular* (Special Issue on Systemic Linguistics) 13(1): 34.

Prabhu, N. S. (1987) *Second Language Pedagogy*. Oxford: Oxford University Press.

Prochazka, V. (1942) Notes on translating techniques. *Journal of the Linguistic Circle of Prague* 8: 1–20.

Rahim, S. A. (1986) Language as power apparatus: observations on English and cultural policy in nineteenth-century India. *World Englishes* 5(2/3): 231–240.

Richards, J. C. and Rodgers, T. S. (1986) *Approaches and Methods in Language Teaching.* Cambridge: Cambridge University Press.

Roochnik, D. (1998) *Of Art and Wisdom: Plato's Undestanding of Techne.* USA: Pennsylvania State University Press.

Rorty, R. (1981) *Philosophy and the Mirror of Nature*. Princeton: Princeton University Press.

Rosenau, P. M. (1991) *Post-Modernism and the Social Sciences: Insights, Inroads and Intrusions*. Princeton, NJ: Princeton University Press.

Rothery, J. (1989) Learning about language. In R. Hasan and J. R. Martin (eds) *Language Development: Learning Language, Learning Culture: Studies for Michael Halliday*. Norwood, NJ: Ablex.

Rutherford, W. E. (1987) *Second Language Grammar: Learning and Teaching.* London: Longman.

Sadovnik, A. R. (ed.) (1995) *Knowledge and Pedagogy: The Sociology of Basil Bernstein.* Norwood, NJ: Ablex.

Sapir, E. (1921) *Language*. New York: Harcourt, Brace and Company.

Sapir, E. (1944) On grading: a study in semantics. *Philosophy of Science* 2: 93–116. Reprinted in D. G. Mandelbaum (ed.), *Selected Writings in Language, Culture and Personality*. Berkeley: University of California Press, 1949.

Sarwar, Z., Shamim, F. and Kazi, A. M. (1985) *A Think-Out on Oxford English for Colleges.* Karachi: Kifayat Academy Educational Publishers.

Saussure, F. de (1966) *Course in General Linguistics*, translated and edited by Wade Baskin. New York: McGraw-Hill.

Sharp, R., Green, A. and Lewis, J. (1975) *Education and Social Control: A Study in Progressive Primary Education.* London: Routledge and Kegan Paul.

Singh, P. (2001) Pedagogic discourse and student resistance in Australian secondary schools. In A. Morais, I. Neves, B. Davies, and H. Daniels (eds) *Towards a Sociology of Pedagogy: The Contribution of Basil Bernstein to Research.* New York: Peter Lang.

Stern, H. H. (1983) *Fundamental Concepts of Language Teaching.* Oxford: Oxford University Press.

Stern, H. H. (1984) Review and discussion. In *General English Syllabus Design: Curriculum and Syllabus for the General English Classroom.* Oxford: Pergamon.

Stoppard, T. (1993) *Arcadia*. London: Faber and Faber.

Street, B. V. (1995) *Social Literacies: Critical Approaches to Literacy Development, Ethnography and Education.* London: Longman.

Strodtbeck, F. L. (1971) Sex-role, identity and dominant kinship relations. In F. Hsu (ed.) *Kinship and Culture*. Chicago: Aldine Publishing Co.

Teruya, K. (2007) *The Systemic Functional Grammar of Japanese, Vols 1–2*. London: Continuum.

Thumboo, E. (1986) Language as power: Gabriel Okara's voice as a paradigm. *World Englishes* 5(2/3): 249–265.

Tickoo, M. L. (1990) Towards an alternative curriculum for acquisition-poor environments. In M. A. K. Halliday, J. Gibbons and H. Nicholas (eds) *Learning, Keeping and Using Language: Selected Papers from the 8th World Congress of Applied Linguistics*, vol. 1. Amsterdam: John Benjamins.

Tillett, P. (2002) *Consider the Heavens. A Guide to Astronomy and its Impact on Our Lives*. Australia: New Holland Publishers.

Tollefson, J. W. (1991) *Planning Language, Planning Inequality: Language Policy in the Community*. London: Longman.

Tomlinson, J. (1999) *Globalization and Culture*. Cambridge: Polity.

Toulmin, S. (1961) *Foresight and Understanding. An Enquiry into the Aims of Science*. New York: Harper Torchbook.

Toulmin, S. (1972) *Human Understanding, Vol 1: General Introduction and Part 1*. Oxford: Clarendon Press.

Trevarthen, C. (1974a) The psychobiology of speech development. In E. H. Lenneberg (ed.) *Language and Brain: Developmental Aspect.* Neuroscience Research Progress Bulletin (Boston) 12.

Trevarthen, C. (1974b) Conversation with a two month old. *New Scientist* 62 (2 May), 896: 230–235.

Trevarthen, C. and Hubley, P. (1977) Secondary intersubjectivity: confidence, confiding and acts of meaning in the first year. In A. Lock (ed.), *Action, Gesture and Symbol: The Emergence of Language*. New York: Academic.

Trudgill, P. (1974) *Sociolinguistics*. Harmondsworth: Penguin.

Trudgill, P. (1978) *Sociolinguisitc Patterns in British English*. London: Edward Arnold.

Tucker, G. H. (1996) So grammarians haven't the faintest idea: recognising lexis-oriented and grammar-oriented approaches to language. In R. Hasan, C. Cloran and D. G. Butt (eds).

Tucker, G. H. (1998) *The Lexicogrammar of Adjectives: A Systemic Functional Approach to Lexis*. London: Cassell.

Tucker, G. H. (2007) Between grammar and lexis: towards a systemic functional account of phraseology. In R. Hasan, C. Mattheissen and J. J. Webster (eds).

Veel, R. and Coffin, C. (1996) *Learning to think like an historian: the language of secondary school history*. In R. Hasan and G. Williams (eds).

Vygotsky, L. S. (1962) *Thought and Language*, edited and translated by E. Hanffman and G. Vakar. Cambridge, MA: MIT Press.

Vygotsky, L. S. (1978) *Mind in Society: The Development of Higher Psychological Processes*, edited by M. Cole, V. John-Steiner, S. Scribner and E. Souberman. Cambridge, MA: Harvard University Press.

Wells, G. (1987) Apprenticeship in literacy. *Interchange*, Vol 18(1/2): 109–123.

Whitaker, A. (2006) *Einstein, Bohr and the Quantum Dilemma: From Quantum Theory to Quantum information,* 2nd edition. Cambridge: Cambridge University Press.

Wilkins, D. A. (1976) *Notional Syllabuses*. Oxford: Oxford University Press.

Williams, G. (1990) Variation in home reading contexts. Proceedings from the 16th conference of Australian Reading Association, held at Canberra.

Williams, G. (1995) Joint Book-reading and Literacy Pedagogy: A Socio-semantic Examination. Unpublished PhD dissertation, School of English, Linguistics and Media, Macquarie University.

Williams, G. (1998) Children entering literate worlds: perspectives from the study of textual practices. In F. Christie and R. Missan (eds.), *Literacy in Schooling*. London: Routledge.

Williams, G. (2000) Children's literature, children and uses of language description. In L. Unsworth (ed.) *Researching Language in Schools and Communities: Functional Linguistic Perspectives*. London: Cassell.

Williams, G. (2001) Literacy pedagogy prior to schooling: relations between social and semantic variation. In A. Morais, I. Neves, B. Davies and H. Daniels (eds) *Towards a Sociology of Pedagogy: The Contribution of Basil Bernstein to Research*. New York: Peter Lang.

Whorf, B. L. (1956) *Language, Thought and Reality*, edited by J. B. Carroll. Cambridge: MIT Press.

Wittgenstein, L. (1953) *Philosophical Investigations*, translated by G. E. M. Anscombe. Oxford: Blackwell.

Index

accent(s) 40, 85, 89, 184–7
anthropology 125, 255, 270, 279
anti-language 214–5, 221–2
Arabic 214, 285
Aristotle 153–4, 156
astronomy 125, 151–3

benefactive 19, 24–6, 28–9, 31
Bernstein, B. 20–1, 37–8, 46, 48, 64–6, 85–92, 99–113, 116–35, 140–9, 152–64, 181, 186, 198, 230, 229–35, 238–9, 243–5, 248, 256–62, 265–9, 279–81
biological 50–2, 125, 147, 160–1, 289, 312
Bourdieu, P. 21, 112, 161, 169, 174, 221, 242, 248
brain 8–10, 19, 25, 32, 45, 47, 50–2, 56, 62–3, 71, 77–8, 125, 140, 155, 338, 364

capitalism 125, 209–11, 215, 227–8, 233–4, 239, 247
  capitalist 210, 213, 221, 225–7, 247
Chomsky, N. 13, 56–7, 97, 109, 155
Christie, F. 37, 41, 161, 188, 314
co-text 27, 31, 71, 137, 349, 355, 370–1
code(s) 85–9, 99–101, 104, 108, 112–3, 132, 135, 149, 160–3, 197, 279, 286
  elaborated 85, 132
  restricted 89, 135
cognition 35, 78, 86, 289, 302, 312, 362, 369–70, 372
cognitive 34, 78–80, 90, 108, 155, 170, 312
cohesion 121, 134, 161
  cohesive 134–40, 378
competence 19, 21, 36–7, 40, 86–7, 104, 128, 248, 317
  communicative 86–7, 317
construal(s) 12–3, 45, 66, 112–8, 131–4, 150, 203, 214, 216, 229, 293–4, 296, 326, 337, 349, 353, 359
contextual 71, 94, 105, 110, 112, 114–5, 117, 160, 184, 296–8, 302, 313, 316, 352
curriculum 41, 49, 63–6, 70, 182, 228–9, 241, 251, 257–60, 280–2
  curricula 38, 65–8, 181, 192, 194, 246, 269

deficit 86–7
delicacy 23, 116, 121, 143, 300, 319, 322, 331
  delicate 23, 32, 113, 135, 220, 331
democracy 96, 146, 211, 222–6, 229, 234, 238, 240
dialect(s) 40, 47, 85, 184–7, 194, 373, 378
dialogic 34, 184, 247, 319
discourse
  horizontal 103–5, 110, 117–8, 120–1, 129–30, 139, 141–2, 147
  instructional 40, 65, 68, 128, 240–4
  pedagogic 41, 66, 101, 119, 132, 146, 172, 233, 240
  vertical 104–7, 124, 126, 129–31, 139, 143–6, 160–1

education 14, 19, 21–2, 25, 37, 39, 41–6, 48–50, 63–70, 90–8, 112, 119, 145–6, 161, 165, 169–70, 179, 187–8, 191–206, 223, 227–30, 233–4, 238–9, 241, 243–7, 251–62, 266–9, 270, 285, 289, 308, 312
  cross-cultural 251, 253, 268
  formal 90, 98, 262
  higher 39, 228, 308, 312
educational
  discourse 174, 187–8
  genres 189–92
  institution(s) 48–9, 64, 67, 90, 247, 257, 259, 265–6, 268
  knowledge 141, 181, 194, 206, 257–8, 261, 265–6, 280–1

process(es) 46, 48–9, 187, 252, 254, 258, 260–1, 268
egalitarian 21, 41, 96, 161, 172, 187, 198, 212
Einstein, A. 149, 156–7, 196
Ellipsis 83, 371, 377–8
Englishes 207, 215, 226, 230–1, 373

gender 69, 246, 364, 378–9
genre(s) 37, 41, 143, 189–92, 203–6, 229, 241, 286
genre-based
literacy 191, 193–4, 203–4, 206, 241
pedagogy 188–90, 192–4, 206, 229, 242, 245, 314
globalization 207–13, 221, 225, 227–9, 234, 238, 242, 286–7
grammar(s) 7, 13–17, 22, 32, 34, 43–4, 61, 66, 89, 109–10, 148, 153, 159, 173, 179, 183, 203, 209, 220, 238, 241, 243, 279, 290, 299, 305–6, 315–22, 327–34, 337–8, 347, 354, 356, 369, 371–7
grammatical
analysis 15–6, 22, 43, 45
category/–ies 164, 245, 339–40, 344–5, 356, 363
functions 46
system 16, 159, 304
grammatics 245, 332
Greek 147–50, 152, 154

Halliday, M. A. K. 8–9, 14–18, 22–3, 28–34, 37, 39, 45–7, 48, 57–9, 63, 71, 74, 76, 79, 85, 88, 93–4, 100, 102, 104–5, 111–16, 119, 123–6, 131–2, 138, 144–5, 158–9, 163–5, 175, 177, 179, 182–5, 189, 198, 205, 214, 221, 230, 241–5, 248, 289–92, 296–7, 301–4, 308–9, 321, 334, 339–40, 347, 352, 354, 356, 362, 364, 368–71, 347–9
Hasan, R. 11–12, 17–26, 37, 41, 44–7, 60–2, 69–72, 75, 80, 84–5, 92, 94, 98, 100, 102, 111–21, 124, 126–7, 129, 131–40, 147, 159, 162–65, 176, 182, 184–7, 193, 197–99, 203, 206, 220, 228, 230, 235, 240–5, 248, 277, 281–2, 291, 295–6, 300, 302–4, 335, 340, 346, 349, 369, 371, 378
history 20, 24, 34, 51, 65–8, 77, 79, 94, 96, 101, 106, 133, 144, 146, 150, 153, 155, 157–60, 164, 169, 177, 189, 195, 199, 208–11, 239, 253, 259, 289–90, 297–8, 322
Hjelmslev, L. 77, 98, 123, 164
humanities 39, 105, 110–11, 124–6, 130, 147, 242–3, 252
humanity 20, 52, 177, 200, 217, 229, 236, 239, 279, 339
Hymes, D. 86, 184, 291, 335

ideology(-ies) 122, 143, 146, 180–1, 186, 201, 207, 211, 215, 218, 221–2, 230, 235, 237, 315
Indo-Pakistani 80, 84, 97, 185, 251, 253, 258–68, 277, 281, 376
innate(ness) 50, 56, 63–4, 127
intelligence 29, 36–7, 64, 70, 198, 203, 217, 236, 312–13, 379
inter(/intra)–lingual 85–9, 92–5
interpersonal 47, 57, 113, 149, 157, 206, 210, 216, 226, 263, 275, 285, 292–7, 302–5, 308, 316, 319, 321, 326, 338

Kachru, B. 207, 230–1, 313
kinship 84, 88, 105, 185, 255, 258–9, 264
knowledge
commonsense 64, 78, 94, 103–4, 106, 117, 120–2, 126–7, 139, 141–2, 146–7, 150, 261, 264
educational 141, 181, 194, 206, 256–8, 261, 265–6, 280–1
hierarchical 105, 108–9, 111, 118–19, 125–6, 143–7, 151, 153, 155, 157
horizontal 105–6, 108–12, 118–19, 122–3, 125, 129, 132, 136, 141–4, 147, 152, 154, 160, 162
segmental 106–7, 162
structured 117, 122–4, 146–7
vertical 126, 130, 146, 241

Labov, W. 85, 87, 184
language
first 308–15
foreign 252, 270, 306, 309, 336, 339
human 54, 56–7, 108, 195, 205, 216, 218, 256, 292, 298, 332, 336–9

learning 9, 14, 58, 62, 306, 308, 329
second 39, 180, 270–2, 282–6, 288, 306, 309–15, 333, 336, 362
teaching 39–40, 203, 316, 375
langue 248, 292, 298
lexical
item(s) 18–9, 24, 81, 89, 178, 209, 216–7, 219, 256, 340–4, 363, 378
metaphor(s) 25, 214, 347, 377
lexicogrammar, lexicogrammatical 15–16, 22–3, 29, 31–2, 40, 43–4, 47, 73, 84, 88, 98, 114, 131, 134, 137–9, 143, 163, 179, 190–1, 202–3, 215, 242–5, 248, 290, 299–300, 303–4, 306, 316–9, 321–2, 325, 328–33, 335, 338–9, 345, 347, 351–2, 359, 363, 377
lexicon 88–9, 143, 299, 337–8, 344
linguistics
applied 312, 317, 334
formal 184, 338
functional 15, 70, 108, 203, 209, 241, 338
generative 108, 162
literacy
action 44, 187, 189–96, 202–6, 229, 241–2
critical 191–2, 197, 201, 203, 206, 242
genre-based 191–4, 203–6, 241
recognition 178–82, 188, 190, 193, 202, 204–6, 228–9, 240–1
reflection 44, 69, 196–9, 202–6, 229–30, 242–7

mathematics(-ical) 39–40, 93, 125, 149, 153–5, 164
Matthiessen, C. M. I. M. 9, 16–17, 29, 32, 37, 45–7, 102, 131, 163, 165, 179, 241, 292, 304–5, 352, 354, 356, 377
meaning(s)
conditioned 348–55, 359–61
connotative 217, 237, 248
default 347–51, 353–4, 356, 361, 365–6
group 59, 63–4, 67, 90, 105, 201
interpersonal 149, 294, 297, 304
linguistic 12–13, 40, 44, 55, 76, 131, 178, 203, 241, 244, 248, 303, 315, 329, 340, 347, 352, 359
making 53–5, 177–8, 183, 186, 198, 243, 272, 317
potential 149, 178, 199, 293, 296, 352
mental
development 49–50, 53, 70
functions 45, 50, 55, 127, 198
process 11, 17, 32–3, 35–7, 46, 353–6, 362–73, 379
metafunction(al) 16, 45, 47, 216, 292–307, 316, 319, 326, 329
metaphor 10, 25, 58, 77, 82, 214
modal 319–22, 327–30, 335, 344–5, 355
modalization 321–2, 327–8, 331
modulation 322, 327–31

network(s)
system 45, 114, 163, 301–4, 320, 323, 331, 335
Newton, I. 149, 153–6, 251
Nigel 57–9
nominal
group 17, 25–6, 30–1, 342, 369–70, 378

pedagogic
action(s) 101–2, 145, 169, 175, 235
context(s) 174–8, 181, 201, 316
device 144, 240, 243–4
discourse 66, 101, 119, 132, 146, 172, 233, 240
grammar 290, 315, 317, 333–4
practice(s) 69, 146, 169, 172, 189, 193, 232–3
pedagogy(-ies) 21, 32, 37, 39, 42, 46, 64–70, 99, 104–7, 111, 118–19, 122, 127–9, 132, 134, 145–6, 160–2, 169–70, 177, 183, 188–94, 196–7, 199–206, 229, 232–5, 238–48, 257, 282, 285, 289, 310–19, 328–9, 332–4, 352, 374
personality 273–9
phonology 40, 73, 131, 178–9, 299, 306, 329, 337
phonological 71, 131, 177, 214, 221, 314, 321, 327, 329–30, 363–4
physics 26, 39, 41, 56, 108–9, 125, 147–60, 164, 251, 375
polarity 321–2, 325, 327–9
proto language 57–9
psychology 47, 125, 279, 285

register(s) 93–5, 97, 133, 144, 184–7, 291–2, 308, 313–4, 322, 351, 359, 377
rhetoric(al) 154, 157, 205, 227, 304

Sapir, E. 33, 47, 74
Saussure, F. de 54, 74, 81–2, 98, 213
science 10, 54, 116, 123, 125, 127, 144, 148, 150, 153–60, 189, 205, 336
sciences
 human 109, 153, 285
 natural 125, 159
 physical 107, 111, 126
 social 32, 39, 99, 105, 109–11, 124–6, 130, 148, 152, 242, 252, 259, 267
semantic
 difference 73–4, 82
 distance 73, 76, 79, 81–97
 orientation 70, 93, 119, 198, 242
 potential 72, 79–80, 88, 215
 reversal 221
 space 73–4
 stratum 301–3
 variation 40, 85, 121, 129, 186–7, 245
semantics 29, 32, 75, 81, 98, 113, 131, 134, 139, 143, 179, 215–16, 237, 299–306, 319, 328, 335, 337, 339, 354, 363
semiosis 102, 159, 171–5, 182, 198, 202, 208, 245, 289, 296–7, 306
semiotic
 mediation 45–6, 48–50, 55–6, 69–70
 potential 79–81
 synergy 33–4
 system(s) 8–9, 12–13, 26, 29, 55, 102–3, 113, 131, 139, 162, 171–4, 203, 213, 240, 289
SFL 13–17, 23, 45–7, 98, 101, 111–13, 116–18, 123, 131–2, 143–4, 216, 290–9, 303, 314, 319, 328, 337–8, 346, 352–3, 362–3, 372, 376
sign 9, 54–5, 76–7, 131, 169–74, 182, 213, 240–1, 243
social
 action 118, 176, 178, 184, 201, 248, 295–6
 activity 49, 64, 112, 184–5, 306, 310, 312–13
 basis 242, 290, 295–300, 315, 332
 being(s) 9, 54, 65, 79, 164, 183, 264
 change 13, 69, 193, 232
 class(es) 92, 185, 187, 201, 262
 context(s) 48, 100, 104, 111, 183, 185, 203, 240–1, 243, 283–4, 296, 298, 306, 309–18, 330, 333–4
 dialect(s) 85, 184–5
 distance 20, 41–2, 47, 140
 environment 8, 63–4, 70, 170, 267, 286, 298–9, 306, 312, 333, 378
 institution(s) 20–1, 49, 77, 255–6, 258, 338
 interaction 49–51, 63, 198, 279, 289, 297
 life 11–13, 50, 76, 100, 102, 174, 176, 190, 193, 196, 232, 244, 298–9, 309, 338
 meaning(s) 242, 252–6, 286
 positioning 129, 175, 177, 185–6, 245
 practice(s) 10, 21, 77, 79, 84, 92, 103–4, 111–14, 120–1, 124, 127–9, 135, 138–9, 242–3, 278
 process(es) 46, 94–5, 117–18, 120, 135, 169, 174, 185–6, 201–2, 241, 248, 292, 309, 311–14
 relation(s) 111, 118, 206, 276, 296–7, 311, 319
 sciences 32, 39, 99, 105, 109–111, 124–6, 130, 148, 152, 242, 252, 259, 267
 semiotic 70, 96, 101, 176, 178, 181, 188, 191, 202–3, 298
 structure 68–70, 94–5, 169, 191, 244–6, 280–1, 284–5
 universe 91, 126, 161, 180, 275, 308, 311
socialization 76–8, 90, 101, 126, 129, 132, 251, 262–3, 265–9, 286, 308–9
sociolinguistic(s) 60, 68, 85, 186–7, 201, 214, 317
sociology 47–8, 64–5, 101, 106, 108–13, 119, 125–7, 134, 146, 148, 161–4, 203, 232, 248, 255, 270, 285
 sociological 101, 110–11, 129, 132, 144, 161–2, 232, 270, 280, 282, 286
speech
 community(-ies) 82–3, 120, 131, 186, 214, 219, 235, 237, 270, 298, 359

event(s) 289, 295, 297, 344–5, 377
fellowship(s) 9, 64, 105, 120–1, 138–9, 142, 183, 185–6, 197, 200–1
syntax 56, 58–9, 109, 317
syntactic 56, 95, 256, 285
systemic functional 15, 70, 102, 108, 159, 203, 241, 288, 290, 376–7

tense(s) 82, 178–9, 336, 340, 343–79
textual 47, 71, 112, 133–4, 138, 141, 157, 159, 190–1, 248, 292–7, 302–5, 316, 338, 343, 352

verbal
group(s) 17, 286, 344–5, 352, 356–7, 364–5, 370, 378–9
process(es) 28–37, 44, 46–7, 372
Vygotsky, L. S. 8, 10, 37, 45, 49–51, 55–6, 67, 70, 102, 119, 124–7, 176, 195–8, 202, 206, 308, 334

Whorf, B. L. 75, 78, 82–3, 86–8, 102, 119, 124, 218, 231, 255–6, 341
Wittgenstein, L. 102, 161, 308

www.ingramcontent.com/pod-product-compliance
Lightning Source LLC
LaVergne TN
LVHW010443080826
844660LV00026B/1201

9781904768388